The Wisdom of the Ego

The
Wisdom
of the Ego

George E. Vaillant

Harvard University Press
Cambridge, Massachusetts
London, England

First Harvard University Press paperback edition, 1995

Pages 385-386 constitute an extension of the copyright page.

Library of Congress Cataloging-in-Publication Data

Vaillant, George E., 1934–
    The wisdom of the ego / George E. Vaillant.
        p.   cm.
    Includes bibliographical references and index.
    ISBN 0-674-95372-X (cloth)
    ISBN 0-674-95373-8 (pbk.)
    1. Defense mechanisms (Psychology)—Case studies. 2. Resilience
(Personality trait)—Case studies. 3. Adjustments (Psychology)—Case
studies. 4. Maturation (Psychology)—Case studies. 5. Creative
ability—Case studies. 6. Self-deception—Case studies. I. Title.
BF175.5.D44V35   1993
155.2′4—dc20   92-37342
                          CIP

For Leigh
whose wisdom, love, and companionship
bring much joy

Contents

Tables

Figures

The Wisdom of the Ego

Introduction

The mind is its own place, and in itself
Can make a heav'n of hell, a hell of heav'n.

John Milton, *Paradise Lost*

Our lives are at times intolerable. At times we cannot bear reality. At such times our minds play tricks on us. Our minds distort inner and outer reality so that an observer might accuse us of denial, self-deception, even dishonesty. But such mental defenses creatively rearrange the sources of our conflict so that they become manageable and we may survive. The mind's defenses—like the body's immune mechanisms—protect us by providing a variety of illusions to filter pain and to allow self-soothing.

Often such emotional and intellectual dishonesty is not only healthy but also mature and creative. Such defensive self-deception reflects the ego's—the integrated brain's—best synthetic effort at coping with life events that otherwise would be overwhelming. Equally important, such self-deception evolves throughout our lives. Our development does not end with childhood but continues through adulthood. The maladaptive defenses of adolescence can evolve into the virtues of maturity. This psychic alchemy helps to explain the resilience of individuals who are abused and disadvantaged during the first decades of life and yet become valued and useful adults. In short, our ego's defenses can be creative, healthy, comforting, and coping. Yet when we are observers—rather than users—of defenses, they often strike us as downright peculiar.

Sixty years ago the physiologist Walter B. Cannon wrote a landmark book, *The Wisdom of the Body*, in which he described the invisible response of the human digestive tract to distress.[1] He clearly identified the checks and balances employed by our bodies' parasympathetic and sympathetic nervous systems to maintain *homeo-stasis*—the term he used to describe a body at peace with itself. In his research Cannon capitalized on what was then a recent invention, X-ray photography, to monitor hitherto invisible physiological processes. Echoing Cannon, I have called this book *The Wisdom of the Ego*, because I believe the invisible responses of the human mind to distress—the defenses deployed by the ego—are as healing, and as necessary to health, as the autonomic nervous system that he did so much to elucidate.

Like Cannon, I capitalize on a recent scientific advance—in my case the availability of records of prospectively gathered human lives. I draw my evidence from the Study of Adult Development, in which large numbers of people have been followed from adolescence through their adult lives. Such prolonged study helps to render visible the healing power of the ego's defenses. In addition, the rich database of hundreds of lives provides statistical support for generalizations made from individual lives. Because one question of interest is the relationship of the ego's adaptive self-deceptions to human creativity, I also examine the life histories of several creative artists.

In this book, then, I weave together three threads. One thread is the mind's—the ego's—modes of self-deception and denial, sometimes referred to as mechanisms of defense. To use a Piagetian term, the deployment of such defenses reflects our adult efforts to *accommodate* to life. The use of ego mechanisms of defense alters the perception of both internal and external reality; and often, like hypnosis, use of defenses compromises other facets of cognition. Awareness of instinctual wishes may be greatly diminished; antithetical wishes may be passionately adhered to; our consciences or our awareness of other people may be obliterated. I shall offer evidence that a person's choice of defenses is critical to mental health.

The second thread is an examination of creativity—the peculiarly human capacity for putting in the world what was not there before. Such a capacity for creativity seems closely interwoven with the alchemy of the ego to bring order and meaning out of chaos and distress. Such creative capacity can allow grief to be mitigated by an esoteric hobby, and it can allow self-deception to be viewed as a virtue rather than a sin. In Piagetian terminology, creativity reflects how we *assimilate* life, take life in, make it our own, and share it with others. Creativity is how we experience life and pour it forth.

The book's third thread is the unfolding of adult development.

The study of lifetimes allows reexamination of cross-sectional views of adult development. Such study permits us to see how people bud and flower, and how human caterpillars evolve into butterflies. It allows us to trace how the capacity for intimacy makes possible the commitment essential for a gratifying career identity, and how such fulfillment from a career makes possible a capacity for generative care. It also allows us to see that this developmental sequence of love-to-work-to-care appears to hold for both men and women.

More important, prospective study of lifetimes demonstrates the resilience and the continuing maturation of adults. Freud diminished human hope by suggesting that the first five years of life were destiny. The evidence I adduce in this book restores hope. The data from the Study of Adult Development demonstrate that mental health and choice of defense are *not* static. Rather, choice of defense may evolve throughout adult life and may transmute irritating grains of sand into pearls. Nor is choice of defense determined by social class, education, or gender.

The modern psychoanalytic use of the term *ego* encompasses the adaptive and executive aspects of the human brain: the ability of the mind to integrate, master, and make sense of inner and outer reality. Or, in Freud's words, "We have formed the idea that in each individual there is a coherent organization of mental processes; and we call this his *ego*."[2] The term *ego* addresses the capacity of the integrated mind to accommodate and assimilate the world.

On the one hand, personality development and maturity occur through the interaction between the person and his or her social environment. On the other hand, as John Milton reminds us, experience is not what happens to the mind (and heart) but what the mind (and heart) does with experience. How the mind manipulates experience is at the core of ego development.

We are accustomed to thinking of ego development as something that occurs in childhood. The developmental psychologist Robert Kegan has described watching the ego development of a young child as follows: "Being in another's presence while she so honestly labors in an astonishingly intimate activity—the activity of making sense—is somehow very touching." Such development, as Kegan notes, is social: "Our survival and development depend on our capacity to recruit the invested attention of others to us."[3] To develop, a child needs a loving caretaker, one who creates for the child what D. W. Winnicott has called a "holding environment"—that is, an environment that provides the child with the secure foundation it needs to mature and to develop a sense of self. Eventually, the caretaker's love comes to dwell inside the child, where it supports the capacity of the ego's self-deceptions to turn life's leaden moments into gold, as it were, instead of into self-detrimental distortions and illusions.

But this book is not about children. Although Kegan expresses a fear that adolescents and adults less frequently "display themselves in these touching and elemental ways," he realizes it may only be that in adults "we are less able to see these ways for what they are."[4] This book is about adults who have exposed their entire lives to scrutiny and have been seen in similarly vulnerable and intimate activities. This book is about middle-aged men and women wrestling with learning how to love, with making meaning, with reordering chaos, and with discovering, often inadvertently, how to put in the world what was not there before. Their life stories offer example after example in which maturation and the internalization of a holding environment occur in adulthood, not in childhood.

Finally, quite unashamedly, I wish to argue for preserving the baby of psychoanalysis even as we discard its bath water. I wish to remind the reader that we have limbic systems as well as cerebral cortices, and that the brain cannot be separated from the heart. This book is an effort to undo some of the excesses of the so-called cognitive revolution, of the medicalization of psychiatry, and of what has been called the "decade of the brain." Howard Gardner, in his lucid history of the cognitive revolution, notes the deliberate decision of cognitive scientists to exclude certain factors that "would unnecessarily complicate the cognitive-scientific enterprise. These factors include the influence of affective factors or emotions, the contribution of historical and cultural factors, and the role of the background context in which particular actions or thoughts occur."[5] *The Wisdom of the Ego* reflects my studied effort to recomplicate such an enterprise.

The prospective study of human lives makes it possible to look closely at psychological experiences and to trace their similarities and differences in large groups of men and women. In the words of the psychiatrist John Nemiah, "The difficulty many people have in accepting the validity of psychodynamic concepts lies not in their lack of a cognitive ability to understand the theory, but in their incapacity or unwillingness to observe the clinical facts on which the theory is based.

Those who reject psychodynamic theory refuse to take subjective human psychological experiences as phenomena worthy of serious attention and study, and consequently they cannot or will not allow themselves to observe them."[6] This book, using data from the prospective, long-term study of many lives, renders those subjective, human psychological experiences visible to even the most intransigent empiricist.

Throughout the book, I will point out the distortions that occur between the actual and the remembered past, between the artist's life and her creative product, and between current reality and our perceptions of it. My intent will be to make the hidden visible, and to retrieve the dynamic "unconscious" first popularized by Freud and Janet from the parochial grip of the "Freudian" humanists so that it can be reinserted into the grasp of natural scientists. It is time for the ego and its defenses to be seen as facets of psychobiological reality, not as articles of psychoanalytic faith.

I

Why Praise the Human Ego?

The striving to master, to integrate, to make sense of experience is not one ego function among many but the essence of the ego.

Jane Loevinger

Not long ago at an amusement park in California, I viewed the riders on the loop-the-loop roller coaster with astonishment. As I watched the excited passengers gather speed, sweep up the loop, and hang suspended upside down with their arms waving, I saw that for them the experience was one of joy, release, and exhilaration. Yet I imagined that for myself such a ride would be anything but enjoyable. I contemplated only the physical assault that might ensue. The stress of such a roller coaster ride might fill my bursae with calcium, crater the lining of my stomach with ulcers, deposit cholesterol within the walls of my coronary arteries, and compromise my immune system with an outpouring of corticosteroids. The experience, I reflected, might take years off my life.

By what alchemy had the brains of the laughing riders mitigated an experience that would have provoked in me only fear and distress? The difference between us, had I ventured to join them, would not have been in our understanding of the risks. Most of the time, after all, nothing really bad happens in amusement parks. I *know* that. Nor would the difference have been in our conscious understanding of stress management. I am, after all, a professor of psychiatry, and I understand quite a lot about stress. I can breathe deeply and visualize placid, blue lagoons as well as the next person. The difference would not have been in the external stress we experienced, for we would all have shared the exposed helplessness of hanging upside down a hundred feet above the ground. The difference would have been in the ways our minds, our egos, *distorted* the experience.

The ego is an elusive metaphor. Psychologists and psychiatrists are hard put to define a good ego in objective terms or to describe how they would go about measuring it. In part this is because our conceptions of mental health exist as theoretical constructs and not as operational behaviors. But even when we take time to define what we mean by mental health, the ego still remains the mysterious god in the machine.

The wisdom of the ego referred to in the title of this book is not the wisdom of vanity but the widom of the integrated adaptive central nervous system. The concept of the ego conveys the mind's capacity to integrate inner and outer reality, to blend past and present, and to synthesize ideas with feelings. I use the term *ego* as Sigmund Freud used it, to convey the self-preservative executive ego, the agile rider of Plato's two horses: selfless conscience and selfish instincts. However, the ego also encompasses all those complex behaviors in which our brains can engage but in which the finest computers in the world cannot. For example, the recognition of faces, of signatures, of counterfeit Renoirs—tasks well beyond the power of computers—are readily performed by an only modestly well trained human brain.

Originally, Freud described the ego as analogous to Plato's horseman trying to ride two horses at once. Goaded on by the selfish impulses of the id, hemmed in by the moral constraints of the superego, rebuffed by reality, the ego struggles to cope and to reduce the forces that work on it into some kind of harmony. The ego institutes delay in our instinctual behavior: Look before you leap. In so doing, it can "neutralize" instinctual urges. Usually this occurs as a gradual transformation, but in cases of religious conversion the development of the capacity for instinctual delay may be sudden.

Over time Freud's model of the ego has evolved. What is outside of us is as threatening as what is within. Interpersonal relationships and external reality are now considered just as important to unconscious conflict as the id and the superego. Thus the ego must control four horses: desire, conscience, people, and reality.

Modern attempts to define the ego include the work of neuropsychologists like Michael Gazzaniga, who studies patients whose left and right brain hemispheres have been surgically separated. Gazzaniga tells us: "Studies on split-brain patients have revealed the presence of a system in the left hemisphere that interprets these actions, moods, and thought processes that are generated by groups of modules that are acting outside the realm of our conscious awareness. The left-brain 'interpreter' constructs theories about these actions and feelings and tries to bring order and unity to our conscious lives. It is a special system that works independently from language processes and appears to be unique to the human brain and related to the singular capacity of the brain to make causal inferences."[1]

But Gazzaniga is really talking about "self." The self has subjective experiences, the self has thoughts and bodily feelings. The ego does not have experiences; it is an organizing mental apparatus that is the sum of the integrated central nervous system. It remains invisible and can be identified only through its footprints. We can visualize and appreciate the results of ego function, but the ego will forever remain an abstraction.

Nor is ego just for adaptation and mental synthesis. Its wisdom also encompasses defense and adult development and creativity. The ultimate developmental ego tasks are wisdom, the fusion of care and justice, and the capacity to consider the needs, rights, and past histories of others even as we pay heed to those same facets in ourselves. Such ego tasks involve not only the mastery of intimate relationships and identification with mentors but the capacity to compare, and to sustain paradox and ambivalence. The ego allows us to distinguish that which we must gather the courage to change from that which we must gain the serenity to accept.

I certainly do not use the term *ego* to convey narcissism. There is, after all, a world of difference between being self-centered (being egotistical) and being centered in the self (possessing ego strength). To survive we must find the important realm that exists between selflessness and selfishness, between reckless disregard for self and paralyzing self-absorption. Thus, ego strength encompasses self-care, and self-care knows neither selflessness nor selfishness. Rather, self-care must employ the long-range view and expand into areas where one can aggrandize self without diminishing others. The adaptive ego must learn to cast its bread upon the waters so that the bread will return tenfold; it must learn to spin straw into gold. But as with the case of the roller coaster riders, such an ego must also develop a capacity for judicious self-deception. And, as we shall see, whether such self-deception leads to art or to insanity, the alchemy of the ego is nothing short of miraculous.

Finally, ego development is not dissimilar to moral development. The poet Edward Arlington Robinson wrote to a friend, "The world is not a 'prison house' but a kind of spiritual kindergarten where millions of bewildered infants are trying to spell God with the wrong blocks."[2] Change D to E and those kindergarten blocks spell EGO as easily as GOD. Consider the difference between the paranoid and the altruist. Both claim to discern intuitively how other people feel. The difference is that the altruist is right and the paranoid sees only an image of himself. Yet over time paranoids can develop into altruists. As adaptive capacity matures, paranoia evolves into empathy, projection evolves into altruism, and sinner evolves into saint. Ego development reflects our ongoing striving to allow the self-diminishing sin of *projection* to evolve toward the self-expanding virtue of *empathy*. This process of ego development simultaneously involves self-deception and the growth of wisdom and creativity.

The ego possesses a remarkable capacity for life-preserving distortion. As I ha ... distortion can take the form of
projectio
riders, o
venerati
and as
often he
physiol
its self-
of the
because
like rol
adapta
pilot C
ment,
becom
pilots.
For h
too w
a mo
an op
of in
balan

this boo
a parallel
the mastery
cope with an in
has three choices.
sanatorium like Trude
Mann's *Magic Mountain*.
tuberculosis was social; cure
and experience of others. The s
I had a brave, warm hand to hold,
roller coaster.

Second, the tuberculous patient ca
nals and follow a wise regimen for treatment

There are three very different means by which our minds can cope with stress and danger. First, we can receive help from others: test pilots can receive empathic and skilled flight instruction. This aid to coping is often called *social supports*, and it is generally voluntary. Second, we can employ voluntary, learned methods to help ourselves: test pilots can rehearse the management of stress and of emergencies. Such maneuvers are sometimes called *cognitive coping strategies*. Third, we can deploy involuntary, unconscious strategies. These are often subsumed under the psychoanalytic term *ego mechanisms of defense*. But, as with the fearless roller coaster riders, this third kind of coping process, the use of defense mechanisms, alters perception of both internal and external reality in a largely involuntary way. Often the result of such mental distortion of reality is to diminish anxiety and depression, and thus to reduce the physiological and psychic wear and tear of stress.

But defenses work not just against the scary reality of roller coasters but also against scary relationships, desires, and taboos. At the same time that defense mechanisms can diminish awareness of instinctual "wishes," loves, and desires, they can also cause passionate adherence to antithetical or neutral desires. Consider how 9-year-old boys flee the kisses of exciting girls and yet eagerly seek out neutral baseball cards. Defenses can also diminish awareness of cultural prohibitions. Consider how adolescents can ignore the most reasonable of parental prohibitions and yet create the most preposterous rules for behavior in their place.

To illustrate the three kinds of coping and to emphasize that in ok I focus only on the third, most involuntary kind, let me draw between the mastery of stress by the wisdom of the ego and f tuberculosis by Cannon's "wisdom of the body." To fectious disease like tuberculosis, the afflicted person First, he can seek help and social support from a au's in the Adirondacks or the one in Thomas In the days before antibiotics the cure of derived in part from the strength, hope, ame is true of resistance to stress. Had I might have survived a ride on the

read the latest medical jour- and convalescence, which

may need to be carefully rehearsed. Learned cognitive strategies for coping with stress are important and have led to Americans' current interest in "learning" stress management. Obviously, this was the course I took in the amusement park. By wisely deciding not to buy a ticket, I spared myself untold misery.

Third, the patient can depend upon the wisdom of his body; he can involuntarily deploy white blood cells and "unconsciously" manufacture antibodies against the invading mycobacteria. In similar fashion, the roller coaster riders had, without effort and without volition, dissociated themselves from fear and danger. Defense mechanisms are for the mind what the immune system is for the body. When Hans Selye, the great Canadian student of stress, wrote that stress can kill us, he emphasized only half of the equation. Of perhaps greater importance is the fact that defenses can allow us to survive.

The ego is to the mastery of stress as the immune system is to the mastery of tuberculosis. If the tuberculous patient deploys immune mechanisms "wisely," his illness will never become serious. But if his immune system either operates ineffectively or becomes overactive, the outcome may be disastrous. Indeed, many of the chronic complications of tuberculosis arise not from the infectious mycobacteria but from the body's efforts to combat them. Similarly, much of what is labeled mental illness simply reflects our "unwise" deployment of defense mechanisms. If we use defenses well, we are deemed mentally healthy, conscientious, funny, creative, and altruistic. If we use them badly, the psychiatrist diagnoses us ill, our neighbors label us unpleasant, and society brands us immoral. But I hope it is clear that when I use the traditional term *defense mechanism* I use it in the sense of coping—of *adaptation*. Even insanity, like our dreams, reflects the striving of our ego to master, to integrate, to make sense of aberrant brain function. If we could not cough and manufacture pus, we would die. If we do not unconsciously distort inner and outer reality, we are condemned to anxiety and depression.

But, reader, beware. I am only a few pages into the book, and I am already trying to discuss science with metaphor. In the understanding of ego defenses the term *mechanism* does not mean anything quite as concrete as immune mechanisms. A defense is not an invariant physical pattern of brain activity. A defense is a descriptive metaphor for the temporary clouding of reality through thoughts, feelings, and behaviors. Since defenses involve the highest integrative regulatory processes of the central nervous system, they are not easily distinguished from ordinary behaviors, thoughts, and feelings. There is the rub. As Melvin Konner, a very thoughtful sociobiologist and anthropologist, has written, "Adaptation is thus that most puzzling of all scientific phenomena: an inherently unprovable, yet eminently useable idea."[3] Rainbows are a useful metaphor with which to discuss such phenomena. The too thoughtful scientist may dismiss rainbows as an illusion. Indeed, when examined closely, they do disappear. Certainly, rainbows have no true location in space, and they are without a beginning or an end. However, unlike flying saucers, rainbows show up in photographs and are seen by everybody. Yet the full appreciation of rainbows—and of ego defenses—requires occasional recourse to the language of painters and poets rather than that of scientists.

Early in my career the chairman of my department of psychiatry warned that my efforts to teach defense mechanisms to first-year medical students would prove unrewarding. He thought that such abstruse tenets of psychoanalytic psychology should come later in psychiatric training. He was wrong, for belief in unconscious psychological defenses is no longer confined to those who religiously adhere to psychoanalysis. Heads of state are aware of projection. Ethologists speak freely of displacement. Sublimation and repression have long been familiar to biographers, and more recently to social historians.

Academic psychology, however, retains a mistrust of the unconscious in general and of defense mechanisms in particular. The "cognitive revolution" has ignored defenses, and only recently has modern experimental psychology been groping to reinvent a language for regulatory self-deceptions. The reasons for such mistrust stem both from the rigorous, if sometimes limiting, empiricism of academic psychology and from the often self-serving excuses given by psychoanalysis for ignoring empiricism.

In many respects the mistrust of defense mechanisms is unwarranted. Modern experimental psychologists often forget that Freud, too, began life as a scientific empiricist. Many modern psychologists try to study personality as if trying to understand operas by just reading the libretto. Freud insisted that we attend to the music as well. The metaphors of John Keats, Guiseppe Verdi, or William Shakespeare are simply better equipped than the literal-minded prose of Immanuel

Kant or B. F. Skinner to describe the scientific realities of a colorful sunset or the pain of a broken heart. Freud reaffirmed that humans are the guardians of forces they cannot see or perfectly control. Modern investigation of the hypothalamus and the limbic system has left the central importance of these forces unquestioned. The good news is that psychologists have recently begun to rediscover defense mechanisms. But their terminology differs from mine: they try to operationalize defenses as "self-deceptions," "comforting denial," and "cognitive regulatory mechanisms."

At the same time, in many respects the mistrust of defense mechanisms is entirely warranted. In conceptualizing defenses, Freud made many errors. At first he saw defenses as only pathological. To be fully analyzed supposedly meant to give up defenses. Thus, Freud did not always appreciate that defenses were homeostatic and could help even the most psychologically healthy adult keep from being immobilized by anxiety and depression. Second, he erroneously believed that all pathogenic defenses had their roots in childhood. In addition, because of events in his own life and historical epoch, Freud saw defenses as too exclusively related to sexual conflict; he ignored their equally important role in regulating aggression, grief, dependency, tenderness, and joy. Finally, having studied people in the solitude of the consulting room, Freud ignored the role of ego defenses in modulating relationships. He placed too much emphasis on a psychology of drives and too little on a psychology of relationships. Among others, Melanie Klein, Harry Stack Sullivan, and Otto Kernberg have worked hard to broaden the limited role that Freud granted to the defenses. They have taught clinicians to appreciate that defenses modulate and distort external relationships and internalized representations of people as well as drives and emotions.

It was nineteenth-century advances in biological science that made it possible for Freud's elucidation of defense mechanisms to be taken seriously. Toward the end of the nineteenth century, for the first time, the brain came to be seen as an anatomically discrete sense organ made up of individual cells whose organizational patterns and connections could be stained and studied under the microscope. In 1897 Sir Charles Sherrington demonstrated that these cells were connected by synapses and arranged into sensory tracts.[4]

The discoveries of Sherrington and others permitted a well-trained neurologist, as Freud was, to demonstrate that the mind could deceive itself—that a "hysterical" patient could possess a normal central nervous system and yet suffer from crippling anesthesias and palsies. For example, once the distribution of the "real" sensory tracts of the hand was charted, neurologists were able to prove that cases of anesthesia that had the distribution of a glove (rather than that of a stripe from elbow to fingertip) had no biological basis. Instead, these anesthesias were the involuntary creations of the patients' imaginations. Yet such patients were not malingering, for they did not flinch from pinprick. The integrated nervous system could practice adaptive, even creative, self-deception. Teeth could be painlessly pulled out under hypnosis, and yet the patient could talk about the process. It is true that twentieth-century neurobiology has proven that much of what Freud wrote about dreams was false; nevertheless, Freud's knowledge of nineteenth-century neurobiology has allowed many of his writings to remain biological classics.

Freud also pointed out that in understanding human conflict, much of which is nonverbal, only a poetic—and by that I mean also only an affect-laden—science will do. Such a science must keep in consciousness the poet's imagination and the poet's sensitivity to nonverbal feeling and affective color. In the words of Melvin Konner, both a sociobiologist and a poet, "The 'unconscious' described by Sigmund Freud is indeed a marvelous metaphoric organ. With its ebb and flow of emotion, its stored record of salient experience, its concourse with the body and its well blazed trails of feeling and expression, it can generate dreams, errors, beliefs, symptoms, lifelong patterns of word and deed, while its mechanisms remain unbeknownst to us."[5] But *unconscious* is really a misnomer. It often merely refers to those aspects of human experience for which we have inadequate language or understanding.

Nevertheless, modern experimental neurobiology supports Freud's metaphor of unconscious conflict and, more important, describes such conflict in a way that permits replication of experiments. In the laboratory, psychologists can identify meaningful mental activity that exists in the mind without words. A considerable body of research has made it clear that for most people language ability and logical analysis seem to be localized in the left hemisphere of the brain. Michael Gazzaniga, working with patients with surgically separated left and right hemispheres, has devised ways to investigate what happens when the left (verbal, logical) hemisphere does not know what the right hemisphere is seeing. In one of his studies, we showed the right hemisphere a series of film vignettes that included either violent or calm sequences. We used a device that permits prolonged exposure of visual pictures to the right [cerebral brain] hemisphere while the eyes remain fixed on a point. The computer-based system keeps careful track of the position of the eyes, so that if they move from the fixed point, the movie sequence is electronically turned off. For example, in one test a film depicting one person throwing another into a fire was shown to the patient's right hemisphere. She [that is, her surgically separated left brain hemisphere] responded, "I don't really know what I saw; I think just a white flash. Maybe some trees, red trees like in the fall. I don't know why but I feel kind of scared. I feel jumpy. I don't like this room, or maybe it's you getting me nervous." As an aside to a colleague, she then said, "I know I like Dr. Gazzaniga, but right now I'm scared of him for some reason." Clearly, the emotional tone associated with the movie had crossed over from the right to the left hemisphere. The left hemisphere was unaware of the content of the movie . . . and had to deal with it. The left-brain interpreter responded by making up a story that explained the newly felt state of mind.[6]

All the woman admitted to seeing was autumn leaves, the color of fire; but they certainly made her nervous. A psychoanalyst might call her response repression, but that interpretation would give the brain's synthetic capacities too little credit.

In the early 1960s, research psychiatrists documented that increased stress caused increased production of corticosteroids (cortisol) by the adrenal gland. The measurement of blood levels of these steroids seemed to offer scientists an objective way to measure stress. If going away to college for the first time or entering the hospital raised blood levels of steroids a little, what kind of stress, the scientists asked, might raise them a lot? The researchers moved from the polite laboratories of Washington, D.C., to the battlefields of Vietnam.[7] What would happen to blood levels of corticosteroids among men pinned down by incoming artillery shells at the so-called fire bases? To find out, researchers collected the urines of soldiers under sustained fire in Vietnam and flew them back to Washington for analysis. When their corticosteroid levels were found not to be elevated, the soldiers at the fire bases were interviewed. They explained that they felt quite safe in the terra firma of their besieged fire bases, and they suggested that the ones under real stress might be the pilots and crews who manned the helicopter gunships. The urines of these men, too, were duly collected and analyzed. Once again, their steroids were not elevated. When asked why, the air crews pointed to their mobility, their capacity to evade enemy fire. They suggested that perhaps the investigators, if they truly wished to measure stress, should collect the urines from soldiers pinned down at the fire bases. Each group denied that they were experiencing stress, and their bodies believed them. In other words, twentieth-century endocrinologists encountered evidence for the same sort of adaptive self-deception in hormone production that nineteenth-century neurologists had discovered with pain and sensation.

Michael Rutter, a distinguished British child psychiatrist and investigator of psychological resilience in children, notes that merely trying to sum the sources of stress and subtract the protective factors fails to explain the enormous variation in response to stress by different individuals. He refers to "the universal observation that even with the most severe stressors and the most glaring adversities, it is unusual for more than half of children to succumb . . . Although the risk of depression following disturbing life events is increased, it is usual for most people *not* to become depressed."[8] In other words, because of differences in the competence of their immune systems (that is, their defense mechanisms) individuals show wide variation in their resistance to infection (that is, their ability to cope with stress). Stress does not kill us, for defenses permit us to survive.

importance of healthy development

If I admit that defenses are as illusory as rainbows, I had better prove that defenses are just as real as rainbows and far more important. If I wish to preserve the Freudian "baby," I must take care to throw out the "bath water." Fantasy, poetry, free association were the stuff on which Freud came to depend, but they are fallible. Somehow, like Gazzaniga, we must leave Freud's psychoanalytic couch for the laboratory, or better yet, for the real world. Throughout this book I shall turn from poetic examples to numerical tables; but even the tables, however scientifically respectable, will only underscore the limits of science in elucidating rainbows and the human ego. In general, the phenomena of the ego will become most apparent when I provide case examples. Many of these case examples will come from the fifty-year-old Study of Adult Development, which I shall describe in Chapter 5. But first I must define the fundamental properties of defense mechanisms—of involuntary regulatory coping processes:

1. Defenses reflect creative synthesis. The mind creates a perception that was not there before and that did not come just from external reality. In this regard, defensive behavior resembles art.
2. Defenses are relatively unconscious and their deployment is relatively involuntary.
3. Defenses distort inner and/or outer reality.
4. Defenses distort the relationship between affect and idea and between subject and object.
5. Defenses are more often healthy than pathological.
6. Defenses often appear odd or startling to everyone but the user.
7. Over time defenses often mature and allow the mentally "ill" to evolve into the mentally well.

Let me offer a concrete illustration of a defense—a photograph of a rainbow, if you will, obtained through my metaphorical telescope, the Study of Adult Development. I was interviewing an internist who had participated in the study for thirty years. He told me, with vividness and enthusiasm, about his hobby: growing tissue cultures in his basement. He then told me with still more enthusiasm that the cells for one of these tissue cultures had been taken from a lesion on his mother's leg. He described his interest in tissue cultures as if it were the most ordinary pursuit in the world. But I have yet to describe his hobby to an audience without an uneasy ripple of laughter sweeping the room. Audiences have found the fact that this doctor was growing his mother's cells in his basement, as a child might raise flowers, extraordinary, even pathological. In short, the doctor saw his own behavior as normal; outsiders saw it as odd and, as we so often view other people's religion, politics, and dreams, possibly improper. Thus their laughter.

But anyone can have an unusual hobby. What made this internist's avocation particularly noteworthy was that near the end of the interview he revealed to me—in the most matter-of-fact way—that his mother had died only three weeks earlier. Knowing that he had been very fond of her, I asked him how he had coped with her death. He said that, since he was a physician, he had spent his time comforting his father. On a conscious level, this man had rationalized—and he was good at rationalizing—that he had borne the grief of losing his mother by caring for another person. Put differently, by his self-report he had used altruism as a coping strategy. Had I been interested only in conscious coping strategies, I too might have classified his means of mastering his mother's death as altruism. Instead, I located his source of solace by making a connection of which he himself was probably unaware. I deduced that the knowledge that somehow his mother was still alive and living in his basement might be providing a secret source of comfort. Certainly, he had described his scientific hobby to me with an enthusiasm and a warmth usually allotted to people and to art. Certainly, he had described the loss of his mother by death with the blandness usually allotted to leaves dropping off a tree in autumn—or to tissue cultures.

In short, defenses are creative, healthy, comforting, coping, and yet often strike observers as downright peculiar. But that is why defenses—like immune mechanisms—serve adaptation. That is why defenses integrate experience by providing a variety of filters for pain and mechanisms for self-deception. Defenses creatively rearrange the sources of conflict so that they become manageable. On the one hand, a grown child's very real love was detached from his deceased mother and reattached to his living tissue culture. Ego psychologists often call such a process *displacement*. On the other hand, the dispassionate, intellectual interest that doctors find useful in managing tissue cultures and in bearing the mortality of their patients was attached to his mother's death. Ego psychologists often call such a process *isolation of affect*. Like projection and dissociation, displacement and isolation are part of the repertoire of defense mechanisms.

Defenses result from creative synthesis. Defenses often manifest themselves in paintings and in dreams, in phobias and in hallucinations, in humor and in religious experience. As such, defenses are the building blocks of interesting behavior, of madness, and of art. They help explain the unreason of both the sinner and the saint. But if defenses integrate, make sense of, and master conflict, they remain difficult to describe. As with rainbows and shooting stars, now we see them, now we don't.

Defenses cannot be fitted, as can the chemical elements that make up the tangible world, into a periodic table. Creative synthesis, after all, is a result of the <u>highest order of brain activity.</u> Mozart's magic cannot be explained as merely an aberration of the wiring of his brain or the result of socialization by an ambitious and musically talented father. Similarly, we know much about the basic physics of crystal formation, and yet we cannot fully classify the complexity of the shapes of snowflakes—each one of which is unique, a new and beautiful creation. The explanation of the legerdemain of the art of both Mozart and snowflakes requires a higher order of complexity than our understanding of neurons and crystal formation.

Nevertheless, I shall try to schematize the defenses. I shall treat them as if they were as real and as readily classified as colors—the colors of a rainbow. Indeed, in the next chapter I shall offer for the defenses a periodic table of sorts. But like the colors of the rainbow, and unlike the chemical elements, defenses blend into one another. And just as a thesaurus lists a vast number of words for colors, the psychological literature provides a bewildering assortment of names for these regulatory coping processes. But however idiosyncratic our language for color or for involuntary regulatory coping processes may be, both rainbows and creative adaptation do exist.

Defenses are "unconscious." If the distortions of defenses are as creative as dreams and poetry, they are also as imperceptible to the user and as difficult to believe in as a round world was to Columbus's detractors. The internist I interviewed could not see the discrepancy between his enthusiasm for his hobby and his bland description of his mother's death. <u>To have seen it would have destroyed the utility of his self-deception.</u> Defenses, by necessity, are "unconscious." By this I do not mean that the defensive behavior itself is invisible to the user, only that the user does not recognize <u>the defense *as* a defense.</u>

<u>If we understand that we are using a given defense, it no longer works.</u> Dental surgery performed under hypnosis would become agonizing if we breached the trance and reminded the patient of the pain. Had the internist noted the association between his hobby and his mother's death, he might have wept. However, it must be kept in mind that the term *unconscious* is relative. Imaginative experiments by cognitive psychologists can illustrate that most comforting self-deceptions are only partially repressed. For example, after we blow out the candles on a birthday cake, the secret of making our wish come true is to tell no one. Secrecy strengthens the self-deception. Fantasies comfort only so long as they are secret, and yet the self-deceit is only partial.

Defenses distort, deny, and repress reality. Defenses effect denial and self-deception by altering inner and outer reality. The common response to hearing that a beloved or famous person has suddenly died is "Oh, no! It's not true. I don't believe it." For a more dramatic example of denial consider a physician acquaintance of mine who fell victim to barbiturate dependence. Heavy use of barbiturates leads to slurred speech, unsteady gait, a characteristic tremor of the eyes on looking to the side (nystagmus), and unexplained seizures. Since the doctor could not bring himself to acknowledge to another person or to himself that he had an addiction, he sought help from a neurologist for his symptoms. His neurologist, who could not believe (that is, would have been made anxious and depressed by believing) that a fellow physician could be addicted to barbiturates, tentatively diagnosed another but equally plausible cause for such symptoms, a brain tumor. Since at the time computer-assisted tomography (the CAT scan) had not yet been invented for diagnosis, it was necessary to insert air into the ventricles of the patient's brain. This meant drilling burr holes through his skull and inserting needles into his brain. Even at this point he did not acknowledge his addiction, but meekly allowed the holes to be drilled—a totally unnecessary and unrevealing diagnostic procedure. Such behavior by a physician can only be described as a frank distortion or *denial* of *external reality*. Unlike the examples I have offered of displacement (the internist) and of dissociation (the roller coaster riders), we usually associate such ignoring of external reality with psychosis. Yet in this instance the physician was not crazy, only severely addicted to barbiturates and profoundly ashamed.

Defenses alter the relationship between affect and idea. Defenses can alter the links between emotion and ideas and between the owner of the emotion and the person toward whom the emotion is directed. Affects, which are emotionally tinged mental representations, are thought to be made manifest by the brain's limbic system or rhinencephalon (smell-brain), a part of the brain highly developed only in mammals. Love and hate, disgusting smells and sentimental songs, evocative memory and epileptic auras all are elaborated by the temporal (limbic) areas of the mammalian brain. In contrast, ideas, logical mental processes, and abstract pattern recognition are thought to be most dependent upon the uniquely evolved human cerebral cortex.

The temporal or limbic region of the brain is particularly linked to emotional recognition. To link an odor, or a melody, with another person is to retain the person indelibly in memory. But we remember a person's smell very differently from the way we remember his or her name. We remember the melodies of songs differently from the way we remember lyrics. The former are more likely to make us cry or sing. Such is the nature of affect. An affect can bind a feeling and an object (usually a person) together for eternity. A major task of the ego is to balance and mediate the interchange between the peculiarly mammalian limbic system and the peculiarly human cerebral cortex.

Figure 1 diagrams the distortion of integration of feeling and idea that occurred in the internist's use of his hobby of growing tissue cultures as a defense against his grief. The transposition of idea and emotion was effected by his use of the specific defense mechanisms that psychiatrists label isolation and displacement.

This model of the mind illustrated in Figure 1—sometimes referred to as Freud's "topographic" model—suggests that the task of the defense mechanisms is to reduce the internist's conflict. Defenses

---

Actual, but unconscious, mental reality: "I grieve for my mother, whom I loved!"

Idea (loss/attachment)
Self (doctor) ⟶ Object (mother)
Affect (*Grief!/Love!*)

Conscious reality: "I love my tissue culture! My mother is dead."

Idea (loss)
Self (doctor) ⟶ Object (mother)
Affect (none)
Idea (attachment)
⟶ New object (tissue culture)
Affect (*Love!*)

Figure 1. A model of the adaptive mind at work, illustrating the defenses of isolation and displacement.

achieve this by the systematic alteration of conscious awareness of one or more of four components: subject, object, idea, and feeling. In Figure 1 an idea, *loss*, is separated from its affect, *grief*, and the affect is then removed (isolated) from consciousness. Another idea, *attachment*, and its affect, *love*, are separated from a dead, but important, person and reattached to (displaced onto) a still living, but more neutral, tissue culture. The first process is often called *isolation* and the second process *displacement*. The figure assumes that there is one version of inner and outer reality in awareness, and another truer unconscious version that is out of awareness, that is "repressed." But note that I use the term *repression* here in a very broad way. In Chapter 2 I shall redefine repression more narrowly, as a specific defense mechanism in which the affect is conscious but now separated from the associated idea, which is repressed. Sometimes Freud made this distinction; sometimes he used the term *repression* to encompass all defensive process. As we shall see in Chapter 2, the semantic problems surrounding defenses are formidable.

Defenses are healthy. However disordered, sick, sinful, or unreasonable defenses may appear to the observer, they reflect an adaptive response and an intact, working brain. By themselves defenses are not evidence of illness. As in the case of immune mechanisms, however maladaptive the results, defenses are deployed in the service of coping. The distinction between "defending" and "coping" is quite as arbitrary as a distinction between the unhealthy pus of acne and the healthy ingestion by our white corpuscles of intruding bacteria. The situations that call forth defenses and those that call forth white corpuscles are perilous; we cope as best we can. The distinction between adaptive and maladaptive is often in the eyes of the beholder.

The manifest unreason and self-deception of defenses are as healthy as a possum playing dead or a mother quail scuttling off into the underbrush feigning an injured wing. Only a possum or a quail with a healthy central nervous system can accomplish such a deception. Stalin and Hitler may have been severely paranoid. We can call their projections "sick," but the two men were among the most gifted leaders of this century. Their use of projection and their mental behavior, however peculiar and destructive to others, made them far more effective leaders than did the more moral but tangibly damaged brains of King George III and Woodrow Wilson. The latter two men were made ineffective by illness (porphyria and cerebral stroke respectively).

Stalin and Hitler were rendered all the more socially dangerous by their skillful paranoid distortions of inner and outer reality by brains functioning, if not wisely, all too well.

The use of defense mechanisms is analogous to the deployment of fever, cough, and white blood corpuscles. We worry and deem ourselves ill when we have a fever or boils, but without them we would be dead. The only Nobel Prize ever won by a psychiatrist was awarded to Julius Wagner von Jauregg for his discovery that giving malaria to patients with general paresis (syphilis of the brain) was lifesaving. He had discovered that the fever of paroxysmal malaria killed the syphilis-producing spirochetes and arrested the patient's illness. The pathologic symptom, fever, was in the service of health. In like fashion, defense mechanisms, too, strive for homeostasis and keep people confronted by sudden conflict from being immobilized by depression and anxiety.

An eight-year-old boy of my acquaintance, when climbing Mount Chocorua in New Hampshire, got within three hundred yards of the top and then developed weakness and spasms in both legs. He could not move either leg without excruciating pain. The only solution was for him to sit down. Miraculously, half an hour later, once the other, older boys on the expedition had achieved the top and it was time to go home, the eight-year-old, like Lazarus rising from the dead, was able to walk. Once they were pointed down the mountain rather than up, his palsied legs again became capable of painless locomotion. The boy was not ill; he was bored, tired, and outnumbered. But he was no willful malingerer; rather, his paralysis fully merited the impressive neurologic diagnosis *astasia-abasia* and also the equally daunting psychiatric diagnosis *hysterical conversion reaction*. But whatever one calls his defensive behavior, it was in the service of adaptation, not of disease.

Defenses appear odd to others. To an observer, defenses appear odd, definitely remarkable, and often downright irrational. Audiences laugh uneasily when told of the internist's tissue culture. The climbing companions of the eight-year-old boy became first worried and then irritated. Observers of such involuntary behavior are tempted to correct or blame the user. The user's first response to having a defense pointed out is usually to claim that the behavior just happened by chance. Next, he may rationalize and "explain" why his behavior has a reasonable motive behind it. Then, if confrontation continues, he may become anxious, angry, or depressed. For to abandon a defense is to expose the conflict. Without their defenses both the roller coaster riders and the internist would have been upset.

An observer may call the user of a defense stupid, or wicked, or mentally ill. All such responses are as useless as scolding a child for sneezing. We can neither condemn a tubercular patient for coughing nor ignore the internal disorder that the coughing portends. Similarly, we must neither condemn the lawful eccentricities of the ego's mechanisms of defense as sins nor dismiss them as mere chance events. As with the cough of the consumptive, attention must be paid to the odd behaviors of people with emotional dis-ease. The wisdom of the ego, like the wisdom of the body, must be understood before we are tempted to meddle.

Understanding defenses is essential to any kind of counseling or psychotherapy, for by understanding defenses we understand *why* people behave irrationally. Attention to defenses trains us to look beneath the obvious. For example, if we know that displacement underlies some phobias, then we know that we are unlikely to find the source of phobics' anxiety by questioning the phobics about the exact object of their fears. Rather, we must look everywhere else for the source of their distress.

Once we start to appreciate the existence of defenses, we will see them used by friends, neighbors, and relatives. The proper response is neither to cry "Gotcha!" nor to worry that there may be something terribly wrong. Rather, by understanding defenses, we can often master what disturbs us about other people. When we understand the whys of irrational behavior, we become less judgmental and can offer social support. If we insist on pointing people's defenses out to them, we must be willing to share responsibility for their ensuing anxiety. Nobody is comfortable being mentally undressed.

In addition, to understand defenses is also to appreciate that in many cases concrete psychiatric diagnosis and illness do not exist. As Adolf Meyer suggested, much of the time psychiatrists deal with *reactions,* not diseases. Human misery is rarely caused by anything as specific as a bacillus. The insurance companies have done neither their clients nor psychiatric classification a favor by agreeing to pay for care only of mental disease and not of dis-ease. In addition, sometimes pain should be used to lead us to the primary cause and not be mindlessly eradicated. Thus, internists no longer thoughtlessly medicate people for cough and bellyache. Instead, they search for cause—the fishbone caught in the trachea or the inflamed appendix that needs removal. The same cause-seeking may be necessary for many so-called anxiety and major depressive disorders, which may be only symptoms of unrecognized distress. Symptoms and defenses must not be confused with disease.

I wish, from the beginning, to acknowledge the problems that arise in trying to identify the nature and reality of a defense. Underlying Cannon's homeostatic wisdom of the body were the tangible parasympathetic and sympathetic nervous systems. Underlying defenses and the wisdom of the ego are processes as ephemeral as rainbows and as diverse and as difficult to describe as the crystalline latticework of a snowflake. Cannon studied simple neural systems innervating the gut that were linear and easy to visualize. In contrast, defense mechanisms are the holographic, synthetic, and evanescent products of a creative, infinitely complex central nervous system.

In order to visualize and to manipulate the body's homeostasis, Cannon could capitalize on a new scientific tool, the use of X rays. But if scientific proof requires experimental manipulation, how can I do that for defenses? Psychoanalysts have long been mocked by their experimental psychologist brethren for constructing a philosophical system in which they can always win. The Freudian dictum that there are "no negatives in the unconscious" allows anything a person says to be rearranged to fit the analyst's thesis. When convenient to psychoanalysts (let me relabel them psychobiographers), normal forgetting can be blamed on motivated "repression." To document intuitive clinical hunch, the analyst can order the content of dreams and poetry as arbitrarily as a fortuneteller orders tea leaves. Clearly, if we are to believe in invisible, unconscious defenses, if we are not to use defenses like demons and poltergeists as a way to justify our own prejudices, if defenses are not just to exist in the eyes of the beholder, then we need some form of experimental validation. In order to study defenses, we need a tool analogous to Cannon's X rays.

The best settings in which to validate defenses are those in which long-term *prospective* clinical observation of normal individuals is possible: the psychobiography of creative artists, and longitudinal studies of the human life span. Among the latter is the Study of Adult Development, based at Harvard University, in which the participants have been studied for longer than the working lives of the original investigators. In this book, in order to validate defenses, I will draw upon both the lives of creative artists and data from the Study of Adult Development.

Each of these longitudinal methods—the prospective study of adult development and the psychobiography of artists—obtains and contrasts three different classes of data. These three are contemporary biographical fact unbiased by memory, autobiographical subjective report, and pathological, creative, even tangible symptom. The three classes of evidence make it possible to triangulate the presence of a defense mechanism. I use the term *triangulate* as it is used in surveying. By studying a mountain peak from contrasting angles a surveyor can estimate its height. By integrating biography, self-report, and symptom, we can appreciate the reality of defenses and estimate the inner workings of the mind. Take as an example the psychobiography of a creative artist. The biographer has biographical facts—concrete, observable, black-and-white facts about the artist. The biographer may also have access to the artist's letters and the artist's own explanations for his or her emotionally driven work. And, if wise, the biographer will pay attention to the artist's creative products themselves—those odd bits of imaginative behavior that are as startling, as colorful, and as individual as the delusions of a madman. By combining these three vantage points—biography, autobiography, and creative product—we can obtain the evidence that we need for a validation of defenses.

Such psychobiographical data are similar to those obtained during prolonged psychiatric observation, for there is no absolute distinction among the creations of artists, the play of children, and the creations of madmen and dreamers. The biographical facts about the artist are comparable to the patient's history compiled from pretrial investigations and laboratory findings from old hospital records and what the nurse noted on the ward. (Note how I cast about both for multiple sources of data and for data gathered at the time rather than in retrospect.) The artist's autobiographical report is analogous to the patient's own subjective, often emotional, recounting of past and present events. Finally, the artist's creative product is analogous to the actual content of a patient's hallucinations, delusions, or obsessions. Such symptoms or creative products correspond to the internist's tissue cultures.

Consider the example of the internist once again. His symptom, or his creative product, as it were, was his imaginative growing of a tumor from his mother in his basement—for most of us no routine task. It was a fact that his mother had died three weeks before our interview. His autobiographical report revealed little emotion, grief, or upset in describing his mother's recent death. Instead, he expressed great enthusiasm, excitement, and caring about an only barely animate tissue culture. Most important, my source of biographical evidence was from carefully gathered facts collected by observers blind to the future. I depended for "fact" neither on memory nor on my interpretation after the facts were all in. I depended upon prospective observation of this man by the Study of Adult Development. Evidence that he was fond of his mother and that he came from a close family had been gathered when he was 18 and had been evaluated by raters ignorant of the future. Finally, this was not the first or the last time that this man would isolate idea from affect and use displacement to shift his attention away from real pain and conflict toward more manageable and less affect-laden fields of concern.

My intent in this book, then, is to examine the wisdom of the ego—a phenomenon so complex, so affect-laden, so peculiarly human that only a metaphor-ridden, poetic science will do. I will try to use biography to show, rather than to tell. Since I mean to explore the ego's wisdom, I shall not use information from psychiatric patients. Rather, to demonstrate that defenses reflect health and creativity and not illness, I shall depend upon prospective longitudinal studies of *normal* adult development.

I shall develop three entwined themes concerning the ego: first, that defenses are as important to our well-being as our immune mechanisms; second, that human creativity also transmutes pain and restores the self; and third, that just as the human body matures during childhood, so the human ego matures during adulthood. I shall try to document that Freud's ego mechanisms of defense deserve the same respect from clinicians as is accorded to immune mechanisms, and that defenses, however ephemeral, deserve the same respect from the natural sciences as is accorded to rainbows—and to thunderstorms.

2

A Matter of Definition

Go to, let us go down, and there confound their language, that they may
not understand one another's speech.

So the Lord scattered them abroad from thence upon the face of all the
earth: and they left off to build the city.

Therefore is the name of it called Babel; because the Lord did there confound the language of all the earth.

Genesis 11:7–9

A clearly understood nomenclature of defenses not only enables
us to understand adaptation to stress; it also offers us a means of
uncoding, of translating if you will, much of what seems irrational in
human behavior. Such translation of unreason can bring humanity to
criminal justice, heightened understanding to group behavior, and
fresh insight to the mysteries of neurosis. By understanding defenses
as a product of conflicting emotions, we can reattach lost affect to
cognitions and ideas. In this way the study of defenses may even be
able to humanize the discipline of cognitive psychology lest it become
entirely abstract and computational. But readers must be forewarned.
The study of defenses will not initially provide much self-help, for our
own defenses are invisible and beyond our ken. Understanding
defenses must remain a largely altruistic endeavor. Others must point
out our own defenses to us before we know that they are there.

Unfortunately, learning the language of defenses is a little like
studying a foreign language. The fun comes at the end, not at the beginning. At first, deciphering defenses is like the tourist's struggle with
a dictionary rather than the "Aha!" experience of being able at last to
understand a conversation or a newspaper. Like a glossary for a foreign
language, this chapter will attempt to make distinctions clear. But
many readers will encounter definitions that differ from the ones they
have learned. To clarify my use of terms, I shall also offer clinical
examples.

But a hierarchy or rank ordering of self-deceptions and denials is as important to our understanding of defenses as is the development of a language with which to discuss them. "Rapid progress," writes the psychologist Richard Lazarus, "in the development of an adequate psychology of coping is unlikely until a theoretically based system of classification for coping responses has been evolved."[1] In this chapter I shall offer a theoretically based system of classification, but first I shall provide a schematic grammar for defenses, by contrasting the ways in which the mind can alter conscious representations of the same conflict.

Figure 2 offers a model for how defenses work. Whereas Figure 1 in the previous chapter modeled the *expression* of a conflict, Figure 2 models the *sources* of human conflict. In other words, Figure 2 represents how conflict is created from multiple sources rather than how the consequences of conflict are mentally attenuated as was suggested by the diagram of the internist's displacement and isolation of affect in Figure 1. This second diagram is analogous to Freud's so-called structural model of the mind: a tripartite model of superego, ego, and id. We all live in a mental universe in which mental conflict is oriented by the discordant tug of four lodestars: our desires, our conscience, the important people in our lives, and reality. Conflict-engendered defense arises when there is a sudden change in one of the four lodestars. Uncompensated, such sudden change (for example, an unex-

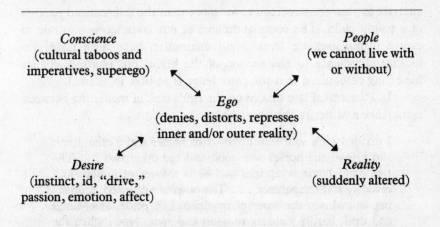

Conscience
(cultural taboos and
imperatives, superego)

People
(we cannot live with
or without)

Ego
(denies, distorts, represses
inner and/or outer reality)

Desire
(instinct, id, "drive,"
passion, emotion, affect)

Reality
(suddenly altered)

Figure 2. The four lodestars of human conflict.

pected death) produces anxiety and/or depression. To the extent that this change cannot be accommodated, to the extent that it creates cognitive dissonance, the ego—the integrating principle in our central nervous system—needs to stall for time until mental accommodation can take place. Such alterations in inner and/or outer reality and emotion must be, in lay terms, denied, repressed, or distorted until the accompanying anxiety and depression can be borne.

By the lodestar *desire* I mean our emotions, our drives, our wishes (hunger, grief, lust, rage, and so on). Psychoanalysts call this lodestar *id,* fundamentalists call it *sin,* cognitive psychologists call it *hot cognition,* and neuroanatomists point to the hypothalamic and limbic regions of the brain. Freud lumped all desire under the term *libido,* but there are many desires. Grief, anger, and dependency loom quite as large as sex as sources of conflict. For the purpose of understanding intrapsychic conflict, the psychoanalytic term *affect* is a useful substitute for *desire.* (An affect is created when an instinct or desire is attached to an object, for example when hunger attaches our attention to a sizzling hamburger.)

By the lodestar *conscience*—the superego of psychoanalysis—I do not just mean the admonitions of our mother and father that we absorbed before age five. By conscience I mean our whole identification with our society, with our culture, and with our own ego ideals. Erik Erikson's view of culture—and, indeed, Freud's own view of "civilization and its discontents"—have led even the most simplistic psychoanalysts to view the superego as far more than the internalized parents of a young child. The commandments of our conscience continue to evolve throughout our lives. Neuroanatomists have been unable to localize conscience to one section of the brain, but pharmacologists have long recognized that the conscience is soluble in alcohol.

In *Phaedrus,* Plato described the ego's task of mediating between conscience and desire this way:

> I divided each soul into three—two horses and a charioteer; and one of the horses was good and the other bad . . . The righthand horse is upright . . . he is a lover of honour and modesty and temperance . . . The other is a crooked, lumbering animal . . . the mate of insolence and pride, shag-eared and deaf, hardly yielding to whip and spur. Now, when the charioteer beholds the vision of love, and has his whole soul warmed through sense, and is full of the prickings and ticklings

of desire, the obedient steed then as always under the government of shame, refrains from leaping on the beloved; but the other . . . forces [the charioteer] to approach the beloved and to remember the joys of love.[2]

In elucidating the defenses, Freud, too, conceived of the ego as mediating only between conscience and desire, between superego and id, between individuals' sexual instincts and their internalized "Victorian" prohibitions. But such a Platonic viewpoint is too parochial. It is not only dissonance between conscience and desire that begets conflict. As soon as psychoanalysts began to look at social interactions and to study their patients within the matrix of other people rather than in the isolation of the consulting room, the stress of interpersonal conflict became clear. The dyadic tensions, first elaborated by Harry Stack Sullivan and Melanie Klein—and by Freud's own concept of transference—are every bit as important as intrapsychic conflict.

Thus, *people* form the third lodestar in Figure 2. People become a source of conflict when we cannot live with them and yet cannot live without them. The death of a loved one is the most obvious example, but there are many others. There are individuals to whom we are peculiarly attached but with whom we are not at peace. Examples are the boss whom we strive to please but also hate, the scapegoat we abuse but would mourn were he to disappear, and the lover who terrifies us by exclaiming "Yes!" to our rather tentative proposal of marriage. People also exist within. Internal representations of important people in our lives continue to haunt us and to cause conflict for decades after we have ceased to live with the people themselves.

By reality, the fourth lodestar, I mean those facets of our external environment that are capable of changing more rapidly than we can adapt. The drought of the Australian outback and the Amazonian damp are not stressful to the aboriginals for whom such drought and damp are predictable and unchanging. But five inches of snow—a mere flurry in Montreal and a blessing at Aspen or St. Moritz—can paralyze Paris or Washington. In similar fashion, good news—graduation from law school or the winning of an unexpected grand prize in a lottery—to the degree that the change wrought is sudden or inadequately planned for, can become as stressful as a flood or a diagnosis of tuberculosis.

Tragic reality for whom no one is responsible—such as a child's leukemia—is too psychically destabilizing to be borne, and thus reality must be distorted. For example, pioneering studies of the parents of leukemic children at the National Institute of Mental Health revealed that almost none of the mothers were able to accept the absence of human causation in their children's death.[3] For their children's leukemia, the mothers blamed either themselves or the hospital; their anger was either projected out or turned on the self.

Curiously, external reality, the fourth lodestar of conflict, was the last to be recognized as such by psychoanalysts. It was not until after World War II that psychoanalytically informed accounts of stress, such as *Men Under Stress* by Roy Grinker and John Spiegel, Kai Erikson's *The Buffalo Creek Disaster*, and Robert Coles's *Children of Crisis*, acknowledged that the same defenses known to mitigate intrapsychic and interpersonal conflicts also mitigated suddenly altered reality.

To mitigate intrapsychic conflict, then, the task of ego mechanisms of defense is to restore psychic homeostasis by ignoring or distorting one or more of the four lodestars. The internist with his tissue culture ignored the importance of *people* in his life; the mothers of the leukemic children ignored the *reality* that leukemia is no one's fault; the roller coaster riders ignored the importance of their *feeling* of fear. In summary, defenses (that is, mental regulatory processes) can accomplish their task in two different ways. First, defenses can alter the *causative* lodestars of conflict by denying or distorting desire, people, reality, conscience, or any combination thereof. Or, as outlined in Figure 1 in the preceding chapter, defenses can alter the *expression* of conflict, by distorting recognition of subject, object, idea, affect, or any combination thereof.

Table 1 illustrates a variety of different ways in which an individual could express his conflictual awareness that he hates his father. Consider a fictional case example. A 30-year-old Chinese-American businessman finds himself dishonored and threatened by his 65-year-old father, who is his business partner and whom he has never before consciously mistrusted. The son discovers that his father has defrauded their customers. The young businessman is confronted with a reality, a fact of life, for which he has had no time to prepare. He finds that he can neither live with his father nor abandon his filial relationship. Ethically, he believes that he should continue to honor his father; but in his limbic system and amygdala, he feels, "I hate my father!"

Changes in the son's reality and in his personal relationships have produced *external* social conflict as dynamically important as his *internal*

Table 1. Contrasting ways of altering the conscious representation of a conflict

Defense	Conscious representation of idea, feeling, or behavior	DSM III Phenomenological diagnosis[a]
No defense	I hate (!) my father.	309.9 Adjustment reaction with atypical features
Psychotic defense		
Denial	I was born without a father.	298.8 Brief reactive psychosis
Immature defenses		
Projection	My father hates (!) me.	301.0 Paranoid personality disorder
Passive aggression	I hate (!) myself (suicide attempt).	300.4 Dysthymic disorder
Acting out	Without reflection, I hit 12 policemen.	301.7 Antisocial personality disorder
Fantasy	I daydream of killing giants.	301.2 Schizoid personality disorder
Neurotic (intermediate) defenses		
Dissociation	I tell my father jokes.	300.15 Atypical dissociative disorder
Displacement	I hate (!) my father's dog.	300.29 Simple phobia
Isolation (or intellectualization)	I disapprove of my father's behavior.	300.3 Obsessive-compulsive disorder
Repression	I do not know why I feel so hot and bothered.	300.02 Generalized anxiety disorder
Reaction formation	I love (!) my father or I hate (!) my father's enemies.	—
Mature defenses		
Suppression	I am cross at my father but will not tell him.	—
Sublimation	I beat my father at tennis.	—
Altruism	I comfort father haters.	

a. Diagnosis assumes that conscious representation of the conflict was carried to pathological extremes and that the other criteria for the diagnosis were met.

conflict over his patricidal impulses. And conflicts over anger, grief, and dependency are just as distressing to him as conflicts over forbidden "Freudian" sexual wishes might be in some other filial relationship. Either the son must consciously experience both the *idea* and the *feeling* of hating his father, which will lead to profound anxiety, depression, and physiological stress, or in some way he must alter his inner and/or outer reality. The table illustrates different ways in which the young businessman's conflict-laden statement "I hate my father" can be cognitively rearranged by the ego to decrease anxiety, guilt, or depression. In the center of the table are phenomena familiar to all. To the left are the idiosyncratic labels that psychoanalysts use to describe the *psychodynamics* of such phenomena, and on the right are the idiosyncratic labels that epidemiologists use to classify such behavior. Thus, Table 1 contains a moral. Often, what psychiatrists label as specific disease is no more than the patient's ego coping with nonspecific dis-ease. Phobias, obsessions, even some psychoses are often more analogous to cough or fever than to diabetes or cancer. It is noteworthy, however, that the denials and self-deceptions that result from the deployment of what I call *mature defenses* result in no diagnosis. Not everyone who practices self-deception appears ill to others. The oyster, after all, deals with the irritation produced by a grain of sand by creating a pearl.

Implicit in my description of Table 1 is a second lesson. The table illustrates several defenses already described in Chapter 1; dissociation, displacement, isolation, projection. It also introduces a few more defenses like reaction formation and sublimation. Although it is important to acknowledge that self-deception and denial exist, it is more difficult to assign mutually exclusive and consensually validated labels for defenses than it is to assign labels for diagnoses. In older literature, the Berkeley developmental psychologist Norma Haan[4] offered us 30 styles of denial. The psychoanalyst and Harvard professor Grete Bibring and her co-workers[5] offered us 40 styles. More recently, a review by Manfred Beutel lists 37 labels used by 17 psychoanalytically oriented cataloguers of defense. For only 5 of the 37 defenses was there reasonable consensus. To make it worse, nonpsychoanalytic researchers have come up with completely different taxonomies. In short, students of personality, like the builders of the Tower of Babel, are in danger of being confounded by a bewildering array of terms.

Table 2 tries to bring some sort of order unto this Kingdom of

Babel. Just as a prism refracts light into distinct colors, just so Table 2 divides up the broadly defined terms into distinct, mutually exclusive defensive styles. The table does this by identifying both which of the four lodestars of the sources of conflict are most distorted by each defense and the different means by which the ego alters the subject's relative awareness of self, idea, affect, and object. In so doing the table ignores the hypothesis, first put forth by Anna Freud in *The Ego and the Mechanisms of Defense* and frequently repeated since, that some defenses deal more with certain affects than with others and that some defenses deal only with people. This hypothesis may be correct, but thus far it has received little experimental confirmation.

Deliberately, I have included in Table 2 defense mechanisms for which reasonable consensus exists.[6] The table groups these defenses into four categories that are based on the relative adaptiveness of these styles of self-deception in adult life. For example, projection is listed as *immature* or maladaptive and altruism as *mature* or adaptive. At first I may seem to be naming, and then assigning value to, the colors of the rainbow. For on the one hand, defenses are but metaphors—a shorthand to describe mental processes whose existence we can only infer. On the other hand, the defenses that individuals use can have profound effects on themselves and others. The word that we use to label the color of a red bandanna is quite arbitrary; but whether, indeed, the color is red or green makes a big difference to a bull. In general, the deployment of mature defenses tends to pacify other people, while the deployment of immature defenses tends to have the same effect upon observers that red exerts upon a bull.

In many ways the three defenses altruism (mature), reaction formation (neurotic or intermediate), and projection (immature) are similar. For example, each defense denies the subject's ownership of desire. In addition, developmentally projection often evolves into reaction formation and reaction formation into altruism. But that is as it should be. What, then, are the critical differences that effect adaptation?

To illustrate this distinction between mature (adaptive, coping) and immature (maladaptive, pathological) defenses, consider the examples of two passionate, famous, self-sacrificing ascetics whose personal belief systems would seem to the majority of the world's population to involve self-deception: Mother Theresa and Adolf Hitler. Reaction formation, the deliberate eschewing of sensual gratification, was present in the lives of both Hitler and Mother Theresa. Mother Theresa has lived in celibacy and poverty. Hitler, too, was often celibate, dressed

Table 2. Mutually exclusive ways of identifying the defenses

| | Sources of conflict | | | |
Styles of defense	Affects/ instinct/ desire	Conscience/ culture	Relation- ships/people	Reality
I. Psychotic				
1. Delusional projection	Externalized	Exaggerated	Distorted	Distorted
2. Denial	Ignored	—	Ignored	Ignored
3. Distortion	Exaggerated	Ignored	Distorted	Distorted
II. Immature				
1. Projection	Externalized	—	Distorted	Exaggerated
2. Fantasy	—	Ignored	Taken inside	—
3. Hypochondriasis	Distorted	—	Devalued	Distorted
4. Passive aggression	Turned on self	Exaggerated	Exaggerated	—
5. Acting out	Exaggerated	Ignored	Displaced	—
6. Dissociation	Altered	Altered	Exaggerated	—
III. Neurotic (intermediate)				
1. Displacement	—	—	Displaced	Minimized
2. Isolation/Intellec- tualization	Minimized	Exaggerated	Distanced	—
3. Repression	Disguised	—	—	Minimized
4. Reaction formation	Ignored	Exaggerated	—	—
IV. Mature				
1. Altruism	Minimized	Exaggerated	—	—
2. Sublimation	Disguised	—	—	—
3. Suppression	Minimized	Minimized	Minimized	Minimized
4. Anticipation	—	—	—	—
5. Humor	—	—	—	—

more simply than any dictator in memory, and was a vegetarian. However, Mother Theresa sacrificed herself for Calcutta's poor and was rewarded with Nobel gold; her belief that she knew what others needed was correct, empathic, and what may be labeled altruistic. In contrast, Hitler's projective efforts to sacrifice himself for the good of the German people were rewarded by his suicide and an ignominious gasoline funeral pyre in the rubble of Berlin—a city destroyed by his intransigence and his unempathic projection of his own needs upon the German people.

The difficulty, of course, is that such a comparison is possible

	Expression of impulse		
Self/subject	Idea	Affect	Object
Made object	Exaggerated	Exaggerated	Made self
Omnipotent	Ignored	Ignored	Ignored
Omnipotent	Altered	Altered	Generalized
Made object	—	—	Made self
Omnipotent	—	Diminished	Within self
—	Altered	Anger becomes pain	Displaced
Made object	—	—	Ignored
Omnipotent	Ignored	Ignored	Generalized
—	—	Altered	—
—	—	—	Displaced
—	—	Ignored	—
—	Ignored	—	Ignored?
—	Reversed	Reversed	—
—	—	—	Made self
—	—	Diminished	—
—	Diminished	Diminished	—
—	Exaggerated	Altered	—

only in hindsight. As in discerning historical truth, long-term follow-up is necessary to distinguish the relative adaptiveness of defenses. In the 1930s might not a partisan German economist have noted that Hitler, as an ascetic, idealistic German politician, had, at least for a while, provided his nation with economic rebirth? Could not Mother Theresa have been viewed by a Hindu psychologist as just another Western religious crank perpetuating the racist credo of the white man's burden and thus, indirectly, contributing to Calcutta's economic stagnation?

But let us use Table 2 to analyze the differing adaptive self-deceptions of Mother Theresa and Hitler. Certainly, both used reaction formation. Both found a source of pleasure in poverty, rather than in wealth; such behavior is in keeping with the fact that the user of reaction formation admits the desire, but its value is reversed. Black becomes white. With both altruism and reaction formation, however, the *self* is not confused with the *object* and other people are not distorted. This was more true of Mother Theresa than of Hitler. With both reaction formation and projection—but not with altruism—we believe ourselves endangered from without by our own most cherished desires, which, of course, in reality reside within. The user of projection, like Hitler, maintains that his own instinctual desires emanate not from himself but from the object. Hitler perceived the Jews and Communists as filled with his own unacknowledged desires; Mother Theresa saw only herself as to blame. Armed with these distinctions, I believe that even in the 1930s the German economist and the Hindu psychologist might have agreed on who would be a better future candidate for the Nobel Peace Prize and probably on whose self-deceptions would ultimately be the most adaptive.

But nuns are not comparable to heads of nations. How can I really hope to distinguish an adaptive ego from a lucky one? Since the question is complex, it is best to approach the answers one step at a time. The first step is systematically to distinguish defensive styles from one another while holding conflict, talent, and protagonist constant. Only by focusing on a single individual can I demonstrate that the kinds of "denial" that people employ have profound implications both for how we regard them and for their own adaptation to life. Thus, keeping the focus on a single fictional individual, I shall try to differentiate the eighteen defenses listed in Table 2 and to illustrate why some modes of denial and self-deception are labeled as relatively mature (adaptive) defenses and others as relatively immature (maladaptive) defenses. The generalizations that I shall illustrate with a fictional protagonist are supported by a significant body of experimental evidence.

For my adaptive heroine I have chosen a 16-year-old girl, Peggy O'Hara, who suddenly finds herself in conflict with her conscience, with her desires, with her reality, and with important other people she can neither live with nor live without. I have deliberately chosen an adolescent girl rather than a middle-aged man. For to talk or write about defenses that come too close to oneself can lead to their breach—and this can lead to depression or anxiety or further self-deception.

Therefore, to discuss defenses dispassionately I must distance myself from my imaginary protagonist.

The external reality of Peggy's life is that for the last twelve of her sixteen years, she has gone to a Catholic girls' school and has been educated exclusively by nuns. She has never been on a date or even held hands with a boy. The instinctual reality of Peggy's life is that at age 12 she went through menarche and since age 14 she has been endocrinologically sexually mature. The cultural reality of her life is that she made her First Communion at age 8 and by age 16 the nuns' beliefs have become her own. Her devout Catholicism is as much a part of her identity as are her sexual stirrings. The interpersonal reality of her life is that in the last few months, while working on church projects, she has fallen in love with an 18-year-old boy. Since she is socially mature, she does not experience mere puppy love but a genuine affective commitment. A final confounding fact is that her boyfriend is as sexually experienced as she is naive.

How can Peggy's ego guide her through a long hot summer without her becoming anxious or depressed? A Catholic conscience (superego) conflicts with impatient biology (id), which conflicts with the reality of her inexperience, which conflicts with her boyfriend's intimate demands. Without mediation from this young adolescent woman's ego, conflict is inevitable. Without some form of adaptive self-deception, her conflict (rename it, if you will, *cognitive dissonance* or *stress*) must make her depressed and anxious and a candidate for one of the psychiatric diagnoses outlined in Table 1.

Yet Peggy's dilemma also reminds us that much of the anxiety and depression in the world does not belong to diagnosable anxiety neurotics and certifiable psychotic depressives. Anxiety and depression belong to ordinary people experiencing ordinary conflict and change. Peggy's problem is by no means as exotic as a Capulet falling in love with a Montague. Indeed, in Peggy's case, such conflict and change are as necessary to her growth and development as are exercise and education. Millions of young women have been in similar situations. Their conflicts have been anything but pathological; and given enough time, their "illnesses" have proven to be self-limiting. The task of Peggy's ego, then, is simply to get her through the summer without her becoming *too* anxious and *too* depressed. But to do so it must employ selective self-deception: it must deploy defenses.

Before tracing Peggy's possible uses of defenses, I must distinguish coping via the ego's involuntary mental regulatory processes (defenses) from other styles of coping. In Chapter 1, I suggested that there are three general classes of coping style by which one can resolve stress. The first general class involves cognitive, conscious coping strategies. For my young Catholic protagonist, one such solution would be for her father to send her to Europe for the summer. But too often such coping strategies are luxuries. Often only the rich can volitionally choose to avoid the slings and arrows of outrageous fortune. And were her father to send her to Europe for the summer, Peggy might become both angry and very depressed.

The second general class of coping styles is social supports. Peggy's boyfriend could be unusually understanding and patient. Or she could turn to some older friend, a trusted priest, a big sister, or even a guidance counselor, for advice and comfort. When someone holds our hand, we all become less anxious under stress. But again, this coping style relies on the luxury of social supports. In many parts of the world guidance counselors are scarce and understanding adolescent lovers scarcer still.

The less privileged of the world must depend on the alchemy, the adaptive self-deceptions, of their egos. Thus, I will focus Peggy's story on the third class of coping styles—the ego mechanisms of defense. In keeping with the models of mental life and the hierarchy of defenses outlined in Table 2, I shall describe various mutually exclusive ways the ego of a 16-year-old girl could distort inner and outer reality. Let me begin first with defenses I have classed as psychotic.

Psychotic Defenses

Table 2 identifies three styles of psychotic defense: delusional projection, distortion, and denial. Psychotic defenses reorganize the perceptions of a defective (for example, sleeping, poisoned, immature, or emotionally overwhelmed) central nervous system. Unlike defenses at other levels, psychotic defenses can profoundly alter perception of external reality.

Delusional Projection

Were she to use delusional projection, Peggy might report to her priest that the devil was shining laser beams upon her genitals. Terror stricken, she might shut herself in the seclusion of her bedroom, a helpless victim of external persecutory demons—demons that no amount of scientific reasoning and religious reassurance would chase away. Her priest might be overwhelmed and refer her to a psychiatrist who would give her a clinical diagnosis of schizophrenia.

In dreams, in childhood, and at times of great danger, such *delusional projection* is occasionally part of our everyday life. Thus, before we dismiss such bizarre behavior as due only to the twisted genes of schizophrenia, we should reflect on what happens in our own nightmares, in children's fairy tales, in great religious paintings, and in the minds of military men too many cultural leaps away from their enemies to test reality. Remember the U.S. officer in Vietnam who reported that he had to "destroy the village in order to save it." Away from the stress of battle such reasoning seems lunatic.

In delusional projection, inner conflicts are externalized and given tangible reality. Until we awake from the dream or remember that the fairy tale is just a story, or until modern tranquilizers calm Othello, or until our subhuman enemy becomes our noble ally in our next military conflict, cure seems impossible.

Delusional projection can be distinguished from simple projection by the fact that in the former reality testing is virtually abandoned. Othello's suspiciousness is more than projection, for Othello does not just wrongly accuse the innocent Desdemona, he strangles her. Similarly, wise leaders believed that unless Vietnam villages were torched, an unruly row of "dominoes" would fall and ultimately crush cherished American freedoms. Future historians may never understand, but insane defenses are sometimes deployed by perfectly normal individuals.

Distortion

Were she to deploy distortion, Peggy might announce to all who would listen that a famous rock star had proposed to her. She could tell from his gestures on television and from his quotes in the movie magazines that she was his intended love. Ecstatic with joy, Peggy would purchase exotic lingerie and extravagant amounts of contraceptives. In her excitement her real boyfriend would fade into the background, and her parents would believe her to be crazy. The value of such a defense would be that the imaginary figure was unobtainable— so she could feel loved without having to face sexuality.

True, such behavior is often associated with the manic phase of manic-depressive illness, but once again distortion like Peggy's can occur in everyday life. Consider the deep conviction with which a child waits for a dead cat to wake or the faith that sustains a deeply religious person faced with inevitable catastrophe. Just days before being massacred by the United States cavalry at Wounded Knee, the Lakota Indians danced a dance to bring the buffalo back to the plains, to give life to their dead ancestors, and to bury the hated white man under a great pile of dirt. The Lakotas were not crazy, only faced with a disaster of unbearable dimensions. Thus, religious faith—someone else's religious faith—provides us all with dramatic examples of distortion in everyday life. But as with the identification of all defenses, observer bias must be controlled. If we believe our own religion to be true, how can we fairly judge the sanity of another's?

With distortion there may also be a pleasant merging or fusion with another person. An angel's gentle guiding voice may "exist" inside one's head. Hamlet's delusional image of his dead father does not come only to arouse his guilt but also to offer comfort. But such hallucinatory fusion differs from the schizoid fantasizer who only "imagines" a conversation with his dead father. In fantasy the comfort is inside one's head; with distortion the comfort is in the real world.

In real life clear distinctions between distortion and delusional projection are not always possible. Nevertheless, the delusional Peggy is miserable from the sexual excitement "caused" by the devil shining laser beams upon her genitals. In contrast, distortion allows the formerly shy Peggy to believe herself more desirable than Marilyn Monroe—reality be damned. In paranoid delusions, the user puts less emphasis on the gratification of desire and more on distorting the dictates of conscience (see Table 2). In contrast, if the individual is manic and not paranoid, sin seems irrelevant, and he may believe that even a truly unfaithful lover still loves him. During the cycle of manic-depressive psychosis, in manic periods, distortion allows instincts to become both virtuous and instantly gratifiable; in depressive periods, guilty delusions allow demons inspired by bad conscience to consume the sinner's liver and even virtues to become sins. Not surprisingly, the comfort of mania and of religion is harder to give up than are nightmares and the paranoid hatreds of war.

Psychotic Denial

Our 16-year-old convent girl could ignore the existence of her boyfriend. Peggy could walk past him on the street and insist that he was a stranger. She might even mourn his "death" and wear black. It is true that such denial of external reality is more common in catatonic schizophrenia than in everyday life. But I can recall such behavior in a woman who by no means could be called mentally ill. When her cook was discovered to have been murdered in the kitchen, she remained upstairs. A devout Christian Scientist, she behaved as if the whole sorry business did not exist. While others below coped with the police, she asserted with great conviction that "No evil can come to my house." Additional examples of such *denial* (of external reality) would be the physician in Chapter 1 who allowed burr holes to be drilled in his head rather than acknowledge his barbiturate addiction and a 5-year-old acquaintance of mine who at zoos treated all cages that contained animals larger than he was as if they were empty.

In short, psychotic denial literally obliterates external reality. Unlike repression, denial affects perception of external reality more than perception of internal reality. The psychotically blind walk into things; the hysterically blind walk around them. In contrast to dissociation (neurotic denial), psychotic denial ignores external painful stimuli; dissociation only transforms our subjective interpretation of painful internal emotions. Schizophrenics have painless heart attacks noticed by no one; that is denial. In contrast, the dissociating macho executive in a coronary care unit who propositions the nurses and maintains that nothing is wrong does so only *after* he is admitted to the hospital; his heart attack is not denied while it is happening—only afterward.

Note that I use the term *denial* here in a very narrow sense. As Table 2 suggests, all defenses deny something. Here I refer to an ego mechanism that denies external reality. Many of us use denial in fantasy; our deceased loved ones come alive in our daydreams. But psychotic denial leads us to set a place for them at the breakfast table. When we learn of a sudden death, most of us impulsively dissociate and exclaim, "It's not true; I don't believe it," but such denial is short-lived. In contrast, a schizophrenic patient of mine, after his hospital's flags had been at half-mast for three days, could watch a television newscast of President John Kennedy's funeral cortege and dismiss the melancholy, yet novel, spectacle as "that old rerun." To oversimplify, denial ignores external reality (Peggy's boyfriend "died"); distortion transforms external reality to conform to our wishes (her boyfriend is transformed into an unattainable rock star); and delusional projection transforms external reality to conform to our conscience (it is the devil doing it, not I). All reduce unbearable conflict.

Examples of delusional projection, denial of external reality, and distortion are found most commonly in our childhoods, in our dreams, and in psychosis. But these defenses also occur in the worlds of our imagination where the test of reality is not necessary (such as in our religious beliefs and our myths and fairy tales). Such self-deceptions do not yield to graduate school, psychoanalysis, Mao-inspired cadres, or Skinnerian conditioning. In his nocturnal dreams, an engineer's knowledge of aerodynamics is quite inadequate to convince him that he is not flying under his own power. No Inquisition or torture is so convincing as to change a psychotic's waking dream. For most individuals, the devout convictions of a member of another religion appear a little crazy, yet no amount of logical argument will cause Catholics and Hindus to exchange beliefs or convince a devout 5-year-old that Santa Claus is an illusion. What is required is some way of changing the state of the brain. Obvious examples are neuroleptics (such as Thorazine) for the schizophrenic, alarm clocks for the dreamer, and the relentless myelinization of the developing brain that drives a child to develop logical thought processes and thus lose faith in Santa Claus forever.

However, the maturation of the ego is as highly dependent upon environment as it is upon biology. On the one hand, it is the graded exposure to social experience (as well as neurological development) that allows small children to abandon the tangible, comforting reality of imaginary friends and Santa Claus. On the other hand, both the experience of nonexperience (for example, severe sensory or educational deprivation) and extreme kinds of experiences (such as physical and sexual abuse) facilitate the retention into adult life of childish, "psychotic" distortions of reality.

The critical distinction between the three psychotic defenses and all other defenses is whether external reality testing *in time present* is impaired. For example, the fears of the nondelusional paranoid who uses projection are rarely completely imaginary, and his capacity for reality testing is not lost. The overly zealous (prejudiced) baseball fan only shouts "Kill the umpire." In contrast, the individual with delusional projection and distortion can act upon, not merely think about, unrealistic obsessions and compulsions. For the delusional manic and the intoxicated religious zealot the laws of society do not apply. In contrast, the psychopath who *acts out* and the paranoid who *projects* and the martyr who *turns against the self* are often exquisitely cognizant of the law—even as they break it.

Admittedly, not all psychotic behavior is in the service of ingenious defense. Individuals can manifest bizarre behavior because of genetic defect or organic brain damage as well as because of their efforts to adapt to noxious environments. Similarly, the displacement of some phobic and compulsive patients can be cured by antidepressant medication better than by psychotherapeutic interpretation. This should not surprise us. Sometimes mother quails have wings that are truly broken. But even when the brain is "broken," symptoms produced by a damaged brain always reflect not just the deficit but the efforts of the still-intact regions of the brain to make sense of biological disorder. Even in toxic delirium, the patient's hallucinations and delusions make order out of chaos. Even a broken brain is ingenious in its efforts to comfort its owner. The ego is the servant of biology.

Immature Defenses

Table 2 identifies six styles of so-called immature mechanisms of defense. These mechanisms are familiar to any high school teacher afflicted with an infestation of tenth graders. Policemen, urban welfare workers, and aficionados of bizarre, truth-is-stranger-than-fiction sagas on the inside pages of their local newspaper will be able to nod in recognition as well; for the immature defenses represent the building blocks of personality disorder. The reader may question my use of the term *immature* to characterize this group of defenses, but the empirical rationale for this generalization will be provided in subsequent chapters. I use the terms *immature* and *mature* not as value judgments but to underscore the fact that the ego develops into adult life.

Projection

Peggy could *project* her own unacceptable, anxiety-provoking feelings onto her boyfriend. "It is a terrible thing," she could tell her girlfriends, "that men are such animals, so oversexed. Half the time they are undressing you with their eyes." Note how such thought processes protect her from taking responsibility for her own feelings, but keep both sexual idea and affect in consciousness. Unlike use of psychotic defenses and unlike going to Europe for the summer, use of projection does not force Peggy to separate psychologically from the person with whom she is in conflict. Even while she declares her boyfriend odious, Peggy believes he is caressing her with his eyes. The paranoid need never feel lonely and abandoned. The isolated injustice collector who imagines himself persecuted by the FBI is at least on somebody's Most Wanted list. The paradoxical result is that projection, like fantasy, hypochondriasis, and passive aggression (described below), can preserve an ersatz interpersonal constancy. Such defenses provide ways to repair and comfort minds that possess too few satisfying internalized loves. Clinicians more influenced by Melanie Klein and Otto Kernberg than by Anna Freud and her father prefer terms like *splitting* and *devaluation* to describe such ego processes.

In projection, subject is turned into object and object into subject. Projection turns self-loathing into prejudice and mistrust of one's own loving feelings into the rejection of intimacy through unwarranted suspicion. If we love someone, after all, we become vulnerable to hurt; if we are vulnerable, then someone must be to blame. God forbid that we should take full responsibility for the tenderness of our own hearts. Unlike the user of delusional projection, individuals using simple projection, however eccentric and abrasive, remain within the law—and are often preoccupied by it. Indeed, it is that delicate line between the real and the imaginary that most sharply distinguishes the immature defenses from their psychotic ancestors. A schizophrenic's threat to sue his psychiatrist and bring her to justice in front of the Supreme Court worries no one; whereas the litigiousness of a paranoid outpatient can strike fear into any physician's heart. In part, we are so sensitive to paranoid individuals because there is often a grain of truth within their suspicious accusations.

All immature defenses make our personal boundaries porous. Thus, projection gets under the skin of the other person. Objects of pathologic jealousy know how strangely intimate, if intrusive, paranoia is. Victims of prejudice often begin to believe their oppressors' delusions. Some call this process of contagion *projective identification*. Anonymous hate mail can force us to fantasize about our correspondent more insistently than can a loving Valentine. Thus, the *object* of a *subject* who uses immature defenses becomes inextricably bound to the user in extraordinary ways and may respond with reciprocal defenses. The duet between the sadist and the masochist is one obvious example.

Projection differs from displacement in that the *object* is turned into the *subject* and not simply into some less threatening object. The distinctions between projection and its more mature relatives, reaction formation and altruism, have already been touched upon in my contrast between Hitler and Mother Theresa. With both altruism and projection the user presumes to know how someone feels and the *object* is made *self*. But the altruist differs from the paranoid in that the altruist is right. In both altruism and reaction formation, but not in projection, conscience is exaggerated.

Fantasy

Peggy might publicly declare her deep religious conviction and retreat to her bedroom for the summer. But there she might gaze at her boyfriend's photograph and write steamy love poetry, which she would not send to him. In her mind's eye she would rehearse imagined delights discovered in a book of Kama Sutra woodcuts and acted out by her promiscuous girlfriends. Although separated from her boyfriend, she would feel none of the grief that she would have suffered had she accepted her father's offer of a summer in Europe. Her boyfriend's absence would evoke no grief, and her fantasies of lust would evoke no guilt. No demons would assail her. The imagined sexual exploits, however unfamiliar, would evoke no more anxiety than a toddler feels when piloting his parent's parked car. Indeed, fantasy entails no internal consequences at all except to light up the world of our mind. But to her boyfriend Peggy would appear eccentric and aloof. He would feel the loneliness from which Peggy, the dreamer, was immune.

Schizoid fantasy allows the user to indulge in autistic retreat for the purpose of conflict resolution and gratification. In fantasy we can face down both tigers and lovers in safety; we can steal diamonds from Tiffany's without guilt. The plain brown wrapper of our imagination lets us rehearse and practice for what lies ahead without becoming even a little bit mad, depressed, or anxious. In fantasy the only essential is to keep real people from intruding upon our minds. Thus, the wish that we make when blowing out the candles of our birthday cake can come true only if we keep it a secret. Children are adamant about keeping private the details of their imaginary friends.

Unlike mere wishes, schizoid fantasies serve to gratify unmet needs for relationships—relationships in which murder, seduction, and infantile gratification can be carried out with wanton abandon. The subject, the object, the idea, and the affect are all in consciousness—but only in the subject's mind. Fantasy serves to obliterate the overt expression of aggressive, dependent, and sexual impulses toward others. In the secret life of Walter Mitty, all vices are possible.

But despite their power to comfort the user, immature defenses are judged by others to be misdemeanors. Just as a most forgiving person cannot forgive the projection of a bigot, just so in real life entirely harmless schizoid individuals make us fear or abuse them. For example, society has always mistrusted the dreamer who marches to a different drummer; and masturbation, which never made anyone pregnant or HIV positive, has been classified as sin for thousands of years. By her erstwhile boyfriend, then, the gentle, schizoid Peggy might be labeled a snob or frigid or a creep.

Because schizoid fantasy does not externalize conflict, it is quite distinct from projection. Projection places one's emotions and conflicts in the outside world. Schizoid fantasy peoples the inner mind with imaginary relationships—and they stay there. In contrast to psychotic denial, the schizoid individual does not fully believe in or insist upon acting out his fantasies. The dreams of fanatics (delusional projection) and of sociopaths (acting out) are enacted with the real world as a stage, whereas the conquests, rapes, and murders that take place in drivers' minds as they daydream (use fantasy) at traffic lights remain forever secret within the antiseptic loneliness of their automobiles.

Schizoid fantasy can be distinguished from its two closest relatives, the isolation used by obsessive compulsives and the displacement used by social phobics. For fantasy, unlike isolation of affect, excludes rather than limits contact with other real people. By way of compensation, the user of fantasy usually has a richer affective and interpersonal inner world than the obsessional. In *The Glass Menagerie* Laura's love for her crystal pets is perhaps deeper than an obsessional philatelist's displaced affection for his stamps. But the passion of a socially timid stamp collector can be politely shared with other equally preoccupied souls (displacement), whereas Laura's imaginary glass friends must be kept secret. "Head jollies" are a lonely business.

Hypochondriasis

After every movie date, rather than rebuff her boyfriend's advances, Peggy might develop terrible migraine headaches. Her nausea and intolerance of light would require beating a hasty retreat home. She would belabor her mother with her cranial misery, never hinting of the conflict in her heart. By unconsciously magnifying her physical distress, Peggy could remain oblivious to her conflicts over unrehearsed intimacy. At the same time she could make her boyfriend feel sufficiently responsible for her plight that he would continue to visit her in her well-chaperoned sick room.

Contrary to common belief, hypochondriasis is not an effort to obtain gratification and secondary gain from the sick-role. Rather, at the heart of hypochondriasis lies covert reproach. Reflect for a moment. Hypochondriacs are help-rejecting complainers. Hypochondriacs display extraordinary capacity to complain to those who come to comfort. Hypochondriacs bite, as it were, the hand stretched out to feed them. Hypochondriacs are sure to experience painful side effects, not balm, from any help that is proffered; and paradoxically, they rarely reveal their *true* pain. The caregivers and critics of hypochondriacs seldom learn that she was a sexually abused child or that he spent years in Buchenwald. Rather, the medical charts only note that he makes too much of his low back pain and she of her recurrent suicidal thoughts. In short, hypochondriasis transforms reproach toward others arising from grief or aggressive impulses first into self-reproach and then into complaints of pain, somatic illness, suicidal preoccupation, and neurasthenia.

Unlike the displacement-using conversion hysteric, the hypochondriac requires an audience. On desert islands there are no hypochondriacs. Again, in hypochondriasis, unlike conversion hysteria, pain and distress are amplified. In conversion hysteria, with its *la belle indifférence*, pain and distress are ignored. Phobic or obsessional concerns, which are also mediated by the defense of displacement, are usually a problem only to the user. In contrast, the ardor of the hypochondriac's concern may seem unreasonable, delusional, even assaultive to others. The kindest physician learns to hate the hypochondriac. The hypochondriac never understands why. The invisible answer is that the unacceptable subterranean rage of the hypochondriac now becomes the conscious burden of the caregiver. The abusive mother and the concentration camp guards, hidden by the mists of time, escape scot-free.

Frequently, hypochondriasis is associated with introjection. Introjection is a mental process in which the facets of an ambivalently regarded, threatening, or suddenly absent person are perceived within the self. I have arbitrarily included introjection—often deemed a distinct defense mechanism in its own right—with hypochondriasis. In part, my decision reflects the observation that hypochondriasis, like introjection, involves fusion (for example, a mourner bitterly complaining of symptoms of the heart condition that has just killed his father). In part, my decision reflects a wish to distinguish the defensive (that is, the coping/self-deceptive) aspects of introjection from the ego developmental aspects of introjection (that is, the capacity of introjection to take loved ones inside), which will be discussed in Chapter 13. Hypochondriasis and introjection must be distinguished from the *delusional* fusion of distortion and of incorporation, which, as it were, swallows the tormentor whole (for example, the mourner hearing his dead father speaking inside his head). Introjection internalizes part of a person; incorporation takes the whole person inside. Both processes serve to manage our reproach and outrage toward our loved ones who are so cruel and inconsiderate as to die or by some other means to abandon us forever.

Passive Aggression (*Turning against the Self*)

Peggy could play hard to get. She could tease her boyfriend and annoy him. She could be perennially late and cancel dates unexpectedly. She could eat garlic or not wash if she feared they would be alone too late at night. When her friends suggested to her that she was shooting herself in the foot (masochism) or when her boyfriend told her she was being deliberately cruel (sadism), Peggy would be genuinely astonished. All the above misfortunes, she would maintain to herself and others, occurred by accident. Besides, she might tease her boyfriend, how could she be self-defeating and abusive at the same time?

Parents of adolescents, jailors in high-security prisons, and children tortured by masochistic mothers know the answer to Peggy's question only too well. Masochism is not the opposite, but merely a variant, of sadism. Evidence to support this unorthodox statement is found in the most un-Christlike suggestion that Jesus ever made. He recommended that by turning the other cheek one might dump burning coals upon one's adversary's head. Thus I use the term *passive aggression* rather than *turning against the self* to capture the paradoxical nature of masochism. Suicide punishes (and binds) the self *and* the other at the same time. Gandhi starved himself to punish England—and to free India. Winston Churchill, feeling himself a victim, not an oppressor, complained that it cost the British Empire a million pounds a year to keep Gandhi poor. For the observer of immature defenses, truth is often stranger than fiction.

Passive aggressive behaviors are common in everyday life. Running away and playing hard to get are part of the foreplay and the delaying action of many courtships. With their fear of and longing for both dependence and intimacy, adolescents survive through the teasing, self-defeating quality of their love affairs. The heroine of Erich Segal's *Love Story* begins by devaluing her future lover as a "preppie." And consider the infuriating adolescent heroine of Frederick Herbert's play *Kiss and Tell*. In romantic moonlight, she asks her love-struck boyfriend if he does not feel that he can reach up and touch the stars with his hand. When he succumbs and blurts out "Yes!" she mocks him for being oblivious to the fact that the stars are trillions of miles away. But however painful, such teasing binds.

Passive aggression includes failures, procrastinations, illnesses, and often silly or provocative behavior employed to get attention. Sadomasochistic relationships allow the subject to convert "dangerous" intimacy and sexual excitement into the less morally reprehensible but equally enthralling sensations of being taunted, beaten, or abused. By definition, the tease attracts attention and expresses hostility without being taken too seriously. There is no better way to maintain a relationship with someone you can neither live with nor live without. No wonder downtrodden privates and adolescents become such experts at passive aggression. Without officers and parents to provoke, their lives would be unmanageable. Self-effacing clowning allows us to avoid assuming a competitive role or betraying sadness. Indeed, the sad downward turn of a clown's real mouth is literally effaced by his painted, his ludicrously painted—his tragically painted—smile.

Passive aggression (or turning against the self) must be distinguished from its close relatives, hypochondriasis, reaction formation, and altruism. In part, passive aggression differs from hypochondriasis in its selection of object. The passive aggressive individual often punishes *and* suffers at the hands of the real source of his conflict. Peggy punishes her real boyfriend; the recruit punishes his tormenting top sergeant; the angry failed suicide punishes her lover or his vacationing doctor. In contrast, the woes of the hypochondriac are often old news and the recipient of the covert reproach is often innocent. Peggy's mother, not her boyfriend, hears of her migraines in minute detail.

Reaction formation, in contrast to passive aggression, also leads the user to suffer, but at least the object is appeased. With passive aggression the subject gives away the biggest piece of cake in such a fashion that the recipient ends up feeling punished. With reaction formation, the recipient regards receiving the cake as a fortuitous or generous gift. Reaction formation rewards, passive-aggression punishes the object. Altruism differs from both of these other defenses in that the rewards to the subject outweigh the suffering. The altruist casts his cake upon the waters and it returns tenfold. Empathic pastry chefs grow fat and well loved, even as they give the biggest piece of cake away. Mother Theresa wins a Nobel Prize even as she gives all that she has to the grateful poor. The altruist's confusion of self and object provides pleasure for all.

Acting Out

While ignoring her erstwhile boyfriend, Peggy could inexplicably engage in promiscuous sexual behavior with four members of the football team. An illegitimate child put up for adoption might follow. Her friends, parents, and guidance counselor would be incredulous; her boyfriend would curse the perfidy of women; and yet Peggy would experience neither sexual excitement nor guilt. Observers would imagine Peggy insane or morally defective. She herself would remain consciously unaware that her boyfriend's attentions had threatened to recapitulate her painful abuse by an incestuous uncle, and the football team would pass through her bed as ephemerally as the people of her dreams.

It is almost impossible for observers to believe that such behavior can occur without either conscious reflection or insanity. How can a 15-year-old prostitute fearlessly turn tricks in Times Square? Through some neurological anomaly, has she no conscience and no sense of terror? No. The fact is that her ego is delivering her from an even greater affront to her conscience, from a pain too acute to be held in consciousness. More often than not adolescent streetwalkers are running from the risk of incestuous molestation or other abuse at home. More than one heinous child abuser remains consciously unaware of the childhood beatings he himself once received.

In short, the defense of acting out is defined by the direct expression of an unconscious wish or impulse in order to avoid being conscious of the affect, and often the ideation, that acompanies it. In addition, the objects of acting out, for example Peggy's football players, are usually nonspecific or anonymous. Acting out is rarely carried out toward the person(s) with whom the individual is most attached or most angry. Thus, acting out includes many impulsive delinquent acts and temper tantrums that occur with such rapidity as to allow the user to be unaware of their passion. Neither awareness of the conflict-laden affect nor the guilty ideation that accompanies it is conscious. Charles Whitman's behavior in the Texas Tower murders, William Calley's behavior at the Mai Lai massacre, Josef Mengele's behavior at Auschwitz, all are more extravagant examples of Peggy's acting out. Most of their victims were strangers. In killing his own wife and mother as well as strangers, Charles Whitman spared his father, the person toward whom he had most tangible reason to be angry, the person with whom he was about to go on a hunting trip.

The defense mechanism of acting out is not uncommon, yet it leads to behavior so irrational that in the nineteenth century the psychiatrist James Pritchard called it "moral insanity," and Hervey Cleckley, in an influential book, maintained that psychopaths wore only the "mask of sanity." But acting out does not reflect insanity; rather it reflects the tantrums of grownups and often masks the grief of children. Most users of acting out are by no means insane or without conscience. For forensic reasons, I was once asked to interview an intelligent New Hampshire woman who had murdered her two sons in premeditated fashion. It was chilling. Her methodical motiveless act was done without tears, but also without the confusion of insanity or the amnesia of a fugue state. In fact, she was a nice woman, who like Medea before her, was angry at an unfaithful husband, not at her murdered offspring. Perhaps because by chance she had known me in a social context, our prison interview temporarily relinked her to her feelings and breached her psychic anesthesia. For a moment, in my presence, she could appreciate, with great pain, the dreadfulness of her deed. She remembered that her son as she fired the rifle had cried out, "Mummy, you are hurting me." Yet her actions, like those of an adolescent boy breaking windows or snapping off car aerials, had seemed like a good idea at the time. At the time of the shooting, her slaughter of her children was as methodical, as impersonal, and as without affect or doubts as were the actions of a World War II bombardier over Tokyo or Rotterdam or Coventry.

Unreflectively giving in to impulses avoids the rumination, the frustration, and the self-awareness that often accompany delay of conflicted gratification. Remember the triumph of patriotism that allowed Winston Churchill and his air commander, "Bomber" Harris, to perceive the civilians of Dresden as such mortal enemies of the Free World that a hundred thousand of them needed to be sacrificed in a firestorm produced by systematic incendiary bombing. Yet the Nazis who had terrorized and abused England for five long years were in many places in Germany but not in Dresden. (In reality, Dresden was of so little danger to the Allies that for most of the war it had remained quite untouched as a primary bombing target. Indeed, it was the lack of prior bombing that made the city such an effective funeral pyre.) Readers of *Slaughter House Five*, Kurt Vonnegut's empathic and outraged novel about the Dresden massacre, must wonder how Churchill and Harris could possibly have ordered the raid. But moral outrage toward acting out is always easy for the observer. In the midst of a tantrum, none of us feels guilt.

Acting out is the very opposite of reaction formation, for with acting out the instinct is allowed full sway and conscience is absolutely removed—if only temporarily. Acting out allows "sex, drugs, and rock and roll" to become venerated as the very fount of well-being rather than as a clear danger to one's immune system, one's sanity, and one's hearing. Yet developmentally, the frequency with which acting out in youth is followed by reaction formation in midlife highlights the kinship of these seemingly opposite defenses. For example, Leo Tolstoy the spendthrift rapist, college dropout, compulsive gambler, and voyeuristic militarist became Tolstoy the ascetic protector of serfs and the pacifist devoted to public education. His developmental sequence reminds us that the user of acting out can have a hypertrophic, if subterranean, conscience. Promiscuity with strangers can be more driven by the incest taboo than by amorality. Charles Whitman's murderous rampage from a Texas University tower may have reflected his strenuous unconscious efforts not to commit patricide on his upcoming hunting trip.

Conversely, with alcoholism or organic brain disease, reaction formation gives way to acting out. Having lost control over alcohol, Wilbur Mills, a U.S. congressman and a pillar of moral rectitude, made a spectacle of himself jumping into fountains with a striptease dancer, Fanny Foxe. Fatigue, alcohol, and senility make delinquents of us all.

On the positive side, acting out lacks the obliviousness to reality that occurs among chronic users of distortion and psychotic denial. If met socially, the serial murderer or the daring streetwalker may seem quite normal—certainly they are not to be confused with psychotic street people and soapbox injustice collectors. Acting out is different from delusional projection because acting out spares the real tormentor but is accurate about who owns the pain. In contrast, schizophrenics may misconstrue loving attention as torment and then wreak vengeance on their loving "tormentor." This dichotomy between the acting out of the sociopath and the delusions of the insane creates the following paradox. Young men in prison for violent acting out against utter strangers not infrequently have "Mom" tattooed inside a heart upon their chest and take violent offense to criticism of their mothers by others. Yet many of these same young men were physically abused by their mothers in childhood. In contrast, schizophrenics who have been relatively well treated as children may physically attack their own parents when adult; yet their parents remain, alas, the most central figures in their lives. Such schizophrenics may remain quite passive and compliant toward abusive strangers.

Acting out differs from displacement in that the impulse, although directed toward a less intimate object, is not attenuated. Indeed, in a tantrum we say and do things more angrily than we can possibly mean; while in the displacement of play we murder our father on the tennis court six-love, and he survives to love us in return. Acting out differs from the isolation of affect of obsession in that although with both defenses the impulse is not *felt*, with acting out the impulse is not thought about either. Instead, the act is given direct expression. The user of acting out murders but does not worry before or during the act. In contrast, someone who suffers from homicidal obsessions worries incessantly but does not murder.

Dissociation (Neurotic Denial)

When I have asked college students to devise different ways of solving Peggy's dilemma, more than one male chauvinist has suggested, "Why can't she just put her Catholicism on the shelf, jump into bed with her boyfriend, and be done with it?" My counter to this solution is to ask the young macho sophomore to suppose that he knew that he would not be caught for piloting a jet plane without a flying license. I then ask if he would not feel just a little bit anxious and depressed to find himself alone at the controls thirty thousand feet above the Mojave Desert, flying at the speed of sound, and knowing that he must execute a solo landing. My point is that it is not just the conflicts of her Catholic superego that lead Peggy to experience anxiety and depression in response to sexual arousal. Rather, the dangers of any intense but unrehearsed reality make us anxious. Remember, Peggy has never even held hands with a boy. But Peggy *could* willfully get drunk. In that dissociated state Peggy could fearlessly slip into bed with her boyfriend. Thus, with the help of gin, Peggy could without anxiety accomplish a task for which no amount of willpower would suffice. Ogden Nash's immortal couplet summarizes such a solution to courtship well: "Candy is dandy, / But liquor is quicker."

The mechanism of dissociation allows us to replace painful ideas and affects with pleasant ones. The defense allows us literally to *dissociate* our consciousness from our real selves. Dissociation is the one defense that can be employed consciously. Voluntarily, we can escape painful ideas and feelings. We need only alter our consciousness of punishing reality through meditation, through self-hypnosis, through method acting, or through drunkenness. The dissociation of intoxication, Mardi Gras, and trance states can make Pollyannas of us all.

Dissociation evades depression and anxiety by distraction; but distraction, like the prestidigitator's art, is a difficult process on which to focus. Thus, dissociation is the defense most difficult to define and most difficult to identify reliably. Like the captivating, dramatic, distracting hysterics who use the defense most often, dissociation is easily mistaken for something else. Often termed *neurotic denial,* dissociation is the mechanism underlying multiple personality, fugues, many hysterical conversion reactions, and much counterphobic behavior. It can involve a sudden unwarranted sense of superiority or a devil-may-care attitude. The defense of dissociation can transform a roller coaster ride from terror to joy; it can allow the victim of indescribable torture to leave the reality of his tormented body and view the process as a spectator.

Dissociation is distinct from psychotic denial in that it denies only *internal* reality, not external reality. Mr. Hyde becomes Dr. Jekyll, but the outside world remains unchanged. Dissociation differs from repression in that the painful affect is transformed at the same time that the painful idea is banished. Dissociation differs from acting out in that acting out does not spare the displaced object; indeed, in acting out the object is often treated as just that, like a wooden doll in a child's play session. In contrast, if the defense of dissociation, like acting out, ignores the conscience, it also transforms the dangerous affect into play; and if dissociation alters the subject, it does not ignore the object. Thus, of all the "contagious" immature defenses, dissociation has the greatest power to charm and enthrall the observer. Abused children who do not bring danger to our streets often bring entertainment to our theaters. With dissociation, the prostitute becomes a courtesan and the pirate becomes a charming riverboat gambler. Dissociation differs from reaction formation in that it turns the idea-feeling complex into something different, something playful, something distracting, whereas reaction formation turns the idea-feeling complex into its exact, and very earnest, opposite. If reaction formation denies *desire* and if acting out denies *conscience*, dissociation denies both. Perhaps this is why dissociation, the least irritating of the immature defenses, is often just as maladaptive as the others.

Nevertheless, were it not that empirical evidence documents that dissociation is maladaptive, it would merit inclusion in the next level of defenses—intermediate or neurotic. Unlike other immature defenses, dissociation is not more common in adolescence than in middle age. Unlike other immature defenses and similar to the intermediate-level defenses, dissociation distorts feelings more than people. Unlike other immature defenses and similar to the intermediate-level defenses, dissociation can be interpreted. Finally, dissociation does not annoy observers. Unlike the paranoid and the hypochondriac, the hysteric is an attractive, if exasperating, patient. The problem, of course, is that although the dissociating Pollyanna can escape pain unscathed, she is seldom granted victory, comfort, true joy, or requited permanent love. Scarlett O'Hara, Voltaire's Dr. Pangloss, and *Mad Magazine*'s Alfred E. Neuman all put off living "until tomorrow."

The immature defenses share many characteristics. With the exception of dissociation, they are irritating to others and benign to the user—at least over the short term. Often such defenses represent violations of conventional morality or of the law. For example, attempted suicide, at least until recently, was a felony in some American states. Immature defenses also share a peculiar capacity to bind user and object. Immature defenses get under other people's skin. Thus, such defenses help the user maintain an illusion of interpersonal constancy and attachment. In their different ways the suspicious bigot, the schizoid dreamer, the passive aggressive adolescent, and the reproachful hypochondriac all hug their love/hates tight even as they hold them at arm's length. Such two-faced behavior is essential to adolescents who need both protection and separation, but it is trying for their parents. Remember how Brer Rabbit became irrevocably stuck to the Tar Baby, who, he felt, was taunting him. In short, provocation and masochism make separation a sticky business.

Unlike neurosis, immature defenses do not yield to psychiatric interpretation and may even be made worse by such efforts. If we refer the user of immature defenses to psychiatrists instead of to the courts, the user feels misunderstood. He wants a fair trial, not "help." Group confrontation by loving peers is more useful in the treatment of immature defenses. Thus, the adolescent and the character-disordered individual often "get by with a little help from their friends." By this I mean that the well-intended youth worker cannot convince the acting-out adolescent that a shared needle or crack is dangerous, but often a friendly peer can. In the supportive group solidarity of Alcoholics Anonymous, the admonitions of recovering alcoholics can be heard by still-active alcoholics; yet these same alcoholics are deaf to the reasoning, threats, or entreaties of their loving nonalcoholic relatives and their expensive psychiatrists.

Unlike psychotic defenses, the immature defense mechanisms do not usually yield to pharmacological treatment. Rather, immature defenses are often exaggerated by drug use. For example, sedative drug intoxication and alcohol intoxication both increase projection and tantrums. And too often antidepressant medication provides impulsive individuals not with comfort but, instead, with a means of suicide.

There are other popular terms that have been used to describe immature defense mechanisms. This competing nomenclature includes *splitting*, *devaluation*, *idealization*, and *projective identification*. These terms are intrinsic to object relations theory, and the defenses they describe are sometimes referred to as *image-distorting defenses*. The terminology reflects the fact that if the neurotic defenses manage drives, the immature defenses manage relationships. Projective identification, a term defined differently by almost every chronicler of defenses, nevertheless captures the fact that in the presence of a user of immature defenses the ego boundaries of the observer become blurred and porous. A dyadic contagion of affects occurs that makes separation of what is mine from what is thine difficult. Like those afflicted with contagious disease, those afflicted with immature defenses often transmit their shame, impulses, and anxiety to those around them.

The image-distorting defenses are excluded from Table 2 for three rather arbitrary reasons. First, these defenses, later popularized by Otto Kernberg, were conceptualized by Melanie Klein without reference to Anna Freud at the same time that Anna Freud was writing her compendium of defenses, *The Ego and the Mechanisms of Defense*, without reference to Melanie Klein. Thus Klein's and Anna Freud's nomenclatures describe the same intrapsychic universe but from different conceptual frameworks, and to some degree Klein's terms are redundant with the terms in Table 2, which are largely borrowed from Anna Freud. Second, the image-distorting defenses are more complex, for they describe dyadic communication and reciprocal interactions. Their manifestations reflect the interactions of two egos, not one. Thus, projective identification and splitting are to projection and acting out what conversation is to speech. In short, the image-distorting defenses address ego function at a level beyond the simple units of analysis that I wish to use for this book and have outlined in Table 2. My third reason for excluding these Kleinian defenses is that they are used exclusively to manage interpersonal relationships and thus they are narrower in application than the terms in Table 2, which include adaptation to all four sources of conflict—people, desire, conscience, and reality.

Neurotic Defenses

Table 2 defines a third class of defenses, the intermediate or neurotic mechanisms. The use of neurotic mechanisms is more private and seems less intrusive to others than the use of immature defenses. To oversimplify, whereas immature defenses perform legerdemain with relationships, neurotic defenses magically rearrange ideas and feelings. Thus, the limitations of neurotic defenses may be that, because they do not make the other person feel so involved, they lack the power of immature defenses to control relationships. Because they do not get under the observer's skin, neurotic defenses can only protect individuals who are able to form sustaining relationships by other more adaptive means. Put differently, paranoid spouse-beaters and their masochistic spouses may have far more durable, if less enjoyable, marriages than "neurotic" flirts and obsessional accountants.

The advantage of neurotic defenses is that they are closer to reality. The self-deception is not so gross. The user feels responsible for his or her conflicts, and neurotic defenses often reflect compromise, not all-or-nothing solutions. Compared to immature mechanisms, neurotic mechanisms seem less foreign to the observer. They are morally neutral. Their use does not make the tabloids. They are less dependent on the interpersonal field. It is hard to imagine a castaway on a desert island being paranoid or hypochondriacal, but easy to imagine him or her being phobic or compulsive.

Displacement

To the relief of her father, Peggy could distract herself from her boyfriend by devoting her affections to a beloved horse or to a younger, less mature, less sexy boyfriend. She could detach both the *idea* and the *affect* of love from a dangerous, sexually experienced boyfriend and reattach her affection to a more neutral love. Were Peggy never to outgrow preferring horses to men, some might call her "obsession" for horses maladaptive. More likely, Peggy's displaced passion would win her praise and acceptance as an accomplished equestrian, and would reassure her father as well. Besides, since defenses are reversible, Peggy's ingenious summer strategy for containing her conflict might well be abandoned by autumn, by which time her ego might be able to accommodate the novelty of her sexy boyfriend.

Much of the work of psychotherapy involves making use of displacement. Analogous to the use of attenuated viruses to immunize patients against dangerous viruses, an important goal of psychotherapy is to provide an attenuated, displaced approximation of reality. In psychotherapy, the transplantation of attachment from former loves and former hates to the therapist is formalized by the term *transference*—a variant of displacement. But the value of displacement in therapy goes far beyond transference. Consider play therapy with children. Parent dolls are murdered and put in garbage cans. The result is relief, not guilt. Indeed, it is no accident that wordplay, affect-laden associations to dreams, and metaphor—all examples of displacement—enjoy such important roles in psychotherapy. It is through displace-

art therapy

ment that client and therapist alike achieve Wordsworth's goal for poetry: emotion recollected in tranquillity.

Wit, caricature, and parody also involve displacement, and so do some cases of prejudice. Prejudice, of course, links displacement with its immature relative, projection. The critical difference is that displacement alters only the direction of the idea-affect complex, while projection also alters the ownership of the complex so that the subject imagines himself the object.

Displacement is often present in phobias. Thus, in their painstaking work to desensitize phobic patients, behavior therapists, too, appreciate the value of displacement. They begin by exposing their clients to distant, only slightly believable, dangers, and gradually make the dangers more immediate. Unlike psychoanalysts, however, some learning theorists have never fully appreciated the difference between learning as the linking of neutral ideas (as in red light equals stop) and learning as the linking of ideas to affects (red light equals brothel and sexual arousal). Freud's poetic science goes far beyond Skinner's rational science. The cerebral cortex is connected to the brain's limbic system. The head bone is connected to the heart.

Isolation of Affect (Intellectualization)

As an avid reader of D. H. Lawrence's novels and Anaïs Nin's diaries, Peggy might make a conscious decision to lose her virginity. Much like the character Esther Greenwood in her favorite novel, *The Bell Jar*, Peggy might have the concept of sexual intercourse very clear in her mind and might carry it through mechanically without any pleasure whatever but also without any anxiety. In this context *isolation* or *intellectualization* sounds like a dreary means of adaptation; but for surgeons and Strategic Air Command generals, such divorce of affect from idea is an adaptive necessity. Indeed, the defense of isolation is the process by which *rituals* allow us to perform bloody surgical operations and organize funerals without interference from our feelings.

The term *isolation* encompasses the many ways that the mind has of denying the affect that accompanies ideas. Users of isolation exhibit an extraordinary capacity to keep painful ideation in mind but in black and white, as it were, and stripped of all affective coloring. Thus, isolation allows us to think, to intellectualize about instinctual wishes in formal, affectively bland terms. Isolation of affect includes paying attention to the inanimate in order to avoid too close an involvement with the living. Isolation involves paying undue attention to irrelevant detail to avoid conscious recognition of inner feeling. Counting sheep is a familiar example of this process. A more dramatic example of isolation of affect is the use by psychoanalysts of the sterile term *object relations* in lieu of *intimacy* or *love*. Psychoanalysts, as well as surgeons, need ways to keep from being overwhelmed by their hearts' contents. They need to temper the intensity of four-letter emotions.

Although many glossaries of defenses treat *undoing* as a separate defense, I have rather arbitrarily chosen to treat undoing as a subtype of isolation. Undoing involves expressing a wish and then denying it. An example of undoing is knocking on wood after remarking, "I have not seen a doctor in years," or "Our house has never been robbed." The knocking on wood serves as a ritual to undo or to atone for what appears too assertive. Having first boasted of health, we ritually bring to mind the possibility that we may become ill. Another classic example of undoing is the child who carefully steps in the center of sidewalk paving blocks while chanting, "Step on a crack, break your mother's back." His blatantly hostile ideation is verbally expressed, but his hostile idea is both stripped of negative affect and ritually undone by his behavior—*not* stepping on the lines. When I go on vacation, my patients sometimes tell me that they hope nothing bad will happen to me. When I am responsibly at work and "minding their store," as it were, they never seem to worry about such accidental retribution.

I have chosen not to distinguish undoing from isolation for three reasons. First, a frequent user of one of the two defenses almost invariably uses the other. Second, the clinical correlates of the two defense mechanisms are the same. Third, both defenses involve thinking or speaking about conflict without consciously feeling it. We can take back an idea; we cannot take back a feeling.

Individuals troubled by obsessions and compulsions chronically display isolation. Having trouble attaching feelings to their thoughts, they often come to psychotherapists. Indeed, more than a few psychoanalysts, now total converts to the cult of the passionate unconscious, were themselves once inhibited by chronic isolation from their feelings. If in medical school they could stare without giddiness at flowing blood in the operating room, they could not feel the blood coursing through their own guts. Such individuals welcome their psychotherapists' dynamic interpretation, and are grateful to discover their own passions.

Clinically, isolation merges imperceptibly into displacement. In displacement, feelings are attenuated and remain in consciousness while reattached to a less significant object. Displacement and isolation combine to create obsessions. Isolation and displacement are more socially adaptive than their close relative, fantasy. For example, consider an obsessional entomologist who first *isolates* all feeling from his lust and then *displaces* his still lusty ideation onto the vicarious study of the reproductive life of a cockroach. He betrays none, and perhaps enjoys none, of the passion or the human preoccupation experienced by the schizoid loner with a copy of *Playboy* engrossed in sexual fantasy. But the entomologist can publicly discuss his displaced sexual interest before a hundred of his closest colleagues at professional meetings. Unlike the loner, he earns a living, airfare to interesting world capitals, and an audience with whom he can shamelessly discuss his sexual preoccupations. In contrast, the user of fantasy may be on welfare and dares share his secret centerfold loves with no one.

Repression

Were Peggy to deploy repression rather than isolation, she would dress provocatively, talk romantically, and yet be outraged at her boyfriend's first sexual advance. "Why," she might exclaim, "the idea never crossed my mind!" In the presence of her boyfriend, her heat, her color, the perfumed scent of her feminine mating display would fill the room. Her friends and mother would note her interest. The limbic lobes of her boyfriend's brain would resonate with sexual and olfactory recognition. Only Peggy's own intellectual realization of her attachment, only the cold black-and-white ideation of conscious awareness, would be lacking. At first even Freud thought such an extraordinary lack of awareness must be deliberate. Since the beginning of time, smitten men have cursed hysterical Peggys for being dreadful teases. They could not imagine that the sexually provocative behavior of such women was unaccompanied by conscious lust.

With repression affect is everywhere, but the associated idea is not "in mind." The idea is repressed. But unlike the focused taunting of the passive aggressive adolescent, the teasing of the hysteric—the chronic user of repression—may be almost touchingly naive. The passive aggressive adolescent who "innocently" shoots himself in the foot is never totally surprised when he gets an angry response from his father. The hysteric may be genuinely astonished that his platonic girlfriend has misread his intentions. The two forms of teasing, hysterical and passive aggressive, can also be distinguished by the response of the observer. The passive aggression of the martyr always gets under our skin; in contrast, all but the most churlish are a little charmed and somewhat forgiving toward repression. We do not take the defense of repression personally, and may remain bemusedly fond of the attractive flirt. The neurotic defenses compromise and create a truce. The immature defenses attack and enmesh even as they defend. Nevertheless, with maturation passive aggression often evolves into repression.

The "forgetting" of repression can be distinguished from most nondefensive forgetting in that the lack of awareness of repression is often accompanied by telltale symbolic behavior—such as Peggy's low-cut dress. Repression differs from the defense mechanism of suppression in that repression affects unconscious inhibition of impulse to the point of losing, not just postponing, cherished goals. In contrast to the hysteric, the stoic, using suppression, minimizes and looks for the bright side, but does not ignore. A stoical Peggy would ask her boyfriend to postpone his ardor, but she would not be surprised that such a passion had been evoked.

As anyone who works in the theater knows, dissociation and repression often occur together. Repression per se is different from its closest relatives, dissociation (neurotic denial) and reaction formation, in that the honest affect accompanying the repressed idea remains in consciousness. The temptress using repression knows that she likes to look pretty and thus is different from the dissociative "airhead" who gets the giggles every time she sees an attractive man. She is also different from the religious fundamentalist who is suddenly smitten with feelings of piety and the dangers of sexuality every time she sees an attractive man. Repression differs from isolation, of course, in that repression excludes idea, not affect, from consciousness. With repression the hysterical subject can hear the music but forgets the words; with isolation the obsessional subject can think the words but recalls no melody. Thus, to the observer, the obsessional usually appears more "repressed" than the manifestly flamboyant hysteric. Following Freud's example from 1905 to 1926, psychoanalytic authors have often lumped repression and isolation together under the generic term *repression* and thus have sacrificed the important distinction between the lack of awareness of affect and lack of awareness of cognition.

Reaction Formation

Like many another parochial high school student, Peggy could announce to her boyfriend that sex was bad and that he would love her more if she remained "pure." Like many an ascetic before her, she could explain that denying her boyfriend her virginity was a far, far better thing she did than she had ever done before. Their love would be better served if they waited until marriage. Reaction formation keeps both idea *and* affect in mind; only the value is reversed. In short, reaction formation turns white into black, and turns a wish into its opposite. Sex is bad precisely because it is so enjoyable. Cold showers are better for you than warm ones precisely because they make you suffer more. With reaction formation, not only is the dam against the forbidden wish complete, but the very opposite of the wish is valued for allegedly the best reasons in the world. On the bright side, reaction formation allows us to care for someone else when we wish to be cared for ourselves, allows us to love hated rivals and unpleasant duties. Successful reaction formation is often highly moral. Reaction formation is highly valued in nurses, policemen, servants, and roommates. On the dark side, in intimate relationships reaction formation rarely leads to happiness for either party. Those who wear hair shirts feel abrasive to those who come too close.

As noted previously, reaction formation can be distinguished from altruism in that reaction formation gives the user little pleasure. The self-deception or "denial" of reaction formation is different from that of dissociation (neurotic denial) because dissociation distracts us from and ignores our internal feelings while reaction formation notices everything but reverses its value. Similarly, the "denial" of reaction formation is different from psychotic denial because with reaction formation nothing in the external world is ignored, only its value. It is not that sex does not exist, only that sex is dirty.

Reaction formation differs from projection in that it condemns the impulse but leaves responsibility with the user, while projection shifts responsibility for the origin of the impulse or affect from subject to object and may or may not reverse its value. Reaction formation is usually more adaptive than projection. The paranoid inquisitor who burns witches for their "bad" sexuality is assailed at night by succubi or incubi in the most seductive guises and sleeps badly. Safe in his reaction formation and his hair shirt, the celibate ascetic who condemns only his own sexuality sleeps surprisingly well. We cannot be masters of our passions until we take responsibility for them.

As already noted, reaction formation is often the natural descendant of, but is never confused with, acting out. However, where neurotic reaction formation ends and the distortion of religious belief begins is more problematic. Does a Muslim warrior really believe he is immortal (distortion), or only that he is very lucky to die in battle (reaction formation)? I do not know; I suspect it depends on the warrior.

Neurotic defenses, unlike immature defenses, can be therapeutically interpreted. When someone accuses us of projection, we become angry; but when someone reminds us that we forgot a feared and thus repressed dentist appointment, we are ambivalent, then we have an "Aha!" experience: "Thank you so much! How could I have forgotten?" Neurotics pay their psychotherapy bills.

Immature defenses are contagious; neurotic defenses are not. Put differently, the user of immature defenses is analogous to a person in a crowded elevator who, subsequent to a dinner laced with garlic, lights up a cigar. A fellow passenger feeling crowded, invaded, and emotionally aroused perceives the smoker as disgusting, intrusive, and immoral. Angrily, he points to the "No Smoking" sign; the cigar smoker, delighted with his own inner feelings, is outraged. Immature defenses, like garlic-induced halitosis, exist only in the sensibilities of the beholder. In contrast, the user of neurotic defenses is analogous to a passenger on the same crowded elevator who has a cinder in his eye. He feels mortified and in pain. His fellow passengers hardly notice his distress except perhaps to wonder intellectually why his face is so contorted. Were one of them to notice, interpret the source of distress, and deftly remove the cinder with the corner of a tissue, the sufferer would perceive him as a savior, not a nag. Over the short haul, neurotic defenses make the user suffer; immature defenses make the observer suffer.

Mature Defenses

Finally, as depicted in Table 2, there is a fourth level of defenses, which I have labeled *mature*. Because mature defenses involve the synthesis, rather than the denial, of the four sources of conflict in Figure 2, they are more difficult to diagram. Unlike repression, which ignores the *idea,* or isolation, which ignores the *affect,* or projection, which ignores the *subject,* or displacement, which ignores the *object,* the mature defenses effect a delicate balance and allow subjects to experience themselves, their objects, their ideas, and their feelings. Unlike acting out, which ignores *conscience,* or reaction formation, which ignores *desire,* or schizoid fantasy, which ignores real *people,* or psychotic defenses, which ignore *reality,* mature defenses elegantly balance and attenuate the four lodestars of reality, people, conscience, and desire. Thus, the results of mature defenses are closer to harmony, counterpoint, or alchemy than to mental illness. Straw is spun into gold, despair is forged into poetry, and the whole is rendered greater than its parts. Because all of the components of conflict are allowed to be somewhat conscious, mature defenses provide the illusion of being voluntary. No wonder that readers may start to grumble at me for calling such virtuous coping strategies unconscious defenses.

Mature defenses are different from defenses at the other three levels in still another way. They integrate sources of conflict, and thus these modes of self-deception require no interpretation. Even the psychotherapist feels that the solution could not be improved upon. The denial involved in the deployment of mature defenses requires no treatment—only applause. The pity is that usually they cannot be deployed "on purpose." Usually the development of mature defenses requires the loving intercession of or identification with another person.

Altruism

Peggy could become an initiate in a convent. She could work toward becoming the bride of Christ, a ritual in which she would receive a real ring, a real wedding dress, and real praise from both nuns and her conscience. Her first assignment might be to work in the convent kindergarten or nursery school. If she could not conceive children, she could still play with and be loved by them. If she had to share her possessions and her labor with the poor, she would also receive their love, their tithes, and their admiration in return. Such a fate contrasts sharply with the shame and impersonality of having sex with the football team, the grief of giving up the resulting child for adoption, and the loneliness that is so often companion to promiscuity. There are worse fates than becoming a nun.

Altruism allows doing for others as one would be done by. Unlike reaction formation, which also gives to the object what the self desires, altruism leaves the self at least partly gratified. Unlike reaction formation, altruism tempers asceticism with pleasure. Unlike passive aggression and martyrdom, altruism allows the object to feel blessed and not afflicted. Altruism attracts people to the user; martyrdom repels them even as it holds them close in chains.

Altruism resembles projection in that the self's feelings are attributed to the object; but with altruism, unlike projection, such attribution is empathically correct. In projection the subject's *sins* are wrongly attributed to the object; in altruism the subject's *needs* are correctly attributed to the object. Thus, projection makes us helpless victims of our own self-loathing, while altruism grants us self-efficacy. The paranoid looks at the houses of the rich and feels abused that they have so much and he so little. Sister Peggy helps the poor and gains comfort by viewing herself as more fortunate. Gratitude is more fun, more moral, and usually more mature than envy. How wonderful if we could transform ourselves from injustice collectors to saints by an act of will. Unfortunately, like the other defenses, altruism is essentially involuntary. But no wonder altruism is sometimes called Grace.

Sublimation

With sublimation, Peggy might spend an engrossing summer playing opposite her boyfriend in the parish production of *West Side Story*, Leonard Bernstein's popular musical modeled on *Romeo and Juliet*. Peggy the repressor would wear perfume and a provocative red dress and maintain that the *idea* of sex had never crossed her mind. Peggy the sublimator, playing Maria, would wear a provocative red dress and through music and romantic language keep both the feelings and the idea of sexuality forever in mind. At the same time, the sexuality of Peggy-as-Maria would be so exquisitely attenuated that the ingenuous Peggy would be without anxiety and her 18-year-old man-of-the-world Tony/Romeo would forget his frustration as he, too, was transported by the music and Peggy's real kisses.

Sublimation channels and harnesses the torrent of our affects rather than merely dissipating them as in acting out or merely damming them as in reaction formation. In contrast to dissociation, the feelings in sublimation are not bogus or camouflaged. On stage Peggy kisses the man she really loves. Thus, sublimation allows the indirect or attenuated expression of instincts without either adverse consequences or marked loss of pleasure. The tortured childhoods and young-adult conflicts of some actors and playwrights are legendary; yet the stage allows their pain finally to win them love, applause, and, better yet, catharsis. As Freud wrote, sublimation "enables excessively strong excitation arising from particular sources of sexuality to find an outlet and use in other fields, so that a not inconsiderable increase in psychic efficiency results from a disposition which in itself is perilous."[7] Such is the magic of sublimation.

Humor, displacement, and sublimation are all ingredients of play. However, unlike the regression in the service of the ego that occurs with humor and unlike the make-believe of some displacement, the playfulness of sublimation often has real consequences. Our heroine dresses like Maria, behaves like Maria; but because her true boyfriend plays opposite her, her behavior is not make-believe or fantasy. With displacement, one's feelings, if allowed, are directed toward a less significant or frightening object. Whereas what is so extraordinary about sublimation—and what makes its use so perilous—is that often one's feelings and attention may be directed toward an even grander and more challenging person.

Suppression

With suppression, Peggy would remain aware of both her Catholic heritage and her surging desires, of both the strength of her attachment and the limits of her experience. She would progress anxiously and slowly—as many have done before her—from handholding to kissing to petting to the long weekend spent away from parents' prying eyes. For suppression involves the capacity to keep the idea and the feeling and the person in mind while waiting—uncomplainingly—a finite, not an infinite, length of time. No wonder that of all the defenses, reliance on suppression as the dominant defensive style correlates most highly with ego strength.

Suppression involves the semiconscious decision to postpone paying attention to a conscious impulse and/or conflict. But evidence that such a decision is not simply voluntary is provided by the fact that jails would empty if delinquents could learn to "just say no" or even to count to ten before they robbed a gas station, punched a policeman, or purchased cocaine. Freud once commented that the postponement of gratification is the hallmark of maturity. The delicate balance of suppression is as voluntary—and as involuntary—as the ability to walk a tightrope. Such balance seems so easy for the accomplished, coordinated acrobat, and yet so utterly impossible and anxiety-provoking for the rest of us.

Unlike the user of repression, the person who uses suppression remembers the conflict. At the end of *Gone with the Wind*, Rhett Butler, unlike Scarlett O'Hara, will remember to "think about it tomorrow." But always, a critical difference between suppression and repression, between suppression and isolation, between stoic suppression and Spartan reaction formation is that with suppression all the components of conflict are allowed to exist at least partially in consciousness.

The distinction between suppression and dissociation is more complex. At the heart of the distinction is maturity. The wise stoicism of Ecclesiastes is certainly very different from the childish dissociation of Pollyanna. Both the stoic and Pollyanna note that clouds have silver linings, but Pollyanna leaves her umbrella at home. Both dissociation and suppression allow us to look at the bright side, but suppression notes that the glass is *half* full. In contrast, dissociation characterizes the proverbial optimist who, upon finding his Christmas stocking full of horse manure, starts searching for the wonderful pony he is sure Santa has brought him. Suppression and dissociation differ in another way as well. Essential to suppression is the postponement of gratification: the user of suppression saves now for next summer's air travel. Even if deeply in debt, the user of dissociation flies now and has no doubt that he will be able to pay later.

Anticipation

It could be that soon after she met her boyfriend, Peggy began to worry. What if she grew to like him a lot? What if he tried to kiss her? Her friends might not understand how a romantic crush could lead to so much fretting; her mother might be puzzled why Peggy sometimes looked depressed. But Peggy would be paying her dues of anxiety and depression in advance. She would hold in consciousness the knowledge that at first petting might be as guilt-provoking as it was exciting; but when the anticipated event occurred, she would not be overwhelmed and she would not walk away.

Anticipation involves realistic and affect-laden planning for future discomfort. As Table 2 suggests, of all the mature defenses, anticipation rearranges outer and inner reality the least. Rather than use self-deception, anticipation spreads anxiety out over time. It involves the self-inoculation of taking one's affective pain in small, anticipatory doses. Anticipating that he might be assassinated, King Mithridates VI became a legend by taking small doses of poison every day to build up his tolerance and protect himself from dying of poison. In the words of the psychoanalyst Heinz Hartmann, one of the pioneers of ego psychology, "The familiar *function of anticipating* the future, orienting our actions according to it and correctly relating means and ends to each other . . . is an ego function and, surely, an adaptation process of the highest significance."[8]

Like suppression, anticipation may seem voluntary until one realizes how hard it is to remember to mend one's roof while the sun still shines. Most of us, like Scarlett O'Hara, would prefer to "think about it tomorrow." Making a list of worries before embarking on a trip seems like a reasonable cognitive coping strategy. But nobody likes to worry; thus, we "forget" to act on such advice. We would never miss planes or forget to floss our teeth if we had consciously pondered the unpleasant consequences in advance. Moreover, it is far easier to plan voluntarily for neutral events like plane trips and tooth decay than for affect-laden events like funerals and the real costs of war. Thus, without social supports, relatively few people can plan for tomorrow's emotional distress. Without the help of another person—a coach or a therapist—it is hard voluntarily to rehearse emotional pain. Even highly paid boxers train for fights through the mediation of a trainer. Pilots and ships' crews prepare for emergencies through shared group protocols. States must impose laws to get people to wear seat belts and motorcycle helmets. Churches, pastors, and extended families make it possible for us to take part in funerals. These observations support my argument that the capacity to worry and grieve in advance unassisted is an ego skill rather than an easily learned coping strategy. They also illustrate the importance of social supports in the maturation of the ego. Flossing our teeth is so much easier when we find ourselves loved.

Anticipation is different from isolation and intellectualization in that it does more than just the busywork of cognitive planning and making lists. Anticipation involves thinking *and* feeling about affective issues. Anticipation is different from fantasy in that the subject experiences modest affective distress during realistic worrying rather than the autistically bland daydreams of disasters and/or wish-fulfillment.

Finally, it is important to distinguish the dissociation that leads to the "laid back" behavior of cockeyed optimists and Pollyannas from the capacity to remain calm under stress that results from anticipation. Legendary aviators like Charles Lindbergh and Chuck Yeager calmly survived flying careers that would have killed all but the most wary. Lindbergh and Yeager dealt with stress as Mithridates did with poison. To have underestimated danger would have been fatal. To have exaggerated danger would have been incapacitating. Thus, they worried in advance, made lists, practiced, and then, appreciating that they had prepared as well as they could, they relaxed. So easy to say, so difficult to do.

Humor

The mechanism of humor is a defense so subtle and so elegant that words fail. How can I even begin to make the reader imagine the use of humor by a 16-year-old adolescent caught in a stressful dilemma other than to assert that wise Peggys have found ways to mitigate their predicaments with humor since the beginning of time. But humor can be convincingly portrayed only in real life; I cannot illustrate it in a fable as I can the other defenses.

We all recognize that humor makes life so much easier. As with suppression and anticipation, humor keeps idea and affect and object in mind. "Humor," Freud suggested, "can be regarded as the highest of these defensive processes."[9] Humor, like anticipation and suppression, is such a sensible coping device that it ought to be conscious. But humor, in contrast to "the best-laid plans," cannot be invoked on demand. Almost by definition, humor pops up where we least expect it; humor always surprises us.

Yet if humor always *seems* accidental, it never occurs by chance. Like the equally involuntary beating of our hearts, the behavior of our egos is neither random nor lazy. Humor, like suppression, requires the same delicacy as tightrope walking or building a house of cards. It is no accident that many great comedians have had extraordinarily unhappy childhoods. Nor is it an accident that most people with unhappy childhoods do not become even minor comedians. The artistic mastery of such childhoods through humor by individuals like Charlie

Chaplin, Marilyn Monroe, and Jackie Gleason did not happen by conscious choice. Like artistic creation, like Mozart's ability to control a keyboard at age 8, humor appears voluntary until we try to imitate it.

Humor permits the overt expression of feelings without individual discomfort or immobilization, and without unpleasant effect on others. Unlike the mindless dissociation present in hysterical laughter, humor can never be deployed without some element of an observing ego. As any comedian knows, timing is everything. Dissociaters, like Dickens's Mr. McCawber and Voltaire's Dr. Pangloss, are forever hiding reality behind illusion. In contrast, the humor of great comedians, like gallows humor, allows us to face reality and yet respond as if it were a game. Why, Mark Twain asks us, do we rejoice at a christening and weep at a funeral? Answer: We are not the ones involved! Humor allows us to look directly at what is painful, whereas dissociation distracts us to look in some other direction.

A friend once wrote to me, "Humor can be marvelously therapeutic. It can deflate without destroying; it can instruct while it entertains; it saves us from our pretensions; and it provides an outlet for feeling that expressed another way would be corrosive." Or, as Freud wrote, humor "scorns to withdraw the ideational content bearing the distressing affect from conscious attention, as repression does, and thus surmounts the automatism of defense . . . humor is a means of obtaining pleasure in spite of the distressing affects that interfere with it."[10]

In contrast to practical jokes and clowning and other forms of passive aggression, humor allows pleasure to both the observer and the user. Unlike wit, a form of displacement, humor lets you call a spade a spade. Caricature and parody displace idea and affect away from the dangerous object onto a more neutral target. In contrast, humor, like hope, permits one to focus upon and to bear what is too terrible to be borne. But the safety of humor, like the safety of dreams, depends upon cataplexy. We see all, we feel all, but we are paralyzed. Finally, humor, like stoicism, empathy, and great art, only comes with maturity. Humor reminds us that the wisdom of the ego depends upon adult development and creativity as much as it does upon defense.

Let me digress to discuss two facets of defenses at which I have been hinting all along. First, mature defenses seem as moral as immature defenses seem immoral. Thus, the five mature defenses in Table 2 can be reframed as (1) doing as one would be done by (altruism), (2) artistic creation (sublimation), (3) a stiff upper lip (suppression), (4) planning for the future (anticipation), and (5) not taking oneself too seriously (humor). Second, by definition mature defenses are less common among the young. The reader may object to my definition of humor. She may say, "But all humor is not benign. It can be malicious and maladaptive. What about satire, or, worse yet, what about the practical, even sadistic, joke?" Such objections are addressed by two points I wish to make about defenses: defenses mature; and, as they mature, they become increasingly moral.

A thumbtack in a teacher's chair is hilarious to a 6-year-old but is profoundly irritating to and, in more ways than one, gets under the skin of the teacher. The hostile impulse is so obvious as to fool nobody. Only the user laughs. Thus, the sadistic humor of *passive aggression* is both childish and a sin.

As the years pass, the student's hostile impulse becomes more covert. The irate student's aggression becomes *displaced* into wit, parody, and satire. The medical school faculty attend the student's skit. If they are not actually delighted to be lampooned, they still laugh, applaud, and control their displeasure—a reasonable compromise. No one is fooled by political cartoons, but in totalitarian countries, the distinction between displaced wit and passive aggressive mockery can make the difference between livelihood as a journalist and martyrdom in a concentration camp. Yet one does not need to be a Freudian psychoanalyst to appreciate that in medical school skits and in *Mad Magazine* wit is not all as it seems. Anger, sadness, and sexuality have been wittily displaced.

Mature humor differs from both such displacement and passive aggression. First, mature humor requires sophistication (that is, social maturity) before the observer even "gets" the joke. People who laugh at *New Yorker* and *Punch* cartoons are older than people who laugh at thumbtacks in a teacher's chair or at cartoons of pigeons defecating on dignitaries. Second, in most adult humor the joke is on us, not on someone else. In the displaced, even sadistic wit of Tom and Jerry cartoons, the cat is the butt of the joke, and *we* identify with the mouse. In contrast, at Woody Allen movies and in viewing *New Yorker* cartoons, we laugh because it is our own foibles that are lampooned. Third, in mature humor, even the Freudian can never be certain from whence springs the secret energy of the joke.

The parallel maturation of fantasy through displacement to sublimation can be easily illustrated. At age 10, Peggy might have played out lonely fantasies with Ken and Barbie dolls and mooned over pop stars as distant as the real stars in the sky. At 13 she might have befriended and sent Valentines to a shy boy one year her junior but soon forgotten him when she undertook her exciting, if displaced, task of taming a skittish horse. Now at 16 she spends her summer as the heroine Maria/Juliet opposite a passionate Tony/Romeo in the summer stock production of *West Side Story*. Nightly the goal of consummated love, if repeatedly sublimated, is kept in mind in time present and with a real person.

3

Self-Deceptions of Everyday Life

The delusions of paranoia were seen by him [Freud], not as primary, but as attempts (however misguided) at restitution, at reconstructing a world reduced to complete chaos.

Oliver Sacks, *The Man Who Mistook His Wife for a Hat*

The psychologist Robert White wrote in 1952, "We know a good deal about the ways in which conditions mould men, and this knowledge is important; we know very little about the ways in which men mould conditions, and this knowledge can hardly be called less important."[1] This statement by an early pioneer in the study of adult development carries a double meaning. On the one hand, the social sciences are relatively ignorant about how individuals make history and thus create their own outer environment. On the other hand, we also know all too little about how, within their own minds, individuals mold and reconstruct inner worlds and conditions which they fear would otherwise become chaos.

In this chapter I shall offer six examples of self-deception, or reconstruction of conditions, that range from the sublime to the psychopathic. I shall also introduce the two themes of creativity and adult development that besides defenses make up the wisdom of the ego. Each of the true stories that I am about to tell has more than one moral. Together they illustrate the principal point of Chapter 2: that denial and self-deception come in very different flavors. They also suggest that, in general, defenses that appear pathological also appear immature *and* maladaptive *and* immoral, and defenses that appear healthy also appear virtuous *and* adaptive *and* mature. In short, maturity, virtue, and mental health are inextricably entwined. These six examples show that the phenomena of defenses deal with cognition that is hot and with affects that are interesting, and they suggest that in order to understand human behavior psychology must learn to identify and interpret defenses. In telling these stories I wish to underscore the creativity of the ego and to point out that creative science, like creative art, often serves to bind up the creator's wounds. Finally, I wish to reemphasize the paradox that all defenses are unconscious and yet conscious at the same time. Our brains are capable of parallel processing—of being of two minds about important subjects.

What I do not wish to do is to suggest that all behavior is defensive—only odd behavior. And by odd behavior I mean activities like growing tissue cultures in one's basement or, as we shall see in a few pages, like dynamiting schoolhouses in the middle of the night.

I shall start with an example of what Freud calls the psychopathology of everyday life, an example of reaction formation. On February 16, 1976, *Time* magazine quoted the following fundraising letter: "Dear Friend: After years of shock and sorrow over the decline of morals and decency in our country, I thought I had become shock-proof . . . Can you believe it: complete color films of sexual acts between women and men, including homosexual acts, using your children. Unless you and I act today . . . our children and our children's children will be exposed to perversion so sinister that good will become evil and evil will become good."

The letter was from Reverend Billy James Hargis, as part of a fundraising appeal from the Tulsa Crusade for Christian Morality. In 1950 Hargis, president of the American Christian College, had founded the Christian Crusade to promote far-right political and religious causes. He published a weekly, the *Christian Crusade,* and his organization honored at its rallies two totems of 1960s liberal scorn, Major General Edwin Walker and Governor George Wallace.

At this point, the reader's critical hackles may start to rise. On the one hand, the reader may suspect that I am about to project my politics into scientific discourse. On the other hand, the reader may already be snickering, suspecting Hargis of covert sexual prurience, of Bible-belt reaction formation—a defense mechanism in which good becomes evil and evil good. Now it is the scientific reader's turn to snicker. Maybe it is psychoanalysts who use the defense of projection; maybe I imagine my own prejudices in others. How can one bring truth out of such a potential shouting match?

Let us use the experimental method to demonstrate the ego at work. Let us try to use the triangulation of long-term follow-up and psychobiography, and let us collect evidence. Previously, Hargis had helped to write a best-seller (250,000 copies) entitled *Is the Schoolhouse the Proper Place to Teach Raw Sex?* Why could not the title of his creative product (or symptom) have just been *Is the Schoolhouse the Proper Place to Teach Sex?* Why make sex "raw"? Perhaps Hargis was more preoccupied with sex than his reaction formation would seem to allow. But how can we be sure? Only by letting the whole story unfold.

Hargis's letter was written in January 1976. Fourteen months earlier a student had gone to the vice president of the American Christian College and confessed that on his honeymoon—which followed his wedding at which Rev. Hargis had officiated—"The groom and his bride discovered that both of them had slept with Hargis." According to *Time*, the trysts had taken place in Hargis's office, at his farm in the Ozarks, and even during his tours with the college choir, the All-American Kids. "Hargis had justified his homosexual acts by citing the Old Testament friendship between David and Jonathan"; and then, for good measure, had threatened to blacklist the youths for life if they talked. Confronted by college officials, Hargis acknowledged his guilt, and then blamed his behavior on his "genes and chromosomes." Since at that time there was no more evidence that homosexuality was caused by genes and chromosomes than that it was caused by sin and the devil, I can argue that it was Hargis who denied. I can argue that Hargis could live with passion too "raw" to bear only by projecting it somewhere else. If reaction formation fails to deceive, try its less mature close relative—projection.

Within a year after the scandal broke, the ingenuity of Hargis's ego defenses proved more compelling and adaptive than the "sinful" instincts that they had tried to conceal. Because of his formidable fundraising skills, Hargis was invited back to his college. He promptly announced that he was "led of the Lord to come back to Tulsa." Shortly afterward he purchased a six-story building for his downtown headquarters, and for the next ten years he remained active as an educational administrator. Surely such political legerdemain is incompatible with mental incapacity. However odd Hargis's behavior, society was not ready to brand him either ill or bad.

The lesson of Hargis and his defenses was summed up by the father of one of his students. The father reported that his son's three-year sexual involvement with Hargis had begun when the boy was 15 or 16 and said, "I will forgive him his sin because God's Word tells me what I must do, but I will never forget his acts against my son." We, too, need to remember that if there are sins, there are no sinners. In understanding the wisdom and the distortions of the ego, there is no reason to be permissive toward misbehavior. But our human dilemma becomes how we, like the trustees of the American Christian College, can employ the creative fundraising of a Hargis and yet not let his maladaptive defenses abuse our children.

A second example of the psychopathology of everyday life illustrates a very different sort of denial from reaction formation: *sublimation*. Some time ago, a 30-year-old musician, afflicted with progressive deafness, was debating suicide. He wrote to a friend that he was "living an unhappy life, quarreling with nature and its creator, often cursing the latter for surrendering his creatures to the merest accident which often breaks or destroys the most beautiful blossoms." Yet he begged his friend "to keep the matter of my deafness a profound secret, to be confided to nobody, no matter whom."[2] To another friend he confessed, "For two years I have avoided almost all social gatherings because it is impossible for me to say to people, 'I am deaf' . . . Already, I have often cursed my Creator and my existence."[3] If he fantasized abuse from God, the flesh-and-blood father who had created him had been a chronic alcoholic who had repeatedly humiliated him.

The following year this musician composed a will in which his low self-esteem and suicidal ideation became more apparent still. "Ah, how could I possibly admit an infirmity in the *one sense* which ought to be more perfect in me than in others? . . . What a humiliation for me when someone standing next to me heard a flute in the distance and I *heard nothing!* . . . Such incidents drove me almost to despair, a little more of that and I would have ended my life . . . With joy I hasten to meet death." One might legitimately ponder how such a musician was to live out a full life. Certainly, one might doubt that he would ever work up to his full capacity. One might predict that he might indeed commit suicide; for as he wrote at the time, "It was only my art that held me back."[4]

Predictions can only be tested by follow-up. If I am to assert that this musician's art allowed him to sublimate his pain, grief, and humiliation, tangible proof is required. A quarter of a century later, the musician was still alive and still involved with his art. Age 53 found him standing at the Royal Imperial Court Theater of Vienna, staring at the score of a symphony whose premiere he had just finished co-conducting. One of his soloists plucked his sleeve and directed his attention behind him, to see what he could not hear, the clapping hands, the waving hats and fluttering handkerchiefs. An observer recorded proudly in his own diary, "Never in my life did I hear such frenetic and yet cordial applause . . . When the parterre broke out in applauding cries the 5th time, the Police Commissioner yelled, 'Silence!'"[5]

But the miracle was not that the totally deaf Ludwig van Beethoven was now hurrying to meet life. It was not that his art had allowed a misanthropic crippled bachelor the admiration of his two beautiful female soloists. (When he first interviewed his lead soloists, Beethoven confessed that "since they wanted by all means to kiss my hands and were really pretty, I proposed that they kiss my mouth.")[6] Nor was the miracle that, thanks to Beethoven, Vienna, besotted with Rossini's Italian lyrics, could finally applaud a choral work in its native German, or that Beethoven had used his art to "mould conditions" and to heal his own self-esteem.

No, the miracle was none of the above. The miracle was that Beethoven's Ninth Symphony had put Schiller's "Ode to Joy" to triumphant music. Twenty-three years before, Beethoven had written in his will, "As the leaves of autumn fall and are withered—so likewise has my hope been blighted . . . Oh Providence—grant me at least but one day of *pure joy*—it is so long since real joy echoed in my heart—Oh when—Oh when, Oh Divine One, shall I feel it again?"[7] At the same time the progressively deaf musician had confessed the bargain that he wished to make with his accursed creator: "Oh, if I were rid of this affliction, I would embrace the world."[8] But his affliction had not disappeared, it had worsened. Nonetheless, the lyrics that the totally deaf Beethoven had put to music were "Be embraced, all ye millions, with a kiss for all the world. Brothers, beyond the stars surely dwells a loving father." The miracle of Beethoven's Ninth Symphony was that the self-deception, or should I say the magic, by which his ego had transformed an alcoholic and an "accursed creator" into a "loving father" had indeed spun dross into gold—not just for himself but for others and for generations to come.

Among the lessons to be drawn from these first two examples is that there are many kinds of denial, many forms of self-deception. Ludwig van Beethoven's denial was very different from that of Billy James Hargis. If Hargis's reaction formation was both adaptive and maladaptive, Beethoven's sublimation brought joy to all. Behind Beethoven's feat of psychic alchemy lay the unrelenting honesty of his ego. Pain was not concealed but only rendered bearable. Beethoven's despair was not transformed into dissociated joy but only into music. Indeed, as Beethoven wrote and rewrote his score for Schiller's "Ode to Joy," over the draft of one instrumental recitative he scribbled, "No, this would remind us too much of our despair."[9] Throughout everything, he had remained conscious of his pain. And he was no aging misanthrope given to seducing pretty playmates by the use of rose-colored glasses or by an evangelical preacher's confidence tricks. On his own merits, Beethoven personally coached his pretty soloists for their performance in his Ninth Symphony. Nor did he abuse them; he only recorded in his journal that he had wished to kiss their lips.

The distortion of the Ninth Symphony was not that of a psychotic or even that of a dissociated Pollyanna. I doubt if anyone ever leveled at Beethoven the epithet "What a cornball!" that a college student, sotto voce, once leveled at me and my classroom efforts to retell Beethoven's story. But, then, the ego's wisdom suffers in translation.

Beethoven died in bed at his appointed time. His death was accompanied, we are told in legend, by thunder and lightning from without and by both the composer's hands being balled into fists from within. But that is only legend, and I wish to honor fact. The historical facts were that in Vienna, in honor of Beethoven's death, even the schools were closed.[10] Nineteenth-century Vienna did not close its schools for lunatics or for cornballs.

To make another point, let me look at the relationship between creativity and play. Unlike Hargis's reaction formation, Beethoven's act of writing the Ninth Symphony seems an almost conscious act of will—until one tries to emulate the example. Always, mature defenses *seem* more conscious than immature defenses. But, in fact, people cannot *make* themselves happy. People cannot make themselves creative; but unhappy children sometimes become happier when they play. We cannot will creativity, yet it is conscious. Play is certainly conscious and voluntary. That is the paradox. Through play our interior worlds change, and imaginary games can elicit real smiles. Sometimes play becomes creativity and creativity turns anger and despair into something beautiful. Such is the ego's alchemy. Adults need to relearn how to play, and as they do, sublimation and humor may become more salient in their repertoire of defenses.

Over the years, Beethoven had told himself many stories to alleviate a painful childhood spent with his abusive, alcoholic father—his accursed creator. But in the performance of the Ninth Symphony, Beethoven's painful imagination became transformed into liberating reality. Play allows us not just to wish but to throw ourselves into life. By becoming lost in play, we are found; and so both creativity and play are different from fantasy. The denial of Beethoven's sublimation seems incontrovertibly more adaptive than the denial of Hargis's reaction formation and more fun than my own cognitive strategy of avoiding loop-the-loop roller coasters.

Clearly, not all denial, not all self-deceptions are the same. Despite his suicidal inclinations, Beethoven took responsibility for his own angry despair and transmuted his rage into chords of joy for his audience. There are certain risks, however, to deciphering defenses. At the end of one lecture in which I referred to Beethoven's melancholy, a college sophomore marched to the podium. What right did I have, she challenged, to call Beethoven depressed? Who, indeed, has the right to say that at the center of something beautiful lies despair? Perhaps only another artist.

Thus, Adrienne Rich, listening to Beethoven with a poet's hyperacuity, reflects on the creation of the Ninth Symphony:

> A man in terror of impotence
> or infertility . . .
> howling from the climacteric
> music of the entirely
> isolated soul . . .
> trying to tell something the man
> does not want out, would keep if he could
> gagged and bound and flogged with chords of Joy
> where everything is silence and the
> beating of a bloody fist upon
> a splintered table.[11]

It takes an artist's sublimation to hold another artist's pain for the rest of us to see—and to bear. As a method of denial and of truth telling, sublimation is nothing short of miraculous.

———

The value, however, of our understanding defenses is not just to understand art. The value of understanding defenses is to understand the ultimate humanity, and even the ultimate decency, in behaviors that, too often, we dismiss as either mental illness or sin. We all need to become less paranoid toward people in pain.

Robert Coles, a Pulitzer Prize–winning psychiatrist, tried to look beneath the surface of a sinner, not an artist. No great fan of psychoanalysis, Coles did not ignore history and ideology and how they molded men, but he listened to more than that: He paid mind to how women and men mold conditions. As a fledgling child psychiatrist, Coles went south in 1960 to try to understand how Mississippians were adapting to the pain and turmoil of the court-ordered desegregation of the public schools. Coles tried to understand not only how young black children adapted to taunts and hate-tinged racial slurs but also how white adults, dismissed by pious bigoted northern liberals as "rednecks," adapted to a changing world.

Coles asked himself the question: Why should anyone have nothing better to do in the middle of the night than plant dynamite in schools and churches? So he met with John, a Louisiana mob participant, who marched outside schools with a placard reading "Fight Integration. Communists Want Negroes With Whites." As Coles explained to John, "I am a physician . . . a research physician specializing in problems of human adjustment under stress."[12] He met with this man, whom I shall call John-the-Bigot, weekly. Coles listened and tried to comprehend the feelings—rather than the ideas—that fueled John's hate. He sought the meaning behind the paranoia of John's placard.

Certainly, John's *ideas* did not make sense. They would have conveyed little meaning to a rational cognitive psychologist. Depending upon the observer's own prejudices, the substance of John-the-Bigot's cognition was patently crazy, wicked, or paranoid. John's bizarre *ideas* could not explain for Coles why people would have nothing better to do in the middle of the night than plant dynamite. For among John's peculiar ideas was the notion that residents of New Orleans would do well to beware of the Greeks and Lebanese who were infiltrating the city by boat. Blacks, John believed, should be returned to Africa—

except for a few who should be sterilized and kept on in America as manual laborers. Similarly, Jews should be stripped of their power and exiled to Russia. And to top it off, the fluoridation of water supplies was a threat to American freedom. John's world of ideas was an insane battlefield between God and the devil. On the devil's side were Negroes in league with Communists and, presumably, with the advocates of fluoridation. John's ideas did not initially encourage even Freudian forgiveness; for as John explained to Coles, his parents were "the nicest parents anyone could ever want."[13] How was Coles to translate what John said into what John felt and meant? How was Coles to follow Oliver Sacks's suggestion and to understand John's words as "attempts (however misguided) at restitution, at reconstructing a world reduced to complete chaos"?

In looking beneath the surface meaning, Coles, like his mentor Erik Erikson, tried to blend sociology and psychoanalysis. Unlike many psychiatrists, he was able to portray society as being as important as the unconscious: "We must all know that the animal in us can be elaborately rationalized in a society until an act of murder is seen as self-defense and dynamited houses become evidence of moral courage."[14] America's patriotic dynamiting and burning of whole Vietnamese towns in order to preserve them was still to come.

In short, Coles ignored John-the-Bigot's ideas and, instead, paid attention to both his societal and his affective reality. John's earliest memory was being whipped by his father when the latter had returned from World War II. In contrast to his earlier statement about his parents, John finally admitted that he had hated his father for as long as he could remember. His father was dark, short, and belonged to the Louisiana Cajun minority. John, too, was short and dark-complexioned. His mother and brother, both preferred by the father, were blue-eyed, taller, and closer to the Anglo-Saxon southern ideal. John's father was chronically angry, both because he was an alcoholic (biology) and because he could not always earn a day's pay (economics). His son John became a convenient scapegoat. Prejudice allows us to transplant what we believe to be our own unforgivable feelings into others. Our prejudices begin against ourselves and only later are projected onto others, often others who remind us of ourselves. Thus, John, a dusky scapegoat, hated the dark-skinned minorities.

John-the-Bigot had a second problem. In his childhood his mother had delegated much of his care to his black nurse, Willi Jean.

John was a sickly child, and his mother blamed him for his own illness. In contrast, Willi Jean took care of him and made him feel loved. But she committed two unforgivable sins. She allowed John to love her, and she died when he was still young. Thus, with the unreasonable, grief-relieving illogic of projection and its first cousin, reaction formation, John grew up convinced that God had punished him for nigger-loving. He confided to Coles that blacks were like children, dirty children. He described the inherent sinfulness of Harlem: "I've been there and seen it." It was clear that John had gone to Harlem as a yearning voyeur and then triumphantly concluded, as if to prove the wisdom of his segregationist philosophy, "You wouldn't let a wild animal go free in your home or in school with your kids, would you?" [15] At this point in his interview Coles confides to the reader that "each of us tired suddenly, and hardened." The previously trusting, accepting child psychiatrist who had "found myself knowing him" was finally repelled by John's defenses. Without trust, projection destroys relationships; and John's unreason had become momentarily too hot. There is no legal brief, no mathematical equation, no cold idea that would make two individuals "tire suddenly." John's projection, though it regulated his conflicted love for his nurse and his distorted internalization of his father's own self-hatred, had become invasive, divisive, and explosive. John's denial was clearly maladaptive. It could infuriate even a humane clinician. His defense became equated with sin. Most of the time, Hargis's denial (that is, his reaction formation) went unnoticed. Beethoven's denial (sublimation) inspired the world for centuries. Beethoven died at his appointed time, and the schools of Vienna were closed in his honor. In contrast, John's paranoid placards and his passionate efforts to make others responsible for his own painful rage had no effect upon the New Orleans school system at all.

In his narrative, Coles steps back and reflects that the contagion of individual prejudice depends not only upon inner conflict but also upon the society and the culture. He points out that at the same time that John was carrying his placards in New Orleans, neighboring and equally rabid segregationists submitted to racial equality on Louisiana air bases as a condition of federal employment. Coles's implication is that the defense mechanism of projection, the sin of prejudice, can be suppressed in the face of suitable economic incentives. He also appreciated that part of John's difficulty was his jobless panic, and that his place in the school picket line provided him with a chance "to speak his mind." Individual psychopathology, social conflicts, and economic instability have separate causes; each plays an important role in human behavior. We must learn to empathize with the prejudiced, even as we condemn their prejudice.

_____

Let me introduce yet a fourth form of denial. In *Children of Crisis*, Coles describes another youth, also called John. This John's surname was Washington. He was one of ten black youths assigned to integrate the local high school. While witnessing the hatred aimed at both Washington and himself at a basketball game, Coles became alarmed and anxious, but Washington did not. Coles was puzzled by this John's "altogether remarkable composure"—his apparent immunity to stress. His appetite, his humor, his expression were controlled. Rather than demonstrate fear in response to the segregationist threats, on one occasion he stoically confided to Coles, "I am going to have to get used to that, so we might as well start now." [16] "But it's sweet pain this time," he explained on another occasion of threat and danger, "because whatever they say to me or however they try to hurt me, I know that by just sticking it out I'm going to end the whole system of segregation . . . Yes, when they get to swearing and start calling me 'nigger,' I think of the progress we're making." [17]

What reframing. What denial. What suppression! Note that Washington's statements do not reflect dissociation, the denial of emotion by the roller coaster riders. Nor is he like the placard-carrying John-the-Bigot, denying his own feelings by placing them in others. He is able to keep in consciousness both the cloud and its silver lining. John Washington accurately noticed and acknowledged that he was in pain, but it became "sweet pain" because his ego allowed him to include its past, present, and future significance in the same mental gestalt. Clearly, in the dictionary sense of the term, his behavior could be called *denial* just as could Beethoven's sublimation and the roller coaster riders' dissociation. But John Washington's pain did not hurt because its owner could imagine the future as well as the present.

The case of John Washington raises another problem: explaining where such resilience in the face of adversity comes from. Coles, too, asked where his resilience came from and looked for an answer in the obvious places. Perhaps, unlike John-the-Bigot, he had had a happy childhood. But John Washington, it turned out, had not had a happy childhood. He came from a family genetically (and environmentally) blighted by maternal psychosis and environmentally (and genetically) cursed by paternal alcoholism. Since the old standbys of nature and nurture were no help, Coles wondered if the solution lay in the historical moment. Certainly, war is less frightening if within its context you feel like a hero rather than a victim. In the national television coverage of desegregation John Washington sensed a whole world cheering, while John-the-Bigot sensed a whole world sneering. If you have a place to stand in the world, you can bear its pain.

But Coles also touched on the wisdom of the ego when he described John Washington's ego in the following fashion: "The tough side of his personality, the stubborn, crafty, inventive qualities that poor and persecuted people often develop simply to survive, found an event, a challenge that could draw upon them—make them qualities that could guarantee success rather than, as before, keep chaos at arm's length."[18] True, conditions mold men, and Coles appreciated that this is important; but the ways in which the human ego can mold societal stress into a challenge that can draw out its own strength are equally important.

_____

For my fifth example of the psychopathology of everyday life, let me take an episode from the life of the man who has contributed most to our understanding of defense mechanisms. Like John Washington, Sigmund Freud was crafty and inventive. I believe that Freud's greatest contribution to modern psychology was not only to acknowledge man's capacity for self-deception but also to identify the regulatory processes by which such denials, repressions, and distortions take place. But along the way Freud simultaneously used his science as an art and as a creative self-deception to heal pain of his own. Freud may have been wrong when he suggested that dreams were the royal road to the unconscious. Rather, it may be waking acts of creativity, such as his own, that offer us such an avenue.

Since the days of its nineteenth-century founders, Wilhelm Wundt at the University of Leipzig and William James at Harvard, academic psychology has focused too narrowly on cognition and on cognitive dissonance and its resolution. Both Wundt and James wrote long and influential textbooks of psychology,[19] but each text devoted only a single chapter to emotion. In sharp contrast to almost every other nineteenth-century psychologist, Freud did not ignore the role of emotions in shaping experience. Rather, he gave to the emotions pride of place, a priority that made possible his elucidation of the ego.

In 1894 Freud, the contemporary of Wundt and James, observed not only that emotion (affect) could be "dislocated or transposed" from ideas and people but that such affect could be "reattached" to other ideas and objects by mental regulatory processes which he chose to call displacement and sublimation.[20] At the time these were most novel concepts. Yet within this act of scientific creativity was also evidence of a self-deceptive, a healthy, even an inspired ego at work.

When Freud branched out into psychiatry in 1894, he was still a hard-nosed scientist, a practicing neurologist and the secretary of the Society of German Naturalists and Physicians. Yet that very year he was hard at work describing defense mechanisms for the first time. Referring to his ground-breaking essay "The Neuropsychoses of Defense," Freud promised his friend Wilhelm Fliess, "I shall send off a manuscript full of the most beautiful brand-new discoveries."[21] Four months later, still savoring his paper's insights, he wrote to Fliess, "I have the distinct feeling that I have touched on one of the great secrets of nature . . . I know three mechanisms: that of affect transformation (conversion hysteria), that of affect displacement (obsessional ideas) and that of exchange of affect (anxiety neurosis and melancholia) . . . The impetus to them is not in every case something sexual."[22] In 1895 Freud suggested to Fliess that such creativity was not easy: "Psychology is really a cross to bear . . . hunting for mushrooms is, in any event, a much healthier pastime. All I was trying to do was to explain defense, but just try explaining something from the very core of nature!"[23]

Yet the years 1894–1896, in which he published his two seminal papers on defense, were the most anxiety-ridden of Freud's life. During this period he was convinced that he would not live to see age 50. In the same letter to Fliess in which he boasted of his discovery of differentiated defense mechanisms, Freud wrote with all the self-absorption of a hypochondriac, "I promise you a detailed report on my illness next time."[24] In fact, he had been complaining to Fliess about his health for some time. Just two weeks earlier, Freud, the neurologist who was busy identifying symptoms in his neurasthenic patients as imaginary, wrote to Fliess, "Then suddenly there came a severe cardiac misery, greater than I ever had while smoking. The most violent arrhythmia, constant tension, pressure [*Pressung*] and burning [*Brennung*] in the heart region, shooting pains down my left arm; some dyspnea . . . the dyspnea is so moderate that one suspects something organic, and with it a feeling of depression, which took the form of visions of death."[25] (A half-century later Max Schur, Freud's physician, pointed out that not only Freud's symptoms but even his language reflected his ego's creativity. Freud's terms *Pressung* and *Brennung*, which have been translated into English as "pressure" and "burning," do not exist in the German language.[26]

In the summer of 1896 Jacob Freud, Sigmund's father, became fatally ill. In a letter dated November 2 of that year, Freud wrote, "The old man's death has affected me deeply. I valued him highly, understood him very well . . . By the time he died, his life had long been over, but in my inner self the whole past has been reawakened by this event."[27] In the letter Freud then described a "nice dream I had the night after the funeral." Freud's actual description of his "nice" dream was somber and anything but pretty. Perhaps it may have been an outlet for feelings of self-reproach, which death often leaves among the survivors. Freud's dream was of his father's funeral; and he had seen a short notice, "You are requested to close the eyes." Marianne Krull, one of Freud's biographers, suggests that the notice did not mean just putting pennies on the dead man's eyes to close them, but that "Freud felt that his father wished him not only to render him a last service but to shut his eyes to certain facts. In other words, this dream must have reminded Freud of an unspoken taboo Jacob had passed on to him in early childhood, namely, not to delve into his, Jacob's, past."[28]

In February 1897 Freud inferred from the existence of some hysterical symptoms in his brothers and several sisters (but not himself) that even his own father had to be suspected of the incest to which Freud was attributing the cause of hysterical symptoms. "Unfortunately," he confided to Fliess, "my own father was one of those perverts and is responsible for the hysteria of my brother and those of several younger sisters."[29]

Three months later, still unable to close his eyes, Freud began instead to experience writer's block as well as "cardiac misery" and lost all interest in his "self-analytic" dream book. He became concerned with primal scenes (children witnessing parental intercourse) and suggested that such traumatic experiences could be linked to fantasies. At this point, his own self-analysis began in earnest. Freud began to focus on the resentments that children entertained toward their parents. He proposed that "Hostile impulses against parents (a wish that they should die) are also an integrating constituent of neuroses. They come to light consciously as obsessional ideas . . . this death wish is directed in sons against their fathers, and in daughters against their mothers."[30] In the same month, Freud interpreted one of his own dreams: "The dream, of course, shows the fulfillment of my wish to catch a *Pater* as the originator of neurosis and thus puts an end to my ever-recurring doubts."[31]

By June 1897 Freud's writer's block had worsened: "I have never before even imagined anything like this period of intellectual paralysis. Every line is torture."[32] Even his handwriting was altered. In August he arranged for his father's gravestone, and wrote to Fliess, "The chief patient I am preoccupied with is myself. My little hysteria, though greatly accentuated by my work, has resolved itself a bit further."[33] The next month he retracted his seduction theory, thus exonerating his father. "And now I want to confide in you immediately the great secret that has been slowly dawning on me in the last few months . . . There are no indications of reality in the unconscious so that one cannot distinguish between truth and fiction that has been cathected with affect."[34] A month later he wrote to Fliess that the "Oedipal" relationship of the child to its parents was a universal event in early childhood and might explain the gripping power of *Oedipus Rex*. In fantasy, everyone in the audience had once been a budding Oedipus, and such fantasies might explain the power of *Hamlet* as well. "How does Hamlet, the hysteric, justify his words, 'Thus conscience does make cowards of us all'?" Freud asked.[35] For his answer, he needed only to turn within. His own conscience had led him to retract his seduction hypothesis. As soon as he obeyed his "nice dream's" injunction, "You are requested to close the eyes," his writing paralysis disappeared. Freud renounced his seduction theory and replaced it with his own version of the Oedipus legend in which lustful children are the abusers and murderers of innocent parents.

By February 1898 Freud was fully recovered and his creativity freed. "I am deep in the dream book," he wrote Fliess, "am writing it fluently and enjoy the thought of all the headshaking over my indiscretions and audacities that it contains."[36] But for all its displaced audacities and indiscretions, *The Interpretation of Dreams*—considered by Freud himself to be the apogee of his lifetime of creativity—was a eulogy to his father. It blamed the victim, Oedipus, and allowed Laius to escape judgment. In the actual Oedipus legend, a legend of which Freud was undoubtedly aware, Laius was a notorious pederast and a heartless father who could order his infant son to be mutilated, his feet pierced by a spike, and left by henchmen on a mountainside to die. Thus, if we pay attention to the historical legend, Oedipus's murder of his father could be viewed as justifiable homicide. But Freud chose to ignore the facets of the Oedipus legend that made Laius the perverse one; and Freud's self-deception healed his neurasthenia. For the next forty years, Freud was quite free of writer's block, of dyspnea, and of heart disease. He also was quite unconscious of how much reaction formation and displacement were embodied in his great book.

For eight decades Freud's renunciation of his seduction theory was taken as an example by many observers, and not just by his orthodox admirers, of his enormous courage in seeking scientific truth. However, in the past twenty years biographical research, from Max Schur's loving book to Jeffrey Masson's polemical *The Assault on Truth: Freud's Suppression of the Seduction Theory*, has made it clear that Freud deceived himself. In most cases, patients' accounts of parental incest are *not* fantasy.

Freud himself admitted that his entire scientific reorientation was connected with his father. In 1908 he wrote, "This book [*Interpretation of Dreams*] has a further subjective significance for me personally—a significance which I only grasped after I completed it. It was, I found, a portion of my own self-analysis, my reaction to my father's death."[37]

By 1905 Freud had found at least one more facet of what he had called his psychological "cross" too heavy to bear. He tried to forget all about—to close his eyes to—differentiated defenses: "'repression' (as I now begin to say instead of 'defense')."[38] In 1926 his "repression" lifted and he wrote, "I have revived a concept . . . of which I made exclusive use thirty years ago when I first began the study of the subject [of anxiety] but which I later abandoned. I refer to the term 'defensive process' . . . it will be an undoubted advantage, I think, to revert to the old concept of 'defense.'"[39] In the same book, *Id, Inhibitions and Anxiety*, Freud pointed out the utility of distinguishing the defense of isolation from repression. He had clearly defined this distinction in

1894, but in 1926 he asserted, "We are setting out to describe [it] for the first time."[40] Even psychoanalysts use repression.

To summarize, if Freud's 1894 career switch from neurology to the study of defenses and psychoanalysis was a scientific advance, perhaps facilitated by anxious conflict, Freud's abandonment of the seduction hypothesis in 1897 and of the concept of differentiated defense mechanisms in 1905 were almost certainly illustrations of defensive response to anxious conflict and were *not* scientific advances. Freud's own uncovering of the human unconscious was in part his creative way of mastering hostile ambivalence toward his ineffective father, an ambivalence that surfaced at the time of his father's approaching death. Freud branded himself a budding Oedipus and therefore a guilty perpetrator, not a victim, of childhood pain. But beneath the surface of Freud's conscious statements lay his very real contempt for his father. At first glance, Freud's *mea culpa* might look like masochism, turning against the self, and appear to be quite maladaptive. But no one suffered from his self-deception. Besides, you cannot usefully punish a dead man. Rather, Freud's self-deception produced a book, *The Interpretation of Dreams*, that won him immortality and raised the consciousness of humanity to the fact that children do lust after their opposite-sex parents.

Nor does the accumulating biographical evidence that Freud unconsciously defended himself and distorted his evidence diminish the scientific validity of his discovery of the "neuropsychoses" of defenses—his discovery of the wisdom of the ego. Thus, as epigraph for his biography of Freud, Peter Gay quotes from Freud's own biography of Leonardo da Vinci: "There is no one so great that it would be a disgrace for him to be subject to the laws that govern normal and pathological activity with equal severity."[41] Nor would we doubt the validity of Charles Darwin's *The Origin of Species* if we discovered that his own distant ancestors had been monkeys.

Finally, let me offer an example of yet another kind of denial—repression. In so doing I hope to illustrate how complex and paradoxical a defense repression is. I hope to illustrate why the cognitive psychologists can dismiss repression as an artifact of diminished attention and why at the same time psychoanalysts view it as such a central concept. Whether one believes that the "unconscious" is unconscious depends upon one's point of view. The truth is by no means black or white.

On a snowy winter Tuesday, a psychology intern was lying on his psychoanalyst's couch. It was the end of the hour, and he was planning future appointment times. "But Thursday is a holiday," the patient said. "It's Washington's Birthday."

"That's all right," the psychoanalyst replied. "I will be able to see you on Thursday."

"Well, you'd better not save the time," the patient insisted. "You see, I'm not sure if I'll be in town. I may go away."

"Well, maybe we can talk about it tomorrow," said the analyst, ending the hour. "You can let me know then."

The patient walked out of the office, and in his conscious mind, he was thinking: How very singular, it is up to me whether or not I can see this busy physician on a holiday. It is wrong that he should have to wait on my uncertainty. (It would not be overstating matters to suggest that the psychology intern had a strict conscience.)

In any case, the patient reassured himself that he would discuss the matter further the next day. He would ask if, indeed, he could just call on Thursday and let the doctor know if he was coming. Yet it was wrong of him to ask this, he mused. Such last-minute planning would be an outrageous inconvenience to his doctor.

The next day, Wednesday, the intern arrived ten minutes late. He said he had had a dream that he had missed his appointment, that he had just forgotten all about it until it was too late. The analyst, noting that his patient was late and believing that sometimes such mistakes occur unconsciously on purpose, inquired, "Was the appointment you missed today's appointment?" "No," the patient replied, "it was on the afternoon of Thursday." He explained that his dream had been mostly about how hard it had been for him to ask a social worker from his clinic for a ride home. He remembered that in actual fact a week ago he had kept thinking all afternoon that he needed a ride home, but then at the crucial moment he had forgotten to ask the social worker for a ride. She had left without him. It was always hard for him to ask people for help. He associated to his dream for quite awhile.

The Wednesday hour was up and the patient got off the couch to leave.

"See you Friday," said the doctor.

The psychology intern was disappointed. Now he wanted to come on Thursday. He realized that now, of course, it was too late. The hour was over. He could not ask for the Thursday appointment . . . ask for the Thursday appointment so he could continue to analyze how hard it was for him to ask for things. But as he got up to leave, he had trouble finding his books—almost as if he did not want to leave.

In summary, the intern's plan to ask for an appointment on Thursday had been in the back of his mind all during the Wednesday hour. His actual life problem, asking for help, was not kept out of consciousness, nor was the yearning affect behind his need for help. The *subject*, the *affect*, the *object* were all *in mind*. Even the defensive process—to forget until too late to ask—had been clearly spelled out in the dream. All that the intern had forgotten was the *idea* of talking about what he had consciously resolved the day before to talk about— to ask for a Thursday appointment. His forgetting was all the more extraordinary because the previous weekend he had written a graduate school paper on *repression*. As Anna Freud wrote, "The obscurity of a successful repression is only equaled by the transparency of the repressive process when the repressed material returns."[42] As a method of denial, repression is so common, so much a part of the self-deception of everyday life, that we all can own it.

This book is a view from within. I do not intend, like Robert Coles and Erik Erikson, to integrate biology and society. I shall present a one-sided view of how humans mold conditions rather than of how conditions mold humans.

I will examine individuals in conflict and trace a variety of solutions to conflict: some crazy; some irritating to others like those of John-the-Bigot; some, like the psychology intern's repression, irritating only to the self; and some, like Beethoven's, brilliantly adaptive, bringing survival to the user and joy to the world. I wish to differentiate adaptive denial and self-deception from maladaptive denial and self-deception. But I shall ignore the philosophical underbrush surrounding the value-ridden term *adaptive*. Instead, I shall listen to Claude Bernard, a brilliant student of physiological adaptation, who warned us, "The words fever, inflammation, and the names of diseases in general have no meaning at all in themselves . . . Our language, in fact, is only approximate, and even in science it is so indefinite that if we lose sight of phenomena and cling to words, we are speedily out of reality. We, therefore, only injure science by arguing in favor of a word which is now merely a source of error, because it no longer expresses the same idea for everyone. Let us therefore conclude that we must always cling to phenomena."[43]

4

Necessary Questions

> The concept of adaptation, though it appears simple, implies . . . a great
> many problems. The analysis of this concept promises to clarify many
> problems of normal and abnormal psychology, among them our concep-
> tion of mental health.
>
> Heinz Hartmann

As soon as we decide to take unconscious mental regulatory processes seriously, as soon as we try to reify adaptive self-deceptions,
several questions come to mind. The questions most often raised by
intelligent audiences pondering the implications of different adaptive
styles include: (1) How many defenses are there? (2) How do you
identify a defense? (3) Can you use defenses on purpose or teach
others how to use more adaptive defenses? (4) When is a defense a
symptom and when is it adaptive? Are some kinds of denial or self-
deception healthier than others? In other words, is a coping mechanism different from a defense mechanism? (5) Are some defenses
limited to specific situations, specific affects, or specific relationships?
Are some defenses specific to gender, culture, or historical epoch? (6)
Does each personality type use a characteristic defense? (7) How do
we cope when we do not use defenses? In other words, if a defense
becomes conscious, what takes its place? (8) Can breaching a person's
defenses be helpful to therapy? If so, how do you tell someone that
they are using defenses? (9) Are defensive styles immutable, or do
they change over time? Does adult development affect choice of
defenses?

This list does not exhaust the possible questions, but it is long
enough for one chapter. Quite deliberately I shall postpone the most
interesting question of all—Where do mature defenses come from?—
until the end of the book.

How Many Defenses Are There?

There are as many defenses as there are colors in a rainbow. Like the colors of a rainbow, the variegated legions of defense mechanisms make up a constant whole. It is our language and our vantage point that changes—not the rainbow. There are as many defenses as we have the imagination, the temerity, or the linguistic facility to catalogue. Freud, in his *New Introductory Lectures,* listed only four defenses.[1] By convention, Anna Freud is said to have listed ten defense mechanisms in her now classic compendium *The Ego and the Mechanisms of Defense.*[2] However, in studying that work I counted at least twenty. Grete Bibring and her co-workers, in a study of young mothers, compiled a list of forty defenses.[3] But that is only a beginning. Our language of coping, adapting, and defending has produced a vocabulary as multifarious as the tongues of the builders of the Tower of Babel.

My most instructive lesson in this babble of tongues occurred in 1977, when the American Psychiatric Association was planning for the third edition of its Diagnostic and Statistical Manual (DSM III). I was one of a group of psychoanalysts interested in both diagnosis and defenses who were brought together in a conference room at the New York Psychiatric Institute in uptown Manhattan. Our task was to reach consensus on what were the most important defenses for possible inclusion in DSM III, and to provide tentative definitions. It should have been easy. We were a very homogeneous group—American East Coast psychoanalysts. But the result was chaos. The dialogue soon revealed a remarkable absence of consensus. In such a context, to include defenses as explanatory concepts within a diagnostic manual seemed scientifically preposterous. What if the room had included English psychiatrists, biologic psychiatrists, cognitive psychologists? Not surprisingly, DSM III went to press without mention of defenses.

Were we trying to provide names for imaginary concepts, or was our difficulty simply linguistic? Were we like ancient Greeks and Romans, arguing over the correct names of the gods of mythology? Or were we like automobile manufacturers competitively naming the colors of our products? No one would deny that the color blue exists, but whether it is called azure, aquamarine, or heavenly blue is a matter of semantic choice. Colors are real; only their names are imaginary.

So too, the phenomena underlying defenses are real; only their names are imaginary. Defenses reflect a spectrum of largely unconscious mental regulatory processes that permit mastery (or avoidance) of psychic conflicts (or cognitive dissonance). In Chapter 2, I selected eighteen labels from the compilations of defenses produced by others. Such a list is arbitrary and idiosyncratic. However, thirteen of these eighteen defenses are included in DSM III-R, the revised version of DSM III. Those thirteen mechanisms, plus an additional seven only briefly discussed in this book, reflect the efforts of American psychiatry to devise a consensual Esperanto with which to discuss defenses. It is a promising start to achieving a real consensus in the field.

My own rules for selecting the eighteen defenses defined in Chapter 2 were simple. First, the term should have been used and described by several respected investigators. Second, each mechanism named should be clearly differentiable from the others. Third, the eighteen terms should encompass most of the different ways our minds have of distorting the perceived relationships among subject, affect, idea, and object.

But over the years, discussions of defenses have grown more sophisticated. Just as in real life pure colors rarely exist, just as in nature chemical compounds are more common than pure elements, and just as many musical compositions involve parts for more than one instrument, just so compound or blended defenses must be used to describe real-life behavior. The tale of Peggy O'Hara, then, is as over-simplified as the lives of Aesop's characters. The labeling and reification of defenses is reductionistic; but, then, so is labeling a complex woodland biome a birch or a pine forest.

Let me provide a simple example of a complex defense. In many obsessions, isolation of affect and displacement occur as an amalgam. It is not uncommon for women to come to clinicians and report that they have a phobia of knives and that they are obsessed with the idea of hurting their children. These thoughts frighten the mothers very much, but the thoughts are rarely accompanied by angry feelings. Rather, the mothers' thoughts of hurting their children are experienced as illogical. These women usually feel very fond of their children and cannot imagine why they should feel compelled to do them harm. Such individuals do not become child abusers, but their phobic obsessions may prevent them from ever using knives. As their clinicians learn more about these women, they find that they have displaced real anger toward their husbands onto their children. These husbands have often been abusive or failed to meet their wives' needs for care. However, anger is frightening to these often overtly dependent women, and thus their anger is transferred (displaced) onto their children. Then, the ugly idea is stripped of its affect (isolated), so that it appears in their minds as an unmotivated obsession.

Often defensive behaviors are determined as much by the other person as by the subject. Defenses such as identification, hypochondriasis, projective identification, devaluation, and splitting are examples of such higher-order interpersonal defenses. With the exception of hypochondriasis (and of reversal, listed by Anna Freud but not by me), these more complex defenses are used most frequently by clinicians influenced by Melanie Klein and Otto Kernberg. These two writers have been more interested in how human beings manage intimacy and the people they can neither live with nor live without than with how they manage conscience, reality, and desire. In this book, however, I shall try to confine my discussion to defenses at the simplest, most generalized level.

How Do You Identify a Defense?

Many psychoanalytic writers since Sigmund Freud have tried to examine defenses under higher and higher magnifications. In so doing they have obfuscated phenomena that they wished to examine. As with studying a rainbow or an Impressionist painting, looking at defenses too closely makes them disappear into meaningless detail and ambiguity. One reason why *The Ego and the Mechanisms of Defense* has remained a classic reference on the subject is Anna Freud's unusual capacity for simplification. She described defenses to the psychoanalyst Joseph Sandler as follows: "If you look at them microscopically, they all merge into each other. You will find repression anywhere you look . . . The point is, one should not look at them microscopically, but macroscopically, as big and separate mechanisms, structures, events . . . [Then] the problem of separating them theoretically becomes negligible. You have to take off your glasses to look at them, not put them on."[4]

But even if I keep things simple, how can the reader know if my suppositions about Beethoven and Billy James Hargis are correct? Like some primitive aboriginal, am I perhaps making up a mythology to explain events that I cannot comprehend? When we talk of defenses are we not always in danger of confusing the mote in our neighbor's eye with the beam in our own? If we make suppositions about people's unconscious conflicts, are we not in danger of projecting animals into inkblots and the future into tea leaves?

Certainly, it is as difficult to prove a defense as to prove a sense of humor or paranoia. Certainly, I lack Galileo's telescope and Darwin's fossil evidence. But as with invisible planets, the presence of a defense can be demonstrated by its predictable and consistent distortion of the events surrounding it. As with distant mountains, the salience of a given defense can be assessed by the triangulation of repeated observations from multiple vantage points. That is, if self-report is checked against objective biographical data and symptoms are checked against both of these, the reliability of the resulting observation can be confirmed by an independent observer.

But notice that in order to praise the cleverness of the ego I personify it. Note how I reify intangible defenses. The oxidation of carbon is invisible; the flame we can all see. The cough reflex is an invisible neural process, the cough a tangible sound. Just so, the neural act of self-deception, the process of projection, is invisible, but John-the-Bigot's paranoid placard is visible for all to see.

Alone, clinical judgment *or* self-report *or* projective and associative techniques are quite inadequate to identify such inferred unconscious processes. But used together, as they are by the skilled clinician or biographer, these three sources of information become quite powerful. As in the case of Beethoven, we have the biographical facts: the year when he began going deaf, the historical fact that the Ninth Symphony is considered a work of art rather than a madman's delusion, and the actual text of Schiller's "Ode to Joy" and Beethoven's rewriting of it. We also have Beethoven's own autobiographical view of things: how he wrote about himself in his diary and his "testament." Finally, we have that extraordinary creative distortion, the Ninth Symphony. Putting all three sources of information together allows me to conclude that for Beethoven to say at one time "If I could recover my hearing, I would embrace the world," and twenty years later, totally deaf, to put to soaring music "Be embraced, all ye millions, with a kiss for all the world"—and more miraculous still, for the world to consider itself embraced—is neither coincidence nor delusion but sublimation.

In clinical psychotherapy research, television has replaced the longitudinal study of biography. Investigators have used videotapes to capture complex behaviors for study and replay. Then independent raters, equipped with manuals outlining operationalized descriptions, have been able to obtain good success in the reliable identification of the patients' defenses included in the video. In both the methods of prospective longitudinal study and of videotape, the key to the reliable identification of defenses is to replace words with behavior.

Can You Use a Defense on Purpose?

This question is one that has been posed by most students of defense, including Freud. Can we use defenses on purpose? Repression seems so self-serving. Passive aggression seems to be deliberately done to annoy. And nobody would want to absolve a young punk who acts out and willfully snaps off fifty car aerials from having to pay for the consequences of his behavior. However, the illusion that defenses are used on purpose stems from our simplistic notion that the brain is only a cognitive brain, a marvelous tabula rasa that first is educated and then behaves in a purely rational way. But the brain is much more than a rational voluntary organ. We sneeze, cough, dream, and fall in love with a minimum of conscious planning or freedom of will.

Our temporal lobes and limbic system, arguably the least understood parts of our brain, serve to attach meaning to beloved objects, people, and memories in ways that defy cold reason. We forget that our memory is not under our conscious control. We can memorize the multiplication tables by decision, but the melody that suddenly makes us cry two years after an ended love affair comes as a surprise.

A second way of introducing the fact that defenses are not deployed on purpose is to ask: Are feelings on purpose? Can we laugh, cry, or fume on command? Indeed we cannot, and in some tragic situations where we expect to cry we find ourselves stony faced or laughing. Similarly, we may find ourselves furious and acting very badly in situations where we really meant to be on our best behavior. Only method actors are capable of producing emotions at will; and, not infrequently, such individuals are susceptible to inadvertent hysteria as well as advertent histrionics. Even our thoughts are not under conscious control. We may rejoice at kissing our lovers' lips but scorn their toothbrushes; we cannot explain why some people regard raw oysters as a delicacy and others find them disgusting. These distinctions are based upon the delicate interaction of our memories, our viscera, and our loves and hates. Like feelings, the defenses that protect us from mental illness can be inadvertent and yet conscious.

The fact that defenses modulate what is outside of voluntary control becomes clearer if we consider the differences between ideas and feelings. First, ideas, detached from feelings, are neutral. They mean just what we believe them to mean. They lend themselves to symbolic expression. We can think and write about ideas and make them, as we would mathematical formulas, obey reason. In contrast, as soon as we endow an idea or an object with feeling, we lose our reason. The object may be overvalued or shunned like the plague. Things that we endow with feeling, we grow attached to. A telephone book is ever so much more useful than a Valentine or a grandchild's scrawled drawing, but we treat the telephone book with far less reverence.

Unlike ideas, feelings are within our bodies. Anxiety is derived from the old French word *angere*, to choke up. Sorrow produces an ineffable ache in our heart. Anger produces a pain in our necks or in our tails. In contrast, the telephone book, filled with important and reasonable numbers, produces no sensation in our bodies at all. A dramatic illustration that ideas and feelings reflect separate phenomena occurs when a stroke affects Broca's area, the so-called speech center in the cerebral cortex. Individuals so affected are incapable of initiating language of any sort until someone, for example, steps on their toe or spills hot coffee on their lap, whereupon they are fully capable of profane and scatological expletives. Despite a dense aphasia, such individuals can shout a perfectly enunciated "God damn you to hell!"

Feelings have temperatures, but ideas do not. Cognitions are at most cool, whereas feelings can be boiling, tepid, or icy. Sexual desire makes us grow hot and blush; fear makes us tremble and grow cold. Again, ideas and numbers occur in black and white, whereas feelings are colorful. Anger makes us see red, envy makes us green, and grief renders our once gaily pigmented world gray or black. I remember a 6-year-old boy discovering a colorful copy of *Playboy* on the coffee table. He thumbed through it for a little bit, expressed an opinion that the jokes were not funny, and then, suddenly, he left the room. Ten minutes later he returned with a seeming non sequitur: "Guess what, Dad, I just counted to a thousand." By counting—higher than he ever had done before—he had successfully distracted his mind from the stimulating photographs of naked breasts. His ego brought order to conflicting feelings by dampening them in a shower of neutral numbers. In similar fashion, when the anxieties and feelings of a disturbing day do not let us sleep, we cannot voluntarily put our minds at ease but instead must count sheep to distract our minds.

Ideas are not dependent on other people for their intensity; feelings are. We can learn calculus by ourselves. We can appreciate its power, utility, and symmetry. A gifted calculus teacher makes only a small difference. Prisoners teach themselves law, and artists learn anatomy without teachers. But teachers are more important when we learn poetry, art appreciation, or clinical medicine. It is hard to get angry without the participation of another person, and there are few jokes which do not include people. Tickling ourselves is almost impossible, but we giggle and squirm involuntarily when tickled by someone else. Although sexual gratification can occur through self-masturbation, fantasies of other people are almost always present. Eating alone is far less fun than eating in company. Yet it is also people who make us lose our reason.

Ideas can be made objective, and they can be voluntarily passed from generation to generation, whereas feelings are always subjective and difficult to teach. *De gustibus non est disputandum.*

Finally, and most important to my argument, conflicts are resolved differently in the presence and absence of feelings. How does conscious, rational conflict resolution differ from unconscious, affect-laden conflict resolution? Should I buy a Toyota or a Ford? A marvelous Hegelian dialectic ensues. Thesis is countered by antithesis, and if all goes well synthesis ensues. Some light, little heat, and no color.

But let me change the scenario. Let me ask you, the reader, to put a penny in your mouth. You are likely to reply: "That is a disgusting idea. You must be some kind of an eccentric." In such a dialogue, nothing has been clarified. There is little light, only heat and confusion. The causes of your dislike of licking pennies are out of sight. But it is a safe bet that whereas the contest between the Toyota and the Ford will come out roughly fifty-fifty, hardly any readers will put pennies in their mouths. Why? We do not arrive at our opinions about licking pennies by conscious choice. Our parents' admonitions come to mind. Our reasoning becomes at best poetic, at worst irrational, and we may never fully understand our revulsion toward licking pennies.

In summary, the brain's ego is more than its parts. The ego creates involuntarily, and what it creates, it defends and regulates. The ego brings order out of chaotic feelings and yet at the same time distorts inner and outer reality. Paranoids cannot become altruists by an act of will. But, through therapy, maturation, and loving relationships people learn more mature styles of self-deception.

When Is a Defense a Symptom and When Is It Adaptive?

How do you tell when a defense is healthy and when it is pathological? When are defenses in the service of adaptation and when are they the building blocks of mental illness? Many psychologists feel that the term *defense mechanism* is pejorative. They insist that if an unconscious adaptive style is beneficial it should be called a *coping mechanism*. My own view is that the distinction between coping and defense cannot be made so clearly.

Consider the white corpuscles and their association with pus. In the case of acne, the accumulation of white corpuscles is superfluous, annoying, and an intrinsic part of the pathology. In the case of the potential infection caused by an intruding splinter, white corpuscles are lifesaving, adaptive, and an intrinsic part of the healing process. A suit of armor provides lifesaving protection in a medieval jousting match, but it becomes a nuisance when the wearer is whitewater canoeing. The ego's armor is no different.

Thus we need to consider both the nature of the defense and the context in which the defense is deployed. First, to be adaptive a defense should meter, rather than remove, affects. Rather than simply anesthetize, a defense should reduce pain. It is no accident that the two most adaptive defenses, anticipation and suppression, result in far more immediate distress than do reaction formation, psychotic denial, and acting out. Each of the last three defenses allows the user perfect (if temporary) anesthesia.

Second, defenses should channel feelings rather than block them. Dammed feelings can be as dangerous to the masochist and the ascetic expert in reaction formation as dammed floodwaters were to the residents of Johnstown and Buffalo Creek. Boiling kettles need vents.

Third, consistent with the analogy of immunology and infection, defenses should be oriented toward the long term, not the short term. Acting out, smashing all the china, going on a two-day binge after an unhappy love affair, relieves tension—for a while. But short-term relief is bought at the price of sustained future distress. In contrast, stoicism and anticipatory mourning allow one to pay now and fly later.

Defenses should be oriented toward present and future pain relief and not past distress. To be paranoid toward doctors and hospitals at age 40 because of an unpleasant tonsillectomy at age 5 can be fatal. Yet during World War II paranoid individuals made superb aircraft spotters.

Fourth, to be adaptive a defense should be as specific as possible. It should be a key that exquisitely fits the tumblers of a specific lock and not a sledgehammer applied by habit to every closed door. Civil disobedience (passive aggression and masochism) in the hands of Martin Luther King, Jr., was such a tool precisely—and quite consciously—used. In contrast, Buddhists who doused themselves with gasoline and engaged in self-cremation to protest the Vietnam War—when not under the gaze of the television cameras—retroflexed their outrage on themselves for naught.

Finally, since the ego's greatest ally is other people, the use of defenses should attract people rather than repel them. The greatest distinction between the mature and immature defenses is that with the mature defenses the subject's regulatory self-deceptions are perceived by those close by as virtuous and attractive. In the case of immature defenses, such self-deceptions are seen by others as irritating, wicked, and repellent. John-the-Bigot and Beethoven both tried to alleviate the pain of having alcoholic, abusive fathers. But their efforts at self-deception affect us in very different ways.

The distinctions I have made so far apply to most contexts. Now let me consider how special situations can affect whether a given defense will facilitate healing or promote disease. First, in some contexts immature defenses can be adaptive and neurotic defenses can be maladaptive. For example, it makes a difference whether the defense reorders the world in the context of imagination or reality. We can all be safely mad in our dreams. When we imagine what goes on in the personal lives of inhabitants of the White House, of the Kremlin, or of Hollywood, we are likely to use projection, distortion, and fantasy. But since we are not directly involved, our use of primitive defenses has no consequences. Children can also distort inner and outer reality without the adverse consequences that would happen were they adults. Modest use of fantasy and passive aggression is probably essential to negotiating adolescence, but those same defenses serve the adult poorly.

Again, within particular cultural contexts, certain defenses are given permission. Compulsive behavior and isolation of affect, harmless enough in everyday life, are virtues in the surgical operating room and in the accountant's office. The same defenses are maladaptive on the stage and on the dance floor. Acting out—impulsive vengeance without a thought to one's own safety—is considered a virtue in war and a crime in peace. Dissociation—believing that we are someone we are not and that our impulsive behavior can have only joyful consequences—ceases to be maladaptive at Mardi Gras.

Finally, whether a defense is normal or abnormal depends upon the eyes of the beholder. We always regard our own vigilance toward our enemies as adaptive, but we view their mistrust of us as an unwarranted projection of their own shortcomings.

Are Some Defenses Specific to Certain Situations?

I think the answer to this question is no, but many would disagree with me. My own belief is that since defenses reflect higher-order phenomena like intelligence or creativity they are relatively nonspecific. Indeed, it is the very nonspecificity of defenses that makes them so essential to the wisdom of the ego. Their purpose is to reduce the cognitive dissonance—the anxious depression—produced by sudden change or conflict. What is a thoracic surgeon who smokes two packages of Camels a day to do when suddenly confronted by the realization that cigarette smoking results in lung cancer? What was the 16-year-old convent-educated Peggy O'Hara to do when she fell in love? These very different situations facing very different individuals at different stages of the life cycle could evoke any of the eighteen defenses outlined in Chapter 2.

Defenses are called forth whenever there is *sudden,* unrehearsed change in any of the four lodestars: people, reality, instinct, or conscience. The sudden change in reality can be a heart attack, integration of a school system, reading Darwin for the first time, or graduating from college. The sudden change in people can be that they have moved too close or too far away—too quickly. The sudden change in emotion can be any unexpected surge, whether from unanticipated grief, rage in the heat of competition or battle, sexual desire in puberty, or dependent yearnings in sickness or in love. Examples of sudden increases in the intensity of our conscience and culturally created values can be as varied as killing in the heat of battle, "pulling the plug" on an incurably ill relative, and feeling rich among Calcutta's poor. In all these cases, any of many defenses can be called into play. To limit a given defense to a particular situation would be like limiting any form of creativity to a single arena of human experience. On the one hand, immature defenses seem more often to be used to manage conflicts about people and neurotic defenses seem more often to manage conflicts about feelings. On the other hand, conflicts about people almost always involve feelings, and conflicts about feelings usually involve people.

With defense choice, as with creativity in general, it is the protagonist and not the situation that determines the mode of expression. Exceptions exist, but they *are* exceptions. Put differently, choice of defense profoundly affects outcome, while social environment only modestly affects choice of defense. The findings from the Study of Adult Development detailed in the next chapter support this surprising generalization. Of course, personality, motivation, and behavior all reflect a person-situation interaction, but some people use some defenses in preference to others. Not everybody has the same personality—and this leads us to the next question.

Does Each Personality Type Use a Characteristic Defense?

The chicken-egg question of whether one's characteristic defenses determine one's personality or whether one's personality determines one's use of defenses is perhaps best answered "Yes, to both of the above." Why do some people selectively use certain defenses? What are the similarities between defenses and character? Certainly paranoid characters use projection, phobic characters use displacement, histrionic characters use dissociation and repression. Charlie Chaplin, Will Rogers, Mark Twain, and Marilyn Monroe all used humor and so we regard them as comedians. But nobody uses a single defense all the time—or exclusively. People, unlike textbook examples, exhibit a complex repertoire of personality types and defensive styles. A good analogy is to compare a person's chosen defenses to an acre of forest. There are birch forests and pine forests. In the wild a birch forest will contain many other trees and so will a pine forest; nevertheless, we can characterize them by their dominant tree. Sometimes the acre is so heterogeneous as to defy classification, but usually generalization is possible. But to generalize we must walk through the acre, looking for patterns. So it is with defenses and personality. We must study lives and watch for an individual's dominant defensive patterns. But other observers may follow different paths and come to different conclusions.

How Do We Cope When We Don't Use Defenses?

To cope fully is to experience reality fully. To keep conscience and impulse, interpersonal attachment and reality fully in mind is the ideal. When we cope fully, we cry and assert, we love and feel joy or grief. We need defenses only when we cannot bear conflict or when change in our lives happens faster than we can accommodate it.

In Chapter 1, I suggested that both social supports and cognitive strategies are alternatives to defense mechanisms. In addition, unconscious defenses are less important in the mastery of chronic stress than of acute stress. For example, mothers eventually learn to deal with colicky infants through cognitive strategies (such as reading Dr. Spock) and social supports (such as calling their mothers). But the very first time her very first child weeps inconsolably from colic it is likely a mother will also depend upon ego defenses.

Certainly, there is much to be said for cognitive strategies and conscious coping. By seeking information, by breaking a problem into steps, by reducing ambiguity, and by pacing how fast new information comes in, we can greatly reduce stress and conflict. These are basic techniques that can be taught to all who must learn dangerous or stressful professions. Maturity and intelligence are both important to such conscious methods of coping. So is having freedom to maintain movement and autonomy. Voluntarily withdrawing from the source of conflict is another way to reduce stress. For example, one can choose to abandon the independence of college and return home to one's mother. One can simply avoid taking up tiger hunting, hang gliding, and riding scary roller coasters. Indeed, if one has free choice, one may not need to use it. It is always less stressful to act when one is given a choice.

The difficulty is that choice is not always affordable. Intelligence and freedom of choice are luxuries. Indeed, their very absence often helps to cause stress. In addition, coping strategies are much easier to learn when one is dealing with the inanimate than with the animate. Textbook coping strategies are better suited to learning how to fly a plane than to learning how to fall in love. Parents of adolescents yearn for cognitive strategies as effective as ones that worked when their children were young. But, unlike the rules for surviving a toddler, the rules for surviving an adolescent child keep changing.

Social supports are also often a superior alternative to defense mechanisms. Warm relationships are essential to wholeness, wellness, and healing. We have only to think of the importance of mother, doctor, shaman, and leader to realize how potent other people can be in allaying anxiety and relieving depression. Besides their mere presence, besides the power of the "laying on of hands," there are additional roles that people perform in our emotional homeostasis. First, social support can give us permission to share our conflict, and more important, permission to express and thus to attenuate the associated affect. Another person can help us to reminisce, to confess, and, ideally, to lessen the second-guessing of our conscience. Thus, cognitive strategies for stress management often include another person.

Social supports also provide a "safe house" where affects can be given expression while the conscience is held at bay. Mardi Gras, an Irish wake, a shoulder to cry on are all very social affairs. The rituals of a funeral service and of sitting shivah are examples of social supports as an antidote to unbearable anxiety and depression. Others share responsibility for the mourner's pain. Lastly, another person can offer the individual in conflict a sense of shared competence and unconditional positive regard. Such support can help us achieve mastery, and once that mastery is internalized, it becomes our own. Such learned mastery wards off helplessness and becomes a potent antidote to depression. So the ego is not our only ally in adversity. Cognitive strategies, freedom of choice, and warm hands to hold are invaluable. But the ego is with us even when these others are not available.

Can Breaching a Person's Defenses Be Helpful to Healing?

Understanding defenses is useful precisely because it allows us to provide better social support and better cognitive strategies to others in need. Sympathetic listening depends upon knowing what the person is *really* talking about. But this relationship between understanding defenses and being a good comforter brings us to the next question. When should we intervene in the distortions of another person's ego?

What should we do if we see friends using maladaptive defense mechanisms? Do we tell them? And if we do so, is it likely to help?

In terms of removing defenses, it is well to remember the fable of the wind, the sun, and the overcoat. The wind and the sun were debating which was the more powerful. Spotting a man in an overcoat, they both claimed that they could make him remove it. The wind went first. The harder the wind blew in the man's face, the more tightly the man clutched his coat around him. Finally, when the wind had retired in defeat, the sun came out from behind a cloud and shone benignly but warmly down upon the man's back. In no time he cast his overcoat aside. In other words, the best way to remove defenses is to make the person feel safe and to approach the defenses indirectly. A frontal assault on someone's defenses is rarely successful.

There are several rules to follow in breaching a person's defenses. First, remember that what is annoying, self-defeating, dangerous, or duplicitous about defenses is unconscious. Trying to reason with or discipline adaptive mechanisms is likely to prove as effective as trying to control someone's snoring. Like snoring, defenses are not used on purpose to annoy or to deceive; and, as with snoring, we should understand and forgive defenses but we do not necessarily have to tolerate them. Sometimes the sleeper must be awakened. Sometimes self-deception must be confronted.

In such cases, it is wise not to try to challenge or interpret a defense without first obtaining the user's permission. One does not undress another human being without permission. In addition, when a person is metaphorically without clothes, warmth, empathy, and the Golden Rule are important. How would you feel if similarly exposed? We should remove or point out people's defenses with the same tact and respect for individual choice and privacy that we would use in removing their clothing. Freud's military term for defense, *Abwehr,* is misleading. Defenses are not to be breached by frontal assault but circumvented with tact, play, and metaphor. We all prefer doctors who use warm stethoscopes on our exposed chests.

In addition, do not confront a defense unless you have the time, the patience, and the commitment to share responsibility for the consequences. A person can often surrender his or her own ego's defenses if another person is willing to volunteer as a partial replacement. Social support can take the place of defense. Social support can provide more lasting value when it also becomes psychotherapy. In such cases, the other person not only offers to "hold" the user of defenses while both acknowledge the defense but also clarifies and shares responsibility for the emotional outburst that accompanies the breach of defenses. Underneath the anxiety and depression that accompany conflict lie lust and rage, longing and grief, as well as unacknowledged reality, relationships, and moral standards. However painful the process, the sources of conflict must be acknowledged, tolerated, and validated by the listener.

Even then, the attempt to remove a defense may fail unless we are prepared to offer an alternative mode of coping. Defense mechanisms evolve into other mechanisms, even into cognitive strategies; they do not necessarily just disappear. Thus, in interpreting defenses, we need to offer a substitute. This can be ourselves, a coping strategy, an escape, or the facilitation of another defense. For example, rather than interpreting a Hell's Angel's behavior as acting out, we might help him to become a motorcycle policeman. We might enable him to replace his wish to speed (acting out) with stopping others from speeding (reaction formation). In addition, in such a supportive setting, we may help the user recognize that the cost of a defense is greater than the gain. Such "spoiling" of immature defenses by others may be essential to maturity.

Finally, remember that the ego is wily, resilient, and wise. We are none of us so powerful or so dangerous that other people will give up defenses they need just because we point them out.

Are Defensive Styles Immutable?

If we cannot change our own or another's defenses by an act of will, does that mean they are permanent? Put differently, what is the effect of maturation upon our adaptive mechanisms? Over time our personality and our handwriting change, but like the inexorable march of glaciers and of old age, such alteration takes place incrementally. Similar shifts occur in our preferred choice of defense.

Freud wrote, "The sexual life of each one of us extends to a slight degree—now in this direction, now in that—beyond the narrow lines imposed as the standard of normality. The perversions are neither bestial nor degenerate in the emotional sense of the word. They are the development of germs, all of which are contained in the undifferentiated sexual disposition of the child, and which, by being suppressed or being diverted to higher, asexual aims—by being sublimated—are destined to provide the energy for a great number of our cultural achievements."[5] In other words, unconscious resolution of conflict governs not only perversions but also art; creative self-deception governs not only criminal behavior but also altruism. The sins of the young girl may become mother to the virtues of the grown woman. Such maturation explains how Thomas Merton and St. Francis of Assisi could have been dissolute youths.

It seems likely that the acquisition of more mature defenses results both from a maturing nervous system and from successful identification with other people. As in the development of any skill, the growth of mature defenses requires both biological readiness and suitable models for identification.

Jean Piaget, the brilliant Swiss student of human development, has documented that, as children mature, the might-makes-right morality of Mount Olympus evolves into the harsh talion law of the Old Testament which gives way, in turn, to the more merciful and flexible precepts of the Golden Rule.[6] This maturation of morality occurs from within and takes place whether or not the child attends Sunday School. Expressed differently, acting out and projection evolve into reaction formation which in turn evolves into altruism.

For example, it is not until about age 7 that a child can describe the physical geography of a room as it might appear from the perspective of someone seated in a chair facing the child. Until that age the child "projects" his own sense of right and left onto the other person. He cannot envisage that what is on his right might be on the other person's left. Similarly, perhaps projection (externalization) of one's feelings cannot be given up for displacement (that is, acknowledged ownership) of feelings until a child is neurologically as well as emotionally capable of recognizing that others do not necessarily share his sensations. No one who has raised small children has failed to notice that the impulsive, acting out behavior of toddlers is often suddenly replaced in grammar school by strict prohibitions. Manipulative weeping gives way to "boys never cry." Then in adolescence, when acting out again occurs, the parents who condemn such impulsive behavior most rigidly are often those who have struggled with the very same impulses in themselves (reaction formation). Conversely, when we are very tired or intoxicated, we suddenly see in others feelings that are in fact our own. In other words, if mature cognitive function is impaired by drugs, fatigue, or even deafness, immature defenses may return.

The life of Harry Hughes illustrates the evolution of projection during adult life. Hughes was a member of the College sample of the Study of Adult Development, which will be described in the next chapter. As an adolescent Hughes was dominated by pessimism and self-doubt. In boarding school he was frightened of sexuality and believed that masturbation led to mental illness. But he externalized the blame. He tried to demonstrate that it was the school authorities, not himself, who were afraid of sex. Indeed, he created a campus controversy by asking that the prize he won in an essay competition be an unexpurgated copy of Henry Miller's *Tropic of Cancer*.

In college, although the Study of Adult Development staff felt that Hughes "seems and looks unhappy," the only discomfort to which he admitted was embarrassment that people noticed his blushing. Like many paranoid people, Hughes resented being dependent on people and remained on guard. He found criticism difficult to tolerate, and instead of admitting inner distress he was vitally concerned with air and water pollution. He could blame his early failure to become a successful creative artist on the political unrest in the world. For him, it was easier to focus on unclean air and war-torn Europe than to appreciate the adolescent gloom and war within himself. Nevertheless, in anticipating the need for reform in antipornography laws and the creation of antipollution laws, Harry Hughes was many years ahead of his time. Paranoids often provide the cutting edge for social progress.

In college Hughes profoundly doubted the honesty of other people, and the psychiatrist's opinion was that "Harry projects his distrust and cynicism onto others." Two years later Hughes himself was able to admit that he had felt "paranoid" toward the Study. Nevertheless, just as in 1940 Hughes had been right to fear air pollution, his hypervigilance uncovered a covert truth; several of the Study staff had, in fact, "disparaged" him behind his back. Their notes called him "a real psychoneurotic" and "a sick fellow." If he picked up such judgments in their manner toward him, no wonder he felt misused.

Like many who use projection, Hughes had special difficulty in recognizing where persecution stopped and intimacy began. In his twenties he stated flatly that he had "no intention of getting married." At 29, when he fell in love with his future wife, he saw himself as the one pursued. Years later, in describing his internal grief over his mother's death, he semantically put responsibility outside himself: "My mother's death introduced a period of stress which I am just getting over." Finally, although most men saw their continued scrutiny by the Study as some kind of acceptance, Hughes protested that he had not known he would "be pursued so long" by the Study of Adult Development.

As Hughes matured, he increasingly substituted reaction formation for projection. Instead of becoming a revolutionary, he became a hardworking, obsessive book editor with a very strict conscience. The change came slowly, and at first the boundary between his reaction formation and projection was difficult to draw. As an 18-year-old he declared that dancing was unhealthy and that "band music stirs up people's emotions and is to be condemned for that reason." At 26 he no longer was quite so fearful that sexuality would harm him. Instead, he decided to remain celibate for religious reasons. As he observed, "My religious concerns excluded me from most areas where trouble was likely to arise."

At 19 Hughes tried, both physiologically and metaphorically, to put his own anger outside himself. To feel angry literally made him want to vomit. Then, as he had done with his sexuality, he began to use reaction formation, not projection, against hostility. Thus, at 24 he not only was celibate but had become a conscientious objector during World War II as well. If his daydreams were entirely of fame, in real life he noticed that "I do have a need to run myself down." At 46 he could still insist, "I fear competition from the fear of doing harm." Yet, simultaneously, he admitted that he had very deep competitive feelings. He owned his feelings, but it was his job to quash them.

Finally, at age 50, Hughes was able to confess that he liked winning for its own sake. At last he could seek refuge in altruism. He regarded his success as a trade publisher as "positive activity on the side of the angels." He raised his children with the "belief that service is the way to happiness." In maturity he even proved to be a loyal participant in the Study by which he had once felt persecuted. This one-time loner and religious ascetic was now sought after at parties. Nobody is entirely inhibited who asks for *Tropic of Cancer* as a school prize.

At 65 Hughes continued to suffer inner anguish, but he was free of projection. Instead, he had turned profound inner pain and a life-threatening illness into a beautiful novel that provided pleasure and beauty to the world.

_____

Maturity is many things. Maturity includes having appropriate expectations and goals for oneself and finding a major source of fulfillment in productive work. Maturity includes the capacity to love and to hope. It includes the ability to discharge hostility without harming others or oneself, and the capacity to suspend one's adult identity and engage in childlike play. Finally, maturity includes the capacity to adapt to change, to endure frustrations and loss, and to maintain an altruistic concern for human beings outside one's own group and beyond one's own time and place.

To look at such development as purely embryological is too narrow. Developmental psychologists who have followed in Piaget's footsteps have shown that, in Western cultures, moral development, at least in part, progresses independently of social class, nationality, and religious persuasion. Adaptive ego maturity, not conscience or the externally derived superego, appears to be the agent of morality. The first developmental shift that allows maturation of defenses occurs when locus of control passes from outside to inside (that is, from externalizing, immature defenses to neurotic, intermediate defenses) and the individual is able to say "it is my problem, not your problem." The next shift comes with further maturity as instinctual conflicts cease to be regarded as shameful and guilt-provoking and instead become acceptable internal sources of pain and pleasure not requiring guilt. The appeasement of displacement and reaction formation can then be given up for altruism and sublimation. The ego functions through its capacity for mature reasoning rather than by fixed guilt feelings.

Ego development, a subset of maturity, involves maturation in at least five domains: impulse control, psychosocial integration (interpersonal style), creative synthesis (meaning-making), maturation of defenses, and maturation of cognitive style. The last domain—maturation of cognitive style—has been extensively discussed elsewhere and is outside the scope of this book. But the life of Harry Hughes illustrates why in order to understand the choice and maturation of defenses we must pay attention to the other domains of adult development. If we are to understand the development of defenses and their effect upon the individual, we must try to understand the ontogeny of the ego and its effect upon choice of defenses. Certainly, psychosocial development, creative synthesis, and defense choice are closely linked. Heinz Hartmann, one of the early pioneers in ego psychology, pointed out that what begins as defensive behavior may become a permanent part of our conflict-free behavior. "The works of man objectify the methods he has discovered for solving problems," Hartmann wrote; and "Defensive processes may simultaneously serve both control of the instinctual drive and adaptation to the external world."[7] Certainly, creative acts are a striking example of adaptation to instinctual conflict evolving into sustained behavior. The wisdom of the ego often manifests itself in creative endeavor.

Hartmann himself cited religion as the most outstanding example of the synthesis of instinctual conflict with ongoing psychosocial development and social institutions. This fact of development links defenses to moral development and helps to explain how a young man who once wanted *Tropic of Cancer* as a prize and also wished to remain celibate and uncompetitive could both become happily married and find well-paid work "on the side of the angels." The relation of moral development to ego maturation has been most fully explored by Lawrence Kohlberg and Jane Loevinger, who have studied ego development by tracing the moral development of children, adolescents, and young adults.[8] Stuart Hauser and Robert Kegan[9] have integrated such work with psychosocial development and with the evolution of defenses. For example, common to Kohlberg's least mature stage of moral development and Loevinger's impulse-ridden stages are behaviors reflecting acting out, splitting, and fantasy. Common to Kohlberg's stage 2 and Loevinger's self-protective stage are behaviors reflecting the ego processes of projection and passive aggression. Reaction formation characterizes both Kohlberg's intermediate stage 3 and Loevinger's conformist stage. Altruism is characteristic of Kohlberg's more mature stage 4 and Loevinger's conscientious stage. While empirical study does not reveal a perfect correspondence, ego development per se and the evolution of defense mechanisms appear to be clearly linked.[10]

Ego development is an overarching process under which are included many tasks, among them psychosocial development, moral development, and the maturation of defensive style. All of these processes are interrelated. For example, if we follow a common line of maturation of defenses such as was illustrated by Harry Hughes's shift from projection to reaction formation to altruism and sublimation, we can chart the evolution of creative process through both psychosocial development and the maturation of defenses. In such a sequence, we can follow Hughes's efforts to integrate self, object, idea, and affect, as well as his efforts to link desire, conscience, other people, and reality. In the same developmental line, we can follow Hughes's self-centered adolescent development through the reaction formation often associated with successful career consolidation to the altruism of generativity and see how closely linked are the processes of adult psychosocial development and the maturation of ego development. The evolution of defense choice involves the whole process of maturation.

5

How Can We Prove That Defenses Exist?

Goe, and catche a falling starre,
Get with child a mandrake roote,
Tell me, where all past yeares are,
Or who cleft the Divel's foot,
Teach me to hear Mermaides singing . . .

John Donne

Perhaps the greatest problem faced by the academic social sciences is that what is measurable is often irrelevant and what is truly relevant often cannot be measured. Social scientists tend to study what they can measure rather than what really interests them. In this way they sometimes resemble the proverbial drunk who searched for his car keys, not where he had lost them, but under the street lamp where the light was better. In studying defenses my dilemma is how to assess and measure subjective mental processes of which the owner cannot reliably tell us. The usual solution is to employ clinical intuition, but clinical judgment is notoriously unreliable and difficult to measure. Unless I maintain scientific rigor, how am I to avoid superstition and intellectual dishonesty? And yet, as e. e. cummings warns us, "only sonsofbitches measure spring with a thermometer." Thus, if I try to measure everything as scientists would wish, how am I not to lose track of humanity? In part the solution lies in a scientific method that permits metaphor but does not exclude experiment and hypothesis testing. On the one hand, poetic metaphor successfully describes the unique and the ineffable, but it fails to predict the future. On the other hand, science, for all its reductionistic sins, allows us to predict eclipses and to know that April will be warmer than December.

Sometimes intuition is right. The fact that beauty exists in the eye of the beholder does not render our perception of beauty invalid, only unreliable. Often an individual's free associations to the perceptions of inkblots—or to dreams—are revealing, but we can never know at what level of inference we are gaining data. With inkblots, beauty, and dreams, we can never separate coincidence and prejudice from revelation, and we can never separate revelation of truth from projective revelation. Unlike poetry, science, even if it does not fully encompass truth, allows us to recognize error. Poetry, for all its error, allows us to recognize truth. Thus, a poetic science might allow us to believe in the reality of rainbows and "a falling starre" even as it allows us to dismiss singing "mermaides" as mere wished-for illusions. But we would still need a telescope to separate the science of astronomy from the mythology of astrology.

Sigmund Freud's dynamic psychiatry has provided us with what the Princeton philosopher Walter Kaufman has called "poetic science," but it has failed to provide us with scientific modes of observation. For dynamic psychiatry, with its permission to employ projective tests and free associations and its impertinent inductions about what goes on inside the black box of the mind, has often ignored reliability and predictive validity. And without reliability and predictive validity, poetic science becomes just another religion. Dynamic psychiatry by itself does not provide a telescope to see into the future. For example, projective tests, in theory such a promising means of using metaphor to discover the mind's secrets, have proved disappointing. By and large projective tests (such as the Rorschach and Thematic Apperception Tests) have been consistently too sensitive and too reflective of the user's intuition to permit consensus among raters or to predict future behaviors. In the Study of Adult Development, the defenses the men in the College sample revealed on their Thematic Apperception Tests bore little correspondence to those they deployed in everyday life,[1] and the psychopathology noted in the Rorschachs of the men in the Core City sample was uncorrelated with the men's real-life psychological problems.[2]

If the study of the ego and its defense mechanisms is to be shifted from the realm of quaint psychoanalytic folk belief to the realm of scientific medicine, I believe three questions must be answered in the affirmative. The first is: Can defenses be reliably identified outside of a private psychoanalytic setting? For example, can psychoanalytically unsophisticated independent observers reliably identify defenses in working-class men with modest verbal skills who have never been in psychotherapy? Interrater reliability, often called consensual validation, offers a critical means of validating a science that depends on metaphor. The second question is: If defense mechanisms can be reliably identified, do they have predictive validity? Can a causal link be forged between choice of defense and future psychopathology? In short, do our styles of unconscious stress management really make a difference? Do the ways in which our mind alters inner and outer reality affect our physical health? The third question is: Can maturity of defenses be demonstrated to be independent of environment and not just one more artifact of social class? Can defensive style be shown to be relatively independent of education, ethnicity, gender, and social privilege? Can it be demonstrated that the ego is similar to the body's other homeostatic mechanisms like blood clotting and the immune system?

To address these three questions, I have used the telescope of longitudinal study. Conventionally, the social sciences in general and psychoanalysis in particular have tried to examine human behavior under ever higher magnification. In understanding personality development, however, the use of high magnification has often been as unrewarding as it is in the study of geography. If we study landscapes with a microscope, the forest becomes lost in the trees. To study defenses—and landscapes—we need to view our subject from a distance. If with any confidence we are to label people psychologically "mature" or "sick," we need to take a longitudinal perspective. Therefore, to answer the three questions that I have posed I have integrated three longitudinal studies that have survived for fifty to seventy years.

The Study of Adult Development

The Study of Adult Development comprises three studies, two based at Harvard and one at Stanford University. It includes three cohorts of individuals, each prospectively studied for more than half a century: the *College* sample, born around 1920; the *Core City* sample, born around 1930; and the *Terman* sample, born around 1910.

The College Sample

The Grant Study (College sample) was begun at the Harvard University Health Services in 1938 by Arlie Bock and Clark Heath. These two physicians had received a gift from the philanthropist William T. Grant for the study of healthy human lives because, in Heath's words, "Large endowments have been given and schemes put into effect for the study of the ill, the mentally and physically handicapped . . . Very few have thought it pertinent to make a systematic inquiry into the kinds of people who are well and do well."[3] Bock described the aims of the Grant Study in a press release on September 30, 1938: "Doctors traditionally have dealt with their patients after troubles of many sorts have arisen. The Department of Hygiene . . . proposes to revise this procedure and will attempt to analyze the forces that have produced normal young men . . . All admit that the sick need care, but very few apparently have thought it necessary to make a systematic inquiry as to how people keep well and do well . . . A body of facts is needed to replace current supposition. All of us need more do's and fewer don'ts."

The subjects were chosen from among Harvard sophomores. In the selection process, about 40 percent of each Harvard class was arbitrarily excluded because there was some question as to whether they would meet the academic requirements for graduation (usually this meant that their freshman grade average was C-plus or lower). The Health Service records of the remaining 60 percent of each class were then screened, and half were excluded because of evidence of physical or psychological disturbance. Each year the names of the remaining 300 or so sophomores were submitted to college deans, who selected about 100 boys whom they considered "sound." They chose sophomores who in Bock's words were "able to paddle their own canoe," or in the freshmen dean's words were "boys we would be glad we had admitted to college." About 80 of the 100 students selected each year agreed to participate in the study.

Over the four-year period 1939–1942, 268 sophomores were selected for study. Of these, 12 dropped out of the Study during college and 8 more withdrew later on. For half a century, the rest have continued to participate with remarkable loyalty. They have received questionnaires about every two years, physical examinations every five years, and interviews about every fifteen years.

As measured by their scholastic achievement tests (SATs), the academic achievement of the students chosen fell in the top 5 to 10 percent of high school graduates; but their average test score of 584 was not beyond the reach of many other able college students. Although they were no more intellectually gifted than their classmates, 61 percent of those in the Study were graduated with honors in contrast to only 26 percent of their classmates; and 76 percent, a higher percentage than of their classmates, went on to graduate school. In comparison to their classmates, twice as many of the College subjects were mesomorphs (solid muscular builds), and 98 percent were right handed. Half were either the oldest in the family or an only child.

Reflecting the composition of the 1940 Harvard College student body, all of the members of the College sample were white and all were male. Socioeconomically, they were drawn from a privileged group but not exclusively so. In 1940 a third of their parents made more than $15,000 a year, but one father in seven made less than $2,500 a year. If a third of their fathers had had some professional training, half of their parents had never graduated from college. Almost half of the men had some private education before college, but during college almost half were on scholarship and/or had to work during academic terms to earn at least part of their tuition fees.

Their physical and mental health was clearly better than that of the population at large. Only one-seventh as many of the College men as expected by chance were rejected for military service on physical grounds and only one-twelfth as many for psychiatric reasons.[4] During combat the men reported fewer symptoms of nausea, incontinence, and palpitation than had been found by other studies of men under battle conditions, and they won more than their share of medals. By age 65 the mortality of the College sample was only half that expected of white males of the same birth cohort and only two-thirds that of their Harvard college classmates.

The College sample at age 47 had an average earned income of about $90,000 in 1989 dollars, but more of them were Democrats than Republicans. In 1954, only 16 percent of the College men had sanctioned the McCarthy hearings; in 1967, 91 percent were for de-escalating U.S. involvement in Vietnam. To generalize, they had the incomes and social status of corporate managers, yet they drove the battered cars and pursued the hobbies, politics, and lifestyles of college professors.

The Core City Sample

The 456 members of the Core City sample, also all male and all white, represented a very different socioeconomic cohort. In junior high school they were chosen as the controls for a prospective study con-

ducted by Sheldon and Eleanor Glueck[5] at Harvard Law School that
led to a landmark book, *Unraveling Juvenile Delinquency*. Like the
College men, the Core City men were studied originally by a multi-
disciplinary team of physicians, psychologists, psychiatrists, social
investigators, and physical anthropologists. They have been interviewed at ages 14, 25, 32, and 47. Over the first thirty-five years of
study, attrition due to withdrawal was held at 5 percent, and only 4
subjects (1 percent) were completely lost.

During the 1930s the Gluecks had been conducting important
retrospective studies of delinquency. In 1939 they obtained funding to
conduct a prospective study in order to contrast young juvenile delinquents with their socioeconomically matched nondelinquent peers.
Between 1940 and 1944, the Gluecks selected the Core City men from
Boston inner-city schools on the basis of their not being known to be
seriously delinquent. In order to match the sample with delinquent
youths, the Gluecks used four criteria in their selection. The Core City
subjects had to be of the same age, the same intelligence, and the same
ethnicity, and to reside in a community with the same neighborhood
crime rate as the Gluecks' 500 delinquents whose misdemeanors (and
social disadvantage) were sufficiently severe to have sent them to
reform schools. Thus, 95 percent of the Core City sample came from
the 60 percent of Boston census tracts with the highest rates of juvenile
delinquency. The boys' average I.Q. was 95, and 61 percent of their
parents were foreign born. (The parents or grandparents of 70 percent of the boys had been born in Italy, Ireland, Great Britain, or
Canada; inexplicably, the Gluecks excluded blacks from both samples.)
Although the boys were chosen for nondelinquency, eventually at least
26 percent of them were arrested—usually for drunkenness or minor
misdemeanors—and 19 percent spent at least a day in jail. These
figures attest to their initial social disadvantage rather than to unusual
antisocial tendencies.

In childhood, half of the Core City men had lived in clearly
blighted slum neighborhoods. Half came from families known to five
or more social agencies, and more than two-thirds of their families had
recently been on welfare. Half of their childhood homes had no tub
or shower, and only 30 percent had hot water *and* central heat *and*
electricity *and* a tub and toilet. In order to be matched with the delinquent youths, a third of the Core City men had I.Q.'s of less than 90;
25 percent had repeated two or more grades of school. In spite of their

low average intelligence, which denied them access to Boston's elite public high schools, as the men matured during the 1950s and 1960s they showed marked upward social mobility. While only 10 percent of their parents had belonged to the middle class (social classes II and III),[6] 51 percent of the Core City sample themselves at age 47 did so. At age 47, their mean income in 1989 dollars was about $30,000.

The Terman Women Sample

The third data set included in the Study of Adult Development consists of 90 women (the Terman women sample), a representative subsample of the 672 women in Lewis Terman's study of gifted California public school children. Terman, a professor of education at Stanford University, by adapting Binet's intelligence test for use in America had made I.Q. a household word. Between 1920 and 1922 Terman attempted to identify all of the children in urban California with I.Q.'s of 140 or over.[7] He chose to focus on three metropolitan areas in California: greater Oakland, greater San Francisco, and greater Los Angeles. In 1920 these areas contained 100,000 grammar school children and approximately one-third of the population of California. From all of these urban grammar schools, Terman first selected a 7 percent sample for group testing. This larger sample included the youngest child in each class, the one or two brightest children in each current class, and, in each teacher's opinion, the brightest child from the previous year's class. Terman then retested the most promising children from this group with the Stanford-Binet Intelligence Test. In this fashion he identified 1,000 children with I.Q.'s of 140 and above—the brightest (by the standards of the Binet test) one percent of California's urban school children. Over the next few years, Terman rather impulsively added additional cases of very bright children to his sample. Ultimately, he ended up with 672 women and 856 men.

Originally, the aim of Terman's crude selection net was to capture at least 90 percent of the brightest children in his three-city area. But when he went back and checked entire schools, he found he probably had captured only 80 percent. Ugly children and shy children were the ones who tended to slip through the net. In addition, all children who attended either private schools or Chinese-speaking schools were arbitrarily excluded. Bright children for whom English was a second language were also at risk for inadvertent exclusion, for the teachers of that day harbored enormous ethnic prejudices. For example, the father of one Terman woman was a poet, a chessmaster, and a former mayor of his town and had three years of graduate education in his profession as a horticulturalist. His daughter's teacher, however, referred to him scornfully as a "Japanese gardener."

In 1920 California was still a young state. The population of Los Angeles was 500,000 and that of Oakland 20,000. Thus, although the children came from urban centers, the childhoods of the Terman women were more like the childhoods of East Coast American children in the nineteenth century. Many had grown up on farms or on tree-lined streets; the urban public schools they attended often still had grassy playgrounds. On the one hand, 20 percent of the Terman women's fathers were in blue-collar occupations. On the other hand, 29 percent of the Terman women had fathers in "the professions"; this proportion was ten times that of their public school classmates who served as controls, but Terman's definition of the professions was broad and included high school teachers.

The Terman women were precocious. They had walked one month earlier and talked three months earlier than their schoolmates. More of them than of their classmates had been breast-fed. Twenty percent had learned to read before age 5, and 60 percent graduated from high school at 16 or younger. Their high intelligence—they had a mean I.Q. of 151—did not handicap them psychologically. On the contrary, their mental health was demonstrably better than that of their classmates. In personality traits, they showed significantly more humor, common sense, perseverance, leadership, and even popularity. They were as likely as their classmates to marry. Their physical health was also better: they had better nutrition, fewer headaches, and fewer middle ear infections. Their siblings had suffered only half the childhood mortality experienced by the siblings of their classmates. Up to age 78, the mortality of the Terman women has been only half what would be expected for white American women in their birth cohort.

The opportunities for these highly intelligent women were filled with paradox. On the one hand, their mothers did not have the right to vote until the daughters were about 10 years old. On the other hand, California college tuition was low ($25 to $50 per term for both Stanford and Berkeley), and a college degree was the expectation for bright women. On the one hand, the Depression, which began when they were 20, and World War II, which began when they were 30, put pressures on these women to enter the workforce. On the other hand, the jobs available to them were often limited in scope and opportunity. When asked what occupational opportunities World War II had opened for her, one Berkeley-educated Terman woman replied, "I finally learned to type."

For seventy years, Terman and his successors, first Melitta Oden, then Robert Sears, and finally Albert Hastorf, have followed these 1,528 gifted subjects.[8] The Terman men and women have been followed by questionnaire every five years and by personal interview in 1940 and 1950. In 1940, twenty years after his initial study, Terman made his second concerted effort to interview and retest all of his subjects. Besides death, attrition at that time amounted only to 2 percent. In 1986, after sixty-five years of follow-up, attrition for reasons other than death was still below 10 percent.

In 1987, Caroline Vaillant and I selected a representative subsample of 90 women from Terman's original sample of 672. Of the 90, 29 had died and 21 others were not seen because of poor health or poor cooperation. We reinterviewed the remaining 40 women. Their average age was 78. Since most of the 50 women we did not interview had been followed for half a century, we were able to include them in most of the data analyses. In general, except for inferior physical health, these 50 women did not differ significantly from the 40 women we did interview.

Comparison of the Three Samples

Although each of the three samples in the Study of Adult Development was relatively homogeneous, the three samples were very different from one another. Thirty percent of the College men's fathers, but none of the Core City men's fathers, were in social class I (physicians, successful lawyers, and businessmen). Thirty-one percent of the Core City men's fathers, but none of the College men's fathers, were in social class V (unskilled laborers without ten grades of education). The parents of the Terman women were largely middle class or skilled laborers (social classes III and IV); few of their fathers were as privileged as those of the College men or as disadvantaged as those of the Core City men. For example, among the Terman women's fathers, there was only one unskilled laborer; he was a farmer who had chosen to work as a janitor at the University of California at Berkeley so his gifted children would have access to a college education.

The mean education of the Terman women's fathers was twelve years in contrast to eight years for the fathers of the Core City men and sixteen years for the fathers of the College men. None of the Core City men's mothers, 15 percent of the Terman women's mothers, and 32 percent of the College men's mothers had gone to college. The mean (Binet) I.Q. of the Terman women was 151; the mean (WAIS) I.Q. of the Core City sample was 95; the estimated mean I.Q. of the College sample was 130–135.

Perhaps the most convincing evidence that the Terman women's high intelligence was not an artifact of environmental privilege but based on biologic potential was the fact that their children were clearly more gifted, as defined by standardized I.Q. tests, than the children of the socially and economically more privileged College men. Seventy-five times as many of the Terman women's children as would be expected by chance had I.Q.'s over 170! (While negative environmental factors can profoundly lower tested I.Q. scores, positive environmental factors can elevate tested I.Q. by only a few points.)

Sixty-seven percent of the Terman women, 99 percent of the College men, and 10 percent of the Core City men graduated from college. Thirty-five percent of the Core City men had less than ten grades of education, while 24 percent of the Terman women and 76 percent of the College men attended graduate school. Nevertheless, in contrast to the *men* in the Terman study who as a group went on to distinguished academic or professional careers, the talents of the equally bright and nearly as well educated Terman women were clearly underutilized by society. A look at their income illustrates this dramatically. At least 253 of the Terman women had full-time jobs most of their lives. The mean maximum annual income ($30,000 in 1989 dollars) of these well-educated and gifted women with lifelong employment was the same as that of the undereducated and often intellectually handicapped Core City men.

The greatest negative bias imposed on the Terman women's lives by high intelligence may have been that only 75 percent of them had children and that their mean number of children was 1.8. In contrast, the men in the College sample averaged more than three children each, and the men in the Core City sample averaged four. Of the 30 Terman women who were most successful in their occupations, only 5 became mothers; as a group, these 30 career women produced only seven children.

Taken individually, then, none of the three samples can be viewed as representative of the general population, but the three samples do have the virtue of being vastly different socially from one another, and they were born into historical birth cohorts up to twenty years apart. Yet within each sample there was considerable homogeneity. Thus, the between-group *similarities* and the within-group *differences* may be generalizable to other American Caucasian samples.

It also helped enormously that the three cohorts of the Study of Adult Development had been studied since childhood. Prospective study allowed me to bring the experimental method to bear on my Freudian assumptions. For example, I sent a College sample man the prospectively gathered vignettes that I had assembled in order to illustrate his use of repression over the years, so that he could grant me permission to publish them, for the views he had reported in college differed greatly from those he maintained later on. However, he sent the vignettes of his youth back to me, saying, "George, you must have sent these to the wrong person." He was not trying to be funny; he could not remember his college persona. For him repression *was* a dominant defense.

Prospective study also revealed how creative and unreliable is memory. Let me offer an example from the life of a Terman woman, Matilda Lyre. At age 78, when asked if she had been interested in becoming a doctor, she replied reprovingly, "You have to remember women have come a long way. I never even thought about being a doctor as a possibility." In actual fact at 14 she had told the Terman staff that she *did* want to be a doctor. In college she had majored in premedical studies, and at age 30 her Strong Vocational Interest Test had suggested medicine as her greatest vocational interest.

Again, at age 78, Matilda Lyre was asked how she had dealt with the gap between what she had been allowed to achieve and her potential. She modestly responded, "I never knew I had any potential . . . I had to learn to cook and raise a garden." This was a reconstruction perhaps to soften the fact that as a child, besides wanting to be a doctor, she had wanted to be an astronomer *and* a poet *and* a scientist. Indeed, when she was 20, one of the Terman workers had described her as someone "who seems to adorn anything she attempts." At Berkeley she had been editor of the college magazine, had been on the all-star swimming team, and had gone around the state giving lectures and writing articles. Despite such potential, her subsequent young adulthood was confined to being a part-time physical education teacher in a small town. The limited economic opportunities during the Great Depression had severely limited her career. Yet when young, Matilda Lyre certainly had known she had potential. Even at age 50 she had admitted "I realized early that learning was easy for me and as an adult that knowledge fortifies my desire to do my own thinking."

At age 78 Matilda Lyre maintained that she first learned about being a member of the Terman Study for gifted children only at the end of college. At 50 she remembered learning about being a gifted child at age 10. At 25 she acknowledged that she had learned about being a gifted child at age 6. Her life story, then, became a reconstruction to make bearable a life frustrated by prejudice, the Great Depression, and poverty. To understand the ego, prospective study is essential.

The saga of Matilda Lyre also revealed a relatively happy ending. At age 30 the Strong Vocational Test revealed that besides medicine her outstanding interest was music. She did not allow herself to develop this side of herself until she was 60. At that time she took violin lessons. A little later she divorced her husband, inherited a beautiful violin from her best friend, and found her music finally taking off. For the last six years she has been playing solo concerts in Los Angeles.

With this introduction to the use of longitudinal samples to test clinical intuition, let me return to the three questions to which an affirmative answer is required if I am to demonstrate empirically the validity of ego mechanisms of defense.

Can Defenses Be Reliably Identified and Analyzed?

If some defenses are hypothesized to be more mature—"healthier"—than other defenses, can these defenses be reliably identified? To address the first question of reliability, I shall focus on the Core City men; since the information available for them is the least rich, methods which reliably identify their defenses can be more easily generalized to other samples. For all three samples, however, the methods were essentially the same.

Having been given the operational definitions of the defenses described in Chapter 2, independent raters were first trained on interview protocols that had been rated by many other raters. Next, they were given a twenty- to thirty-page summary of the Core City men's two-hour semistructured interview at age 47. The raters—a medical social worker and a recent college graduate in psychology—had not been psychoanalytically trained. They were blinded to both the Core City men's childhood records and the independent adult ratings of outcome.

Interview protocols were prepared by the interviewer from verbatim notes taken during a two-hour interview of each of the Core City men. These interviews had been designed to focus on difficulties in the mens' relationships, physical health, and work. Numerous direct quotes were included in the interview protocols, but our methodology embodied both the scientific limitations and the advantages of journalism. The purpose was to use the interviewer's summary as the first step in data reduction and to retain interview emphases that are often lost in transcripts of tape recordings. In writing the interview summary to be used by the blind rater, the interviewer was instructed to elucidate, but not to label, the behaviors by which the individuals had coped with their difficulties.

For each interview protocol, the raters were asked to note all possible instances of each of the eighteen defensive styles discussed in Chapter 2. However, the three "psychotic" defenses in Table 2 were noted so seldom as to be irrelevant. The rater paid attention both to known past behaviors and to alleged style of adaptation to past difficulties, as well as to the special vicissitudes of the interview interactions. The examples of Peggy O'Hara's behavior in Chapter 2 illustrate the kind of behavioral data on which the raters focused. Clinical inference was allowed. In this way, in each of the interviews obtained from the Core City men, the raters identified from ten to thirty defensive vignettes.

Once an individual's defensive styles were identified, a systematic procedure[9] was used to wrestle clinical intuition into the computer—to transform metaphors into numbers. Through this procedure each College, Core City, and Terman subject was rated from 1 (most mature) to 9 (least mature) on maturity of defenses. When assessed by two independent raters, these nine-point ratings of maturity of defense differed by more than two points for only 23 of the 307 Core City subjects rated,[10] and differed by more than one point for only 7 of the 37 Terman women rated. In short, independent raters could consistently agree on whether an individual's dominant defensive style was mature (adaptive) or immature (maladaptive).

Are Defense Mechanisms Valid?

Now that we know that maturity of defenses can be reliably rated, the next question is validity. Does the maturity of people's defenses tell us any more about their lives than their handwriting or their astrological signs? To answer this question I used data from the College, Core City, and Terman samples and calculated the correlations between the subjects' ratings for maturity of defenses and their ratings for measures of mental health, psychosocial maturity (see Chapter 6), and their capacities to work and to love. As indicated in Table 3, the associations between maturity of defenses and these other indications of successful adult development are significant. When roughly comparable variables (rated by judges other than those who assessed the defenses) were compared for the three very different samples, the correlations remained equally strong, suggesting that the positive associations between maturity of defenses and mental health are independent of social class, education, and gender. Earlier work by Norma Haan also supports this finding.[11]

Table 3. Correlations between maturity of defenses and measures of successful adult outcome

Variables	Terman women (n = 37)	College men (n = 186)	Core City men (n = 307)
Life satisfaction, age 60–65	.44	.35	n.a.
Psychosocial maturity (Erikson Stage)	.48	.44	.66
Mental health (GAS or HSRS)[a]	.64	.57	.77
Job success, age 47	.53	.34	.45
Marital stability, age 47	.31	.37	.33
Job enjoyment, age 47	.51	.42	.39
% of life employed	.37	n.a.	.39

Note: Except for the three lowest correlations for the Terman women, all correlations are significant at $p < .001$ (that is, the odds that the correlation could be due to mere chance are less than one in a thousand).

a. For GAS see J. Endicott, R. L. Spitzer, J. L. Fleiss, and J. Cohen, "The Global Assessment Scale: A Procedure for Measuring Overall Severity of Psychiatric Disturbance," *Archives of General Psychiatry* 33 (1976): 766–770. For HSRS, L. Luborsky, "Clinicians' Judgements of Mental Health," *Archives of General Psychiatry* 7 (1962): 407–417.

Table 4. Relation of maturity of defensive style and late midlife adjustment of men in the College sample

	Defensive style (age 20–47)		
Psychosocial adjustment at 65	Most mature (n = 37)	Intermediate (n = 105)	Least mature (n = 31)
Top quintile (n = 37)	18	19	0
Middle three-fifths (n = 99)	18	66	15
Bottom quintile (n = 37)	1	15	16

Note: Pearson correlation coefficient $r = .47$; $p < .0001$.

However, it might be argued that, rather than mature defenses making it possible for people to find joy in living, joy in living allows them the luxury of mature defenses. Thus, it is important to demonstrate that maturity of defensive style has *predictive* validity rather than just the *face* validity suggested by most of the correlations in Table 3. Predictive validity was assessed in the following fashion. Raters blind to the past reviewed the College sample's biennial questionnaires from age 50 to age 65 and scored on a five-point scale how they would feel about having the same adjustment at that age. Mature defensive styles assessed from questionnaires from age 20 to age 47 predicted a satisfactory life at 65 for the College men with an r of .35 ($p < .001$).

Table 4 suggests that maturity of defense predicts mental health as well as apparent satisfaction. Raters unfamiliar with the College men's lives before age 50 assessed their joy in working, their use of psychiatrists and tranquilizers between the ages of 50 and 65, the stability of their marriages, and whether their careers had progressed or declined since age 47.[12] No man assessed as using immature defenses before age 47 was doing relatively well at 65. Only one man who used very mature defenses at ages 20–47 was doing relatively badly at 65. Remember that the Rorschachs of the Core City men had predicted nothing.

The defenses of the 23 College men who at some point in their adult lives were clinically depressed were contrasted with those of the 70 least distressed College men (that is, men who in thirty years of observation never used tranquilizers *or* visited psychiatrists *or* appeared to merit a psychiatric diagnosis). The two groups showed a marked difference in overall maturity of defenses. First, as indicated in Table 5,

61 percent of the least distressed men and only 9 percent of the most depressed men exhibited generally mature defenses; whereas 47 percent of the depressed men and only 7 percent of the least distressed men consistently favored less mature defensive styles. Although altruism, a mature defense, was used by many men and women with unhappy childhoods to master adult life, sustained use of altruism was never noted as a major adaptive style among the depressed College men. Instead, the most depressed men were more likely to use reaction formation and to turn anger against themselves. Suspicions are still warranted, however; simple association does not prove cause. For example, immature defenses are associated with but do not cause alcohol abuse and brain damage; rather, both alcohol abuse and brain damage can *cause* regression in maturity of defenses. The association of immature defenses with depression is most likely not such a simple horse-and-cart causal relationship. In some people severe depression probably leads to a regression in maturity of defenses. Immature defenses probably predispose some people to depression. In still others, depression and immature defenses may both be responses to unmanageable stress, disordered brain chemistry, or both. Much more evidence is needed to clarify the relationship between affective disorder and maturity of defenses.

At this point it *is* possible to address a rather more interesting

Table 5. Use of defenses by the most depressed and the least distressed men in the College sample

Defenses	% using each defense as a major coping style	
	Most depressed (n = 23)	Least distressed (n = 70)
Suppression	26	53
Altruism	0	19
Reaction formation	17	4
Displacement	39	6
Dissociation	26	7
Passive aggression	30	16
Most mature	9	61
Least mature	47	7

Note: Differences significant at $p < .05$.

question. Does maturity of defensive style affect biology: that is, does it predict successful aging? Can we demonstrate that the maturity of defenses as assessed in young adulthood predicts future physical health? Unfortunately, the evidence that maturity of defenses predicts physical health is not quite as convincing as the evidence for the prediction of mental health in Table 4.

Figure 3 contrasts the declining physical health of 79 College men with relatively mature defenses (the black bars) with the declining health of 61 College men with relatively immature defenses (the striped bars). As before, maturity of defenses was assessed on the basis of the

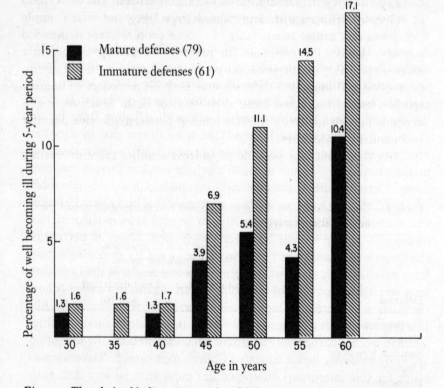

Figure 3. The relationship between maturity of defenses and decline in physical health. (The data on defensive maturity were gathered prior to age 47. The percentage of men becoming chronically ill during each five-year period was based on the total number of men still well at the beginning of the period. Thus poor physical health should not have influenced maturity of defense.)

men's adaptive style between age 20 and age 47. The bars of the graph show only the percentage of men *still in good health* ("excellent" or "minor problems") at the start of each five-year period. For each five-year period prior to age 60, men with immature defenses were much more likely to develop irreversible illness than men with mature defenses. That is, for at least ten years after their defensive style was assessed, the health of the men with mature defenses deteriorated less quickly. Thus, at least for a while, adaptive choice of defense mechanisms may have provided some kind of immunization against poor health. By age 65, however, this association of mature defenses with continued good health could no longer be discerned.

Is Maturity of Defensive Style Independent of Gender, Education, and Social Privilege?

A major task of psychiatry is to try to divorce the homeostatic mechanisms by which human beings maintain mental health from sociocultural artifact. In biological medicine the task is easier. For example, blood clotting factors are distributed in an egalitarian fashion: the Romanov and Hapsburg royal families died young from hemophilia, but their peasants did not. One would hope that biology has been as democratic in its distribution of ego strength as in its distribution of clotting factors and immune mechanisms, but there is room for doubt. Certainly, many parameters of mental health *are* clearly a function of education, I.Q., social class, and/or societal bias toward gender. For example, the use of psychiatrists can be used as an index of mental illness only among socially homogeneous groups. About 40 percent of the College men and only 7 percent of the Core City men sought help from psychiatrists; yet, if anything, the mental health of the Core City men was worse than that of the College men. Again, in a *within*-cohort comparison of Core City men, income correlated with mental health. In a *between*-cohort comparison, however, the equally mentally healthy Terman women earned only a third of what the intellectually less gifted and only modestly better educated College men earned. The responsibility for this intergroup difference lies more with society than with mental health. Finally, the undereducated Core City men (and the least verbally gifted College men) scored a full ego development stage lower on Jane Loevinger's Washington University Sentence Completion test than did verbally fluent College men.[13] However, there is no evidence that verbal fluency reflects mature ego development. Rather, the conclusion must be that Loevinger's widely respected test for ego development is influenced by education and verbal fluency. It is of great interest, then, that maturity of defensive style did not seem affected by socioeconomic status, intellectual ability, or gender. True, the College sample, originally selected for mental health, looked a little better (only 11 percent used predominantly immature defenses), and the Core City men, deliberately matched with delinquents for social disadvantage, looked a little worse (25 percent used predominantly immature defenses). But considering the vast differences between the two samples in intelligence, social privilege, and education, these differences in maturity of defensive style were inconsequential and easily explained by the original selection bias that tried to select only mentally healthy College men.

A less distorted view of the effect of privilege on defensive style can be achieved through within-group comparison—by comparing the members of each group with one another. In this way initial selection bias is circumvented. Table 6 examines the effect of social class, I.Q., and education upon within-group differences in defensive maturity. The associations are insignificant. Even the relationship of a warm childhood environment to maturity of defense is less than one might expect. Such independence from social environment is what one would expect for biological differences such as blood clotting factors.

Everybody I have asked "knows" that women deploy different defensive styles from men. But their knowledge is based on intuition,

Table 6. Correlations between maturity of defenses and biopsychosocial antecedents

Background variable	Terman women (n = 37)	College men (n = 186)	Core City men (n = 277)[a]
Parental social class	−.07	.04	−.02
I.Q.	.18	−.05	.10
Years of education	.09	n.a.	.17**
Warm relations with father	.24	.23**	.01
Warm childhood environment	.39**	.36**	.10
Warm relations with mother	.22	.18**	.04

**$p < .01$.
a. Thirty men with I.Q.'s less than 80 excluded.

not on data. Were there really some individual defensive styles more
favored by the Terman women than by the College men? In order to
obtain a numerical score for the individual defenses used by each individual in the Study of Adult Development, raters noted frequency of
observed use. Each rater scored each defense 0 if it was absent, 1 if it
was noted once or twice, and 2 if it was the most frequently used
defense or was noted three times or more during the two-hour interviews of the Terman women and the Core City men. For the more
intensively studied College sample these ratings were made on all data
gathered between ages 20 and 47. The two raters did not always agree.
Indeed, depending on the defense, in 4–20 percent of the cases one
rater saw a defense as major and the other scored it as absent. To
counteract this problem, the two raters' scores for each subject in each
sample were summed. This provided an individual rating for each
defense that ranged from 0 if both found it absent to 4 if both rated
it as major.

The differences among the three groups in choice of defensive
style were surprisingly small, as indicated in Table 7, which rank
orders the frequency with which each defense was used as a major adaptive style by each of the three study samples. All defenses that more
than 10 percent of any cohort used as a major defense are included.

Table 7. Relative frequency of use of a given defense as a major defensive
style

Defense	Core City men (n = 203)		Terman women (n = 40)		College men (n = 188)	
	Rank order	%	Rank order	%	Rank order	%
Isolation	1	52	2	38	1	46
Displacement	2	47	6	13	4	18
Suppression	3	34	1	43	1	46
Repression	4	16	11	5	5	17
Dissociation	5	15	6	13	6	13
Altruism	6	12	3	33	6	13
Reaction formation	7	10	5	20	9	11
Passive aggression	8	10	8	10	3	23
Projection	9	9	14	3	13	2
Sublimation	10	7	4	30	6	13

The table suggests that relatively more of the Core City men used displacement and projection as major defenses, whereas sublimation was noted more often among the two highly educated groups. Since displacement evolves into sublimation, the difference in the raters' perception of less graceful, less mature attenuation of impulse among the Core City men may be real, or it may be an artifact of the subjects' education or of the raters' bias. For example, writing graffiti on subway cars would be classified as displacement and writing *New Yorker* poetry would be classified as sublimation, but the difference might have more to do with the artist's and the rater's education and I.Q. than with the artist's ego maturity.

The Terman women were somewhat more likely to use altruism and reaction formation and less likely to use repression than the two male groups. This difference is likely to reflect the socialization of women in our culture rather than any influence of biology. But in view of the different methods used and the number of comparisons made, it would be hard to argue that any of the differences in Table 7 is significant. Of greater interest perhaps is that two defenses, passive aggression (masochism) and repression—sometimes thought to be more common among women—were somewhat more common among the College men.

If gender and social class are not important in shaping maturity of defensive style, what about ethnicity? Because of the subtle nuances in idiomatic language and the difficulty of exactly matching samples, it is very difficult to draw valid conclusions about differences in defensive styles between ethnic groups. However, serendipitously, the Core City sample provided a way around this difficulty. Sixty-one percent of the Core City men had parents who had been born in a foreign country; and yet all of the men themselves had grown up in Boston, were fluent in English, and had been sampled and studied in the same way. Thus it was possible to vary ethnicity and culture of rearing while holding other demographic variables constant. In some facets of adult life, parental ethnic differences among the Core City men had exerted a profound effect. For example, men of white Anglo-Saxon Protestant (WASP) and Irish extractions had rates of alcohol abuse five times those of men of Italian extraction.[14]

Table 8 compares the defensive styles of 74 Core City men with parents born in Italy with those of 100 men with parents either of old Yankee stock or born in Great Britain or Anglophone Canada. The similarities are extraordinary. As with gender, the differences in defen-

Table 8. Ethnicity and the use of selected defenses among men in the Core City sample

Defense	% using defense as a major style	
	Italian (n = 74)	WASP[a] (n = 100)
Mature defenses		
Suppression	25	30
Altruism	10	12
Sublimation	6	6
Anticipation	4	5
Humor	6	11
Intermediate defenses		
Reaction formation	8	14
Isolation	50	45
Repression	16	20
Displacement	37	50
Immature defenses		
Dissociation	16	39
Projection	12	12
Passive aggression	19	18
Hypochondriasis	7	4
Fantasy	3	4
Acting out	4	5

a. Men of old American or English or Anglophone Canadian descent.

sive style that we intuitively ascribe to culture may be more apparent than real. Dissociation was the one defensive style noted more often among the WASPs. This difference could not be ascribed to their greater frequency of alcohol abuse. Even among the men who were not alcohol abusers, dissociation was twice as common among the WASPs as among the Italians. Clearly, the question of ethnic differences in defensive styles requires more research, but with improving methods for cross-cultural research on personality, cultural anthropologists have come to similar conclusions. With proper control for observer bias and ignorance, personality differences appear to be relatively independent of ethnicity.[15]

But if culture appears to have little effect on defensive style, biology has a profound effect. The central nervous systems of some Core City men had been impaired by chronic alcoholism. (By this I do not mean acute intoxication, for most men were quite sober when interviewed.) In addition, some men had possible cognitive impair-

Table 9.   Effect of cognitive impairment and alcohol abuse on maturity of
defenses among men in the Core City sample

| | % using defense as a major style | | |
Defense	Unimpaired Core City sample (n = 203)	I.Q. < 80 (n = 29)	Chronic alcoholism (n = 24)
Mature defenses			
Suppression	34	34	11***
Altruism	12	7	0
Sublimation	7	3	0**
Immature defenses			
Dissociation	15	45***	83***
Projection	9	10	29**
Passive aggression	10	31	46***
Hypochondriasis	3	17***	21**
Fantasy	5	0	13**
Acting out	1	10	8***

$**p < .01; ***p < .001.$

Note: In computation of statistical significance, the full sample of 307 men was used
and years of alcoholism and I.Q. were correlated with the full-range (0–4) rating for each
defense. In other words, statistical significance was not computed by using the
percentages shown in the table.

ment, as suggested by I.Q.'s less than 80. Both these groups exhibited
significantly less mature defensive styles than the rest of the Core City
men. As Table 9 indicates, all the immature defenses were two to four
times as common in the two groups with compromised central nervous
systems as in the unimpaired sample. Because the numbers were small,
the differences could not always be demonstrated to be statistically
significant.

Empirical investigation has provided positive answers to the three questions I posed at the beginning of this chapter. First, maturity of
defenses can be rated reliably. Second, maturity of defenses provides
a valid measure of mental health. Third, maturity of defenses is independent of social class but is affected by biology. In short, defense
mechanisms are not just one more tenet of the psychoanalyst's religion.
The study of the ego's mechanisms of defense is a fit subject for serious
social scientists.

6

The Ego and Adult Development

For now we see through a glass, darkly: but then face to face: now I know in part; but then shall I know even as also I am known.

1 Corinthians 13:12

It was a soft June morning at Swarthmore College in Pennsylvania. A brilliant professor had just received an honorary degree from her alma mater. Now she confronted her graduation day audience with simplicity, clarity, and humanity. "Today, I ask the question of you," Sara Lawrence Lightfoot challenged:

> Where do you think you will make your greatest contributions? And I offer you three alternative possibilities. The first and most obvious response lies in the commitment to a distinguished career . . . For me, the far more subtle and complicated work for both women and men is in the two alternative responses—in the commitments of family and in the commitments of community-building.
>
> Nurturing and sustaining relationships in families—the demands of intimacy—are far more complicated than the controlled responsibilities of career. The complications lie in the improvisational nature of family life, in the depth of love that makes us vulnerable, in the daily grinding work that seems to disappear in the mixed conflicting emotions that rise up in us like volcanoes, in the endless forever commitment that is required. I will always be a mother.
>
> The third alternative equally hard to fashion is a commitment of community-building . . . By community-building I mean the broad range—from neighborhood efforts to global challenges, from leading the Girl Scouts and coaching Little League to fighting poverty and homelessness.[1]

A schoolteacher, shortly after his twenty-fifth Harvard reunion, expressed Lightfoot's three alternatives a little differently: he put them in developmental order. Asked how he had changed between college and middle life, this College man wrote, "From age 20 to 30 I learned how to get along with my wife; from age 30 to 40 I learned how to be a success at my job; and since 40, I have worried less about myself and more about the children." For the male schoolteacher there was a linear, almost embryological, progression to adult development; for the female college professor there was free choice. Is adult life more affected by inexorable psychobiological development or by environmentally catalyzed free choice? Perhaps both answers are partly right; but I wish to focus on the answer of the schoolteacher. I wish to underscore an important facet of ego development: its capacity over time to encompass a widening social radius.

Let me turn from twentieth-century Harvard and Swarthmore to another century, to another culture, and to the lifespan development of a college dropout. At age 30, this young man was still very much struggling with issues of identity and still trying to leave adolescence behind him. Nobody would have mistaken him for a grown-up. Incapacitated by what Lightfoot calls "conflicting emotions that rise up in us like volcanoes," he could allow himself intimacy with no one. Between ages 20 and 30, he repeatedly had run away from relationships that threatened to become intimate. In addition, he took no pride in his only talent—writing; instead, he wrote in his diary, "I shall write no more fiction. It is shameful when you come to think of it—people are weeping, dying, marrying—and I should sit down and write books telling how she loved him? It's shameful!"[2] And nobody could have accused this young man, who raped and economically exploited his servants, compulsively had sex with prostitutes, and wandered about Europe sponging off rich female relatives, of community-building. Superficially he appeared selfish and narcissistic; beneath the surface he lacked an abiding sense of self. His ego could not contain the volcanoes of love or work or care.

Four years later, Count Leo Tolstoy, at age 34, overcame his long-standing aversion to close relationships and fell in love with Sonya Behrs. Their marriage endured thirteen children and forty years of Lightfoot's "endless forever commitment." Biographers have portrayed the relationship as a tormented one. But their view is distorted by retrospect and by the diaries in which the Tolstoys recorded their most negative thoughts. As with many diaries, the diaries of Sonya and Leo were responsible for absorbing their split-off negative feelings. Thus, I suspect that even in old age the couple deeply loved each other. In any case, for the first ten years of his married life Tolstoy unmistakably blossomed through and rejoiced in marital intimacy.

At age 36, after two years of marriage, Tolstoy was thrown from his horse while hunting. "When he came to his senses, a thought hit him like a thunderbolt. 'I am a writer!' And joy welled through his mind, while he felt a searing pain in his shoulder."[3] By this time his novel *War and Peace* was well under way. He certainly went on to a distinguished career as a writer.

The next year Tolstoy wrote, "If I were told I might write a book in which I should demonstrate beyond any doubt the correctness of my opinions on every social problem, I should not waste two hours on it; but if I were told that what I would write would be read twenty years from now by people who are children today, and that they would weep and laugh over my book and love life more because of it, then I should devote all my life and strength to such a work."[4] His generative behavior was far more convincing than his words. By the time he was 41, the sixth and final volume of *War and Peace* had appeared. His career as a writer had been consolidated, and his life over the next thirty years illustrated his own idealistic definition of generativity: to so live that others—five successive generations of others—would love life more because of what he had written. Tolstoy spent the rest of his long life setting an example for two of the greatest community-builders of the twentieth century: Mahatma Gandhi and Martin Luther King, Jr. But the journey began with the mastery of his volcanic emotions and his achievement of intimacy with Sonya. No matter that this blissful intimacy did not last forever. As my former editor Louis Howland once patiently explained to me, "George, it is not that divorce is necessarily bad. It is that loving people for long periods of time is good." The capacity to love others deeply for long periods is not granted to everyone. But the point I wish to make about Tolstoy's life is that he did not choose among Lightfoot's three alternatives: like the schoolteacher, he accomplished them all—and in order.

A Model for Adult Development

Lightfoot's words and Tolstoy's life illustrate for me the three most important stages of adult ego development: mastering first the task of intimacy, then the task of career consolidation, and finally the task of generativity. I believe that in general—albeit with many exceptions—the tasks must be mastered in that order, for in sequence they require the ego to achieve increasingly complex integration. For both the all-male College and Core City samples it has been demonstrated that the theory appears to work.[5] While Lightfoot's argument that love is more complex than work is compelling, in this chapter I will present empirical evidence that in most cases it is hard to succeed in the world of work if one has not first achieved intimacy. Second, and less arguably, it is hard to be a mentor and to enable others with generative care unless one has at first succeeded in a career oneself. As an existentialist might suggest, we become what we do.

The most challenging task for me in this chapter will be to show that these developmental steps are equally applicable to women. To do so, I shall integrate data about the Terman women with my earlier work on adult male development from the College and Core City samples. I shall use these three longitudinal studies to provide empirical support for Erik Erikson's intuitively derived model of adult ego development.

Certainly, in any society, the occupational roles that give a woman a sense of competence may differ from those which provide the same sense of competence to men. For example, Terman women who had spent their working lives as housewives epitomized career consolidation if at age 65 they checked "homemaker" under all three career options: "as it was," "as it had been planned," and "as I now would wish." In contrast, a College man who had never mastered intimacy was a financially successful physician, but he lacked commitment. He practiced medicine only for the money while philosophically preferring Christian Science. Since this man abandoned four wives and took no responsibility for his children, he did not qualify for "homemaker" either. His sense of self remained shaky all his life. Like Willy Loman in *Death of a Salesman*, he always felt "kind of temporary" about himself. Like Willy Loman, too, he created nothing; he "had nothing in the ground." He was a chronic deployer of immature defenses, and his life ended by suicide at 50. In short, he found it easy to marry and to become licensed as a doctor, but without ego development such accomplishments become as sounding brass or a tinkling cymbal. He never developed as an adult.

The modified model that I shall use to test Erikson's view of the adult life cycle is portrayed in Figure 4 as a spiral staircase. The model

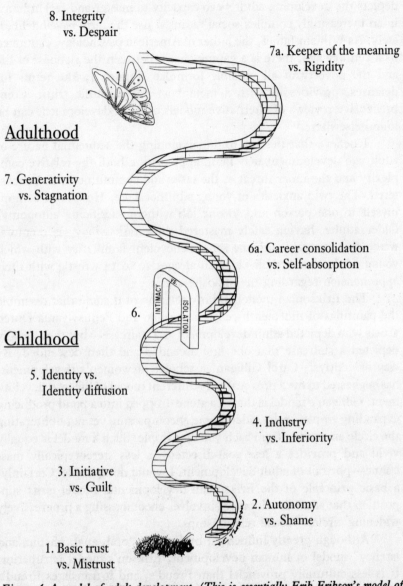

8. Integrity
    vs. Despair

7a. Keeper of the meaning
    vs. Rigidity

Adulthood

7. Generativity
    vs. Stagnation

6a. Career consolidation
    vs. Self-absorption

6.

INTIMACY

ISOLATION

Childhood

5. Identity vs.
    Identity diffusion

4. Industry
    vs. Inferiority

3. Initiative
    vs. Guilt

2. Autonomy
    vs. Shame

1. Basic trust
    vs. Mistrust

Figure 4. A model of adult development. (This is essentially Erik Erikson's model of the adult life cycle with the addition of Stages 6A and 7A.)

depicts the developing adult's ego capacity to master and feel at home in an increasingly complex social radius. I use the term *model* deliberately. As William James, the father of American psychology, cautioned us a century ago, there is a gaping chasm between the richness of life and the poverty of all possible formulae. Figure 4, like terms for defenses, provides us with a metaphor, not scientific truth. Comprehensive reviews of alternative models of adult development can be found elsewhere.[6]

I believe that the key to understanding the sequential nature of adult ego development may lie in appreciating both the relative complexity and the inner threat of the tasks and commitments to be mastered. The twin anxieties of young adulthood are, How can I commit myself to one person and to one job without sacrificing autonomy? Older adults, having safely mastered these tasks, may, as mentors, watch this struggle with the same benevolent familiarity with which young adults watch their children at ages 10 to 14 wrestle with their apprehension regarding the opposite sex.

The Eriksonian model and my revision of it somewhat resemble the paintings of nineteenth-century German and Pennsylvania Dutch artists who depicted adult development as a staircase—but they usually depicted a staircase that one first ascended and then descended. By way of contrast, Carol Gilligan, a scholar of women's development, has suggested to me a provocatively different model of lifespan development. Gilligan's model is that of a stone dropped into a pond producing expanding ripples, each older ripple encompassing yet not obliterating the circle emanating from each younger ripple. Such a model is equally vivid and provides a less goal-directed—a less stereotypically masculine—portrait of adult development. I would not quibble. Certainly, a basic principle of the Eriksonian developmental model is its supposition that adult development involves encompassing a progressively widening circle of social relationships.

Although greatly influenced by Freud's "oral, anal, phallic, and latency" model of human development, Erikson's model is superior. It is less culturally provincial than Freud's, and it translates Freud's poetic metaphors into biological realities. In addition, Erikson extended our conception of human development into adulthood. In Stage I, Erikson replaces Freud's misleading metaphor of *orality* with *Basic Trust vs. Mistrust*. The concept of basic trust better captures the real needs of a young infant for maternal holding, eye contact, and object constancy. Adults who were deprived of these when young may verbally emphasize and symbolically manifest "oral" needs, a metaphor that Freud mistook for biological necessity. As long as basic nutrition is met, gratification of an infant's need to suck is not essential for development. But without loving eye contact and hugging by stable caretakers, the development of humans and other primates is arrested.

In Stage 2, Erikson replaces Freud's misleading metaphor of *anality* with *Autonomy vs. Shame*. Erikson's concept of autonomy better captures the toddler's need to master anger, ownership of self, and a modicum of assertive separation from mother. In contrast, Freud with his concept of anal gratification emphasized the sensual and disciplinary aspects of bowel control, which at age 2 is more relevant to modern Western Europeans than to *Homo sapiens* in general. Just as adult "oral" metaphors convey unmet need for love, so do our Western anal metaphors convey anger and conflicts over autonomy. Eskimo children are potty trained before six months; in their culture parents battle the "terrible twos" over controlling angry outbursts of weeping, not soiling.

In Stage 3, Erikson replaces Freud's misleading and sexist metaphor of *phallic* with *Initiative vs. Guilt*. The concept of initiative better captures the 4- to 6-year-old's efforts to imitate parents, to show off, and to withstand parents' tendency to put down such ambition with "you are not funny and you are not cute." The 5-year-old fears adult retaliation and abandonment if she or he is too cocky, too independent. Thus, Freud's metaphor of castration is vivid, but it is as literally inaccurate as the metaphors of orality and anality. Laius did not threaten to castrate Oedipus; he drove a spike through his feet and left him on a lonely mountainside to die of exposure. Sexual conquest is but one facet of human initiative.

Finally, in Stage 4, Erikson replaces Freud's misleading term of (sexual) *latency* with *Industry vs. Inferiority*. The concept of industry better captures the universal need of 6- to 10-year-olds "to work with and beside" adults, rather than emphasizing, as Freud's does, the parochial cultural need of modern Western technological societies to deny and condemn sexuality in children.

In this book on adult development, I shall not return to Stages 1–4 again. Rather, I shall concentrate on Erikson's Stages 5–8 as I have modified them. Inspection of the spiral depicted in Figure 4 reveals that I have added two stages, 6A, Career Consolidation, and

7A, Keeper of the Meaning, to Erikson's original eight. My reason for these additions is to encompass repetitive patterning that I have observed in examining the lives of adults prospectively followed for half a century.

In describing my revision of Erikson's model, let me begin by noting that for charting adult development a term like Robert Havinghurst's *developmental tasks*[7] is more scientifically correct than *stage*. In adult development the term *stage* is only a metaphor that retains popularity due to its wide use by Erikson and others. Immutable, clearly defined developmental stages belong only to biological embryology, not to adult development. The process of adult development that I have observed in the Study subjects is not nearly as tidy as the cognitive development that Piaget and his students observed in children. Thus, in order to assess adult ego development I have simply charted the mastery of certain selected tasks that I believe reflect the underlying ego development. I use these selected tasks to determine whether a given individual has attained a given "stage."

For research purposes, I have defined Erikson's task of *Identity vs. Identity Diffusion* (Stage 5) as the last task of childhood: sustained separation from social, residential, economic, and ideological dependence upon family of origin. It must be emphasized that such separation derives as much from the identification and internalization of important childhood figures as it does from the ability to master modern life. Nor is identity just a product of egocentricity, of running away from home, or of marrying to get out of the family. There is a world of difference between the instrumental act of running away from home and the developmental task of knowing where one's family values end and one's own values begin. Separation/individuation is a lifelong process and reflects ego development.

Those Study subjects who failed to reach Stage 5, Identity, included men and women who never achieved independence from their family of origin or from institutions. In middle life, they remained dependent on others and never committed themselves either to occupational specialization or to sustained intimate friendship. They did not usually come to psychiatric attention, and some possessed full insight into how far their lives were from what Erikson might call generativity. (Examples will be discussed in Chapter 7.)

Mastery of the task of *Intimacy vs. Isolation* (Stage 6) serves as the gateway to adult development. For research purposes, I have defined intimacy as living with another person in an interdependent, committed, and intimate fashion for ten years or more. For several single women in the Terman sample, the other person was a close woman friend. For the participating men in our study, the other person was almost inevitably a wife. Part of the explanation for this heterosexual emphasis was that only 2 percent of the College sample viewed themselves as homosexual (two men waited until age 65 to tell us) and the homosexual Core City men withdrew from the study.

A Terman woman, Betsy Browning, illustrates the evidence that I used to categorize a person as having mastered the task of intimacy. She had achieved intimacy rather late in life. Asked at age 78 how her marriage to Bob Browning, her second husband, had survived for seventeen years, she replied, "I suppose sex is very important." She added, "I married Bob because I was overwhelmingly in love." She told us that she had learned to enjoy gardens, which were her husband's chief interest, and that, in turn, he was "nice as can be" with her children from her first marriage. As a result of this cooperation, she explained, "We've done some wonderful things together." Asked if they depended on each other, she replied, "We are completely dependent on each other." Their greatest problem, she said, was that as she got older she became tidier and her husband did not. On the one hand, as Erikson suggested, dependence, autonomy, sexuality, identity all must be mastered for intimacy to become feasible. On the other hand, we did not ask that individuals live up to some platonic ideal of intimacy. We asked only that they share an interdependent relationship that had continued for a decade to bring unmistakable, if imperfect, mutual satisfaction.

The task of *Career Consolidation vs. Self-Absorption* (Stage 6A) was defined as making a clear, specialized career identification characterized by *commitment, compensation, contentment,* and *competence.* These four words distinguish a career from a job. Career consolidation involves the transformation of preoccupation with self, of commitment to an adolescent's hobby, and (as Shakespeare put it) of "seeking the bauble reputation" into a specialized role valued by both self and society. As the writer Emily Hancock puts it, "Being home and being married wasn't sufficient . . . I wanted to secure my sense of competence, to be good at something, acquire a measurable skill, something that I could say 'I have learned this, I am good at this, I can do this, I know this.'"[8] Certainly, even extraordinary abilities do not count if

they are not driven by purpose, choice, and intention and if they fail
to bring the owner contentment. Like a sense of personal identity, and
like the sense of merging that is inherent in intimacy, occupational
commitment, too, can seem scary to a young adult. Such commitment
requires ego development for mastery.

Readers familiar with Erikson's work may note that I have split
off certain facets of his theoretical Stage 5, Identity vs. Identity Diffusion, to create Stage 6A, Career Consolidation vs. Self-Absorption. I
have done this in order to distinguish the development of identity within
one's family of origin from identity within one's world of work. One reason for this decision is that selfless generativity cannot be achieved unless
the adult has been able to master both the selfishness (a.k.a. self-mainte-
nance) of achieving stable identity *and* the selfishness (a.k.a. self-actualization) of career consolidation. In a developmental framework to be
selfish (to develop a sense of self) is good, and to be *selfless* (to find
nobody at home within one's soul) is maladaptive. However, to enhance
the self and to consolidate a career one must somehow let others in.
Selfishness and selflessness must alternate. That perhaps is why achieving intimacy is a precursor to being able to accept a mentor and, thereby,
to achieving career consolidation. To gratefully allow another person
to serve as one's model requires trust, maturity, and a capacity to love.

Mastery of the task of *Generativity vs. Stagnation* (Stage 7) was
illustrated by men and women who, through career consolidation, having found themselves, demonstrated a clear capacity for care, productivity, and establishing and guiding the next generation. Generativity
means assuming sustained responsibility for the growth and well-being
of others. Generativity means what Lightfoot calls community-building. Depending on the opportunities that the society makes available,
generativity can mean serving as a consultant, guide, mentor, or coach
to young adults in the larger society. Although we may view deans,
matriarchs, and business magnates as the products of crass ambition
and infantile narcissism, in so doing we ignore the ego skills necessary
to allow one individual to assume sensitive responsibility for other
adults. Leadership looks like nothing more than self-aggrandizement
until one tries to do it.

In introducing the term *generativity*, however, Erikson did not
adequately differentiate it from creativity. Generativity, as the term is
used in this book, does not mean merely raising crops, nurturing small
children, and painting pictures. Pablo Picasso makes this distinction

quite clear: "What do you think an artist is? An imbecile who has only his eyes if he is a painter . . . ? On the contrary, he is at the same time a political being." Having just completed his politically inspired masterpiece, *Guernica,* for the Spanish Pavilion at the International Exhibition in Paris in 1937, Picasso also wrote, "I have always believed and still believe that artists who live and work with spiritual values cannot and should not remain indifferent to a conflict in which the highest values of humanity and civilization are at stake."[9] (I will discuss the ego and creativity in Chapter 8.)

Sometimes the effort to achieve career consolidation excludes care and may lead Ibsen's Nora, or Bullfinch's Narcissus, or Goethe's Faust into permanent self-absorption—the antonym of career consolidation. In such cases, the individual may become permanently mired in Erikson's slough of stagnation, a swamp, in his words, made from "excessive self-love based on a too strenuously self-made personality." In such cases further psychosocial development may be inhibited. Self-absorption is so different from self-enhancement! Anybody can gaze into a mirror, but we cannot hope to teach our children to floss their teeth until we *care* enough for *ourselves* to floss our own.

In Figure 4, I have split off certain facets of Erikson's concept of generativity and relabeled them as 7A, *Keeper of the Meaning vs. Rigidity.* Generativity and its virtue, *care,* require taking care of one person rather than another.[10] Keeper of the meaning and its virtue, *wisdom,* involve a more nonpartisan and less personal approach to others. Put differently, to preserve one's culture involves developing concern for a social radius that extends beyond one's immediate community. This is not a trivial distinction. We can all appreciate the difference in ego development between a wise Abraham Lincoln who tried to heal the wounds of civil war by proclaiming "with malice toward none" and a partisan and successfully generative Ronald Reagan who called the other side in the Cold War "The Evil Empire." Rigidity is the antonym of keeper of the meaning, just as rigidity is the potential vice of the grandparent and the elder statesman.

The tasks of a generative coach or parent of adolescent children are vastly different from those of a Supreme Court justice or the chair of a historical society. The generative person cares for an individual in a direct, future-oriented relationship—as, for example, mentor, or teacher to a student. In contrast, the keeper of the meaning speaks for past cultural achievements and guides groups, organizations, and bodies of people toward the preservation of past traditions. The wise organizers and guardians of the Olympic Games traditions play a very different role from that of the athletes' generative coaches. Similarly, extrapolations from the work of Jane Loevinger and Lawrence Kohlberg on adult ego and moral development also suggest that, with maturation, players become coaches and coaches become referees.[11]

Care and justice, as Carol Gilligan underscores, have always been different dimensions of personality.[12] However, it will be a sad day for humanity if either dimension is ever made the province of one sex rather than the other. In a sense that is why the term *wisdom* is preferable to *justice;* it is less value-laden. We all prefer the image of wise King Solomon to Shakespeare's "justice . . . with eyes severe and beard of formal cut, full of wise saws and modern instances." Yet wisdom cannot be present without justice, nor justice without wisdom.

I shall now discuss the central tasks of adult development in somewhat greater detail. However, for further discussion of the behaviors and ego skills involved at each of these stages, I refer the reader to works by other authors: Erik Erikson for the vicissitudes of identity development;[13] George Goethals for the development of intimacy;[14] Daniel Levinson for career consolidation;[15] John Kotre for the development of generativity;[16] and Virginia Clayton and Paul Baltes for the development of wisdom.[17]

Intimacy

There is a world of difference between the instrumental act of marriage or coitus and the developmental task of intimacy. Although his original formulation of intimacy was "mutuality of orgasm with a loved partner of the opposite sex," Erikson added, "Nor is it a purely sexual matter by any means."[18] Certainly, the concept of mutual orgasm fails to characterize the mastery of sustained adult attachment. Many sociopaths, it turns out, are more accomplished at "mutual orgasm" than some mature, highly intimate marital partners. But if one thinks of mutual orgasm as a metaphor for one adult's willingness to assume responsibility for another adult's vulnerability while at the same time allowing the other to reciprocate, then Erikson is on the right track. If one considers capacity for mutual orgasm as a metaphor to identify a relationship with a person with whom one is physically, responsibly, and reciprocally intimate—then it works. To be willing to enjoy with one's partner both bringing *and* being brought breakfast in bed, as it were, is a more felicitous way of suggesting the mutual interdependence that Erikson (and Freud before him) were trying to express. Intimacy, after all, involves coming to terms with dependency, aggression, *and* autonomy as well as with sexuality. In terms of the tension between selfishness and selflessness, intimacy allows the mutual sharing of self with another in a way that *both* can enjoy.

There is a traditional belief that men have to achieve identity before they can achieve intimacy and that women have to achieve intimacy in order to achieve identity. I believe that this notion is a cultural artifact. If a man believes that he must leave home before he can financially support a wife and if society permits a woman to leave home only after finding a husband who will financially support her, it appears superficially true. But *fiscal* development is not ego development. Certainly, a woman may not want a man who is not yet ready to leave *his* nuclear family, so women tend to marry men who have already left home. It is also true that, in the past, marriage permitted an economically dependent woman to leave *her* nuclear family, so she might need to marry a man with a good job. But such considerations are economic, not developmental.

Career Consolidation

Career consolidation is qualitatively different from the adolescent task of identity formation. In achieving an independent identity, an adolescent need be of value only to herself. In contrast, career consolidation requires an identity that society, too, finds useful. Over the years, Erikson puzzled over where to put the development of stable occupational identity.[19] Although he sometimes tried to link career with adolescent identity formation, he remained uncertain. I believe that the explanation of his uncertainty is that career consolidation is rarely achieved until after intimacy is mastered. After all, many individuals are relatively clear about who they *are* but not about what kind of artisan they wish to *become*. Adult development requires "metabolizing" and assimilating other people throughout the life span. Internalized, albeit highly selected, parental values play an important role in adolescent identity. In contrast, parental mentoring is rarely cited as important in the creation of career identities. Rather, career consolidation is achieved through internalization of a new set of mentors. If fortunate, we never become too old to internalize those whom we admire.

In terms of ego development, the task of career consolidation involves achieving a vocational identity that, like intimacy, reflects reciprocity. To vocational identity one brings *competence* and *commitment,* and from such identity one derives *contentment* and *compensation.* For example, each of the following occupational adjustments fails to meet one of the four criteria for career consolidation. The contented and committed perennial graduate student lacks competence. The amateur full-time golfer, unpublished poet, or solitary birdwatcher who continues an adolescent hobby into adulthood lacks compensation. Ibsen's Nora within her gilded cage of marriage was competent and well compensated, but like an unhappy Wall Street lawyer, Nora felt no commitment toward her self-prostitution and found no contentment in her "paycheck."

The argument may be offered that the insertion of the task of career consolidation into a model of adult development applies only to a modern technological society or only to educated men in upper-middle-class professions. But findings from the Study of Adult Development suggest that this is not the case. Ego development is a reflection of sociobiology and not of culture. Like the role of love, the role of work is important to societies the world around. The medieval hierarchy that led from apprentice to journeyman and from journeywoman to master craftswoman was as clear a thousand years ago as is the path that leads a premedical student to resident to specialist today. The men and women of hunter-gatherer societies still bring commitment and ritual enjoyment to the task at hand. For centuries successful village matriarchs have looked back on their lives and seen within their accomplishments as wife and mother contentment, commitment, compensation, and competence.

Recent popular writers on female development have pointed out that what Erikson called distantiation, or what others have called self-actualization, is intrinsic to adult growth beyond intimacy. Ibsen's play *A Doll's House,* which ends with the developmental epiphany of Nora slamming the door on her patriarchal husband, Torvald, captures the poignancy of this need for a career identity that is as intrinsic to women as it is to men. In her book *The Girl Within,* Emily Hancock describes the issues of career consolidation as they apply to women. One of Hancock's informants reported, "My job had satisfactions to me in defining my ego . . . Work really was a matrix—a very feminine word, for it derives from *womb* and stems from *mater* which means 'mother'—for growing up." [20]

There was an interesting distinction between the Terman women who had worked outside the home and those who had achieved career consolidation solely as homemakers. In response to questions at age 65, only 5 percent of the 300 career women who had worked for most of their lives said they wished they had been primarily homemakers, whereas 30 percent of the 300 homemakers without outside careers said they wished they had also had wage-earning jobs. In other words, although they belonged to a historical cohort of women that preceded the Betty Friedan and Gloria Steinem generations, the Terman women had often wished for careers beyond homemaking. More important, when the Terman women had achieved such careers, they were retrospectively glad. Admittedly, most of the women who had been content with their paid careers also had had careers as successful homemakers.

Many women and men, of course, *never* feel that they have the right to strike out on their own. There is a quality of "selfishness" about career specialization that threatens to corrupt the task. But if both fear of success and selfishness are phenomena that affect both sexes, both society and biology offer men more support for such selfishness. Thus, Hancock warns:

> With a girl's earlier puberty comes a lag in growth; with a boy's comes an increase in mass. As he catches up to and surpasses her in height, weight, and muscular force, the boy, for the first time, is bigger and stronger than she. Her body softens while his hardens. As he gets stronger, smarter, louder, she feels weaker and less certain. The boy's pubertal changes portend an increased ability to dominate; the girl's imply, recurrently, the mandate to nurture and the need for restraint. His experience of adolescence is one of increased power; hers is one of increased risk. [21]

This quote may strike many readers as old-fashioned. But, too often, women may confuse such increased risk with prohibition. Testosterone makes it fun to be first and to compete; estrogen does not. Young Arthur, when he pulled Excalibur from the stone, out from the grasp of the Lady of the Lake, knew he was meant to be king. In contrast, Snow White's acquisition of great beauty led only to the melancholy knowledge that she was in mortal danger. Kipling wrote, "*He* travels fastest who travels alone"; but such selfishness may seem unthinkable to many responsible women.

In terms of career development, vulnerability to pregnancy is another handicap. Childbearing can create for many women what Bernice Neugarten has called "off time" events and make their adult development less orderly than it would be otherwise. For having a child is an experience that has to do with the self but does not provide a self. One of Hancock's informants said, "Having to take somebody else into account at that level means not being able to be selfish. I couldn't choose not to be whatever this baby needed me to be, whether I was tired or sick or lonely . . . life's ordered priorities dictated that I consider his well-being above all else."[22] Even Sonya Tolstoy's wished-for career as a happy wife and mother was destroyed by thirteen pregnancies. In addition, the whole issue of the "second shift" for career women with families makes both tasks more difficult. Unlike men, women with careers must often commit to two full-time jobs. In short, the inequities of biology, as well as of society, may offer women a much narrower channel through which to navigate the two shoals of selflessness and selfishness, on the other side of which looms a satisfying career identity.

Whenever society, or biology, condemns autonomous self-development as "selfish," individuality is sacrificed. Yet as the planned societies of communist, feudal, and monastic communities suggest, there are real short-term societal advantages to the inhibition of adult development. Society does not get its reward until career consolidation finally results in the transformation of a private self into a public self. The recent discoveries by the socialist economies in Eastern Europe are a case in point. The grocery shelves of societies that allow farmers to be selfish have more good things on them for everyone to eat than do the grocery shelves served by forcibly collectivized farms. Too often, the Terman women were led to believe that anything they did that was not selfless was selfish. Like good socialists, they understood that one individual's adult development, as it were, deprived another— at least over the short term. Many of these women did not free themselves from this burden until late middle life.

In the long run, the fact that the Terman women were excluded from the individual careers of their choice was a tremendous loss to American society as a whole even if, as I suspect, their husbands, their parents, and their children were beneficiaries. Consider the fate of

Lewis Terman's own two intellectually gifted children. Both his son and his daughter graduated from Stanford with distinction. Both married. Lewis Terman's gifted son went on to become Stanford University's provost, a distinguished dean of its engineering school, and a founding father of Silicon Valley. Lewis Terman's gifted daughter also worked for Stanford University, but as an unhappy telephone operator in one of the student dormitories.

One of the tasks of mature adult development must be to compensate for hormonal changes and societal imperatives as well as to accommodate to them. In the well-known study by Inge Broverman and her colleagues,[23] both men and women, regardless of their level of education, attributed a specific cluster of traits (independence, rationality, and self-direction) to the ideal man, and both attributed a different cluster (warmth, emotional expressiveness, and relatedness) to the ideal woman. Prospective study, however, suggests that by midlife a major developmental task for women is to reclaim the virtues of any latency child: *independence, rationality,* and *self-direction.* Rediscovery of these strengths often becomes an exciting facet of women's midlife development.[24] Similarly, it is enriching for men in midlife to recover mature virtues that were hormonally and societally denied them during adolescence, such as *warmth, emotional expressiveness,* and *relatedness.*[25] In short, the developmental need to make up for biologically and societally inhibited skills may make career consolidation a more critical developmental task for women and generativity a more critical developmental task for men. More research is needed.

To summarize, career consolidation is the somewhat egocentric passage from apprentice to master craftsman. I believe that the adult developmental sequence of intimacy to career consolidation to generativity is a pattern that extends beyond sex, social class, and historical epoch. The sequence reflects a woman progressing from holding a new baby in one hand, Dr. Spock's *Baby Care* in the other, and a telephone linking her to her mother under her chin to the point, a decade later, at which she is waving one hand at her 10-year-old as the child goes out to play while holding the phone in her other hand to advise a neighbor on the care of *her* new baby. Almost a millennium ago the same transformation might just as well have been epitomized by the same woman's ancestor evolving from novice to master seamstress in order to produce tapestries that would bring humans pleasure for generations and generations to come.

Keeper of the Meaning

In his writing Erikson often fails to distinguish between care and wisdom. The ego develops in stages, and care precedes wisdom. We all can imagine care without wisdom, but not wisdom without care. Wisdom, unlike care, means not taking sides. Wisdom necessitates the appreciation of irony and ambiguity—ego skills that come relatively late in life. How do we learn to keep in consciousness the contradictions and paradoxes that arise within our own minds? Cognitively, how do we develop an intellectual stance that welcomes refutation? How do we retain the competing realities of past, present, and future; and, simultaneously, how do we retain the relativity of our own point of view? These are intellectual tasks thought to parallel the development of wisdom. Yet, as the examples of King Solomon and Portia's judge in *The Merchant of Venice* illustrate, true wisdom always necessitates the fusion of care and justice.

It is for these reasons that, in addition to career consolidation, I have added keeper of the meaning to the sequential psychosocial tasks of adult development. I believe that fulfilling the role of keeper of the meaning is an objective indication of wisdom in older adults. A letter from a 55-year-old College man describes one facet of the process:

> I feel that I have learned more in the last five years than in any preceding ten, and that this is due to a sort of broadening of the future, rather than a narrowing . . . I have finally come through to a realization of what is of critical importance for our future—that we finally come to live in harmony with nature and our natural environment, not in victory over it . . . All of which might make you wonder why I have not designated this as the happiest period of my life, and the answer to that is that the earlier period was one of comparative innocence and youthful exuberance—a celebration more of my physical powers, of unfettered freedom. Those powers I now celebrate are more of an intellectual variety, somewhat tinged by experience of the world; in a way my lately-acquired knowledge and insights—my wisdom if you will, is not an unalloyed blessing, but a burden in some respects.

Another College man was asked at 55 the most important ways in which he had matured. "The process of maturing," he replied, "is pretty well described by Oliver Wendell Holmes in 'The Chambered

Nautilus.' We gradually enlarge our understanding of the world and the people in it,—assuming we *do* mature,—toward the ultimate goal of feeling 'at one with nature',—a goal never totally achieved. I think that at the present time, if I were to be dropped in any part of the world, I could understand and appreciate the people there and make my way among them." His stance is close to what Paul Baltes and Jacqueline Smith describe as one of the basic components of wisdom: "an awareness that all judgements are a function of, and are relative to, a given cultural and personal value system." [26]

Thus, the focus of keeper of the meaning is on the collective products of humanity—the culture in which one lives and its institutions—rather than on the development of its children. As another College subject said at age 55, " 'Passing on the torch' and exposure of civilized values to children has always been of importance to me but it has increased with each ensuing year." In writing about generativity, John Kotre separates the two tasks of care and of keeper of the meaning by observing that ultimately the targets of a potential mentor must be *both* the culture and the disciple, and that the mentor must hold the two in balance. If the mentor puts too much into his mentees (generativity), "he neglects and dilutes the culture's central symbols. But if the preservation of culture is paramount [keeper of the meaning] he makes anonymous receptacles of disciples." [27] This danger is why I suggest that rigidity is the antonym of this stage.

Like generativity, being a keeper of the meaning is characterized by giving away the skills that have been acquired through a combination of intimacy and career consolidation. But now the emphasis is on the skills acquired during the period of career consolidation: organizational skills and informational skills.

One facet of the work of a keeper of the meaning is distinguishing which of one's possessions can be returned to the cultural trust. As an ironic illustration, Henry Ford, having ripped small-town America asunder by his generative creation of the Ford Motor Company, tried to preserve America's past in his wistful construction of Greenfield Village—a museum of how New England looked before the invention of the Model T Ford. Charles Lindbergh in midlife was a pathfinder for Pan American Airlines and a creative architect of global air routes to the far corners of the Pacific; in late life he devoted his efforts to global conservation movements in order to protect the very Shangri-las that he had helped to endanger. And critics of these two controversial men can point to their racial bigotry and thus to their potential for rigidity.

A model of what I am trying to describe by the task of keeper of the meaning is provided by Princeton Project 55. This project was begun December 1989 at a conference sponsored jointly by Princeton graduates in late midlife and the Johnson Foundation and attended by representatives from twelve universities. The men in their late fifties wished to sponsor young adults to "address important societal issues, focus on systemic change rather than treating symptoms, encourage and utilize community participation, and to be non-partisan." The credo of the organizers and their appeal to others between 50 and 60 was as follows: "As we enter our mid-fifties and beyond, we are prepared to devote a larger share of our time and energy to preserving and improving a world from which we have received so much. We believe that the knowledge and experience we have accumulated can be used to find new solutions to the difficult problems which beset our society and the world . . . We came of age together . . . We are all in it together. There is much to be done. Please join us." Since its inception the project has been more than just pious rhetoric. With the active mentorship of its founders, Project 55 has supported young interns to work for a year or for a summer in public school reform, community empowerment, the Environmental Defense Fund, and the World Wildlife Fund.

Other Facets of the Model

An alternative model for adult development, as I have already mentioned, might be Carol Gilligan's metaphor of a stone dropped in a pool, expanding ripples encompassing expanding ripples. But there are several heuristic advantages to depicting the model as a spiral, as in Figure 4. First, this representation underscores that during adult life, individuals evolve rather than merely grow. Second, the spiral conveys the concept that with maturational change, unlike the transformation of caterpillar to butterfly, past progress is not lost. Third, it suggests that, as in climbing a staircase, failure to attain one landing makes it unlikely that one will attain the next. *Yet, as in climbing a staircase, one landing is not better than another.* Consider the study of celestial navigation. Neither sextant nor celestial map can tell us where we *should* go, but both are invaluable in letting us identify where we are. Life is a journey, not a footrace.

I favor the staircase model for yet a fourth reason. As depicted in a two-dimensional drawing like Figure 4, the staircase has a left side and a right side. These sides reflect rhythmic changes in malleability of character that occur during the life span—at least in our own culture. By clinical impression, if not by hard data, the left-hand stages—the Oedipal years (Stage 3), adolescence (5), midlife (7), and old age (8: as lived by passionate elders like Pablo Picasso and William Butler Yeats), are times of personal change and instability. These periods of life are times for reworking ascribed identity and for questioning conventional morality. They are times of heightened introceptiveness, affective lability, and fresh instinctual conflict. These are the times that Susan Whitenbourne would call periods of assimilation.[28] These are the times when humankind provides excellent copy for serious dramatists and pop psychologists, and when relationships and embeddedness may be most important. These are the times during their life span when individuals may appear most impulsive and most like hysterics.

On the right side of the spiral are represented the life periods of autonomy (2), latency (4), career consolidation (6A), and of Shakespeare's judge who keeps the meaning "with eyes severe and beard of formal cut" (7A). By clinical impression, during these periods individuals are preoccupied with the preservation of sameness and autonomy, with following and maintaining rules. They are more likely to be concerned with absorbing, observing, and promulgating past traditions than with reworking their culture. When individuals find themselves on the right-hand side of the staircase, they are relatively less introceptive and less dependent upon forming new relationships. Thus, both dramatists and pop psychologists tend to gloss over these periods of life, and these are the times during their life span when individuals may appear the most obsessional.

A paradox of the model portrayed in Figure 4 is that to characterize maturity by Erikson's "virtue" of *care* runs counter to the view that maturity consists of the capacity to be one's own self-actualizing woman or man. Abraham Maslow, Lawrence Kohlberg, and Jane Loevinger have proposed maturational models that are characterized by an increasing differentiation of self from others and a progressive freeing of self from contextual and social constraint.[29] In contrast, Erikson would agree with Carol Gilligan that "care, then, became the universal obligation, the self chosen ethic of a post-conventional [that is, mature] judgment."[30]

However, whether justice and self-actualization are more or less mature than care and social embeddedness is a debate that should not be resolved. Rather, we must realize that at the heart of both the adolescent's quest for identity and the young adult's quest for career consolidation is the ethic of responsibility to self. But as individuals grow older they move from one side of the developmental staircase to the other. Capacity for intimate interdependence comes *after* adolescents have pulled themselves free from dependence upon their family of origin. Similarly, not until the young adult has consolidated her own career identity is she willing or able once again to subordinate her newly won autonomy in order to assume responsibility for helping others to gain their autonomy. Not until Nora has permission to slam the door and to have a room of her own can she, with love and care, give daughters away in marriage and worry about community-building. Indeed, Gerald Klerman and Daniel Levinson suggest that good administrators (that is, masters of generativity) must first reconcile themselves with the quest of their own adolescent children for independent risk taking and separate identities.[31]

What I am suggesting is that over the life span individuals oscillate from one side of the spiral of Figure 4 to the other. Although they maintain forward motion, adult development may not always seem that way. One member of the College sample, asked what he had learned from his four years of psychoanalysis, replied, "I'm more like I was when I was 4 and less like I was when I was 7." But he had grown up in the process. At the time when he was interviewed he was at the left-hand side of the spiral and being highly generative. It was his adventurousness, not his childishness, that reminded him of being 4 years old.

Finally, over the life span there is an oscillation with a still longer amplitude than the to-and-fro journey depicted in my spiral staircase model. At some point in life there are suddenly more yesterdays than tomorrows. At this point (age 50 in the folk art of the Pennsylvania Dutch), one seemingly retraces the flights one has climbed. If the steps from infancy to childhood to adolescence lead sequentially to mastering one's body, one's external environment, and finally one's emotions, then from 40 to senescence the steps lead in the reverse direction. Like the adolescent, the 40-year-old in crisis struggles with feelings; like the 10-year-old, the 60-year-old struggles to resist the changing times; and like the toddler, the 80-year-old is preoccupied with an unruly, unsteady body. Bernice Neugarten has written that if 40-year-olds "see the environment as one that rewards boldness and risk-taking . . . Sixty year olds seem to see the environment as complex and dangerous, no longer to be reformed in line with one's own wishes and to see the self as conforming and accommodating to outer world demands."[32] At age 65 T. S. Eliot wrote, "If you haven't the strength to impose your own terms upon life, you must accept the terms it offers you."[33] That is the plight, too, of the latency child. To generalize, change is welcome in adolescence and in early midlife and abhorred at age 9 and age 60.

Several investigators prefer to chart adult development in terms of *transitions*, but my model glosses over transitions. From following individuals over time, it is my own impression that the *crisis* aspect of adolescence, of menopause, and of retirement may be overemphasized. I believe transitions are merely by-products of development. Certainly, the process of development cannot be viewed as merely achieving chronological landmarks like graduation, first job, marriage, and first child. Almost anybody can get a job at McDonald's, buy a marriage license, or make a baby. Put differently, obtaining an education may lead to a college degree, but participating in the tradition and experiencing the transition of college graduation does not necessarily create education. Development creates transitions; transitions do not create development.

Indeed, the crises that we associate with transitions may have more to do with three nondevelopmental factors than they do with the process of development itself. The first nondevelopmental factor is psychopathology. For example, people who have a particularly troubled adolescence are also likely to have a particularly troubled middle life. In addition, a tendency to serious depression makes almost any change a crisis. Since psychiatrists work only with individuals in crisis, they gain a false belief in the universality of adolescent and midlife crisis. However, community studies of ordinary people during adolescence and middle life suggest that such assumptions of inevitable developmental crisis are unwarranted.[34]

The second nondevelopmental factor associated with crisis during developmental transitions has to do with changes in role that are poorly mediated by the culture. For example, an uncelebrated retirement or a perfunctory civil marriage ceremony may lead to greater instability of adjustment and crises later on. Primitive tribes often do a far better job of ritualizing adolescence, menopause, and old age than do modern industrialized cultures. Thus, adolescence and menopause in primitive cultures appear less problematic. Smooth transitions are facilitated by cultural ritual and sacramental celebration.

The third, and perhaps the most important, circumstance that makes life transitions into crises is when these transitions occur out of normal developmental sequence. Widowhood is a much greater developmental crisis at 40 than at 80. Menopause may be a crisis at 30 but is often a welcome fact of life at 55. The death of a child is always a crisis because it runs counter to adult development.

Before turning to empirical evidence, I must remind the reader that the model I have presented must be taken with a grain of salt. Who can be sure that Narcissus was unhappy? The lilies—and narcissi—of the field toil not, neither do they spin. Put differently, it is not that failure to master such psychosocial tasks is bad, as much as that mastery of developmental tasks, as in nature, bears fruit. In this regard the Eriksonian model of psychosocial development is different from Jean Piaget's model of cognitive development, Jane Loevinger's model of ego development, and Lawrence Kohlberg's model of moral development. First, the model depicted in Figure 4 represents functional, not structural or cognitive development, and pre-ordered sociobiological development at best plays only a facilitating role. In individual cases, stage sequences may be altered. In contrast to the Eriksonian model in Figure 4, for Piaget, Loevinger, and Kohlberg each new ego stage not only emerges in an invariant sequence but also is a "better" developmental stage.

There is another very clear difference between what Piaget, Loevinger, and Kohlberg call ego maturation in their models and what is implied by my more psychosocial Eriksonian model. The model in Figure 4 is a model of psychosocial behavior, and it reflects affective more than cognitive integration. Psychosocial development is far more vulnerable than cognitive or moral development to social and interpersonal influences, and psychosocial development depends more upon the internalization of role models than do the developmental models of cognitive psychology.

A third difference is that the Eriksonian model reflects performance rather than capacity. In Kohlberg's, Loevinger's, and Piaget's models, people are judged by what they say. In Erikson's model they are judged by what they do.

Empirical Evidence for Adult Ego Development

There are many possible objections to the model I have presented. For one thing, my supposition that mastery of career specialization is a prerequisite to the capacity for care would seem to contradict the folk wisdom that career success interferes with both intimacy and social responsibility. Why should a selfish task like the building of a career serve as a link between a loving task like interpersonal intimacy and a selfless task like generativity? To many, a generative tycoon may seem to be an oxymoron.

Furthermore, are not career consolidation and generativity only relevant to upper-middle-class technocrats? What chance does a high school dropout or a person tied to an assembly line have to be generative? Also, do not women have to master the tasks of caring for the next generation (generativity) *and* career consolidation *and* getting along with a significant other (intimacy) all at the same time? How can I document that Lightfoot's three options, intimacy, career consolidation, and generativity, occur in sequence?

For such a theoretical construct to be tested, studies of random lifetimes are essential. Thus, access to the prospectively studied lives of the College, Core City, and Terman subjects was a necessity. But as I try to identify the specific criteria that allowed raters to decide whether individuals had mastered a given developmental task, thoughtful readers will have further objections. Will not empirical definition of developmental tasks concretize Erikson's elegant, if platonic, language? Will not such definitions sacrifice cultural universality and clinical depth? Certainly, my arbitrary selection of developmental tasks must be viewed in cultural context; other tasks would be more appropriate to other cultures and other historical epochs. Nevertheless, if my concrete definitions of tasks cannot always be applied to other cultures, nobody at all can be classified on the basis of platonic abstractions. Research, like politics, is the art of the possible.

For example, I argue that marriage in an interdependent fashion for at least a decade is evidence of mastery of the developmental task of intimacy. Certainly, ten years of happy marriage is a criterion relevant to many lives in the twentieth-century United States. However, for those in stable homosexual relationships, or in cultures in which marital bonding is unimportant or postponed until late in life, or in highly interdependent institutions like monasteries where rules for communal living take the place of dyadic bonding, criteria for intimacy other than stable marriage would have to be devised. Across cultures, after all, marrying for love has been the exception rather than the rule.

Again, my choice of ten years to indicate mastery of the task reflected a commonsense reductionism designed to help raters reach a black-or-white decision. On the one hand, nothing lasts forever; and on the other hand, ten years seems enough time to distinguish the "real" from the "illusory." However, truth would have been as well served had I chosen eight years or fifteen years as a criterion. Indeed, a problem of selecting so long a time period is that mastery of the next task was begun long before the present one was complete. Also, in a few cases the tasks were not completed in the predicted sequence. For example, in the College sample, 31 percent of men were involved in career consolidation and 10 percent in generativity before intimacy was achieved. *Selfish* career consolidation, however, always preceded *selfless* generativity for the Terman women as well as for the College men.

Before a model of adult development can be taken seriously as a psychobiological process, it must be subjected to four empirical tests. First, if adult development is to be conceived as a psychobiological process then it must conform to biology, and neither to social mores nor to chronological age. This means that, as with shaving and menstruation, not everybody will reach a given stage at the same chronological age. This is in sharp contrast to models like Daniel Levinson's, which assign great importance to chronological age, and to societal models that ordain everybody over the age of 16 an automobile driver. In addition, if adult development is a psychobiological process, it should continue throughout life. As Figure 5 suggests, even as the College men reach age 60 some are still mastering tasks left unfinished earlier in life. The careers of some of the culturally hobbled Terman women blossomed at 65 or 70.

Second, if a psychobiological developmental model is to be taken seriously, it must be generally the same for women as for men, and it must be relatively independent of social class, educational opportunity, and intellectual capacity. One of the great limitations of Jane Loevinger's very useful and sophisticated model of adult development is that its assigned ego levels are affected by the subjects' verbal intelligence and education. It is encouraging that recent interview data, summarized in Table 10, suggest that the College men, the Core City men, and the Terman women, in spite of differences in sex, education,

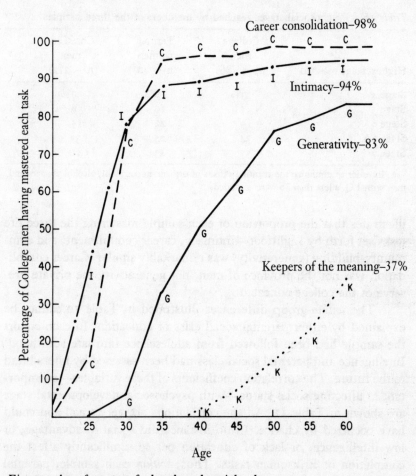

Figure 5. Age of mastery of selected psychosocial tasks.

verbal intelligence, and social opportunity, did not differ greatly in level of Eriksonian development.

Indeed, the selection bias involved in the selection of the three cohorts makes the differences observed *between* cohorts appear trivial. The Terman and Core City children were selected from whole-classroom samples in grade school; any schoolchild was eligible for inclusion. In contrast, each man in the College sample had to have been mature enough to go away to and gain admittance to a selective college. Then, from that elite sample, the College sample was further selected by including only the healthiest sophomores. Nonetheless, Table 10

Table 10. Psychosocial stages reached by members of the three samples

Highest stage reached	College men (n = 186)	Terman women (n = 40)	Core City men (n = 212)[a]
Stage 4	3%	0%	7%
Stage 5	5	10	4
Stage 6	3	22	15
Stage 6A	34	25	33
Stage 7	55	43	41

a. In order to minimize the stunting effects of organic impairment, alcohol abusers and men with I.Q.'s less than 80 were excluded.

illustrates that the proportion of each sample mastering the three life tasks set forth by Lightfoot—intimacy, career commitment, and community-building (generativity) was remarkably similar. Career consolidation was not the province of men, nor generativity the private preserve of the college educated.

The *within*-group differences illustrated in Table 10 cannot be explained by either parental social class or education. In each cohort the sample had been followed from adolescence into late adulthood. Intelligence and parental social class had been assessed by raters blind to the future. The correlation coefficients of these variables—so important in affecting social status—with psychosocial developmental stage are shown in Table 11. All the correlations are very small and could have occurred by chance. In no instance did social disadvantage, or low intelligence, or lack of education per se significantly affect the completion of Eriksonian tasks. Thus, *within* each sample, parental social class and the subjects' own intelligence and education did not affect the attainment of generativity. This is surprising, because normal growth and development require privilege and protection. Nevertheless, Table 11 suggests that the sources of individual differences in adult maturation seem to come from within and to reflect intrapsychic development as much as a simple response to social environment.

However, the developmental tasks are not entirely immune to social pressure. An impoverished, diseased, totalitarian, or prejudiced society will inevitably dim the bright future that Lightfoot proffered to Swarthmore graduates. And additional data given in Table 11 does suggest that a warm childhood environment facilitates adult development. The quality of each Study member's relationship with each of his

Table 11. Independence of psychosocial developmental stage from social class, intelligence, and education

Background variable	Terman women (n = 85)	College men (n = 187)	Core City men (n = 277)
Parental social class	.05	.06	.04
I.Q.[a]	.01	.00	.09
Years of education	.15	n.a.	.12
Warm childhood environment	.10	.24***	.17***
Warm relationship with mother	.09	.18**	.14**
Warm relationship with father	.21**	.21**	.06

**p < .01; ***p < .001.

a. The Army Alpha was used for the College men, the Stanford-Binet for the Terman women, and the Wechsler-Bellevue for the Core City men.

or her parents was assessed by asking raters blind to the subject's adulthood, "Was the parent-child relationship conducive to the development of basic trust, autonomy, and initiative?" These three traits were selected because they constituted the criteria for Erikson's first three proposed stages of development. In each of the three samples a warm childhood environment predicted psychosocial maturity.

The third test of my model was to demonstrate that adults do develop in orderly fashion. If, as I suggest, the adult developmental tasks must usually be mastered in sequence, then adults who love their work should first love their spouses; and those adults who care for others should be those most competent at and best compensated for their work. At least statistically, the tasks of intimacy, career consolidation, and generativity should have to be mastered in order. Both the College data presented in Figure 5 and the Core City data presented in Table 12 offer evidence for sequential mastery. By late midlife, not everybody had mastered intimacy or even managed to live independently, but virtually everyone placed at a given "stage" had mastered the tasks set for the preceding "stages."

The purpose of Figure 5 is to illustrate both that the percentage of individuals mastering each task increases over time and that mastery occurs in the expected order. As time passed, the percentage of the College men mastering each task increased. The figure was constructed by a rater who read through the several-hundred-page chronologically ordered dossier assembled for each College man. The subjects had responded to identical questionnaires at roughly the same age. Even the face-to-face interview protocols were semistructured. Thus the data sets on which individuals within a given cohort were compared were very similar. Each time a rater found an item or a quotation that illustrated clear mastery of or failure at a stage/task, this evidence and the subject's age at the time were recorded. When the rater had found enough evidence to feel confident that a given task was completed, no more evidence was sought for that task. The age of task completion was estimated from averaging the ages at which the items leading to adequate evidence were recorded. However, task mastery had to last ten years to be regarded as definitively achieved. Figure 5 presents graphically the ages at which the College men were estimated to have completed a given Eriksonian task. The evidence for the sequential completion of intimacy, career consolidation, generativity, and keeper of the meaning was clear for a majority of the sample. Of the 77 men who mastered generativity, 57 (74 percent) first mastered intimacy, then career consolidation, and only then generativity.

The data for the Terman women were equally suggestive. Of the 17 Terman women who attained generativity, 11 had first mastered intimacy, then career consolidation, and only then generativity. Four women mastered two of the stages at about the same time, and only 2 of the 17 women mastered the tasks of intimacy, career consolidation, and generativity in some other order.

Table 12 examines the Core City men's sequential mastery of the three developmental tasks. It is a difficult table and requires some attention. It contrasts the subjective, clinical holistic judgment of two raters with the objective presence or absence of discrete but reductionistic criteria. Thus, the table identifies 121 men who were judged on clinical grounds to be generative. Of these men, 70 percent also met two or more of the three independently coded criteria chosen to provide a black-and-white definition of that ineffable virtue, care: (1) enjoys adolescent children, (2) participates in volunteer activities, and (3) has generally warm relationships with other adults. Of these 121 generative men, 88 percent had also met three or more of the Calvinistic, Babbit-like criteria for career consolidation: (1) not more than one year of unemployment, (2) likes his job, (3) steady job improvement over the past two decades, (4) same employer for ten years, and (5) has not been chronically unemployed or had more than four jobs in the last decade.

Table 12. Percentage of Core City men assigned clinically to Stages 6–7 who mastered a majority of objective criteria reflecting Stages 6A and 7

	Adult life stage achieved (clinical assessment)		
	Intimacy (6) (n = 75)	Career consolidation (6A) (n = 126)	Generativity (7) (n = 121)
Mastered 3–5 Stage 6A criteria[a]	32	68	88
Mastered 2 or 3 Stage 7 criteria[b]	15	22	70

a. Criteria were (1) not more than one year of unemployment, (2) likes his job, (3) steady job improvement over past two decades, (4) same employer for ten years, (5) has not had four or more jobs or been chronically unemployed in last decade.

b. Criteria were (1) enjoys adolescent children, (2) participates in volunteer activities, (3) object relations in top two-fifths.

In contrast, of the 75 men judged on clinical grounds to have mastered only intimacy (that is, they were good at loving their wives but not their jobs), only 15 percent met at least two of the criteria for generativity. These findings lend support to my hypothesis that Lightfoot's three choices bear some kind of sequential relationship to one another. Career consolidation seems an important precondition of generativity. For developing the capacity to love without the capacity to work did not permit the capacity to "care" to become evident. The job stability and job contentment of the 121 men clinically judged to be generative were actually greater than those of the men who were judged to have mastered only career consolidation. Whereas, of the 126 men who were judged on clinical grounds to have achieved career consolidation but not generativity, only 22 percent had met the objective criteria for generativity.

A fourth test of any developmental model is that it achieve a reasonable degree of rater reliability and predictive validity. In general, the stage levels reported in this chapter were estimated from rater consensus. When individual ratings by independent judges were correlated with one another, a correlation of .6 was obtained. This reflects an acceptable, but rather modest, level of reliability. Table 13 shows correlations between the major outcome variables of the Study of Adult Development and Erikson life stages. (The Erikson stages were treated as a 5-point variable: 1 = Stage 4, 2 = Stage 5, 3 = Stage 6, 4 = Stage 6A, 5 = Stage 7.) Most of the variables in Table 13 were

Table 13. Correlations between maturity of psychosocial stage and major outcome variables

	Terman women (n = 50)	College men (n = 187)	Core City men (n = 277)
Concurrent variables			
Maturity of defenses	.48	.44	.57
Global mental health, age 40–50	.48	.65[a]	.77
Job success, age 40–50	.59	.50	.40[b]
Marital satisfaction, age 40–50	.33**	.42	.53
Job enjoyment, age 40–50	.54	.38	.41
% of adult life employed	.10 (n.s.)	n.a.	.40
Children's outcome at age 30	n.a.	.29	n.a.
Creativity	.47	n.a.	.14 (n.s.)
Predictive validity			
Life adjustment at age 77	.47	n.a.	n.a.
Life adjustment at age 65	.58	.34	n.a.
Life satisfaction age 65	.56	.29	n.a.

**p < .01; n.s. = not significant; all other correlations significant at p < .001.
a. On a subsample of 88.
b. Adult social class substituted for job success.

measured contemporaneously with assessment of Erikson life stage—at age 47 for the College and Core City samples and between 50 and 60 for the Terman sample. Although the match is not perfect, Table 13 suggests that the psychosocial development correlates highly with maturity of defenses. However, in contrast to the case for psychosocial development in Figure 5, there does not appear to be consistent maturation of defenses after age 30. In late midlife, for every cohort member who seemed to use more mature defenses, there appeared another whose adaptive style seemed less mature. The reasons for decline in ego maturity were usually alcoholism and organic brain damage.

Three life variables for the Terman women were assessed many years after psychosocial maturity was established: life adjustment at ages 65 and 77, and life satisfaction at age 65. Of the 17 Terman women who at age 60 were called generative by a rater blind to the future, 100 percent were seen as adapting to old age well at age 77 by a rater with no information about the past. Of the 23 Terman women who did not meet criteria for generativity at age 60, 39 percent did not meet independently rated criteria for adapting well to old age at 77. For the College sample, psychosocial maturity (Erikson life stage) at 47 correlated with an r of .34 (p < .001) with objective adjustment to aging at age 65 and correlated with an r of .29 (p < .001) with the men's own subjective satisfaction with their current lives in late midlife.

In summary, the developmental model outlined in this chapter is based on Erikson's extraordinary generalization that "the human personality, in principle, develops according to steps predetermined in the growing person's readiness to be driven toward, to be aware of, and to interact with a widening social radius."[35] Yet despite my own enthusiasm for this particular model, I must remind readers that there is no model for conceptualizing developmental change over the life span that commands consensus. Indeed, all existing models of adult development are methodologically flawed. Most such models either are theoretical like Erikson's, or are derived from cross-sectional data, or are retrospective like Daniel Levinson's. Even the four major longitudinal studies of adults that have survived through the entire adult life span—studies of the cohorts from the Institute of Human Development at Berkeley, the College and Core City cohorts from the Study of Adult Development at Harvard, and the Terman women drawn from Terman's cohort of gifted children at Stanford—are all methodologically flawed. First, they are drawn from a profoundly restricted sampling of humanity. Thus, before the evidence of this chapter can be considered more than suggestive, the findings must be confirmed in other American ethnic groups and in cultures other than American. Second, the longitudinal studies are confined to narrow birth cohorts. The study of a single birth cohort cannot distinguish developmental change from secular or historical change. Third, the studies are flawed by their outdated methods of data collection. Indeed, the two longitudinal studies of adult development that have adhered most carefully to methodological precision, those by Warner Schaie[36] and Robert McCrae and Paul Costa,[37] have found very little evidence for adult development. Thus, proving that the orderly changes that Eriksonian optimists like me have ascribed to adult development really occur will require further experimental controls. Historical change must be controlled. Culture and geography must be controlled. And so must the investigators' unwarranted hopefulness about the capacity of human nature to develop.

Thus, it seems appropriate to close this chapter with Erikson's warning: "The assumption that on each stage a goodness is achieved which is impervious to new inner conflicts and to changing conditions is, I believe, a projection . . . of that success ideology which can so dangerously pervade our private and public daydreams and can make us inept in heightened struggle for a meaningful existence continuously, even as the body's metabolism copes with decay."[38] Biology is process, not task completion. Intimacy is not achieved once and for all, and the seeds of love must be eternally resown. Career consolidation without continued productivity leads to rigidity and stagnation; and more than any other life task, care reflects process—a process that must be eventually relinquished, even as the letting go and renunciation of advancing age become linked with our capacity for wisdom.

7

Life Histories

Basically, clinical psychology as a research discipline is the study of lives or of life careers.

Lawrence Kohlberg

This chapter and the next will illustrate the forces that the ego must master in order to permit growth and creativity. First, let me flesh out Erikson's model of adult growth with detailed life histories from the Study of Adult Development. Since we are too apt to view the search for intimacy as a female quest, the search for career consolidation as a male quest, and the search for generativity as a quest only for the educated and privileged, I shall try to circumvent such stereotypes. Men will illustrate the quest for intimacy; women the quest for career consolidation; and a Core City man the mastery of generativity.

The Failure of Adult Development

What if one never chooses to climb the spiral staircase described in the preceding chapter? What if one tries to remain a grammar school girl forever? Eliza Young was a woman who mastered none of the tasks of adult life and yet was without mental illness. Alone and lacking in confidence most of her adult life, she nevertheless remembered herself as "perfectly happy in a small town up to age 12 . . . In elementary grades I was the favorite storyteller of our room. From age 7 on I put myself to sleep making up stories but *not identifying myself with the heroine* . . . In college, I had my first proposal, my first real story writing; I first fell in love as a college senior." But Young never published the story and nothing further developed from her proposal or her "first love." Heaven forbid that she identify with heroines.

Young's father was vice-president of a midwestern university, and her less gifted siblings went on to enjoy distinguished academic careers. When Young was 27 her mother wrote to the Terman study that her daughter was diffident, standoffish, and "we feel she has not measured up to what we had expected." Until age 40, Young lived at home with her parents and worked in a library. Occasionally she sent short stories off to magazines and almost, but not quite, got them published. In her head she was a socialist, but her only tangible civic activity was giving money to the Community Chest. All her life she supported herself through her library work, but she did not feel that work was a vocation, nor did she ever acknowledge that her work was satisfying.

When Eliza Young was 39, her mother died. But unlike the case of her College counterpart Algeron Young, to be described in a few pages, this death was not a stimulus for fresh growth. Instead, she told the Terman study, "I finally answered the innumerable notes of sympathy and tribute. As the only child living at home, I have many adjustments to make." When she looked back, she saw herself as "slow in learning how to dress, dance and chatter" and "more bookish, creative, peculiar" than other children. "I had to learn to conceal it [her creativity], practice it privately or divert it to group activities like storytelling and editing . . . I joined the Army and the war, saw Paris, danger, and romance . . . home 'till Mother's death last year, now off to Tucson . . ." However, when compared to the World War II experiences of other Terman women, Eliza Young's Parisian adventures appeared rather tame.

At age 44, while remodeling and furnishing her house, a first real effort at independent (Erikson Stage 5) living, Young became ill with nervous fatigue and developed neurodermatitis. "Doctors cured my ailments," she wrote, "advising bland diet and freedom from strain." Yet perhaps no woman in the study had attempted less or suffered less conventional stress. At age 45, when asked about her publications, Young wrote to the Terman study, "Extracts from my annual library department report were printed in the daily paper." At age 50 her principal hobby was "collecting Victorian male children's stories . . . very inspiring and soothing in an atomic age." Vacations were spent entertaining friends and "collapsing" on a beach nearby. Although she did have a pet cat, she maintained no contact with her nieces or nephews.

Asked at 63 how she now felt about her life's work as a librarian, Young wrote, "I dislike it"; and she used her minimal heart disease as justification for early retirement. Although she admitted there were parts of her job that she had liked, even at 63 she felt no real identity with it. She refused to answer Terman study questions about her joy in living and satisfaction with work. Instead, she responded, "I am supposed to be in a new edition of *Who's Who of American Women,* but I did not buy a copy so I am not sure."

Still a "liberal" after her retirement, she described herself as a participant in Common Cause. But her activity in this citizens' group was only to read what they sent in the mail. In similar fashion, she wrote that she participated in the local symphony society. Her participation: attending their concerts. Her principal focus in late midlife was, "I must keep well, avoid stress, worry, and high blood pressure, and care for my body sensibly." God forbid that she identify with heroines—or even with ordinary adults.

There was no medical, social, or economic reason why this gifted child never grew up. At no point in her life did Young evidence serious distress or symptoms that met accepted criteria for mental illness. She did answer yes to the questions "Does some particularly useless thought keep coming into your mind to bother you?" and "Are you troubled with feelings of inferiority?" Certainly, indecision, doubting, worrying, and neurasthenia characterized all of her personality questionnaires. Thus, she might have met diagnostic criteria for obsessional neurosis; but so did Charles Darwin and Florence Nightingale. Eliza Young's life illustrates the lives of roughly 10 percent of the members of each of the three cohorts who, as noted in Table 10, for most of their adult lives were unable to master any of Sara Lawrence Lightfoot's three commitments: to a family, to a career, or to community-building. Commitment to a widening social radius requires ego development that Eliza Young lacked.

Intimacy

A few months before he embarked on what would be a forty-year commitment to marriage, Bob Browning, a College subject, wrote to the study of his own ambivalence about intimacy. On the very cusp of mastery he was aware of the fact that "something held me back":

It would probably be better if I talked this over with the Grant Study counselor rather than rambling on as I am going to. In the last three years I have seen most of my friends take the step. Like the few remaining bachelors I know, I don't know just why I haven't . . . one of my best friends, I think, married because it would be more comfortable and he was feeling left out because all his other law school friends had wives. This is a stupid reason. I don't enthuse over their married life.

I have several friends who have married just because they want a particular girl for their partner and companion in life. They, I think, are the happiest, and them I envy and admire.

As for myself, marriage is an institution which holds few charms. Being married to the right person is my supreme desire. I should very much like to be married for this, and no other, reason.

I am seeing almost daily a girl I think is very close to the right person. She has much of what I want in a wife, such as vitality, intelligence, fondness for me, sense of humor, and health. She likes my friends and family . . . yet I am not ready to ask her to marry me. Gad, I wish I knew why. It may be my lifelong desire always to be looking for greener pastures is the trouble . . . I wonder if there isn't someone who would have all the qualities and perhaps more of some.

Anyway, this bothers me considerably and is the paramount problem of my young life at the present time. I can see very clearly being happily married to Elizabeth, but something—what I don't know—holds me back. I'd give a bucketful to know. This I do know—for three months I have seen her almost constantly and have yet to want to leave her in the evening, even after spending three full days over New Year's with her. If the Grant Study could give me any insights into this strange part of me, I would be most pleased and very grateful.

Not surprisingly, the Grant Study had little to contribute; but maturity and the passage of time allowed Bob Browning to give up looking for "greener pastures." His ego soon harnessed "the mixed conflicting emotions that rise up in us like volcanoes," and without further ambivalence, he married his Elizabeth.

In contrast, Algeron Young, another member of the College sample, did not achieve intimacy until late in his life. In mid-adulthood, like Eliza Young, he epitomized self-absorption, not career consolidation, and stagnation, not generativity. His mother had described him as "a grown man when he was two years old"; yet when he was grown up, Young remained a perpetual boy.

In college, Young wanted to become an automotive engineer. Instead, in thirty years he never rose beyond a low-paying position in a White Plains heating and plumbing firm. This was in spite of a socially privileged mother and a private boarding school education, and in spite of both intellectual gifts and psychological stability that were deemed superior to those of most of his classmates in the study. Young's occupational responsibility—installing furnaces—never changed. He took pleasure in his job only because, as in childhood, he could build things. He told his interviewer in detail and with real enthusiasm about furnaces, but he did not communicate a sense of responsibility for the other people with whom he worked or pride in or commitment to his work role.

Evidence that Young had not dealt with career consolidation is illustrated by his questionnaires. At age 29 he wrote, "The brevity of my answers leads me to believe that my life must have been pretty substandard. It still may be . . . my fondness for my current work has grown less. I seem to be stuck in a rut." At 46, when far less socially privileged and less intellectually gifted classmates were firmly established in the upper middle class, Young still worked for his plumbing firm and wrote, "I feel deeply inadequate . . . I have always felt that I could never sell myself." At age 50, Young was unpromoted and discontented. He still worked twelve hours a day and often on Saturdays. He complained that his work involved the "same old rat race." And at 58, when asked what contribution he had made that would benefit others, he replied, "If there is one, I can't imagine what it would be." He continued to lack commitment and contentment. At age 60, after thirty-five years of work, what he liked best about his job was "the good benefits and the lack of stress."

But Young had not sacrificed success in the workplace in order to maintain rich human relationships. The study anthropologist noticed that Young at age 29 was still "closely tied to his mother, unwilling to make new associations." At 49 he was still unmarried and living only a few blocks from where his parents had lived. His life revolved around his pets, not his relationships with people. He was too busy for the latter. "Catering to six cats," he assured me, "can be a big affair." Like Eliza Young, Algeron Young found commitment to a widening social radius too taxing for his ego to bear.

Nor did Algeron Young ever come to grips with generativity. He perpetually felt too much out of control of his life to involve himself with his community. At 50, his philosophy over rough spots was, "I know I can't be my brother's keeper." However, he tried to be a good citizen and to care for his Westchester neighbors who commuted to work on the parkway. "We try to look out for each other," he told the interviewer, but then added that in his twenty years of commuting he had never actually seen anyone on the parkway except strangers. He had never stopped for another motorist in distress. He then said that one day a drunk had wandered out on the parkway and twenty cars had run over him before anybody stopped. I suspect that Young feared that his world might be equally callous toward him.

It was hard to tell what had stunted Young's growth. In adolescence, both his parents let him down, for both suffered severe depressions. When his father was psychiatrically hospitalized for the first time, Algeron, at the age of 11, stopped believing in God. After his mother became depressed when he was in college, he stopped believing in himself. Yet in the forty years of follow-up there was no evidence that Young ever met criteria for major depressive disorder; he just preferred the certainty and rationality of furnaces to people. My guess—and it is no more than a guess—is that his parents' weakness, not their genes, left him guilty and enraged, unable to take leave of them and unable to absorb what good they had offered him. At age 49, Young could still say, like a 10-year-old boy, "My main interest is in things mechanical."

Certainly, it is not just change in ourselves that drives us to play new roles. The roles that others play in our lives also transform us. Admittedly, such transformation takes place from within and only if we can metabolize, as it were, influential other people. Such maturational change takes place through internalization and identification, not through simple socialization or instruction. (The difference between the internalization of an instruction by another person is the difference between knowing something in one's guts and in one's head.) If internalization fails to take place, or if *things* remain more nourishing than *people*, we fail to grow. Both Eliza Young and Algeron Young lived most of their lives as if they could not let others inside.

At age 50, after the death of a friend, Algeron Young told the study that every time a friend died he lost a piece of himself; then he added, "Do not ask for whom the bell tolls; it tolls for thee." Prematurely, Young had addressed a question that all who survive into old age must answer. How, over the latter course of the adult life span, are losses replaced? How does the ego cope with the death of old friends? We stop growing when our human losses are no longer replaced.

One surprising resource for fresh growth comes from the fact that internalized people and their values are analogous to buried geological strata. Relationships can be laid down—internalized—in one era, covered up for years, and then decades later exposed, in a variant of what George Pollock, a wise psychoanalyst, has called "the mourning-liberation process."[1] Such a process may explain Young's renaissance late in life. In his adolescence Young's parents had been profoundly disappointing, and any earlier contribution they had made to his sense of self remained buried during the first three decades of his adulthood. But then, in late midlife, perhaps with their deaths as a catalyst, Young's parents became a source of identification. Just as in the aging brain the death of neurons may allow the return of old memories, just so in adult life the death of parents may release fresh growth. So it was with Algeron Young.

When Young was in his early fifties, his mother died. A year later he married. For him, intimacy was a developmental task postponed—not abandoned. In addition, for the first time since age 11, Young gave up his agnosticism and returned to the Episcopal church of his parents. At age 60, Young was not just a regular church member but a deacon and also an active trustee of and accountant for an Episcopal retirement home. He donated twenty hours a week of volunteer service to community-building. This man who for thirty-five years had seen his job as "humdrum," valuable only because of its pension plan and not because of its use to others, this man who had concerned himself with cats and heating plants rather than with people, has now been happily married for more than a decade. He is finally playing a sustaining role in passing on a religious heritage that for forty years had meant nothing to him. For the first time, he has used his superior intelligence in order to become the valued treasurer of his church. Young has become an elder at last. To grow, we need to feel enriched by those we have loved. We need to feel gratitude, not envy or resentment.

Career Consolidation

The lives of many of the Terman women illustrated that career consolidation could be fully mastered by women who did not set foot in the workplace. The life of Rebecca Thacher is an example. When she was

11 years old, her mother thought she was most suited for a career as a homemaker. At 12, Rebecca told the Terman study staff she would rather be a housewife than have a career. She graduated Phi Beta Kappa from Stanford, then married immediately after graduation. The biggest change wrought on her by marriage, she wrote, was that "my interests have been tremendously broadened by my husband. He cares very little for music or literature as such, and has taught me the value and fascination of practical interests such as engineering. He always wants to, and usually does, take everything apart."

At age 30 she said she definitely had chosen her life's work. Her ultimate goal was "a home where my husband and children will be free and happy and which they will consider the center and not the boundary of their affections." On the 1940 Terman study questionnaire, she gave her parents' marriage top marks. She checked off that as a child she had greatly admired both her mother and her father, and that she had felt not at all rebellious toward either one. She believed that neither parent had inhibited her independence; instead she said that she enjoyed a feeling of deep affection and understanding with both. (Experience of rating the full lives of ninety Terman women taught us that the women's answers to these 1940 questionnaire queries were generally honest.)

In 1950, at age 40, Thacher gave her marriage the best possible score, a nine. At age 49 she wrote, "My greatest satisfaction and pride is my husband's success. He worked his way through college and has achieved his present position solely on ability." Asked if she was listed in *Who's Who*, she replied, "My husband is listed in *Who's Who*."

At age 62, Thacher checked off that her career had been that of a homemaker and that her choice was "as it was, as I planned it and as I would now choose." She also wrote, "Celebrated fortieth wedding anniversary this year. Grateful for extremely happy marriage, fine sons—both graduated from Berkeley—delightful daughters-in-law, adorable grandchildren." In 1977, at 67, she wrote that she had been married "45 wonderful years to a perfect husband."

At 25, Thacher had said her ambition in life was "to build a home that will be an influence for good in the community, to raise good children, and to live my religion as fully as possible." But if wishes were horses, beggars would ride. She received credit for generativity not for her pious words but because in midlife she chaired the vestry and oversaw the financing and building of a new church in Pasadena.

At age 75, after fifty-four years of marriage, she was asked what changes in her life she would make if she had her life to live over again. "Of course, I would hope to do better," she wrote, "to be kinder—more patient and understanding, more aware of the needs and problems of others. I have had an exceptionally happy life with a perfect husband and many warm relationships with brothers, sisters, cousins and in-laws." A rather selfless life, perhaps, but one that surely illustrated competence, compensation, commitment, and contentment. At 76 Rebecca Thacher remained happy and in almost perfect physical health.

But for most people, the river of life does not run as smoothly as it did for Rebecca Thacher. If life's raging rivers are to drive turbines, they must be neither completely dammed nor allowed to run free. Similarly, the springs of human rage must be channeled and harnessed if they are to release useful energy as opposed to havoc or, as in the cases of Eliza Young and Algeron Young, paralysis. Like loving and grieving, raging also taxes the wisdom of the ego, and the mastery of anger is highly associated with career consolidation.[2]

Let me offer three illustrations. The first comes from my clinical practice, the second from my biography of a Terman woman, and the third from an autobiography of a Terman woman. All three show the psychological and the societal forces that beset these women and threatened to dam—or damn—their quest for gratifying careers.

My patient was a young medical student who burst into my office one morning. In tears, she blurted out that she was overwhelmed with shame. Her background was that her parents ran a small Mom-and-Pop grocery store into which all of their children had been co-opted. High school afternoons and evenings, college vacations and summers were all spent in filial duty working in the business. That my patient had had the temerity to go to medical school, and thus to threaten to escape the family fate, was, to her mind, shameful selfishness, as indeed were all her efforts at self-assertion.

On this particular day, she seemed to feel even worse about herself than usual. With tears streaming down her face, she related the events of the previous day—the first day of her senior obstetrics rotation. She and the obstetrical resident had been caring for a woman about to deliver. The resident had suddenly been called out of the room to assist in an emergency. This had left my patient alone with a woman in the final stages of labor. She had had to deliver the baby by herself! I asked her if her competent and creative act was as exciting as I (recalling my own days as a medical student) imagined that it might have been. She nodded her head vigorously. Her sobs intensified. She had been socialized to believe that self-assertion and independent effectiveness on her part were shameful. But just as part of adult development is to learn that sexual expression is joyful and not scary, just so part of adult development is to learn that effectiveness and victory in the workplace are joyful and not obstructive.

At the end of the psychotherapy hour she was all smiles. After an hour of confessing her shameful . . . I mean aggressive . . . I mean assertive . . . I mean creative . . . misdeed to a clearly cheering audience, her ego could accept the fact that assertiveness and creativity were not quite the same as committing mayhem—even if they used the same primal instinctual energy and provided the same visceral excitement. Delivering one's first baby is one of the most exciting events in any doctor's life and brings her or him dangerously . . . I mean creatively . . . close to playing God. Besides, it was not just from her parents that the medical student needed permission to create.

Collectively, the Terman women repeatedly encountered similar dilemmas. How were they to experience competent, creative behavior as acceptable? How could they publicly own up to such behavior, especially if it was based on intelligence that was already identified as superior to that of their classmates? Especially if until they were 10 years old their mothers had been deemed by a democratic society unfit to vote! Especially if, even at age 75, one Terman woman could not admit to her best friend, also a closet "Termite," that she had been selected over sixty years before for a study of gifted children.

It was not just that the Terman women had been excluded from jobs and systematically underpaid, although that was a part, of course. Rather, I believe that they had also been hobbled by a phenomenon that Matina Horner and her students have elaborated with their research on women's fear of success.[3] Many women—and many men— are not at ease when they are confronted with competitive success. Was the baby the medical student's or the resident's to deliver? Was the medical student violating the taboo of mirror-mirror-on-the-wall in daring to assume the image of a competent adult? Pleasurable competitive competence, like pleasurable sex, requires societal permission and mentoring. Honest anger, not handguns, must be legalized.

I shall use the life of Terman woman Emma Dickinson to illustrate a person who did not master career consolidation. Her father was an electrician who was ill from her mid-adolescence. Her blue-collar household provided her with relatively few books, yet tests revealed that at $8\frac{1}{2}$ she had "the language usage" of someone of age $15\frac{1}{2}$. Her parents considered her sense of humor, her sympathy, and her appreciation of beauty to be her outstanding traits. When she was 10, Lewis Terman, marveling at the balance of her interests, wrote her parents, "This is one of the best reports we have ever sent out."

Although her tested I.Q. was 160, Emma Dickinson could not afford to go to college. At 22 she was receiving between forty and fifty cents per hour as a part-time secretary. When asked about her future career, she replied, "I have no goals except to keep my job and perhaps later to raise a family. These are the only things for which I feel I am fitted." At 27, with "music my most absorbing interest," she was taking night courses in music and gardening. She devoured biographies of Beethoven. But she wrote to the study, "my most marked ability has always been to absorb knowledge. This hasn't a lot of practical value in the business world. During the Depression while job hunting, I nearly died of fright during interviews."

At age 36, when asked for her accomplishments in the area of public service, creativity, and club membership, Dickinson left her questionnaire blank. "I'm really appalled at the blank spaces," she wrote. "In fact I was almost tempted to invent something fascinating to fill in the spaces so I wouldn't sound so dull. However, I appreciate that what you want is the awful truth, so here it is." Her job was buying tools and supplies for a manufacturer of petroleum meters. She received $70 per week in 1950 dollars. Indeed, throughout her entire work career, if converted into 1978 constant dollars, her income never really changed. At age 60 she wrote, "my personal triumphs have been minor and fleeting."

Dickinson never moved out of her mother's house. At 40 when asked if she had encountered any sexual problems, she responded, "No opportunity to find out." After her mother died she married her elderly boss, who lived only for another year. After that she continued to look after her elderly relatives. She certainly never considered her job a career. Developmentally the raters placed her at Stage 4, a master of Eriksonian industry. At age 65, Emma Dickinson, like Algeron Young, became a deaconess of her church; and using her superior intelligence she became an executrix and a conservator of other people's estates. Thus, although single and vocationally unfulfilled, in her modest way she became a keeper of the meaning.

But Emma Dickinson's developmental failures and successes were not unanticipated. At 12 she wrote the following poem:

> The butterfly leads a useless life,
>   is what many people say.
> She does not join the fight or strife;
>   from work she flies away.
> The butterfly does not waste the day
>   but faithfully does her duty,
> She helps the world be bright and gay
>   and she carries a message of beauty.

Let me quote at some length from the book *Forgive Me No Longer: The Liberation of Martha*, written by a Terman woman, Esther Fibush, in collaboration with Martha Morgan, her psychotherapy client.[4] Martha Morgan, though too young to have been included in the Terman study, is, I feel sure from reading the book, of the intelligence level of the Terman women. Both therapist and client serve as examples of the dilemma of young adults confronted by joining the "fight or strife" of career consolidation.

Let Esther Fibush speak in her own voice of a question Emma Dickinson might have asked: "How does a woman handle intelligence?"

> It may sound stupid or insane to suggest that intelligence can be a problem. But it is—for women . . . I used to have a feeling that every time I let my intelligence show—which meant just about every time I let my real self show—no matter how tentatively or distant, I was struck down often by someone who had some kind of real power over me even if only the power to hurt me.[5]

> If there is one main thing that women's liberation is about, it is about the intelligence of women and the need to set that intelligence free not only in the eyes of the world but also in their own eyes; to free women from their own discomforts and inhibitions and prejudices about their own intelligence so they can begin to use it more constructively for whatever purposes they choose . . . I doubt that men are very often afraid of their intelligence . . . for any superiority a man may have is at least

of potential value to him. He is in no danger of being condemned for recognizing it or for being aggressive in using it.[6]

Like many other women, Martha had had trouble handling
her intelligence. As a child she had not been aware of her
own intelligence but simply experienced herself as somehow
different and rejected. When she began to be aware that she
was indeed very intelligent, she did not know how to handle
this recognition about herself. If she hid it or played it down,
she was denying her own Identity. Yet if she displayed it, she
would offend or alienate others. She had never experienced her
intelligence as something that inspired confidence or won admiration and recognition.[7]

She [Martha] felt that she must never compete; for it was as
dangerous to win as it was painful to lose . . . She would veer
from the frightening thought that she was far superior to
everyone else to the sickening thought that she was no good
at all. To escape this dizzying swing, Martha had turned to
the substitute that is not only permitted but actively encouraged if you are a woman: the love relationship in which a
woman makes herself so indispensable to a man and later to
her children, that she need not compete or achieve in the world
outside her home.[8]

Esther Fibush writes also of her own life:

The circumstances of my childhood within my family and
immediate environment had caused me to develop characteristics of dependence and submissiveness which had their useful-
ness in a society that values women for their "femininity."[9]

As a child there were so many things I could not do for myself, that I could not afford to alienate the adults upon whom I
depended; and so I could not allow myself to say or do anything
that would make people angry at me . . . I walked a constant
tightrope, effacing whatever aspects of myself might upset the
careful balance I was maintaining, hardly daring to breathe at
crucial moments. (It's no wonder that my first overt psychoneurotic symptoms came in the form of breathing difficulties).[10]

When they [my family] fought, I would inwardly scream "I
hate you all! I hate you all!" My fear of other people's anger
was thus in part a fear of my own anger, fear that someday I
would let loose and say what I was really feeling which would

be the end of everything—all the false security and love I had been buying for myself . . . eventually I must have lost much of my ability even to recognize anger for I arrived at a point where I rarely felt myself to be angry at all . . . I used to pride myself on my "good adjustment" meaning of course what was considered to be good adjustment for a woman.[11]

Is it any wonder that mastery of a task that reflects competence, compensation, commitment, and contentment is particularly difficult for men and women who have difficulty expressing anger? For how can such a task as career consolidation be labeled *selfless?* But let Esther Fibush continue.

Sylvia Plath was of Martha's generation, not mine; but . . . I found myself in some kind of identification with Plath. I felt I had retreated from competition into the self-effacing role that was the prevailing notion of womanliness in my day, when what I really would have wanted was to win that competition, as it seemed to me Sylvia Plath had done . . . Her career— except of course for her suicide and her suffering—seemed to epitomize what I would have chosen for myself had I the talent and the drive, and the courage to be aggressive.[12]

Plath's famous poem "Daddy" provides a shared perhaps universal female experience . . . It does for me, and I had a father whom I loved very much.[13]

(In "Daddy" Sylvia Plath had chanted, "There's a stake in your fat black heart / And the villagers never liked you. / They are dancing and stamping on you. / They always *knew* it was you. / Daddy, daddy, you bastard, I'm through.")[14] Esther Fibush then asks, "Where does all this freefloating hatred come from, hatred so ready to attach itself to such a song of hatred so extravagant as to approach psychosis? And in so many women? And in me?"[15] Then, in a therapy hour, she tells Martha, her client, the answer, the moral of career consolidation: "If you didn't have anger and didn't use anger effectively you were nobody, you were nothing, you would be wiped out. But anger used constructively . . . you know, it's creative. You absolutely have to have it, without it you can't do anything."[16] Fibush's point is that it is not that fathers are bad or unlovable people; only that at times it is liberating to feel uninhibited rage toward them.

But the mastering of rage is as delicate a balancing act for the ego as intimacy, and it is a developmental challenge that is by no means confined to women. Only half of the Core City men achieved career consolidation. Those who failed the task were three times more likely to report that they handled anger either through explosive outbursts or by burying it within themselves. In contrast, the men with stable work commitments reported graceful and attenuated ways of expressing anger. College men like Algeron Young, who never achieved successful or gratifying careers, also revealed a lifelong inability to deal with anger. Both College and Core City men with sustained careers were two or three times more likely to have had a mentor than those who failed to master career consolidation. In part, mentoring provides a model of identification and societal permission for assertive achievement. But such an observation still begs the question of why some people find and "metabolize" mentors and others, like Eliza Young, never identify with heroines.

Generativity

In his illuminating book *Outliving the Self*, John Kotre succinctly sums up the task of generativity: "To invest one's substance in forms of life and work that will outlive the self."[17] Although the Neanderthal and the Cro-Magnon had the same cranial brain capacity, Neanderthal men and women died before age 40, while many of their Cro-Magnon counterparts lived into the sixth decade. Was their prolonged life span part of their Darwinian capacity to replace their Neanderthal contemporaries? Did their prolonged life span contribute in any way to the unique development by Cro-Magnon men and women of art and culture? Did Cro-Magnon longevity provide their children with the gift of grandparents? I do not know, but I think these questions are certainly worth wondering about. For the differences by which anthropologists distinguish Cro-Magnon from Neanderthal are identical with those that are central to human development during the last half of the life cycle— religion, culture, grandparenthood, and community-building.

Unlike the Neanderthal, perhaps the Cro-Magnon, in Kotre's felicitous phrase, outlived the self. It occurs to me that the earlier stages in the developmental model I have presented—industry, identity, intimacy, and career consolidation—are collecting processes for the self; whereas the later stages, generativity and keeper of the meaning, appear to be giving-away processes. What do I mean by collecting processes?[18] First, there is a sense of *self* that is collected as the adolescent/young adult achieves identity. Further, there are *interpersonal skills* that obtain from mastering the tasks of intimacy—the abilities to live with, depend on, care for, and yet be oneself with another human being. Finally, during career consolidation (which appears to be a more extensive collecting process), people are gathering *technical skills,* role definitions, awards and achievements—a forging of work-enjoyment and work-competence cemented by commitment. We are tempted to call it selfish when Ibsen's Nora slams the door, when Virginia Woolf acquires a room of her own, and when Rudyard Kipling travels fastest by traveling alone. But in reality such career consolidation underlies generativity. For, once mastered, career consolidation provides individuals with an integrated self from which they can speak with authority, a state from which they can safely give themselves away. As Daniel Levinson suggests, with maturity the acquisitive "dream" of youth becomes the casting off of the elder's "legacy."[19]

What allows the giving-away process to begin, that alchemical process by which the career and the autonomy of others become more important than one's own? Certainly, we cannot give away what we do not have. Many Terman women, like Emma Dickinson, became impoverished by giving themselves away too young, by becoming meal tickets to their parents during America's Great Depression or by becoming nannies to their children before they had developed any skills for themselves. There needs to be a healthy, rational (not "selfish") self-interest that facilitates a lot of taking in—only later to be given back. I do not mean to imply that the care of young children cannot reflect a career; I only wish to point out that children need parents who respect both themselves and their children. Yet to refuse to give oneself away is to risk stagnation—Erikson's antonym for generativity. This, I believe, is the logic supporting his hypothesis that adult developmental tasks must be mastered in sequence.

What triggers the giving away? I suspect that the so-called crisis of midlife is one catalyst. Such developmental unrest, really more a midlife task than a crisis, forces us to look with wonder again at where we are and how we came to be here. In this reassessment individuals take stock, noting what they have and wondering why they do not have other things. It is this dangerous doubt, this reorienting opportunity, that helps the giving away to begin. A second catalyst comes with the "future shock" of having adolescent children that makes a person get out the old lists, the old life-achievement criteria, and decide that the painfully won partnership, the parental authority, the mirror-mirror-on-the-wall approval lose their savor unless shared, unless spiced with the new task of becoming mentor to the next generation. Perhaps part of the stagnation of Egyptian culture was that the rich tried to take their wealth with them. In the last millennium, the rich have left their wealth to the church, to the university, and most recently to foundations. Not the ideal, necessarily, but a step in the right direction. But in the last analysis, if you are filled and overflowing, real "passing on" is effortless and unstoppable.

Consider the case of Core City member Bill DiMaggio. Life gave him far less opportunity than it gave to Emma Dickinson. When he was a child his family was in social class V. He had to share a bed with his brother in an apartment without central heating. His father was a laborer who became disabled when Bill was a teenager, and his mother died when he was 16. With a Wechsler Bellevue I.Q. of 82 and a Stanford reading I.Q. of 71, he completed ten grades of school—with difficulty. As we measure intelligence, Bill DiMaggio was exactly half as smart as Emma Dickinson.

Nevertheless, at an interview at age 47 Bill DiMaggio was a charming, responsible, and committed man. If he was short and noticeably overweight around the midsection, he still retained much of his youthful vigor. His face was expressive; there was a twinkle in his eye; and he conveyed a sense of humor and a healthy appetite for good conversation. He maintained eye contact and answered the interviewer's questions directly and frankly.

By consenting to be a continuing part of the Core City study, DiMaggio told the interviewer, he felt he was contributing something to other people; he felt this "little thing" was important. For fifteen years DiMaggio had been working as a laborer for the Massachusetts Department of Public Works. Several years earlier a position had opened for a carpenter, and even though he did not have any carpentry skills, he had been able to get the position by seniority. He had learned the necessary skills as he went along. Of his work he said, "I like working with my hands." Indeed, he had always enjoyed working with wood; and he told the interviewer that he had redone the inside of his own house, rebuilding some door frames and putting up cabinets. He also took pride in his role in maintaining some of Boston's antique but historical municipal buildings.

Asked how he handled problems with people at work, he said

quite simply, "I'm the shop steward in the union, so they lay off me. I'll stand up to them if I feel I'm right." If he believed certain jobs were dangerous, he would not allow his men to work on them. Under union rules, management would listen to him. In short, he had learned to speak with authority.

Over the last year, DiMaggio's bosses had been trying to get along better with him. Because he had become one of the few really experienced men on the job, he noted, "They depend on me more." Management also depended on him to help teach other men. After the age of 40, I.Q. as measured by a school-oriented test like the Wechsler Bellevue Intelligence Test does not count for much. It is what you have learned along the way that matters.

If he had his life to live over again, DiMaggio said, he did not think that he would do anything differently. And, he continued, "It's only a job. I'm more concerned about my wife and kids. Once I leave work, I forget about it." He was too concerned with family matters to worry about work when he got home. But the difference between Bill DiMaggio and Algeron Young was that at work DiMaggio took pride in his job, enjoyed it, and saw himself as enhanced by it.

"I have had more time for my children than my father had for me," he told the interviewer. He described taking his sons fishing and taking them to all sorts of places as they were growing up: "We spent a lot of time together." His own father—chronically unemployed—had never had time to take him fishing or go out with him very much. In other words, if you need help with community-building ask a busy woman or a busy man.

When asked what he felt his greatest problem had been with his children's growing up, DiMaggio replied with a smile, "Do you have about six months?" Becoming serious, he added, "Being worried about drugs." He knew that his children smoked marijuana, and he said he could accept that. But if both parents seemed somewhat tolerant of their sons' smoking marijuana, they did not let them do so in the family house. They were accepting of the fact that their youngest son had moved in with his girlfriend; they chalked this up to "him being very immature," and they felt that he would get more mature as time went on. A vital ingredient of generativity is hope, but such hope is possible only if one's mind can encompass human development.

At various times, DiMaggio joked with his wife with ease and animation. Indeed, the interviewer was moved by the affection they showed for each other. When DiMaggio was asked to describe his wife, she tactfully left the room. He then yelled after his wife that if she stayed out of the room he would tell all the bad things and not the good things. He then offered the interviewer a simple string of qualities: "sweetheart—very understanding—everything you want in a woman—she loves to talk and argue and I like this." He said that probably what pleased him the most about his wife was her "sense of humor—without it we couldn't have survived." Yet when his wife came back into the room and the interviewer asked "which child was most like him," DiMaggio suggested the oldest, but his wife nominated the youngest boy because "he has your sense of humor."

DiMaggio said what bothered him most about his wife was that she seemed to be smoking more lately, and "I want to hang on to her as long as I can." On family disagreements, he said, "We don't settle them readily, but we don't let them overcome us." He explained that when he and his wife had arguments, they did not last very long. "We don't hold grudges." Again, he mentioned using humor to help take the bite out of arguments and disagreements. He said that they tried to respect each other's opinions and not force their own opinions on the other. Asked whether he turned to anybody in times of trouble, he said, "We turn to each other." His wife chimed in, "Bill is my best friend." Referring to deaths they had had in the family, DiMaggio said, "We try to comfort each other." Commitment, tolerance, and humor seemed to be three key ingredients in a contented, long-lived marriage.

In keeping with Loevinger's penultimate task of ego development, respect for another person's autonomy, DiMaggio said that his greatest ambition in ten years was to see his children living independently. The capacity to accept such a generative balance between care and letting go requires intrapsychic maturation. Being forced to reflect—to observe oneself from a different vantage point—a person begins to pause and wonder again. Such self-reflection can never be decreed by society or culture. It comes from within—as does looking where one is going or learning to walk. But, like walking, respect for another's autonomy is a complex balancing act that develops in its own time.

Bill DiMaggio was an active member of the Sons of Italy. He regularly helped out with Bingo night, and he and a friend regularly cooked for the club's Saturday lunches. DiMaggio said he liked to do the cooking; he liked the feeling that people were happy with his food.

Through the Sons of Italy, he also did volunteer work in community activities. For example, he helped with various club activities for children held throughout the year. In addition, he and his wife had signed up to work for one of the candidates for mayor. Such activities involve a very different sort of psychosocial commitment from the one Eliza Young expressed by sending her check to the Community Chest. DiMaggio was also active in the Council of Organizations, a sort of umbrella organization for all the charitable clubs in Boston's North End. Thus, the socially and intellectually limited schoolboy had matured into a leader of leaders, a wise man, and a keeper of the meaning.

The interviewer summarized his impressions: "DiMaggio maintains a close relationship with, and a healthy interest in, people around him. He is tolerant of those who are prejudiced, but not compromising in his principles. On the whole, he is a quite mature and interesting man." The raters had no difficulty agreeing that Bill DiMaggio was generative. One rater scored him 93 out of 100 on mental health. The other rater scored him 94. You do not need to attend Swarthmore, Stanford, or Harvard to engage in community-building. Nor do you need to choose between generativity and the alternative goals of a distinguished career and family commitments. The lives of both the Harvard professor Sara Lawrence Lightfoot and the high school dropout Bill DiMaggio epitomize mastery of all three tasks. Viewed from the perspective of a fifty-year study, the maturation of human beings becomes as miraculous as the birth of a child.

Just as intimacy reflects a capacity for mutual interdependence, just so generativity involves a capacity for a different sort of reciprocity, one that spans generations. The emphasis of generativity is upon the harvesting of intimacy and career consolidation—the ability to be in an individual relationship where one "cares" for the other's needs and simultaneously respects the other's autonomy. In such a relationship, the mentor can say and feel, "I love what I do, or feel, or have, so much that I want you to have it too—if you want it. And, by the way, there is plenty to go around!"

However, Erik Erikson has noted that "the fashionable insistence on dramatizing the dependence of children on adults often blinds us to the dependence of the older generation on the younger one."[20] In Alcoholics Anonymous, a "pigeon"—a newly recovering alcoholic—is defined as "someone who comes along just in time to keep his sponsor sober." In short, the pigeon in need stimulates fresh growth in the just-beginning-to-be-generative sponsor. By accepting a sponsor's proffered assistance, the AA pigeon provides the giver with a new reason for being. As the child's separateness is recognized and as the parental relationship with the child is reexamined, the parent/mentor begins to marvel at the joy of seeing them whole.

We asked both the College men and Terman women after the age of 65, "What have you learned from your children?" Some such men and women could only relate what their children had learned from them; few such individuals had mastered generativity. For example, asked what she had learned from her children, one nongenerative Terman woman became irritated: "This is like a question book," she snapped. There was only one thing she had learned from her children: "If I had them again, I wouldn't let them move away. I miss them very much." But then she added, I suspect as a rebuttal, "But what have I learned? . . . I've learned to mind my own business." Then she became sad and reflective: "Maybe we were too potent," she mused, and that was why her children had had to move away. Despite intellectual gifts and social privilege, she had accomplished little in her life beyond a demonstrated ability to spend money tastefully.

Other nongenerative women were simply incapable of allowing the role of sharing to be reversed. Thus, one woman repeated the question with astonishment to be sure she had understood it, then told us what her children might have learned from her: "I'd like to think I helped them develop honesty." She asked herself again, "What did I learn from them? . . . I don't think that you can change, it doesn't mean that you don't try."

Some of the answers were sadder still. Asked what she had learned from her children, one woman replied, "I learned that I'm not patient, I'm not kind, I'm not a good mother." She told us that she would find herself getting annoyed when her young children intruded on the time that she had set aside to read. In fact her self-accusation was unfair; it was based on faulty attribution. She was a kind and selfless woman who had brought up two very decent children. But part of ego development is the capacity not only to internalize others but also to take credit for one's own successes. If we cannot take credit for our own achievements, we may feel that we have little to give away.

The saddest answer came from another very unhappy woman. When asked what she had learned from her children, she replied,

"I'm glad I only had one. I'm not the mothering type." In her case, it was true.

The majority of generative Terman women understood and had mastered the reciprocity involved in learning from children. One said that she had grown up without touching, but that both her grown sons felt comfortable coming up to her and hugging her: "I hadn't known what I was missing." Another woman answered that from her children she had learned "freshness of outlook . . . We are each made up of all the people we have come in contact with." In this simple way she summed up the very quality which I believe is most important for an individual to develop ego strength and mature defenses. That quality is the ability to allow the hope, strength, and experience of others inside.

A third woman whose generativity and maturity of defenses were dramatically evident responded to our question as if it offered her an opportunity rather than the annoyance of a "question book":

> I'm still learning. Every time I'm with him [her oldest son] I'm learning more about how to get along with people and how to see something good in everyone . . . that's what I've learned from my oldest son, patience and loving people—find something good in them. From my daughter, I think she's taught me to be somewhat passive, somewhat thoughtful before you speak is good . . . from the third one, this little one that was here just now—she's not little but she's just a baby [age 40] and she said "Mom don't call me the baby." That's why I did it in front of you because I knew what she would say. She is so jovial, so warm. She makes me smile and I have to smile more sometimes than I do because I forget to smile. She sings. She makes me sing with her. I love to sing but I don't do it anymore when I'm here alone. I wish I would. I used to sing when I did my housework. They are all just such an inspiration to me.

"Inspiration," too, is a metaphor for the way ego strength is acquired—by taking people inside.

Keeper of the Meaning

At 57, Andrew Mason—a College subject of few words—was asked if he viewed the world as fit for grandchildren. "Yes," he wrote. "Awareness of problems of food, population, ecology will bring solutions." Two years later, Mason, a former corporate president, reported his new duties: "Chairman of State Chapter of the Nature Conservancy, Chairman of the Planning Committee of the Mystic Seaport Maritime Museum, Trustee of the Rhode Island Environmental Trust." Stodgy, perhaps, for a man who had once shot lions in Africa—but better for the environment.

Being a keeper of the meaning is by no means a male prerogative or a prerogative of those who have careers outside their homes. Katie Solomon mastered every task of the developmental model, and she never wavered from the ambition she expressed at age 26—to be a superlative wife and mother. A Stanford graduate, Katie spent forty years happily married to a husband with only a high school education and fewer intellectual aptitudes and interests than she had. Yet at 32 she wrote, "I'm proud of my financially successful husband, three beautiful children and little home and garden." Her perception at age 36 of her career success was "finding a place in society where one is needed, respected, accepted and loved." There could be no question but that she achieved this career goal. At 78, when asked to describe the achievement that gave her the greatest feeling of accomplishment and pride, she wrote, "hardly a week passes that one or more of my grown children doesn't tell me, 'Mom, I love you . . . We were certainly lucky. We had a wonderful childhood. None of my friends can talk to their parents the way I can talk to you . . . I'm glad you have a sense of humor.'" She valued these comments and her grandchildren far more than her prizes in photography and her published articles. Similarly, although by age 60 she had spent twenty years in the work force, she wrote, "I've done work, but I would not call it a career." Rather her perception of her real career was that she was a homemaker. Like Rebecca Thacher, Katie Solomon said that her career of homemaker was "as it was, as I planned it, and as I would have chosen."

Katie Solomon's mastery of the task of keeper of the meaning was indicated by the following evidence. Between the ages of 64 and 68 she became involved in consumer protection for the elderly, in conservation, and in ecology. Most important, she learned how to transcend what she called her "DAR/WASP upbringing" and to learn from the next generation. She wrote at 68 that she continued her old comptroller job half time but now as a consultant. "My advice is sought and followed, and more than adequately appreciated and paid." She perceived her grandchildren not as a source of emotional support but as a source of pride, a not insignificant distinction. At 72 she became the "unofficial secretary" for her deceased husband's extended family of fifty people, who "have their annual picnic at my son's home." She, too, had become a village elder.

Integrity

Successful mastery of the task of integrity, Erikson's final stage of the life cycle, was not synonymous with having mastered all prior stages, although I am sure that mastery of the other tasks helped the mastery of integrity. The task of integrity may be redefined as *successful aging*— a process that reflects effective reaction to change, to disease, and to environmental imbalance. Ultimately, and most bluntly, successful aging means the mastery of decay. Successful aging necessitates a certain acceptance. Robert Hobson, a gifted British teacher of psychotherapy, illustrated this point in a personal communication to me with a story about Carl Jung at the end of his life. The great Swiss psychologist was asked by a journalist how he felt about growing old. "I am old," Jung replied, "so I be's old. I am not a bloody American."

The contemplation of successful aging forces us to reflect upon human dignity in the face of disability. The current adaptation of one of the Terman women, Lisa Eccles, illustrates what I believe Erikson meant by integrity. For the first seventy years of her life she had shown no evidence of mastering the tasks of generativity or keeper of the meaning. True, she could look back on her past success as a career woman: "I am proud that my real estate clients respect me," she told us, and she described her career identity as "owner of Better Homes Realty." But outside of her immediate family her own mastery of intimacy and career consolidation did not touch many people. Instead, as she put it, "I revel in the achievements of others and am a good appreciator." Then, in 1984, Eccles wrote to the Terman study, "I was 70 in 1981 and was hospitalized in October for three blocked brachial arteries and skin graft surgery. A broken hip in early 1982 and a total hip replacement in 1983 have left me disabled but *not* defeated . . . My accomplishments since then have been to stay alive and alert and to be thankful for all the blessings that have been mine." As George Bernard Shaw is alleged to have said, "Old age is not for sissies."

After her 1984 letter to the Terman study, Eccles's vision of the world continued to broaden. She wrote, "Who has the right to dictate another's spiritual life and beliefs? . . . Religion is like buying shoes; most can be fitted comfortably; some get more peace from going barefoot. But it is important for them to keep their feet clean so that they do not offend others."

She also said, "Some of us are happy and content to sit and chew our cuds like so many Carnation cows . . . Our ability to face up to situations and our capabilities of handling emergencies without panic may also be a gift not to be ignored." Ecclesiastes, the inspiration for her code name, could not have said it any better. When a recent questionnaire inquired about her aims for the future, instead of checking whether it was important for her to "die peacefully," Lisa Eccles, now 78, wrote beside that box, "Who has a choice? Death comes when it comes." Ready for death, she nonetheless checked off her assessment of her current state of mind as "happy." Instead of checking whether it was important for her "to make a contribution to society," she wrote beside the box, "In a minor way I have already done so." Her past retained sufficient meaning for her that she could accept the indignity of her failing body.

Clearly, adult development is not as orderly as embryology. Some individuals, often because of great stress, tackle developmental tasks out of order or all at once. Alexander the Great, General Lafayette, Napoleon Bonaparte, and Joan of Arc were inspirational and generative leaders in their twenties. William Osler, one of the greatest physicians of all time, did not confront intimacy or marry until age 40—well after he had established himself as a brilliant professor of medicine and the most generative physician of his era. Ludwig van Beethoven enjoyed a brilliant and committed career, but never enjoyed intimacy. Genius has never needed to follow rules.

An untimely death, a historic catastrophe, a serious illness can also trigger the generative process of giving away. Such "offtime" events, as Bernice Neugarten describes them, can lead to a nonsequential order of reviewing what has been accomplished, of what has been collected, of how one has succeeded or has failed. Consider Martin Carey, a member of the College sample. He was no genius, and his life was not permitted to unfold in an orderly fashion. There can be little question, however, that he mastered Erikson's developmental task of integrity.

Carey began life as a gregarious member of a close-knit family. Both his parents were social workers in the spirit, if not the letter, of the phrase; and at 13 Martin, too, had made a commitment to a life of service to others. He collected a sense of himself early on, consolidated it, and shared it with discretion throughout his forty-five years in the study. All life events—and this man faced severe setbacks—were moderated by his relationships with people, both on a personal and professional level. At age 23, when asked about his "fitness for his present work (medical school)," Carey wrote, "children fascinate me; I enjoy playing and working with them . . . I get along well with children, enjoy taking the time to amuse them or to circumvent their distrust of doctors; . . . I'm patient enough to do with children what many other people do not have time nor patience to do." Carey identified with what a generative pediatrician might do. "It was not just the career," the rater noted, "but the relationship and the skill in the relationship that came through." In short, prior to achieving intimacy or obtaining a medical school diploma, Carey prompted the rater to remark on his capacity for care. Later, at age 26, when asked what was stimulating or interesting about his embryonic career, Carey mentioned "the opportunity for aid to children through increasing parental understanding." In medical school he wrote that the meaning of his work was, "to make a contribution to the community."

Not only did Carey begin the work of generativity at an early age, he began the work of growing old early as well. At 26 he had already told the study about his "philosophy over rough spots": "That no matter what personal difficulty I struggle with, others have survived worse; and that, fundamentally, there is a force of events which will carry us through even though at personal sacrifice."

Just after completing his pediatric residency, Carey developed poliomyelitis. For months he was totally helpless. At age 33, newly liberated from six months in an iron lung and knowing he would never walk again, he responded as follows to the Thematic Apperception Test (TAT) card that portrays a pensive youth contemplating a violin:

> We start with a young boy, who's been born into a family with, perhaps, talented musical parents. Their driving ambition from the start was the creation of musical talent in their child. We see him as the . . . childhood . . . result of his parents' ambition and the driving force that pervaded their life. His face suggests that perhaps that as a result of illness or accident

he has lost his eyesight. There is a cast to his eyes, the way they are closed reminds you of . . . the classical lithograph of Beethoven after he lost his hearing. The child is still able to produce sounds of beauty from it [the violin]. He uses his fingers to . . . express his feelings and emotions.

To another TAT card, Carey responded:

Here is a young boy who . . . started out in college with brilliant prospects, a bright future but he becomes disillusioned with life, morose, despondent . . . and decides to end his life. He is apprehended in the process of jumping from a tall building. As he does so, he closes his eyes. Before them flashes a panorama of his past life, hopes, aspirations, sadness, of failure. Realizing, then, the agony of being cornered . . . the despondency to end his own life.

    He'll be examined by a psychiatrist and placed in a hospital for therapy. After months, his goals will be altered. After being in therapy a little longer, he'll get what he wants. He'll be able to be of use to society again, to go on to achieve that which . . . in later years will be satisfying.

By age 35, crippled by polio, Carey continued to be of use to society both as a pediatrician and as a teacher. He did not use his pedagogic success as an excuse to withdraw from being a full-time clinician. He shared with his patients the advantages of working as an active clinician from a wheelchair: "Others can get not only professional help but some measure of comfort from my carrying on as if nothing had happened." Mentorship means to show and to share, not merely to tell.

    Nor did Carey's pleasure in teaching come from didactic instruction and from self-aggrandizing *telling*. Rather, he wrote that the nurses and the medical students he taught "seem to respond to increased participation and responsibility, in contrast to the passive roles they often play in our clinics." His success as a teacher came from enabling others; his success came from, as it were, giving the self away, a process that was to be vital also to his integrity, to his successful aging.

    Twenty years later the progressively crippled Martin Carey again expressed the challenge of old age: "The frustration of seeing what needs to be done and how to do it but being unable to carry it out because of physical limitations imposed by bedsores on top of paraplegia has been one of the daily pervading problems of my life in the last four years." But three years later, at age 55, he answered his own challenge: "I have coped . . . by limiting my activities (occupational and social) to the essential ones and the ones that are within the scope of my abilities."

At 57, although he was slowly dying from pulmonary failure secondary to his twenty-five years of muscular paralysis, Carey told the study that the last five years had been the happiest of his life. "I came to a new sense of fruition and peace with self, wife and children." He spoke of peace, and his actions portrayed it. During this time he had "let go" of the stamp collection that had absorbed him for half a century; he had given it to his son. A year before his death, in describing to an interviewer his "risky anesthesia" and recent operation, Carey said, "Every group gives percentages for people who will die: 1 out of 3 will get cancer, 1 out of 5 will get heart disease—but in reality '1 out of 1 will die'—everybody is mortal." Although still only middle-aged, he fully accepted that there is a time to be born and a time to die.

At age 32, Carey had written of his work motivations: "to add an iota to pediatric knowledge, the sum totals of which may ultimately aid more than the patients I see personally." But it takes a longitudinal study to differentiate between real-life behavior and facility with pencil-and-paper tests. That Carey's words were not pious good intentions but rather intimations of immortality was confirmed by what happened when he died. An endowment for a professorship in his name was raised to perpetuate his lifelong contribution to pediatrics. Throughout his life his wife, his children, his colleagues, and his patients had loved him. Now, his professorship lives on.

Martin Carey's life violated the generalization that good physical health in itself has something to do with successful aging. Although late in his life his psychosocial adjustment put him among the most successful College sample outcomes, he died before age 60. But while dying he demonstrated a capacity to make meaning for himself and to maintain meaning for others. Thus, his life suggests not that death and retirement reflect failure but that the capacity to remain productive and generative while alive provides pleasure and meaning to all.

We have seen that the wisdom of the ego has more to do with living than simply with the mastery of conflict. In Jane Loevinger's words, "The striving to master, to integrate, to make sense of experience is not one ego function among many but the essence of the ego."[21]

8

The Ego and Creativity

Four facets may be distinguished in the rich personality of Dostoyevsky: the creative artist, the neurotic, the moralist and the sinner . . . How is one to find one's way in this bewildering complexity? Before the problem of the creative artist, analysis must, alas, lay down its arms.

Sigmund Freud

Butchered to make a Roman holiday," she protested to her diary. "Women don't consider themselves as human beings at all. There is absolutely no God, no country, no duty to them at all except family . . . I have known a good deal of convents. And of course everyone has talked of the petty grinding tyrannies supposed to be exercised there. But I know nothing like the petty grinding tyranny of a good English family. And the only alleviation is that the tyrannized submits with a heart full of affection."[1]

The Victorian diary writer was understandably furious. Her plans to learn nursing at one of London's great teaching hospitals had just been thwarted once again. Instead of pursuing her own career, she was to accompany her father for a course of hydrotherapy for pain in his inflamed eyes. But the writer did not submit with a heart full of affection. Instead she wrote a novella, privately printed, called *Cassandra*. Cassandra, the imaginary heroine, spends her day "Sitting round a table in the drawing room, looking at prints, doing worsted work, and reading little books." When night came Cassandra—and all such women, we are told—must "suffer—even physically . . . the accumulation of nervous energy, which has had nothing to do during the day, makes them feel every night, when they go to bed as if they were going mad."[2]

Instead of helping us to see that such women are mad (angry) instead of mad (crazy), the author of *Cassandra* tells us they are forced to retreat into a dream world. "Is not one fancying herself the nurse of some new friend in sickness, another engaging in romantic dangers

with him . . . another undergoing unheard of trials under the observation of one whom she has chosen as the companion of her dream."
Cassandra seems to have no weapons but the defenses of hypochondriasis, fantasy, and passive aggression; so she, "who can neither find
happiness in life nor alter it," dies. As she dies, she cries out, "Free—
free—oh! divine freedom, art thou come at last? Welcome beautiful
death!"[3]

The author, too, was no stranger to fantasy, masochism, and
hypochondriasis. As early as age 23, she recognized the extent to which
the habit that she termed "dreaming" had enslaved her. "Consoling
visions had come to occupy more and more of her time," writes her
biographer Cecil Woodham-Smith. Sometimes, she "could not control
herself and she gave way with the shameful ecstasy of the drug-taker."[4]
By the time she was 28, "dreaming became uncontrollable. She fell
into trances in which hours were blotted out. She lost sense of time
and place against her will."[5]

Fantasy, however comforting, is a perilous defense. We know
that Tennessee Williams's "dreaming" sister, the model for Laura in
The Glass Menagerie, spent much of her life as an incapacitated schizophrenic. At age 31, the author of *Cassandra* foresaw a similar future
for herself, and in her diary she wrote, "I see nothing desirable but
death."[6] But she was no Sylvia Plath; Florence Nightingale died in
bed at the age of 90.

But how did Florence Nightingale's dreams and conflicts lead her
to the front page of the *London Times* instead of to a lifetime of autistic
reverie? How did her fantasy life let her perform such deeds of glory
as to eclipse the charge of the Light Brigade? What were the steps by
which her anguish led to a creative solution? How could this intractable
hypochondriac treat the sick instead of being sick? How could she find
a real "new friend in sickness" with whom to engage in romantic
dangers?

To find the answers we must examine the creative process. This
examination will show that sublimation evolves developmentally out
of schizoid fantasy and obsessional intellectualization and that altruism can evolve out of hypochondriasis. The charisma of the artist is
never far from the character disorder of the confidence man. Andy
Warhol, André Gide, and Oscar Wilde offer examples of individuals
who bridged both worlds. Like character-disordered individuals, successful artists know how to insert themselves into our very marrow,

until we, too, become afflicted with their torment and share in their desires. But unlike the charlatan, the impostor, and the Don Juan, artists, by penetrating our bones, allow us to join them in their salvation. The sublimation of the artist and of the creative community-builder helps us to make sense of our own experience. We curse the person with personality disorder who makes us weep, but when Verdi and Shakespeare make us weep we thank them for catharsis. How do creators transmute their own bitter poison into our medicine?

Arthur Koestler's cognitive view of the creative process moves us one step toward an answer. Koestler, one of the most thoughtful illuminators of creativity, outlines the cognitive steps that the brain takes in order to have an *Ah!*, *Aha!*, or *Haha!* experience. Koestler divides all creativity into three interlocking domains. First, there is the *Aha!* satisfaction of cognitive science, which consists of a Eureka-like decrease in psychic tension as the key turns in the lock, as the puzzle is deciphered, as the paradox is resolved. Second, there is the *Haha!* surprise twist of humor, which consists of the assertive, lustful collision that makes us shake with laughter and allows us to discharge our pent-up desire safely into the open air as the paradox is stated. Third, there is the savoring *Ah!* of our identification with a work of art, which is the grateful, quiet, oceanic feeling that prompts us to pay good money because sad movies and great opera will make us cry. Koestler's *Ah!* reminds us of how Wordsworth described poetry: emotion recollected in tranquillity. Always, Koestler tells us, with artistic originality, scientific discovery, and comic inspiration, "you get more out of the emergent whole than you have put in."[7] That, of course, is the wonder of sublimation.

In terms of ego psychology, Koestler's definition of creativity comes close to defining the mature defenses. In terms of everyday life, Koestler's definition of creativity is equivalent to putting something in the world that was not there before. But Koestler does not fully explain how purely cognitive creativity could have helped Florence Nightingale. Instead, if we are to chart how her anger, sadness, and lust were channeled so that she could die in bed at 90, we must pay attention to the very issues that Howard Gardner in his explication of cognitive science insisted that he would *not* discuss: "The influence of affective factors or emotions, the contribution of historical and cultural factors and the role of the background context in which particular actions or thoughts occur."[8] Appreciation of all of these factors is essential to understanding both Nightingale's creativity and her salvation.

Before the problem of the creative artist, alas, cognitive psychology is even more helpless than psychoanalysis. Affect and context, after all, are essential to explaining the paradoxical power of the artist's pain to heal. Only by paying attention to emotion, to the historical moment, and to her family environment can we understand the process by which Florence Nightingale achieved immortality rather than the oblivion of a neurasthenic Victorian spinster, or of the Terman subject Emma Dickinson.

For these reasons, I shall depend on Sigmund Freud to help me explicate Nightingale's achievement. Freud, however, conceptualized the artist as a man; readers familiar with his text will realize that I must bend it slightly to allow myself to describe the artist as a woman. I believe Freud also was too narrow in his definition of the artist. Community-builders and scientists are also highly creative and in many of the same ways—thus, my choice of Florence Nightingale.

In his *Introductory Lectures,* Freud begins by noting that "an artist is an introvert"—an introvert "oppressed by excessively powerful instinctual needs." Thus, the artist desires to win honor, power, wealth, fame, and the love of the opposite sex, but "lacks the means for achieving these satisfactions." Consequently, like any unsatisfied person, the artist "turns away from reality and transfers all [her] interest and libido too, to the wishful construction of [her] life of fantasy . . ."[9] By age 26, Florence Nightingale was employing not only fantasy but also reaction formation. She had already begun to fear success because she enjoyed it too much. She viewed vanity, love of display, love of glory as her besetting sins, and at the same time she felt paralyzed. Outwardly, she was capable only of being a good and dutiful daughter, a butterfly leading a useless life.

Freud goes on to suggest that artists are not like other people, for "their constitution probably includes a strong capacity for sublimation and a certain degree of laxity in their repressions . . . An artist, however, finds a path back to reality in the following manner . . . Access to the half-way region of fantasy is permitted . . . and everyone suffering from privation expects to derive consolation from it. But the yield of pleasure . . . is very limited."[10] And so it is. By confiding to her diary her vivid fantasies of passive death Nightingale hardly met the folk recipe for healthy retaliation: "Living well is the best revenge."

But Freud points out that the true artist has more going for her than just fantasy. In the first place, she "understands how to work over [her] daydreams in such a way as to make them lose what is too personal about them and repels strangers and how to make it possible for others to share in the enjoyment of them."[11] This delicate process, after all, is at the heart of the battle that goes on between the guardians of public morals and guardians of free speech. How do we allow others to share in the enjoyment of our autistic reverie? When does pornography become beauty? When does the Old Testament's allegedly hellish perversion of sodomy become the inspired heavenly love epitomized by David and Jonathan? With sublimation, paradox abounds. The mature defenses transform sin into morality, but it is a delicate balancing act.

I remember asking a patient of mine, a schizoid vagrant, how he would support himself when he left the hospital. He told me *his* fantasy. "Doctor, I think I'll write a bunch of letters and then I'll publish them. I've seen whole sets of leather-bound volumes of letters. They are in all the libraries. I can live on the royalties." Of course, it is not that easy. Freud reminds us that only the artist "possesses the mysterious power of shaping some particular material until it has become a faithful image of [her] fantasy." Only the artist "knows how to link a large yield of pleasure to this representation" of unconscious fantasy. Only the letters of artists and politicians—those professional masters of deception—merit publication. Only with charismatic spellbinders do we so wish to identify that we will read their mail. The artist's lack of repression allows other people "to derive consolation and alleviation from . . . sources of pleasure" in the artist's unconscious that have previously been inaccessible to the public. Thus, the artist "earns their gratitude and admiration," and so it was that Florence Nightingale won the gratitude and admiration of the British nation.[12]

Let me trace step by step the way Florence Nightingale found some "particular material" and shaped it into a product that would allow her to enter the hearts of her countrymen. Certainly, Florence Nightingale was an introvert, not far removed from neurosis. As a very young child, she had an obsession that she was not like other people. She saw herself as a monster and believed that "Strangers must be avoided, especially children. She worked herself into agony at the prospect of seeing a new face, and to be looked at was torture. She . . . refused to dine downstairs, convinced she would betray herself by doing something extraordinary with her knife and fork."[13] If her biographers may be believed, Nightingale established little intimacy with her mother. Indeed, she described herself and her sister as being literally starved for love from their mirage-like mother, Fanny Nightingale: "It is no exaggeration to say that we should not have been more alone in any African desert. There is (in both) the appearance of food which disappears whenever you stretch out your hand to take it."[14]

There also seems little question that Florence Nightingale desired honor, power, fame, and the love of men even if she lacked the means for achieving these satisfactions. From her access to her half-way region of fantasy she derived great consolation. Her dreams centered around her suitor Richard Milne, to whom she imagined herself married and with whom she imagined herself performing all manner of heroic deeds. But as Freud suggests and much great poetry illustrates, within the artist there is a "certain degree of laxity in the repressions." Thereby, the artist's "access to the half-way region of fantasy is permitted" to take on an almost, but not quite, psychotic vividness. At age 17 Florence Nightingale, like Joan of Arc before her, had the first of her psychotic-like experiences, hearing an objective voice outside herself speaking to her in human words. "God spoke to me," she wrote, "and called me to His service."[15] Later, as she sat up in bed striving to find a way to escape from home in order to work in a hospital and striving to achieve a state of union with God, Nightingale did not blame God or her mother for her painful life; the fault was her own. Thus, unlike the individual with personality disorder, unlike the psychotic, Florence Nightingale refused to blame others for her dilemma. Deploying reaction formation, not projection, she was convinced that "the difficulties which confronted her were God's punishment for her sinfulness."[16] Creative artists do not project responsibility for their distress any more than do true humorists.

Florence Nightingale's solution was to strip her daydreams of what was too personal about them and might repel strangers. In this way her ego allowed her to shape her obsession with drains and her rage toward her mother until they became a faithful image of her ideal to become a good nurse—until her fantasy of being widely loved and admired became a reality. During her sleepless nights as a young adult yearning for death, she read every book she could find on sanitation and the drainage of human waste. She focused her evenings and her daydreams on what was to be her artistic material: statistics and drains. Good obsessive-compulsive that she was, Florence Nightingale became one of the leading sanitation experts in England. Her passionate interest in performing heroic deeds with Richard Milne became displaced into public hygiene and nursing. The fantasy of a schizoid child became the reaction formation, the displacement, and the intellectualization of an obsessive-compulsive young woman.

But her ego's transformational powers continued to evolve. She learned how to paint pictures with numbers: she was one of the first persons to transform statistics into diagrams. Indeed, she has been credited with the invention of the bar graph. Through a press campaign she used colored diagrams to present to the War Office compelling evidence that most deaths in the army, in either peace or war, were due to preventable disease. And so, "She left the British War Office different than she found it,"[17] and put something in the world that had not been there before. According to Dr. William Farr, the founder of medical statistics, a speech Florence Nightingale gave to the War Office was "the best that ever was written on diagrams or on the Army. I can only express my opinion briefly in [that] Demosthenes himself, with the facts before him, could not have written or thundered a better."[18]

But I am getting ahead of my story. Ten years earlier in 1855, through her family's connections and by persistent scheming on her part, Nightingale was sent to the Near East to organize nursing for Crimean war casualties. Only ten days after the Light Brigade made its tragic charge near Sebastopol, she arrived at the British army hospital at Scutari, near Constantinople, which served as the evacuation site for Crimean war casualties. She found a hospital with no soap, a hospital with only twenty chamber pots and a thousand men afflicted with dysentery. The death rate was 42 percent, virtually all of it from diarrhea. For another thousand men, desperately ill with typhus, scurvy, and infected wounds, she found only unwashed blankets alive with fleas, lice, and maggots.

Undaunted, Florence Nightingale made a "faithful image of her fantasy." Unlike some schizoid eccentric, Nightingale made the world around her accept her terms. In her devotion to public hygiene, she personally supervised the emptying of the holding tubs for bedpans twice a day. Before her arrival they had been emptied only occasionally.

She ordered the excavation of the hospital drinking water supply. It was discovered to have been running through the carcass of a dead horse. She instituted a hospital laundry to wash the soldiers' filthy garments and bedding. Her first purchases were two hundred scrubbing brushes and sacking for the washing of floors. By June of 1855, the death rate had fallen to 2 percent. Florence Nightingale's tangible work of art was a dramatic decrease in mortality. As with her creation of the bar graph, the creativity of science merged with the creativity of art.

In her fantasy, Florence Nightingale called herself the "mother" of 18,000 children, but the reality was that 50,000 admiring young soldiers—and their real mothers back in England—learned to worship the ground on which she trod. It is noteworthy, however, that Nightingale's power came from the context of history, the historical moment in which the *Times* of London invented the modern war correspondent. Nightingale's achievement was not just some cognitive tour-de-force. If the achievements of women mold conditions, so also do conditions mold women's achievements. Thus, the *Times* not only spread the news of her exploits but also financed many of Nightingale's changes through a special fund. Her outraged commanding officer, Colonel Sterling, did not understand this and sputtered, "Miss Nightingale coolly draws a cheque. Is this the way to manage the finances of a great nation? . . . Priestess Miss N., magnetic impetus drawing cash out of my pocket."[19] The men at Scutari called it "Nightingale power."

One of the nurses described what it was like to accompany Nightingale on her nightly rounds at the Scutari hospital. In so doing she helped to create the enduring folk tale of the Lady with the Lamp. "It seemed an endless walk and one not easily forgotten. As we slowly passed along, the silence was profound; very seldom did a moan or cry from those deeply suffering [men] fall on our ears. A dim light burned here and there. Miss Nightingale carried her lantern which she would set down as she bent over any of the patients. I much admired her manner to the men—it was so tender and kind."[20] The men in turn kissed her shadow when it fell upon their pillows. "She taught," said an eyewitness, "officers and officials to treat the soldiers as Christian men."[21] Thus, during the winter of 1855–56, the picture of the British soldier as a drunken, intractable brute to be ruthlessly flogged at the slightest infraction faded away never to return. Nightingale Power and the *Times* worked together.

Florence Nightingale was aware that much of her behavior threatened to repel strangers. "There is not an official," she wrote to her British War Office sponsor Sidney Herbert, "who would not burn me like Joan of Arc if he could."[22] But that was not how it happened. The doctors who initially had violently opposed her came to be absolutely dependent upon her; and Colonel Sterling could only sputter in a letter home, "Miss Nightingale now queens it with absolute power."[23] In Nightingale's own words, she had "toiled her way into the confidence of the officials."[24] She succeeded not because she was feared but because she was useful, and she reshaped her material indefatigably eighteen hours a day. Genius is not only divine inspiration; it is also the infinite capacity for taking pains. As we shall see later, the same ego maturity that allows commitment to career consolidation is essential to creativity.

Finally, after a journey to the battlefields of the Crimea, the formerly and subsequently hypochondriacal Florence Nightingale developed a real illness. She developed dysentery at Balaclava and had to be evacuated across the Black Sea, back to Scutari. The love that she had engendered in the men became still more tangible. A sergeant wrote home that when the men heard of Nightingale's illness they "turned their faces to the wall and cried. All their trust was in her."[25] Her biographer tells us: "All the high officials were at the landing stage to greet her . . . Twelve private soldiers divided the honour of carrying her baggage. The stretcher was followed by a large number of men, absolutely silent and many openly in tears."[26] "I do not remember anything," wrote another observer, "so gratifying to the feelings as that simple though grand procession."[27] Thus Nightingale's illness transcended the agony of those dying of cholera around her and made people grateful to weep. So through the ages has it always been with artistic tragedy. Sophocles and Dickens could not have been any more successful. Even Queen Victoria herself publicly rejoiced at her recovery and, on Nightingale's return, invited her to lunch.

Like any artist, Nightingale was able to transcend reality in order to create legend. I, as a biographer, identify her creative products as reducing a hospital's death rate from 42 percent to 2 percent, inventing the patient's nursing call bell (she had previously invented a row of bells on strings that linked the patient with the nurse's station), and discovering that boring numbers could be redrawn as colored bar graphs. I utter a Koestler *Aha!* at her scientific creativity.

But the legend that preceded Nightingale's return to England—
the legend that leads graduating nurses still to light candles on the
night of graduation—was of a different order. But again there is
paradox. Her own sister and the nurses who toiled directly under her
dominion could see Nightingale as unkind. In contrast, the soldiers
and the British public loved her. For the artist can so alter fantasy,
hypochondriasis, and passive aggression that it is "possible for other
people once more to derive consolation and alleviation from their own
sources of pleasure."[28] The Nightingale legend was concocted from
Koestler's oceanic *Ah!* experience that accompanies true art.

If Nightingale vibrated with anger and vengeance, her vengeance
became creative too. Her passion was not for destruction but for
reform, and thus, as with the creative energy of Gandhi and Tolstoy,
only her immediate family suffered. Her martyrdom and hypochondriasis allowed Nightingale from her bedside to guide—and bully—the
British War Office. If she unerringly brought out the worst in her
family, she brought out the best in the staff at the War Office, who
nicknamed her "the commander-in-chief." Anger, for Nightingale, had
always been expressed by invalidism. Within a month after her return
from the Crimea, she again took to her bed. Her writing suggests the
roots of her anger: "For every one of my 18,000 children . . . I have
expended more motherly feeling and action in a week than my mother
has expended on me in 37 years."[29] As an unloved daughter and a
master of masochism, she noted, "I can hardly open my mouth without
giving dear Parthy [her sister] vexation." And she said of her mother,
"Oh dear good woman, when I feel her disappointment in me, it is as
if I were going insane . . . what a murderer am I to disturb their
happiness."[30] Similarly, when Dr. Sutherland, a member of the British
Cabinet, did not do as she wished, she collapsed and fell in an agitated,
half-fainting state and Dr. Sutherland immediately expressed great
penitence. "Let me tell you Doctor," she wrote to him, "that after any
walk or drive I sat up all night with palpitations . . . Now I have
written myself into a palpitation . . . I have been greatly harassed by
seeing my poor owl [one of her former pets and imaginary friends]
lately without her head, without her life, without her talons, lying in
the cage of your canary . . . and the little villain pecking at her. Now
that is me. I am lying without my head, without my claws and you all
peck at me." But if Dr. Sutherland did as Nightingale ordered, he was
also astute enough to perceive that at the heart of her hypochondriasis

was not just a wish for secondary gain but hostility. He pointed out that he, not she, was the recipient of all the pecking, "and your little beak is the sharpest."[31]

By age 42, Nightingale's rage toward her mother had reached such a point that she took to her bed for six full years. Not until eighteen years later, when her mother finally died, did Nightingale recover sufficiently to make her first personal visit to the London Nightingale School of Nursing to which, from her bedroom, she had long served as an inspiration and consultant. But her "illness" did not reflect impaired biology but rather, like the mother quail's hurt wing, only the results of an ego performing ingeniously. Despite her angry invalidism, virtually every serious question concerning the sanitary administration of the British Army for forty years was referred to Florence Nightingale. Only when she was 86 and increasingly forgetful did the British War Office finally cease sending their reports to her for her opinion.

Creativity in the Terman Women and the College Men

Let me return from the stars to earth and consider the creativity of everyday life in the pooled data from the Study of Adult Development. The British author and psychoanalyst Anthony Storr has cautioned us that "Perhaps creativity is more closely bound up with what might be called a 'dynamic of the normal' than with psychopathology; and maybe one weakness of current psychoanalytic thinking is a failure to make sufficient distinction between normal and neurotic in this context as in others."[32] I would heartily agree. A major purpose of this book, after all, is to stress that much of what we regard as psychopathology is like coughing and fever, simply a "dynamic of the normal." Besides, only one person in a million is as creative as Florence Nightingale. What about ordinary creativity in ordinary people? What about the creativity of every day? To examine this, I will contrast the most creative Terman women and College men with the least creative.

But first, I must put their creative accomplishments in actuarial perspective. On the one hand, we may regard a friend who writes poetry and in twenty years has come no nearer to publication than a rejection slip from the *New Yorker* as creative. On the other hand, we may regard the two Nobel Prize winners Sinclair Lewis and Pearl Buck as not very creative. Thus, in judging creativity, we forget the odds.

Probably not one person in a hundred ever submits a poem for publication, but the chances of winning a Nobel Prize in anything, let alone in literature, are about one in twenty million. Each year in the United States, twenty to forty thousand books are published; perhaps that many people also give individual public musical recitals or exhibit their paintings and sculpture in public galleries. By those odds, over a lifetime, Americans have roughly one chance in a thousand of writing a book or of showing off their art or musical skills in public. If we decide, then, that the Terman and College subjects are in the top one percent, one in ten might be expected to publish a book or to exhibit their art or music in public. The creativity of both the Terman women and the College men exceeded these optimistic odds. Nevertheless, even in these samples of relatively gifted people, creativity must be judged in relative amateurs.

In an effort to study creativity empirically in such amateurs, I shall define creativity as "bringing into the world something that was not there before." For both the Terman women and the College men I arbitrarily defined four categories of creative people. Let us look first at the Terman women. In the most creative category (scored 1 on a four-point scale) were those who won statewide recognition through their creativity. In the next category (scored 2) were those who had won local community recognition (for example, who had published two or more papers, articles, or newspaper columns, or given public musical recitals or art exhibitions, or created a community organization, such as a children's symphony or a social agency). Half of the Terman women fell in these first two categories. The third category (scored 3) included those who had creative hobbies that they kept to themselves. The least creative category (scored 4) comprised those who, throughout their lives, had provided no evidence of sustained creativity of any kind.

I shall contrast the 20 women in the more creative two categories with the 20 women in the two relatively uncreative categories. But before doing so let me offer two portraits: one of a highly creative woman and the other of a woman who, although she could certainly not be called mentally ill, never allowed herself to create at all.

The life of Florence Knight illustrates the close relationship of creativity with altruism and generativity, but her life also underscores what I mean by the creativity of every day. In college and for ten years afterward, she had been interested in little theater and in helping advance the careers of successful novelists. She admitted, "I saw it was more important to support an artist than to do it myself." She next worked as a script editor, and in her thirties she helped to found a pioneering interracial church. As she put it at the time, "I spent most of these last three years in intensive race relations which have helped me work out some of my own problems." As tangible evidence that her creativity was recognized by others, she was honored by being invited to work on the staff at the founding of the United Nations.

In her twenties and thirties, Florence Knight also freelanced, worked as a ghost writer, and composed unpublished short stories. For the next nineteen years of her working life she was a teacher of journalism and English in the Mendocino school system. The counselor, she said, "always sent me the oddballs. I liked to rescue people that others turned down." She served as a judge for an essay contest for California high school writing and was nominated as one of the best teachers in the United States. Many former students, now successful journalists, come back to thank her for her help.

The imaginative and generative quality of Knight's creativity was also illustrated by her playfulness at her high school retirement ceremony. She received not a gold watch but a silver bowl. Her Janusian response was to place her new grandson in the bowl. What better symbol of immortality, of the link between death and rebirth, than to place her newborn grandson in the bowl that was supposed to symbolize her retirement. Five years later she confessed to the Study that "part of my delight with my grandson is watching my son become the kind of father he never had." In many ways throughout her life she had helped to put into the world what had not been there before.

After her retirement, Knight organized a continuing education workshop for imaginative teaching. At age 75 she presented an original and provocative paper. No mere keeper of the meaning, she was still shaking up the stereotyped thinking of 30- and 40-year-old teachers. Her house was filled with good original American art. In her desk drawer was a book that she was writing but that she might never find the time to finish. Florence Knight was not very good at being selfish. To summarize, her creativity was manifested by generativity, by creating both organizations and papers, by appreciating and judging the art of others, and by displaying Koestler's bisociation.

The life of Willa Loman provides a contrapuntal example to that of Florence Knight. Loman had a bleak childhood, a depressed mother, and a brother to whom she was not close. Like her namesake in Arthur Miller's *Death of a Salesman,* Willa Loman lost her father at four and also always felt "kind of temporary" about herself. Only in school was she a stunning success. When she was 12 her teacher described her to the Terman study in very positive terms: she was "bright and level-headed." When she was 18 her teacher wrote that she had "marked leadership, executive ability . . . unusually attractive, winsome personality." Loman's own recollection of school was, "I loved adolescence, I was wildly alive . . . I loved the high school years." She had many friends, belonged to a sorority, wrote poetry, and as an adolescent even published one of her poems. She went on from being her high school class valedictorian to graduate from UCLA and then spend a year in graduate school.

After graduate school, however, Loman's light seemed to go out. Like many a gifted kitten before her, she became a stodgy cat. Having been raised by a depressed mother and in a hellfire-and-brimstone church, she always felt guilty and ashamed. As she put it herself, "Someplace in there I got scared." In college, she remembered, there was a room in the library she could not go into. It was too beautiful— too "overwhelming in its elegance." Perhaps what was missing in her life was internal safety. Perhaps she needed to achieve external safety by taking none of the chances that go with creativity. Bringing into the world what was not there before is a Promethean task that does not suit the timid. At the same time, *most* people are destined to become stodgy grownups, not innovative Bohemians.

There is no evidence that Willa Loman created anything in the next fifty-five years. In a lifetime of hospital laboratory work—a job she obtained by getting the top score on a civil service exam—she never advanced beyond her "peon's job" of washing glassware and counting red blood cells in the hospital pathology lab. As she explained, eventually her job came to be recognized as work that could be done by the educationally handicapped.

During her marriage, Loman and her husband had separate bedrooms. Asked how they depended on each other during their marriage, she said they gave very little to each other emotionally. "We weren't supportive. I would lose myself in a book and he would lose himself in television." Willa Loman is the woman who, when asked what she had learned from her children, replied, "That I am not patient and that I am not kind." Her only participation in community activities was contributing money by mail. She had no hobbies, and during the interview she would admit only to reading magazines and junk mail.

At 50 Loman wrote to the Terman study, "I discovered I had nothing of particular value to contribute to the world." At 60 she wrote, "I have never been a participant." At 78 she began our interview with "I am a phony." Shame seemed absolutely at the core of her being. As she put it, "I am a totally forgettable person."

Yet there was nothing eccentric or inappropriate about Willa Loman. If she had social anxiety, she did not reveal it during the interview. There was no evidence of obsessions, compulsions, phobias, severe depression, or autistic thinking. In 1950 her score on the Concept Mastery Test (a test used by Terman that was analogous to the Graduate Record Examination) was 178, one of the highest in the Terman study; such ability ruled out her having some crippling organic brain disease. Rather, her high concept mastery could only have come from her having also read the serious magazines and well-worn books on her shelves; but she could not tell that to her interviewer.

Her Los Angeles apartment was "absolutely lovely," according to the interviewer: "It was extremely simple. There was no sign that money had been spent—only taste and elbow grease. The floor was without rugs and exquisitely clean. There was a single vase of sunflowers that in their vivid dominance in their corner of the room could have been painted by Van Gogh." However, all of the attractive handcrafts and artwork that decorated her apartment had been created by her relatives. "In summary," wrote the interviewer, "she was a plain, intelligent, and perfectly competent woman." But Willa Loman had never learned to drive a car—or to internalize another person's strength.

Table 14 contrasts the more and the less creative Terman women. Nineteen of the 20 women who had been categorized as creative had either published something or begun a community organization. The single exception was a woman who was a serious amateur painter *and* a community leader *and* a trustee of art museums *and* a serious art collector. The 20 women categorized as less creative included many who had hobbies such as sewing, gardening, pottery glazing, or flower arranging, or who were active in pastimes like dog shows, stamp collecting, or ornithology, or who enjoyed taking courses in art or folk dancing. However, none of these less creative women had ever affected others outside of their immediate families and close friends with their creative efforts.

Table 14. Major differences between the more and the less creative Terman
           women

	Creative (n = 20)	Less Creative (n = 20)	Significance[a]
Basic differences			
Generative	75%	10%	***
Published something	60	10	***
Published a book	25	0	**
Public art or music	40	0	***
Started an organization	55	0	***
Antecedents			
No career plan, age 26	10	30	—
Work satisfaction, age 40	50	20	*
Active outside home, age 45	80	50	*
Poor use of leisure, age 45	30	70	***
Consequences			
Joy in living (subjective), age 60	40	10	**
Adapted to old age, age 65–75	85	50	**
Adapted to old age, age 75–78	65	35	*
Defenses			
Altruism or humor or sublimation a major defense	85	15	***
Sublimation a major defense	55	0	***
Repression not noted	65	40	—
Fantasy not noted	80	50	*

$*p < .05; **p < .01; ***p < .001.$
a. Calculated using the 4-point scale of creativity outlined in the text.

Creativity, putting in the world what was not there before, and generativity, manifesting care for the development of those younger than yourself, are not synonymous. Yet the link in Table 14 between creativity and generativity is obvious. Fifteen creative Terman women and only two of the less creative women met Study criteria for generativity. While there are definite theoretical differences between the creative artist and the creator of social organizations, in fact Lightfoot's community-building and artistic creativity often went hand in hand. Of the 20 women deemed creative, 5 had *both* published or given public recitals *and* started a community organization. Only 2 of the 20 less creative women had ever published anything, and only one had been active in starting a community organization.

When young, the creative women were more interested in accomplishing an active life for themselves outside the home: the creative women were less likely to be without career plans at age 26 and *more* likely to enjoy their job or homemaking at age 40. At age 45 they were more likely to be engaged in some activity—occupational, volunteer, or creative—that took them outside of their homes. The creative women—many of whom had been placed in this category for creativity at work—appeared also to make more imaginative use of leisure time than women who just had creative hobbies.

It is also clear from Table 14 that choice of ego defenses sharply distinguished the two groups of women. Virtually all of the creative women and virtually none of the less creative women deployed altruism, humor, or sublimation as a major defense. Each of these three mature defenses alone was also more common among the creative women. (Significantly, however, these three mature defenses were the mature defenses *least* highly correlated with mental health.)

As Freud would have predicted, repression was less frequently noted among the creative women. Because the numbers are small, however, the differences are not statistically significant. Similarly, as Freud would have predicted, the creative person was characterized by daydreaming made publicly acceptable. Thus, in our sample creative women were noted to use autistic fantasy *less* often than uncreative women. After all, if your daydreams are allowed to become real, they no longer qualify as daydreams. Florence Nightingale became an effective artist only as she abandoned pristine fantasy for involvement in the vermin-infested reality of Scutari.

Table 14 also notes a difference in *joie de vivre* between the two groups of women. In midlife creative women were more likely to have had activities outside of the home; and at 60 they were more likely to express joy in living. Most interesting was the fact that creative women were twice as likely as less creative women to manifest "successful aging." "Successful aging" was measured by a five-point scale with good rater reliability. A score of 5 indicated a woman who at 75–78 enjoyed life, was cheerful, realistic, and open to new ideas, and maintained utility, a sense of humor, and an acceptance of what had been. Florence Nightingale at 80 was still advising the British War Office. A score of 5 also indicated a woman who helped others, was willing to take charge if appropriate, and yet was graceful about her own dependency needs and limitations. If physically ill, she would be a

patient that a doctor would want to have. A rating of 3 on this adjust-
ment-to-aging scale reflected someone meeting only half of the criteria
for a 5. A rating of 1 indicated the kind of elderly person whom doctors
do not like, whom young relatives withdraw from, and who manifests
depression, complaining dependency, or social withdrawal. A rating
of 1 reflected a woman who was rigid, self-centered, and unable to
accept indignities of old age.

Among the 20 most creative women were 9 who achieved their
greatest public success after the age of 60. Such late-life creativity is
in opposition to Harvey Lehman, who believed that creativity, in men
at least, peaks before age 50.[33] Among the 20 creative Terman women
were 2 who became more serious painters after 60 than they had been
before, and 2 who after age 60 gave their first public musical recitals.
In addition, there was a previously inhibited writer who became the
editor of a small newspaper at 75, a woman who published her first
serious book at 65 and her first book of poems at 78, and another
woman whose public literary achievements peaked at 75. The ninth
was a woman who won her first sculpture prize after 70. The explanation for this late efflorescence of talent is most likely that the respon-
sibilities of childrearing and the triple jeopardy of the Great Depression, World War II, and sexism in their young adulthood had forced
the Terman women to postpone expressing potential that had been
always present.

As dramatic as these differences between the women in the high-
and low-creativity groups, however, were the many similarities
between them. For example, with the exception of the levels of happiness and generativity, there were *no* differences between the two groups
in mental health. Creativity was the hallmark neither of mental illness
nor of mental health. Only the women who were unable to play, who
had no creative outlets at all, even private ones, showed poor mental
health. Suppression and anticipation, the two mature defenses most
highly associated with mental health, were not more common among
the creative women. Nor, contrary to our stereotypes of the Bohemian
artist, were the creative women more likely to use immature defenses.
The recollected childhood happiness of the creative women was neither
better nor worse than that of the less creative. Creative women were
neither more nor less likely to be psychiatric cases or to enjoy sustained
marital satisfaction. Several of the less creative women had helped to
create very successful families and gardens, but in this chapter I am

examining only that creativity that wells up from within. I am not discussing organic creativity that requires close cooperation from biology. Besides, if anything, the children and gardens of the creative women turned out even better than those of the less creative.

There were no differences in intelligence between creative and less creative women. Whether their intelligence was measured by I.Q. in childhood, by the Concept Mastery Test in middle life, or by years of attained education, the two groups did not differ. About half of the women in each group had no education beyond college, and in adult life about half of each group confined their reading to popular magazines and light fiction. Nor did these women differ in terms of opportunity. The creative women did not come from a higher social class; their mother's education was not greater; there were not more books in their childhood homes; their parents did not offer them greater parental support for achievement. As with maturity of defenses and psychosocial maturation, the creativity of amateurs seems to come from within rather than to reflect a blessing from the environment.

Admittedly, the numbers are small and the sample is very skewed in the direction of education and intelligence. Certainly, both intelligence and education have something to do with creativity. Indeed, by the standards set for the Terman women, very few of the underprivileged Core City men would have met criteria for creativity. But the point is that the creative Terman women *were* only being compared with their peers.

As a male counterpoint for the Terman women, let us look at the equally well educated College men. Again, their creativity must be judged in comparison to one's own most creative friends, not against famous artists. For example, both Norman Mailer and Leonard Bernstein were classmates of the men in the College sample; but, sadly, they were not selected for study. Only 2 of the 268 College men actually made a living out of writing fiction or acting or painting pictures or playing music.

The four-category research definition of creativity for the College sample differed slightly from that for the Terman women because of differences in available data and in the men's opportunities for creativity. The men received one point for each of four domains in which they were creative. One domain was sustained creative achievement:

being able to make a living as a writer, actor, or artist, publishing more than two books, mounting several one-man art shows, or winning prizes for creativity. The second domain, and this one was deliberately the most inclusive, was having put something in the world that had not been there before. This was defined as holding two or more patents, publishing two or more articles in newspapers or journals, starting an organization, or being a minister who had to give sermons, an architect who had to design houses, or an advertising man responsible for creating copy (in contrast to the account executive who marketed the ideas of another). By definition, success in the first domain meant success in this second domain also. The third domain was having a serious creative hobby. This could be an unpublished but completed novel, privately printed poetry, amateur theater, serious weekend painting, photography good enough to have been occasionally published. The fourth domain was commitment to art in the public arena. This included becoming a literary critic, a trustee of an art museum, a serious art collector, an editor, or a member of prize board for creative activity. Such a definition of creativity clearly does not take into account being the loving father of four or the witty creator of birthday poems and after-dinner toasts. The evidence I have obtained, however, suggests that creativity in the public arena is usually paralleled by creativity in private life. Picasso sketched brilliantly on his friends' restaurant napkins as well as painting pictures on canvas.

Of the 51 most creative College men, 13 achieved points in three or all of the four domains. Among these 13 men were 1 professional actor and 1 professional novelist. There were 5 gifted, nationally known humanities professors, most of whom had published more than one book. There were an unusually gifted architect; 3 highly creative editors, 2 of whom had achieved national acclaim; and 2 men who, although earning their livings as businessmen, had both created organizations *and* achieved serious amateur recognition for their art—one as a playwright and the other for several one-man art shows. The other 39 men in the creative group resembled the 20 most creative Terman women in their achievement. These 39 had achieved points in two of the four domains.

At the opposite end of the spectrum were 60 College men who received points in none of the four domains. These men tended to be good in sports and interested in people; and, in contrast to the least creative Terman women, they tended to have many outside interests.

This difference between the two samples was probably because the College sample had been originally chosen for mental health and self-reliance; the Terman women had been selected only for their I.Q. test scores.

Table 15 excludes the College men who were creative in only one domain and contrasts the most and the least creative men. In general, the differences between the most creative and least creative men were similar to those noted for the Terman women. The men who had published anything were usually creative in at least one other domain. Not surprisingly, the creative men were more likely to be in *Who's Who in America* and to use sublimation as a defense. The creative men were somewhat more generative than the noncreative men and less likely to use repression, but these distinctions were not as marked as for the Terman women. Like creativity in the Terman women, creativity in the College men was associated with successful aging. Unlike the Terman women, the creative College men were not more likely to use altruism and humor.

When the College men were in college, they were evaluated for a number of personality traits. Two of these traits were highly predictive of perceived mental health in college: "vital affect" predicted good

Table 15. Major differences between the more and the less creative College men

	Creative (n = 51)	Not creative (n = 66)	Significance
Generative	61%	45%	—
Published something	80	0	***
Published a book	18	0	***
Enjoyed job, age 50–62	82	55	**
Died by 1989	4	21	**
Sublimation a major defense	27	0	***
Repression not noted	63	50	—
In *Who's Who in America*	40	17	***
Cultural interests in college	41	18	***
Creative and intuitive in college	22	0	***
Verbally fluent in college	33	12	***
Practical/organizing in college	20	52	***

$**p < .01; ***p < .001.$

college adjustment, and an "unintegrated personality" predicted maladjustment. Neither of these traits was related in any way to creativity. One trait, "practical organizing," in college was weakly predictive of mental health at the time and strongly predictive of mental health later in life. The trait was thought to describe sophomores "better in organization than in analytical or creative work. They describe an interest in . . . getting things done."[34] In keeping with common folk wisdom, Table 15 suggests that being viewed as sensible and organized militated against future creativity.

To summarize, mental health was associated with both common sense and generativity, but not with creativity, altruism, or sublimation. Creativity was positively associated with generativity, sublimation, and altruism, negatively associated with common sense, and relatively independent of mental health.

Three traits, however, that were quite independent of mental health—in college or later in life—were four times more common among the College men who later engaged in creative behavior. The first of these traits was having "motivations toward the *creative and intuitive*. A group characterized by high ability for self-expression or who are original and creative in their thought . . . This group is largely composed of those contemplating artistic or literary careers." The second trait was having "motivations towards the *cultural*. A group for whom enjoyment of participation in literature or the arts is predominant . . . it leads them either to follow an artistic career or to consider any form of life work as a means of existence in order that they may satisfy their cultural needs." The third trait was *verbalistic*, which was applied to sophomores "who have a facility with language or an ability to verbalize their thoughts in rich or well formulated language."[35] In other words, being interested in being creative in college predicted being creative later in life.

The observation that for the College men, as for the Terman women, creativity and mental health were unrelated contradicts two widely held beliefs. On the one hand, the tortured poet attracts our attention; and, thus, erroneously we believe that mental torment is a necessary muse. On the other hand, we believe that, since creativity in a child is a sign of health and that play reflects joy not pain, creative adults will be mentally healthy. In opposition to both sets of beliefs, creativity in the gifted amateurs in the Study of Adult Development did not seem to be associated in any way with either the presence or the absence of mental illness. The numerical measures used to assess warm childhood environment and childhood neuroticism and those used to assess adult depression and psychopathology when adult correlated at less than .02 with the four-point scale of creativity assigned to the College men. Similarly, the global dimensions that the Study used for mental health in terms of success at working and loving in college, at age 30, at age 47, and at age 65 were insignificantly associated with mental health. It was only in the *enjoyment* of late midlife that creativity appeared associated with good psychological outcome in the College men, just as it had been for the Terman women.

Nancy Andreason, a highly literate professor of psychiatry, has published the most convincing study thus far that creativity *is* associated with mental illness.[36] She studied 30 professional writers at the University of Iowa Writers' Workshop and their immediate relatives, comparing them to matched controls and their immediate relatives. Andreason found that clinically significant depressive disorder was roughly three times more common in the writers and their relatives than in the controls and their relatives.

The results from the Study of Adult Development were less clear-cut. On the one hand, among the 11 serious writers in the College sample, 3 had experienced clinically significant depression (three times as many as expected) and only 3 seemed completely free of psychological problems. While these numbers are too small for statistical significance, they do agree with the findings of others that writers of fiction—and especially of poetry—may have more depression than the population as a whole. But none of the three college personality traits most closely associated with creativity—cultural interests, verbal fluency, and a creative/intuitive nature—were even suggestively associated with major depressive disorder. In other words, it may be only the poets and the playwrights, among artists in general, that make us equate creativity with mental illness.

Two variables—alcoholism and athleticism—that I expected to be negatively associated with creativity were not. It was easy for me to imagine that if a man was afflicted by alcoholism this would impair his work life sufficiently so that he would be unproductive. In general this was true, but not with regard to creativity. Indeed, alcoholism has been the curse of many successful American fiction writers and professors of English. Second, the idea of the artist/athlete seemed incongruous to me, but not to the College men. Marked athletic involvement in college or in midlife was in no way antithetical to achievement by the men in any of the four domains that I used to assess creativity.

Thus far I have discussed creativity as an adaptive operation by the ego and as a means by which the ego resolves conflict and legitimizes omnipotent fantasy. But this is to sell creativity short. In some ways the ego and creativity are one and the same. For example, essential to creativity are the same ego skills essential to career consolidation: the capacity to find sustained interest and faith in one's own abilities. What my examination of creative amateurs has suggested is that creativity requires much besides conflict. The conflict-laden lives of Nightingale and Beethoven (and of the protagonists of the next three chapters— Sylvia Plath, Anna Freud, and Eugene O'Neill) are perhaps the exception not the rule. Rather, the sources of creativity are multiple, complex, and fascinating, and they will probably never be fully understood. Painful childhoods allow the psychobiographer to illustrate the alchemy and the wisdom of the ego, but inner torment is by no means a necessary or a sufficient cause for creativity. Nor is there a clear linkage between insanity and creativity. Rather, there are many other places besides defense mechanisms where we can look for the sources of creativity. After all, we all have the capacity for creativity within us. We all have the capacity to experience life deeply and to share our unique experience with others—if only we can find a means of expression.

First, for the expression of creativity, there is a need for talent. Thus, Florence Nightingale's unusual intelligence undoubtedly played a role in her achievement. But to develop talent, as already noted, requires commitment, energy, perseverance, and the capacity for taking pains. Like intelligence, talent is a necessary but never a sufficient cause of creativity.

Second, the expression of creativity involves maintaining the capacity to play. And play is a way of having fun, not a way of resolving psychopathology. Defenses (and the life tasks of keepers of the meaning) involve accommodation and compromise; in a sense, defenses are *reactive* to life. Play in children and creativity in adults are *proactive*. Thus, if creativity is not essential to mental health, it is often part of resilience. If creativity does not make one whole, it still provides active mastery over passively experienced trauma.

Thus, one of the conditions that make creativity possible is that mysterious process by which some adults continue to know how to play; for if commitment is in the domain of the mature, play is in the domain of the child. It is a fact that only about one-tenth of musical child prodigies remain virtuosos as adults. The same is true of gifted child graphic artists. As adolescents, all of the Terman women, even Willa Loman, were creative, but only a few were highly creative as grown women. Many of the College men, when young, put new creations in the world, but over time they stopped doing so. At best, they became keepers of the meaning; at worst, they became unimaginative, rigid curmudgeons.

Dreams and play have to do with developing the new, whereas maturity, like it or not, has a lot to do with maintaining the status quo. "As people grow up they cease to play," wrote Freud, "and they seem to give up the yield of pleasure which they gain from playing."[37] Or as Ogden Nash, another poetic student of the human condition, put it, "The trouble with a kitten is that / Eventually it grows up and becomes a cat." As I copy out these quotations from Nash and Freud, I watch from my desk my family's two house cats. The five-month-old kitten engages in self-sustained battles with imaginary mice and performs backward somersaults such as the world has never seen. The twelve-year-old tabby dozes; occasionally she opens one eye as if to signal there is nothing new under the sun. Perhaps she is as wise as Ecclesiastes; perhaps she has only forgotten how to play. From a developmental point of view, the task of youth is to innovate, the tasks of middle life are commitment and perseverance, and the task of old age is to pass on what has been learned in the past. Perhaps by a sport of nature these three tasks occur simultaneously in the creative artist. The wisdom of age and the playfulness of childhood occur in the same person. No wonder creative artists are not common.

But talent and play are still not enough. A third requirement for the expression of creativity is ritual. Ritual serves to create the peace needed to let the inner out. Ritual, patterned behavior, and discipline are essential to art. As Storr suggests, "Symbolic, ritualistic activity can be seen as a link between the inner and outer worlds of the subject; a bridge which facilitates the transfer of emotional energy from one world to the other."[38] Johan Huizinga captured the same link between ritual, play, and creativity somewhat differently: "The profound affinity between play and order is perhaps the reason why play, as we noted in passing, seems to lie to such a large extent in the field of aesthetics. Play has a tendency to be beautiful."[39]

Florence Nightingale had a passion for neatness, method, and order. Instinctively, she reached out for facts. In her family, she was the one who helped people find things. She was most meticulous about the exact contents of her own bureau drawers. She even made a detailed comparison in tabular form of the score, libretto, and performance of every opera she attended. Like psychiatrists and art critics, she tried to bring order out of Koestler's *Ah!* experiences. Unlike most psychiatrists and art critics, she was also able to create the *Ah!* experience in others.

Fourth, both creativity and play involve appreciating paradox and the unexpected. As Koestler points out, scientific discovery, humor, and good art must all be able to turn the commonplace on its head. To put something in the world that was not there before, you have to be able to see that which others before you have overlooked. Children enjoy being surprised, adults do not. To be a Florence Nightingale you have to be able to see romance in sewage, as it were. Albert Rothenberg, a psychoanalyst who has spent a career studying creativity, calls this toleration and appreciation of paradox *Janusian thinking* after the god Janus, whose head faced in opposite directions at the same time.[40] Koestler has termed this same process of actively conceiving two or more discrete entities occupying the same space *bisociation*. A simple everyday example of this is the unsung genius who first thought cheese would taste good with apple pie. The bisociative aspect of creativity is also essential to adaptation. The capacity to produce paradox—to spin straw into gold, to find hopeful silver linings in storm clouds, and to find laughter in dispute—is part of the wisdom of the ego.

Fifth, creativity requires the harnessing of feeling as well as thinking. For all their abstract musical genius, Beethoven and Mozart, without passion, would have been but "sounding brass or a tinkling cymbal." But often such harnessing of passion requires mentorship and some sort of identification with another person. Florence Nightingale, the first woman elected to the British Statistical Society, first became interested in mathematics in a most unlikely manner—through her unrequited lesbian love for her cousin. Having first learned Latin and Greek from her own father, Nightingale then became absorbed in mathematics. But she chose to learn mathematics from her cousin

Henry Nicholson, as a way to be safely close to his sister, Marianne Nicholson. Florence expressed her devotion to Marianne with simple clarity: "I never loved but one person with passion in my life, and that was her."[41] This passion, however, was not expressed in a mutual love affair but in a lifelong love of numbers. By linking idea and feeling, creativity can serve as a means of achieving intimacy from a distance.

Sixth, creativity not only links thought and emotion but also links the right brain to the left brain. Koestler puts this a little differently and refers us to a "vague visual imagery [that] seems to follow Wordsworth's advice: 'Often we have to get away from speech in order to think clearly' . . . Language can act as a screen between the thinker and reality. Creativity often starts where language ends, that is by regressing to preverbal levels, to more fluid and uncommitted forms of mental activity."[42] Claude Bernard said much the same thing when he advised us to replace words with phenomena.

Seventh, creativity is catalyzed by a certain shyness. The artist wishes to communicate but is often rather indirect about it. Creativity touches our heart but may do so after the artist has slipped out of the room. This facet of creativity can serve as a social escape, an addiction, a use of fantasy that is almost masturbatory and certainly schizoid in its intensity. We only need to think of the lucid love letter that we may get from someone who is incoherent in our presence. But the distinction between creativity, on the one hand, and fantasy and compulsions, on the other, is that creativity has lost what is too personal and what repels strangers. Using no scientific equipment and little mathematics, Albert Einstein imagined the universe in a novel, almost autistic way. Subsequent experiments, however, legitimized his fantasy. Van Gogh believed he was an artist with something very important to say. If during his lifetime he sold but one or two paintings and the world judged him a lunatic, posterity has vindicated his message as particularly valuable. After their deaths Van Gogh and Emily Dickinson were finally as beloved as they had wished to be when alive. They were not very adept at telling people face to face that they loved them.

Eighth, it is not enough for an artist to want desperately to communicate. Creative communication requires the discovery of a medium. Creative *Homo sapiens* had to postpone becoming an artist until Cro-Magnon culture discovered the media of colored clays and ochre and the receptive walls of the Lascaux and Altamira caves. The technological discovery of the groined vault and improved engineering skills for cutting and lifting stone allowed medieval architects to transmute the humble beauty of barrel-vaulted Romanesque churches into the transcendent grace of Gothic cathedrals. In similar fashion, Florence Nightingale needed an audience. For other people to be able to derive consolation and alleviation from the products of her unconscious, she needed both cultural permission and the willingness of her audience to identify. For sewage to become romantic, war had to be made real to the public. Had it not been for the introduction in the 1850s of the war correspondent, she might have been remembered as simply one of several inventors of the bar graph. It was the £40,000 relief fund—largely raised by the *Times*—that gave Nightingale her "purse strings." It was the *Times* correspondents sending their dispatches home, as much as anything else, that provided the "Nightingale power" and inspired the legend that was essential to Nightingale's subsequent creative meddling in War Office politics.

Finally, creativity can never be explained by appeal to reason alone. Like the birth of a child, creativity compels us not to explanation but to wonder and awe. Before the creative artist, not only psychoanalysis but sweet reason, too, must lay down its arms. As the spinster author of "A Treatise on Sinks," Florence Nightingale nonetheless inspired young men to kiss her shadow as she passed; and as an overcontrolling nursing supervisor she still managed to create a legend that even today inspires young nurses to weep at candle-lit ceremonies. Myth is stranger than fiction.

Indeed, play, art, and sublimation as a defense all go far beyond relieving primitive desires. They reflect a far higher order of mental complexity. They all enhance and transmute mental function. Imagine the bland image that the high-intensity bulb inside a movie projector casts upon a screen; then consider what happens to that image when an intricately detailed movie film passes between the light and the screen and the resulting cinematic illusion captures our hearts and minds. Just so the ego creates meaning where before there was only blinding light. As Freud observed, "The creative artist does the same thing as the child at play. He creates a world of fantasy which he takes very seriously—that is, which he invests with large amounts of emotion—while separating it sharply from reality."[43] Creativity, as we shall see in the next chapter, is anything but simple.

9

Sylvia Plath: Creativity and Psychotic Defenses

Much madness is divinest sense
To a discerning eye . . .
                  Emily Dickinson

Driven to express her psychic pain in words, Sylvia Plath provides us with an excellent illustration of psychotic defenses—an illustration that reveals that psychosis is not only a defect but also an effort at repair. Plath's psychological vulnerability, her extraordinary perseverance, her great verbal talent, and her compulsive journal writing allow us to piece together biographical fact and creative product and to appreciate the adaptive process. Therefore, I shall use episodes from Plath's life both to demonstrate techniques for elucidating, even proving, the existence of defense and to examine four defenses uncommon in the psychopathology of everyday life. Three of these defenses underlie psychosis: delusional projection, psychotic denial, and distortion. The fourth is the mechanism of splitting, a defense mechanism that is mentioned elsewhere in this book only in passing because it is used exclusively to manage conflictual relationships.

Sometimes psychotic defenses, like the creative productions of our dreams, simply make order out of the biochemical aberrations that occur within our brain. Toxic deliria and epileptic psychoses are obvious examples. At other times psychotic defenses appear to be called forth by intact brains to deal with unbearable reality. At such times the results can appear almost healthy. Elvin Semrad, the Harvard psychiatry professor who first drew my attention to a hierarchy of defenses, maintained that "Religion is the only benign form of distortion." The fact that there are no atheists in foxholes allows psychotic defenses to keep us sane in insane places.

Usually, as is the case with our most meaningful dreams, the use of distortion, delusional projection, or psychiatric denial is provoked by biologic vulnerability *and* personal crisis occurring together. August Strindberg, Vincent Van Gogh, William Blake, and Sylvia Plath strove with all their creative might to mend the ravages and disorder of broken brains. Their brains were not only pulled asunder by the lodestars of psychological conflict but also disordered by the poorly understood neurobiology of insanity. Their efforts to create order out of such chaos must lead any thoughtful observer to gain fresh respect for the synthetic capacities of the human ego.

Let me begin with a brief outline of the life of Sylvia Plath. Plath was the only daughter of an autocratic German father, Otto Plath, who taught at Boston University as a biology professor specializing in bees. Her father was an isolated, distant, austere, schizoid man more interested in insects than in people, and thus he was not an easy father for a daughter to know or to internalize. Professor Otto Plath spoke German, and yet on her way to a *summa cum laude* degree at Smith, the only college course with which Sylvia Plath had trouble was German. Rather than seek medical care in the last year of his life when he was ill with diabetic vascular disease, Otto Plath retreated to bed and to Christian Science. He allowed his diabetes to progress unchecked and thus died a slow, gangrenous, and unnecessarily premature death.

Sylvia Plath was 8 years old when her father died. She had loved her father deeply, but he had died through a lack of self care which Plath perceived consciously as suicide and in her poetry as murder. Such confusion is by no means unique to Plath's unconscious; one reason that suicide leaves such pain behind is that the survivors blame themselves. If we turn to the autobiographical record, her closest friend tells us that Sylvia Plath said of her father, "I probably wished many times that he was dead . . . and he obliged me and died. I imagined that I killed him."[1] Or we can turn to her poem "Daddy," written shortly before her death: "Daddy, I have had to kill you . . . Daddy, daddy, you bastard, I'm through."[2] Yet "Daddy" is also a love poem, written from the memory of a sensitive, passionate little girl who, as she recalled her feelings for her father, poignantly protested that he had "bit my pretty red heart in two."

Plath's mother was a strong-minded, long-suffering secretary who, from the beginning, supported her daughter's use of intellectualization as a defense. Plath learned the alphabet to distract and/or to comfort herself while her younger brother nursed; in an autobiographical essay she remembered that this brother's birth had indicated that "my beautiful fusion with the things of this world was over."[3] Plath never saw her Christian Scientist mother cry. Nor was she permitted to attend her father's funeral. Instead, shortly after her father's death, she published her first poem. She went through high school, never getting less than an A. She wrote poetry by schedule and always did her homework on time. "After all, I wasn't crippled in any way," says Esther Greenwood, Plath's alter ego in her autobiographical novel *The Bell Jar;* "I just studied too hard. I didn't know when to stop."[4] Esther Greenwood, and probably her creator, Sylvia Plath, lost her virginity more as a self-imposed intellectual laboratory assignment than as an act of passion. As a result, the consequences were both frightening and bleakly sterile.

Then, at 20, after Plath had won a guest editorship to a New York fashion magazine, she had a prolonged psychotic episode. For three weeks she wore the same clothes, did not eat or sleep, could not concentrate, withdrew under her mattress, and finally tried to take her life with her mother's barbiturates. For three days she lay in coma in a cranny in the basement. At last, hearing her moans, her brother discovered her; and her mother took her to a general hospital from which she was transferred to a psychiatric hospital. If Plath's exact diagnosis remains arguable, few would deny that she was psychotically depressed. A year later she recovered, returned to Smith College, and graduated *summa cum laude*.

At age 23 Plath married Ted Hughes, a distinguished poet in his own right who would later become England's Poet Laureate. After teaching brilliantly for a year at Smith, she moved to England, bore two children, and wrote *The Bell Jar* between the ages of 25 and 29. In 1962, the year before her death, Plath published *The Bell Jar* under an assumed name—as if she needed to isolate herself from ownership of her anger even in the sublimated form of her novel. That fall she also separated from her unfaithful husband, moved from Devon to London, and again became increasingly psychotically disturbed. As she had at age 20, Plath again began neglecting her personal self. But instead of her earlier writer's block she engaged in a frenzy of creativity that, like Van Gogh's creativity during the last two years of his life, illustrates the lack of a clear boundary between art and psychosis. In the five months before she killed herself by putting her head in her gas oven, Plath produced her most luminous art, the *Ariel* poems. "I am living like a Spartan," she wrote to her friend Ruth Fainlight, "writing through huge fevers and producing free stuff I had locked in me for years."[5] The art of both Plath and Van Gogh moves us through their color, feelings, primary process, as it were, and not through their logic, reason, or ideas.

Such close juxtaposition of art and madness keeps alive the illusions that in the white heat of creation the artist confuses art with death and that to be an artist one must be a little mad. Sometimes it seems almost inevitable that Keats, Plath, Van Gogh, and Mozart should burn themselves up with their art and thus die young. We forget that creativity can occur only when the mind is working well, and that genius springs from an infinite capacity for taking pains. Samuel Coleridge's famous poem "Kubla Khan" did not spring full-blown, as he alleged, from a single opiate-inspired reverie. Rather, as John Livingston Lowes has documented,[6] "Kubla Khan" arose from the integration of a lifetime of assiduous reading and as the end product of several drafts. In addition, unlike insanity, art has an altruistic as well as a self-soothing purpose. Thus, Plath could write, "For me, the real issues of our time are the issues of everytime—the hurt and wonder of loving; making in all its forms—children, loaves of bread, paintings, buildings, and the conservation of life of all people in all places."[7] Art owes more to such perceptions of universal sanity than it does to individual insanity.

Both the biographical record and Plath's own diaries support the assumption that the life of Esther Greenwood in *The Bell Jar* may be treated as only barely disguised autobiography. In Plath's words, the novel was "an autobiographical apprentice work which I had to write in order to free my self from the past."[8] Plath's autobiographical protagonist provides us with useful illustrations of psychotic defenses at work.

If we are to regard psychosis as more than the manifestation of disordered chemistry, what does Esther/Sylvia defend against? At first it seems easiest to view Plath's novel as about depression. But, I wonder how many people are moved to tears by *The Bell Jar*. As in schizophrenia and in much of the unbearable anger of everyday life, the "depression" described in *The Bell Jar* is often a polite cover-up for rage and terror. True enough, Esther begins with the existential, developmental dilemma of the star college student having to contemplate entering the real world: "The one thing I was good at was winning scholarships and prizes, and that era was coming to an end. I felt like a racehorse in a world without racetracks, or a champion college footballer suddenly confronted by Wall Street and a business suit, his days of glory shrunk to a little gold cup on his mantel with a date engraved on it like the date on a tombstone."[9] But Esther's feelings are not those of sadness or even hopelessness. She is angry and afraid. When I ask an audience of college students, "What does Esther/Sylvia defend against?" it often takes them a little while to recognize that throughout the novel the dominant emotional themes are anger and terror and not the hopelessness and helplessness of melancholy.

Let me clarify the distinction between anger and depression. In the winter and spring of 1958, Plath found herself becoming consciously angry, seemingly over trifles. She felt guilty over her decision to leave Smith College, where she had been a popular English teacher. In response to her own inner anger she wrote, "In polite society, a lady doesn't punch or spit. So I turn to my work . . . I am justifiably outraged. Spite. Meanness. What else. How I am exorcising them from my system. Like bile . . . Threw you, book, down, punch with fist. Kicked, punched. Violence seethed. Joy to murder someone, pure scapegoat. But pacified during necessity to work. Work redeems."[10] Plath, with her exquisite sensitivity—paranoia if you will—perceived the sadness and regret of fellow faculty members over her leaving Smith as simple reproach. Indeed, reproach is one of the components in the complex emotional amalgam that makes up anyone's grief. But grief, which makes most of us sad, terrifies the schizophrenic and enrages the so-called sociopath and his female counterpart, the "borderline." Two months later Plath wrote, "I was taken by a frenzy a week ago, Thursday, my first real day of vacation, and the frenzy has continued ever since: writing and writing: I wrote eight poems in the last eight days . . . poems breaking open my real experience of life in the last five years."[11] She continued to note in her journal how out of control she felt. Her biographer Anne Stevenson writes, "A late-night brush fire in the neighborhood caused her to burst out suddenly in the same journal entry, 'I longed for an incident, an accident. What unleashed desire there must be in one for general carnage. I walk around the streets, braced and ready and almost wishing to test my eye and fiber on tragedy—a child crushed by a car, a house on fire, someone thrown into a tree by a horse.'"[12] Six months later Plath wrote in her journal, "Fury jams the gullet and spreads poison, but, as soon as I start to write, dissipates, flows out into the figure of the letters; writing as therapy?"[13] On December 12, 1958, her journal's "Main Questions" included "How to express anger creatively?"[14] A year later she began construction of her "hellishly funny"[15] novel, *The Bell Jar.*

In the novel, in the section leading up to Esther Greenwood's (and Plath's) attempted suicide, Plath writes of her father so that the anger beneath her manifest depression can be discerned: "My mother hadn't let us come to his funeral . . . so the graveyard and even his death had always seemed unreal to me. I had a great yearning, lately, to *pay my father back* [italics added] for all the years of neglect, and start tending his grave."[16] She goes on, "Then my legs folded under me, and I sat down in the sopping grass. I couldn't understand why I was crying so hard. Then I remembered that I had never cried for my father's death . . . I laid my face to the smooth face of the marble and howled my loss into the cold salt rain."[17] If we didn't also have her journal and her poetry, this event leading up to her suicide attempt could be construed as simple depression. The facts that Sylvia then broke into her mother's strongbox and swallowed an overdose of her sleeping pills and later wrote the poem "Daddy" suggest an alternative meaning for her impulse to "pay my father back." But perhaps the real world is not as black and white as I suggest. Anger often cloaks depression; depression often camouflages anger. As Freud wrote, "Anyone turning biographer commits himself to lies, to concealment, to hypocrisy, to flattery, and even to hiding his own lack of understanding, for biographical truth is not to be had, and even if it were it couldn't be used."[18] Thus, not all sensitive students of Sylvia Plath's life and art will agree with my formulations.

Delusional Projection

Besides anger, the other dominant emotion that Esther Greenwood describes is raw terror, the same affect that forms the core of schizophrenic misery. She tells us, "I couldn't get myself to react. I felt very still and very empty, the way the eye of a tornado must feel, moving dully along in the middle of the surrounding hullabaloo." That is not the imagery of depression. "I was so scared," Plath's novel tells us, "as if I was being stuffed farther and farther into a black airless sack with no way out." And so, suicidal, Esther Greenwood stuffs herself into a hidden corner of her mother's dark cellar. Later, in response to her psychiatrist's efforts to help her, she describes her frightened thought process as halfway between delusion and projection: "I turn the words over suspiciously, like round, sea-polished pebbles that might suddenly put out a claw and change into something else." [19]

In the hospital after her suicide attempt, Esther is offered a meal of string beans and baked beans: "Now I knew perfectly well you didn't serve two kinds of beans together in a meal. Beans and carrots or beans and peas, maybe, but never beans and beans. The Negro was just trying to see how much we would take . . . I drew my foot back and gave him a sharp, hard kick on the calf of the leg." [20] Righteously, Esther kicked her persecutor with the same aggressive energy that, through sublimation, her creator, Sylvia Plath, had harnessed to compete for prizes while at Smith. The same aggressive energy that Esther unleashed on a man who was trying to help her was the anger that led Sylvia with pathological jealousy (the delusional projection of everyday life) to burn all of her husband's poems in progress and then to destroy his favorite copy of Shakespeare. In so doing, Sylvia was not fighting off an enemy, but, like Othello, killing precisely that which she most loved. To try to master conflict in such a fashion is crazy.

If we turn from Plath's imaginary protagonist to her own poetry just before her own real death by suicide, we find not poems of grief but poems preoccupied with Hiroshima and concentration camps—poems of unharnessed anger and terror. Before her first suicide attempt, Plath had been preoccupied with the trial and execution of the Rosenbergs as spies. In "Daddy," she perceives her father as the source of her terror: "An engine / Chuffing me off like a Jew. / A Jew to Dachau, Auschwitz, Belsen . . . / I've always been scared of *you*, / With your Luftwaffe, your gobbledygoo." [21] Plath's terror and rage were the stuff of which delusional projection is made—and sometimes great poetry, too.

Psychotic Denial

One example of the psychotic denial of everyday life is Plath's decision to commit suicide by hiding herself in a cubbyhole in her mother's cellar. In so doing she believed that she would not be found, almost as a child hides by covering her face. Another equally pathological example of denial of external reality was Plath's response to self-mutilation. Before her suicide attempt, Plath's mother had noticed razor slashes on her daughter's legs, and in *The Bell Jar* Esther Greenwood, having just cut herself with a razor, says, "I felt nothing. Then I felt a small deep thrill and a bright seam of red welled up at the lip of the slash. The blood gathered darkly, like fruit, and rolled down my ankle into the cup of my black patent leather shoe." Esther also demonstrated denial in the way she dealt with her terror in the psychiatrist's waiting room anticipating electric shock treatment. "Then my gaze slid over the people to the blaze of green beyond the diaphanous curtains, and I felt as if I were sitting in the window of an enormous department store. The figures around me weren't people but shop dummies, painted to resemble people and propped up in attitudes counterfeiting life." [22] If real people frightened her, she could—in her mind's eye—render them unreal, and she could perform this transformation in time present when the people were right in the room with her.

The religious equivalent of Sylvia Plath's own psychotic denial can be found in her parent's deployment of their religious convictions. Otto Plath had died a slow, frightening death, denying his need for medical care; Aurelia Plath had not let her daughter, Sylvia, witness her own father's funeral or burial. If you don't see it, it is not true. As Plath has Esther Greenwood put it, "At home, all I ever saw was the *Christian Science Monitor*, which appeared on the doorstep at five o'clock every day but Sunday, and treated suicides and sex crimes and airplane crashes as if they didn't happen." [23] Despite Plath's angry contempt, however, Christian Science, indeed all religiously catalyzed denial, comforts far more people than it dismays.

Distortion

Distortion of reality is also an intrinsic part of poetry and of religious belief. The most obvious example in *The Bell Jar* is Esther's belief that she is committing suicide to rejoin her father. In another example, just before her visit to her father's grave and her suicide attempt, Esther describes her life as a hospital volunteer: "I steered the trolley to a wash basin in an alcove in the hall and began to pick out all the flowers that were dead. Then I picked out those that were dying. There was no wastebasket in sight, so I crumpled the flowers up and laid them in the deep white basin. The basin felt cold as a tomb. I smiled. This must be how they laid the bodies away in the hospital morgue. My gesture, in its small way, echoed the larger gestures of the doctors and nurses."[24] Thus, on the one hand, Esther Greenwood reveals how her suicide might also be construed as a pleasant game and conveys how close creativity and psychosis can sometimes be. On the other hand, in sharp distinction to a user of play, fantasy, or passive aggression, both Esther and Sylvia made a real effort to kill themselves. The "play" of distortion is classified psychotic precisely because it ignores reality and suffering ensues. In contrast, the play of a child unerringly avoids confronting reality and results in no tangible real-world consequences, only joy.

Schizoid Fantasy and Projection

Both as Esther becomes ill and as she recovers, we see in her the more mature cousins of the psychotic defenses: projection and schizoid fantasy. During the era when the sale of contraceptives was still against the law in Massachusetts, she describes her trolley ride home from the drugstore with her newly purchased diaphragm: "As I rode back to the asylum with my box in the plain brown paper wrapper on my lap, I might have been Mrs. Anybody coming back from a day in town with a Schrafft's cake for her maiden aunt, or a Filene's Basement hat. Gradually, the suspicion that Catholics had X-ray eyes diminished, and I grew easy."[25]

Like many individuals with schizoid tendencies, Sylvia Plath was frightened by intimacy. Like many an adolescent before them, Sylvia and her imaginary Esther felt most comfortable having autistic relationships with their boyfriends, ones that existed inside of their heads. While still at Smith College, with the omnipotence of schizoid fantasy, Plath had written "A Mad Girl's Love Song" about her boyfriend Perry Norton:

> I shut my eyes and all the world drops dead;
> I lift my lids and all is born again.
> (I think I made you up inside my head.)
> I dreamed that you bewitched me into bed.
> And sung me moonstruck, kissed me quite insane.
> (I think I made you up inside my head.)[26]

In similar fashion, Esther Greenwood describes her adolescent attraction to Buddy Willard (Plath's fictional name for Perry Norton): "I spent a lot of time having imaginary conversations with Buddy

Willard." "I'd adored him from a distance for five years before he even looked, and then there was a beautiful time when I still adored him and he started looking at me; and then just as he was looking at me more and more I discovered quite by accident what an awful hypocrite he was; and now he wanted me to marry him, and I hated his guts."[27] The term that Melanie Klein and Otto Kernberg use for this same defensive behavior is *devaluation*.

Splitting

Splitting is a defense that developmentally lies somewhere between the everyday neurotic defense of *undoing,* a variant of isolation, and the psychotic *ambivalence* that Euger Bleuler perceived as one of the pathognomonic "4 A's" of schizophrenia. (The other "A's" were autism, flat affect, and loosened associations.) The task of splitting is to alleviate affective ambivalence and assign all the good feelings to one person and all the bad feelings to a scapegoat, as it were. For most of us, splitting takes place demurely out of sight and mitigated by fantasy. Most of us confine our use of splitting to our imaginations and behave in a more integrated fashion toward those we love. Certainly, in our imaginations we read with greater interest about the exploits of uninhibited stars like Elvis Presley and Madonna than we do of the good deeds of Mother Theresa and Eleanor Roosevelt, but in real life we try to behave more like the latter. The small child has no difficulty cuddling up to good Mummy while she reads to him or her about imaginary wicked witches and stepmothers who serve as convenient receptacles for most of Mummy's faults.

Splitting is different from reaction formation because in reaction formation the user is oblivious to ambivalence, and black is truly treated as white. With splitting, a world that is appropriately gray is separated into all black and all white, and the individual is left divided against himself or herself. Anger and love, when they come together in one person without blending, create the sadomasochist, the pervert, and, on psychiatric wards, that infamous creature known pejoratively to psychotherapists around the world as the *borderline*. The so-called borderline is the master of splitting and divides the staff on a psychiatric ward up into "good guys" and "bad guys" so invasively that the staff begin to believe it.

The double-entry bookkeeping of splitting is not as benign as the compromise of undoing and does not isolate the user from loved ones as completely as does schizophrenic ambivalence. An example of neurotic undoing verging on splitting is Beethoven's words to a friend about his ambivalent relationship with his nephew Karl: "He is a monster . . . my love for him is gone . . . You understand, of course, that this is not what I really think. (I still love him as I used to . . .)."[28] An example of psychotic ambivalence verging on splitting is a schizophrenic woman who told me that her life had been shattered because "I had to leave home, but we were too close for comfort!" She had had to kill the thing she loved; in contrast Beethoven could speak from both sides of his heart at the same time.

Beethoven also provides us with an example of the middle ground—of splitting. During the same years in which he alternated between loving and hating his nephew, Karl, and Karl's mother, Johanna, all humanity became the receptacle of his mixed emotions. During the same period in which he was setting to music Schiller's "An die Freude"—"Be embraced all ye millions! / with a kiss for all the world"—he could write with unalloyed misogyny to his loyal friend Karl Bernard, "Oh, may the whole miserable rabble of humanity be cursed and damned."[29] The world was all black, and all white, and in the same mind.

Sylvia Plath's efforts to integrate positive and negative feelings toward the same individual in the real world produced a similarly incongruous struggle. Occasionally, she was able to bring these conflicting feelings together and link what she felt publicly with what she felt privately. The results could be terrifyingly beautiful; at other times her use of splitting deeply wounded those she most loved.

We can begin with the autobiographical evidence that Plath gives us regarding the birth of her novel, *The Bell Jar*. The evidence provides a contrast between the public self epitomized by her effusive, optimistic *Letters Home* to her mother and the private self epitomized by her feelings toward Esther Greenwood's mother in *The Bell Jar*. Sylvia's polite public response to her mother was that her novel was a "potboiler really, but I think it will show how isolated a person feels when he is suffering a breakdown."[30] Yet her fictional description of the novel's creation was Esther Greenwood announcing, "I'd spend the summer writing a novel. That would fix a lot of people."[31] Plath's fictional description accurately predicted the way her mother experienced the book. "As this book stands by itself," her mother wrote, "it represents the basest ingratitude."[32] In the novel, the fictional Esther, after throwing her mother's roses in the wastepaper basket, blurts out,

"I hate her." In her journals, Plath wrote that her own psychotherapist, the real Dr. Ruth Beuscher, had been as permissive toward her hatred of her mother as the fictional Dr. Nolan had been toward Esther's hatred of her mother: "Like a shot of brandy went home, a sniff of cocaine hit me where I live and I am alive and so-there. Better than shock treatment: I give you permission to hate your mother." Two weeks later, Plath's journal splitting gave way to intellectualization and undoing as she asked her journal, "WHAT IS THE MATURE THING TO DO WITH HOSTILITY FOR MOTHER? Does the need to express it recede with a mature awareness?"[33] Once again we see a less mature defense evolve into a more mature one. Splitting becomes undoing.

Plath's mother, like most observers of splitting, did not always appreciate the careful emotional bookkeeping of her daughter's ego operations, the balancing of all the prizes and honors Plath had won for her and all the overly loving letters Plath had mailed home against the debit side of the rage in *The Bell Jar* and the *Ariel* poems. Occasionally, despite her pain, Aurelia Plath did have a sense of Sylvia's double-entry psychic ledger. In the published edition of her daughter's journals Aurelia Plath wrote, "I have no doubt that many readers will accept whatever negative thoughts she reveals here as the whole and absolute truth, despite their cancellation on other, more positive pages."[34]

Some days Sylvia Plath saw her mother as all good, other days as all bad. She also used splitting toward her benefactor, Olive Prouty. In an unsent 1953 letter to one of her boyfriends, Eddie Cohen, Plath wrote, "Suffice it to say that by fairy-godmother-type maneuverings, my scholarship benefactress at Smith got me into the best mental hospital in the U.S., where I had my own attractive private room and my own attractive private psychiatrist." In a letter to her mother written simultaneously with the publication of *The Bell Jar*, she wrote a decade later, "Mrs. Prouty called me. I was thrilled. I am dedicating my second book of Poems [*Ariel*] (almost done) to Friede and Nicholas in England . . . I'll dedicate it to her in America if it gets taken there." A fortnight later she wrote to her mother, "I have written Mrs. Prouty, yesterday, enclosing a copy of my children's book review, telling her about the lovely Jaeger clothes I bought with her first cheque and asking if I may dedicate this second novel I am desperate to finish this winter to her."[35] Yet at the time the printing presses were turning out *The Bell Jar*, a novel that told a very different story. Plath's novel contemptuously renames Mrs. Prouty Philomena Guinea. "I wasn't quite sure why Mrs. Guinea had turned up," Esther Greenwood tells us. "I knew I should be grateful to Mrs. Guinea, only I could not feel a thing." She continues, "Philomena Guinea wasn't at all satisfied with what the doctors were doing and kept telling them so. I hated those visits."[36]

In 1956 Plath wrote to her "Dearest Mother": "You have borne daddy's long, hard death . . . You have fought your own ulcer attacks, kept us children sheltered, happy, rich with art and music lessons, camps and play . . . Think of your trip here as a trip to the heart of strength in your daughter who loves you more dearly than words can say. I am waiting for you . . . I feel with all my joy and life that these are qualities I can give you from the fulness and brimming of my heart . . . Your own loving Sivvy."[37] The sentiment is touching. There is little doubt Sylvia loved her mother, but the letter feels like a lie. Sylvia Plath was too full of rage and longing to be anybody's "loving Sivvy."

In exact opposition to this invitation for her mother to visit her in England were several poems that played with her mother's name. One such poem was "Medusa." (*Medusa Aurelia* was a type of jellyfish—with tentacles—that, when Sylvia was a child, her mother, Aurelia Plath, pretended was named for herself.) In part the poem "Medusa" reflects Plath's fears, also described in her journals, that her mother would appropriate all of her accomplishments; and in part the poem refers to her mother's visit to England during the summer in which Plath and her husband, Ted Hughes, were getting ready to separate.

> In any case, you are always there,
> Tremulous breath at the end of my line, . . .
> Touching and sucking.
>
> I didn't call you.
> I didn't call you at all.
>
> Nevertheless, nevertheless
> You steamed to me over the sea,
> Fat and red, a placenta
> Paralyzing the kicking lovers.
>
> . . . your wishes
> Hiss at my sins.
> Off, off, eely tentacle!
>
> There is nothing between us.[38]

The very same day Sylvia Plath wrote this poem, she told her mother the "good news," as it were: "Dear Mother . . . I am a genius of a writer; I have it in me. I am writing the best poems of my life; they will make my name."[39] Perhaps if she had shared the affective truth with her mother she would have lived.

The danger of splitting is that the user does not realize that the negative side of unmitigated ambivalence threatens, like acting out, to destroy the person the user loves. Plath's biographer Anne Stevenson tells us that a serious boyfriend of Plath's wrote of her, "What she said, what she alleged, the ways she loved, lacked credibility." When Plath shrugged him off at the end of the summer, he "was left feeling 'used' and even 'despised.'"[40] It is hard to forgive people who make us the sole receptacle of their negative feelings. At the same time we must remember that Sylvia Plath's pure elemental anger and mistrust toward her mother were no greater than the affective liabilities that make up many of our relationships with our own mothers. Plath was not an abused child. Nor were the assets of tender, unalloyed love expressed in her letters home any greater than the love that we, too, feel toward our mothers. But in her splitting, Plath failed to commingle the assets and debits. Such bookkeeping can lead to emotional bankruptcy. It also can lead to great art.

It was in 1957, in her poem "The Disquieting Muses" that Plath was first able, with sublimation, to bridge the extraordinary split that existed in her conflicted feelings toward her mother. In the poem she links the two poles, the fury of the "muses" in her inner life and the saccharine sweetness of her "letters home" to her mother. She tells of the New England hurricane of 1938, which had battered her childhood seaside home in Winthrop, Massachusetts:

> In the hurricane, when father's twelve
> Study windows bellied in
> Like bubbles about to break, you fed
> My brother and me cookies and Ovaltine
> And helped the two of us to choir:
> "Thor is angry: boom boom boom!
> Thor is angry: we don't care!"
> But those ladies broke the panes . . .
>
> And this is the kingdom you bore me to,
> Mother, Mother. But no frown of mine
> Will betray the company I keep.[41]

Anne Stevenson sensitively describes this transformation of Sylvia's defense of splitting into sublimation and in so doing documents that splitting is not just evidence of "borderline" personality but is a tribute to the ego's adaptive legerdemain. "It seems," Stevenson writes,

> that in writing "The Disquieting Muses," Sylvia, for the first time, discovered a way to fulfill two warring subconscious drives in a single, subversive poem. Her resentment, instead of blocking the gift intended to win love, was enfolded within it. In her unrelenting bid, both for unqualified love and for complete self-realization, Sylvia had at last hit on what was to be a secret mechanism of her finest work: she offered an exquisitely wrought, poisoned chalice. It was as if the only way open to her for free expression in her poems was to write pleas for love whose themes were subtle shafts of hate.[42]

After her daughter's death, Aurelia Plath boasted, "As soon as my children were old enough to comprehend it, I shared with them the belief my husband and I had held concerning the importance of aiming and directing one's life toward an idealistic goal in order to build a strong inner life."[43] In her poem "Ariel," whose title like "Medusa" played with her mother's name, Sylvia uncharitably reframed her mother's loving instructions:

> And I
> Am the arrow,
> The dew that flies
> Suicidal, at one with the drive
> Into the red
>
> Eye, the cauldron of morning.[44]

Less than four months after writing this poem, Sylvia Plath herself crawled—not flew—suicidal into her gas oven. Her mother, always adept at ignoring funerals, airplane crashes, and incipient divorces, later wrote of her strained visit that previous summer to Sylvia and Ted just weeks before they separated, "On July 9 when Sylvia and I left Ted with the children . . . Sylvia said proudly, 'I have everything in life I've ever wanted: a wonderful husband, two adorable children, a lovely home and my writing.'"[45] Her mother's words utterly ignored the already festering, soon to be lethal pain in her daughter's heart. "And this is the kingdom you bore me to, / Mother, Mother. But no frown of mine / Will betray the company I keep."

All this brings us to the thorny question: What is the association between art and psychosis? When in a college course on defenses I lectured on *The Bell Jar,* many of the students wondered if suicide was the price a woman had to pay for being a creative artist. They perceived art as having driven Virginia Woolf, Anne Sexton, and Sylvia Plath mad rather than imagining the reverse, that threat of madness could sometimes drive one to art. Great poetry does not cause suicide; but great art, perhaps like Van Gogh's last paintings and Sylvia Plath's last poems, can stave off insanity—for a while. Art is not dangerous; it is the circumstances that bring it forth that are perilous, and it is failure to harness the passions with mature defenses that may be fatal. In his review of Sylvia Plath's poetry for the *Reporter,* George Steiner acknowledged, "These poems take tremendous risks, extending Sylvia Plath's essentially austere manner to the very limit. They are a bitter triumph, of the capacity of poetry to give reality the greater permanence of the imagined."[46] As Freud wrote, "Sublimation enables excessively strong excitation arising from particular sources of sexuality to find an outlet and use in other fields, so that a not inconsiderable increase in psychical efficiency results from a disposition which in itself is perilous."[47] Perhaps Freud should have written, "from particular sources of sexuality, rage, terror, sadness, and longing."

The wonder is that creativity and psychosis can become, on occasion, commingled. The wonder is that instead of a laborious developmental march from psychotic defenses to immature defenses to neurotic defenses to mature defenses, Plath's "hellishly funny stuff" allowed her psychosis to merge directly with mature sublimation.

———

Anna Freud, the heroine of the next chapter on mature defenses, and Sylvia Plath, the heroine of this chapter on psychotic defenses, were both victimized by their fathers. Both daughters tried to capture their fathers' essence in their art, and the books of both women continue to sell long after their deaths. In her gift of *The Ego and the Mechanisms of Defense* to her father on his eightieth birthday, Anna Freud's defenses preserved and enriched his work; unseemly love, competition, hostility, and ambivalence are nowhere to be found. In contrast, Sylvia Plath in her poetry identified literally with "the patricidal Oedipus" and the too loving Electra. In her poetry, her father's work is mocked; competition, hostility, and ambivalence are everywhere. Yet if Sylvia

Plath was in some ways so much less well adapted than Anna Freud, she arguably led a less counterfeit life. She married, had children, and could admit that sometimes her father was a "bastard." But adaptation is not a question of either/or. What is important to appreciate is that creativity can be lifesaving. For Plath the lifegiving benefits of creativity could be measured in months; for Anna Freud they could be measured in decades. One woman was not greater than the other. It is true, however, that Anna Freud lived longer, was more fully loved, and caused those who loved her less pain.

Albert Einstein, James Joyce, and Bertrand Russell, three giants of human creativity, all had schizophrenic children. Perhaps that is coincidence, perhaps not. In any case, in Plath's life she was both the creator and the madwoman. In contrast to her, her father, Otto Plath, was frozen. Sylvia Plath's Daddy who stood at the blackboard was an utterly forgettable, if world-class, expert on bees. It was his "crazy" daughter who wrote poems that gave him, his bees, and his daughter immortality. We have no evidence that Professor Otto Plath was an inspiring teacher, whereas, according to one biographer, Sylvia Plath was remembered as "one of the two or three finest instructors ever to appear in the English department at Smith College."[48] In addition, the lessons of her *Ariel* poems are certain to live on for decades to come. The reasons for this have only a little to do with insanity, and much to do with the incandescent wisdom of her ego.

10

Anna Freud: Mature Defenses

Anna Freud: You mean you don't think anyone is born altruistic.

Joseph Sandler: Or even *becomes* altruistic, out of the goodness of his heart.

Anna Freud: No, it's out of the badness of his heart.

The Analysis of Defense, 1985

Sigmund Freud took upon himself responsibility for the shortcomings of a rather contemptible father; Anna Freud took upon herself responsibility for the shortcomings of a rather great one. Both wrote their "confessions" of their responsibility for their fathers' shortcomings in books—*The Interpretation of Dreams* and *The Ego and the Mechanisms of Defense,* respectively. But such is the legerdemain of the creative ego that their respective confessions made them immortal. At first glance, the books were manifestos of their authors' central philosophies and not intended to have anything to do with their fathers, but, as Nietzsche has noted, all philosophical writing reflects "involuntary and unconscious autobiography." Or as Elisabeth Young-Bruehl, Anna Freud's gifted biographer, put it, "But for individuals, it is true that expansions of theory and expansions of self-insight coincide, and greatness is a matter of growing for and through the work."[1]

It seems fitting to illustrate the use of defenses through the life of their greatest elucidator, Anna Freud, but such a process will involve identifying circles within circles. Thus, this chapter will make many points at once. It will offer evidence that defenses are both visible and invisible to the user: that defenses, paradoxically, are simultaneously conscious and unconscious. It will underscore that deployment of defenses is not pathological but can be extraordinarily adaptive and human. It will continue to demonstrate how the coming together of individual autobiography *and* creative product *and* biography helps us to identify defenses as existing in real life and not just in the imagination of psychoanalysts. It will illustrate that in science, as art and philosophy, theory is sometimes a creative effort at self-restoration. Perhaps most important of all, the life of Anna Freud will vividly illustrate four of the most mature defenses; sublimation, suppression, altruism, and humor.

If Anna Freud's life reflects the victory of love, of enduring fame, and of triumphant and creative aggression, her life was also one founded upon pain such as we often associate with the lives of creative artists. At age 36 she confessed to a friend that, during her childhood, "I always sought out children who gave me up, and it always had the same effect on me as now. It was as though I looked at myself with the others' eyes and was of just as little worth to myself as I was to them. Now it is almost all right, because I know it." A year later she told the same friend, "Tonight I dreamed that I killed our cook, Anna. I cut off her head and cut her to pieces and had no feelings of guilt which was very peculiar. Now I know why: because her name is Anna, and that means me."[2] With such a capacity for turning her own anger in toward herself, and with so little support from others, Anna Freud might have ended up a suicide like Sylvia Plath. But Anna Freud died famous and beloved at age 86. How did her life work out that way? What were the sources of her invincibility?

Sigmund Freud's youngest daughter, born in 1896, began life as the unplanned and unwanted sixth child of an exhausted mother. She was named after one of her father's favorite patients, Anna Hammerschlag Lichtheim. In 1900, when Anna was 4, her father immodestly wrote, "A girl's first affection is for her father," and added a page later, "A particularly gifted and lively girl of four . . . declared quite openly: 'Mummy can go away now. Then Daddy must marry me and I'll be his wife.'"[3] The alternative possibilities that daughters might also be rather fond of their mothers and that fathers might also be devoted to their daughters were never very important themes in the writings of either Freud.

Anna was not breast-fed, and her mother clearly preferred her three older brothers and two older sisters. Perhaps in response, Anna comforted herself with a rich fantasy world in which she played the role of a young male hero, whose moral efforts to excel led only to more loneliness. For example, as a child she wrote:

> For all the glory my sword has won,
> The old and the young do envy me,
> But my heart still hungers after Love,
> Which in the forest there I sacrificed.[4]

If in her fantasy Anna Freud felt condemned to loneliness, in her everyday life she retained a sense of abiding shame. By age 16 her posture was already starting to stoop forward; she believed that her ankles and her waist were too fat and that there could no longer be any question that her prettier older sister, Sophie, was her mother's favorite. At 19 she wrote to her father that she had dreamed "that I had to defend a milk farm belonging to us. But [my] sword was broken; so that as I pulled it out, I was ashamed in front of the enemy"; and at 20 she reported to him sadly that her hiking shoes "are so big that when the Hausfrau saw them she said that a man must own them."[5]

Sigmund Freud, the oldest son in a nineteenth-century Jewish family, became his mother's "Goldener Siggi." In contrast, his metaphor for Anna, the youngest daughter in a nineteenth-century Jewish family, was a casket made of lead. When Anna was 17 her father wrote a paper developing the theme of the three caskets in Shakespeare's *The Merchant of Venice*. In the paper, having reminded the reader that Bassanio won Shylock's daughter, Portia, by choosing the leaden casket, Freud retells the stories of Cordelia and Cinderella, each the youngest and humblest of three sisters. He asks his audience, "Is not this once more the scene of a choice between three women, of whom the youngest is the best, the most excellent one? Cordelia makes herself unrecognizable, inconspicuous like lead, she remains dumb." Then he rephrases Bassanio's justification for choosing the leaden casket: "That is to say: thy plainness moves me more than the blatant nature of the other two."[6] The summer after he wrote this essay, Freud confessed to his friend Sandor Ferenczi, "For each of us fate assumes the form of one (or several) women . . . [This summer] my closest companion will be my little daughter, who is developing very well at the moment (you will long ago have guessed the subjective condition for the 'Theme of the Three Caskets')."[7] True, like Cordelia in *King Lear*, Anna Freud was ultimately her father's favorite; but her path was almost as difficult as Cordelia's, and it required as much self-sacrifice. Besides, most of us would prefer that our opposite-sex parent perceive us as beautiful.

Although as a child Anna Freud loved to tell her own fantasies, she rejected fantastic stories by others. She only liked stories that "might be true." Thus, talking animals, witches—anything that came too close to primary process—were rejected. Indeed, it was probably the practical Anna who added the concrete term "mechanism" to her father's more poetic "defense." Of more importance, she was appalled by the possibly irrational consequences of puberty. At age 40 she described puberty as a time when "The id, now grown strong, may overcome the ego, in which case no trace will be left of the previous character of the individual, and the entrance into adult life will be marked by a riot of uninhibited gratification of instinct."[8] Adolescence seemed a dangerous world. In 1907, when Anna Freud was 11, her father wrote a paper called "The Sexual Enlightenment of Children" in which he underscored the importance of honesty with children. Yet the very next year, having been told she was merely going to the hospital for an examination, Anna was anesthetized and her appendix was removed. In her mind, her mother received the blame for the deception, but the parental lie continued to rankle. Years later, both in her practice and in her writing, she went to considerable pains to protect future generations of children from such cruel deceptions. Anna Freud was to practice honesty with her child patients as well as to preach it.

There was a still more important instance of her father's not practicing toward his daughter what he preached to others. In 1918 the 22-year-old Anna Freud began her psychoanalysis with her own father. Her analysis lasted until 1922 and then was probably resumed for a few months in 1924. Sometimes her hour came at the end of their day—as late as 10 P.M. In May of 1920, at age 25, she received a ring from her father similar to that given to his closest male supporters, but nevertheless, a gold ring is an unusual gift to an analysand. With some justification, Paul Roazen surmised that Anna Freud's analyst was "A genius who was also naturally an immense figure in his daughter's fantasy life; as her analyst, he tied her permanently to him."[9]

Despite outstanding grades in school, Anna was not encouraged by her father to attend the Gymnasium. Instead, when she was 16 her education was deemed complete. She was apprenticed to become an elementary school teacher. The next year her father wrote to Ferenczi that since his older two daughters had married, "my closest companion will be my little daughter, Anna."[10] Thus, as the only daughter left at home, Anna, at age 18, became her father's secretary. From age 19 to 24 she also taught school.

For a long time, however, Anna Freud had been secretly and independently preparing herself for her future career as a child psychoanalyst. Decades later she wrote to a friend, Joseph Goldstein, "There were some wooden steps belonging to my father's library, and I used to sit on them very quietly and listen to his discussion with visitors. That was very useful."[11] So it was. Anna Freud also never forgot her father telling her at age 14, on a walk through Vienna's Prater, "You see those houses with their lovely facades? Things are not necessarily so lovely behind the facades. And so it is with human beings too."[12] At 18 she sat in on her father's lectures at the University of Vienna, and in her twenties she went on ward rounds with Julius Wagner von Jauregg, who won a Nobel Prize for discovering malarial fever treatment for general paresis; his assistant Helene Deutsch; and his residents Heinz Hartmann and Paul Schilder. The last three later became famous psychiatrists in America; few psychiatric residents have ever enjoyed a more distinguished faculty.

In 1923 her father endured the first of what would be almost annual operations for pharyngeal cancer. Anna Freud became his nurse, as well as his secretary and his analysand. In 1926, contrary to their custom in previous years, the Freud family took a vacation at the Cottage Sanatorium. Anna Freud slept in the room adjacent to her father's, and she undertook his care for half of each day, alternating with her mother and her Aunt Minna.[13] "To the end of his life," Ernest Jones reminds us, "Freud refused to have any other nurse than his daughter Anna. He made a pact with her at the beginning that no sentiment was to be displayed . . . all that was necessary had to be performed in a cool matter-of-fact fashion with the absence of emotion characteristic of a surgeon."[14] Easy to say, but how difficult to carry out. Such an experience had once driven another upper-middle-class Viennese daughter, Bertha Pappenheim (Breuer's famous patient Anna O.), to hysterical hallucinations and years of invalidism. Like Anna Freud, Anna O. had a brother who received the education. She too resorted to compulsive daydreaming. But unlike Anna O., Anna Freud did not succumb. Deprived of a first-class liberal education by her father, and yet given—by private tutorial—an education that many modern psychiatrists might covet, Anna's ego could discern both the cloud and its silver lining. She chose the latter, but her ego did not ignore her mistreatment.

In 1926, having for three years nobly assumed the burden of being both her father's secretary and his nurse, Anna Freud wrote to her father's psychoanalytic colleague Max Eitingon, "I run across the fact that I do not succeed in doing something to or for others without immediately wanting to have something for myself." [15]

At first, being analyzed by her father only furthered Anna's humiliation. She had to confess to him her sexual fantasies of being beaten. Later she described these fantasies in her first published paper, "Beating Fantasies and Daydreams." In her clinical report, she told how pleasurable fantasies could coexist with fantasies of being beaten. She described how a young woman daydreamed of herself as a male protagonist who was locked in a dungeon and very strictly brought up. He was at the mercy of a cruel and powerful knight who "threatens to put the prisoner on the rack to force him to betray his secrets." "The fantasy ends," she continued, "with the father's forgiveness, and its hidden meaning was always that the father loves only me. By renouncing her private pleasure in favor of making an impression on others, the author has accomplished an important developmental step: the transformation of an autistic fantasy into a social activity." Thus, in creating a good definition of what makes sublimation so adaptive, Anna Freud created a good metaphor to sublimate the shame of being put on the rack of an analytic couch by one's own father. In her paper she also noted, "The sublimation of [a daughter's] sensual love [for her father] into tender friendship is of course greatly facilitated by the fact that already in the early stages of the beating fantasy the girl abandoned the differences of the sexes and is invariably represented as a boy." Although allegedly this paper was about her first patient, a 15-year-old girl, it was written in 1921, before Anna Freud had any patients of her own. Besides, she tells us that her patient's beating fantasy was "proved in a rather thorough-going analysis." [16] Thus the most likely source of her paper was her own analysis.

Anna Freud's paper, in large part, was written to fulfill the requirements of her application for membership in the Vienna Psychoanalytic Society. In May of 1922, having given the paper, she was made a member of the Society. The implications of her paper were far-reaching and helped to shift the attention of psychoanalysis from night dreams to daydreams. Anna Freud, both as patient and as colleague, was one of the influences that shifted her father's attention, and indeed the attention of the whole psychoanalytic movement, from id psychology to ego psychology. Just as Anna preferred to read real-life children's books, so her professional career was devoted to demonstrating that the human psyche could be studied in the real playroom rather than in the dreams of sleeping adults and the myths of ancient Greeks.

In 1925, because of his own illness, Sigmund Freud encouraged his daughter to read his paper "Some Psychical Consequences of the Anatomical Distinction between the Sexes" at the ninth International Psychoanalytic Congress. By today's standards, asking Anna Freud to read such a paper by her own analyst seems cruel and humiliating almost beyond belief. But there is no written evidence that at the time any of the participants at the conference perceived anything unusual about the event.

Today the text that Anna Freud was entrusted to read is notorious; epitomizing Sigmund Freud's sexism, the essay is sometimes nicknamed "Anatomy Is Destiny." Consider the following excerpt:

> Every analyst has come across certain women who cling with special intensity and tenacity to the bond with their father and the wish in which it culminates of having a child by him . . . They [women] notice the penis of a brother or playmate, strikingly visible and of large proportions, at once recognize it as a superior counterpart of their own small, inconspicuous organ, and from that time forward fall victim to envy for the penis . . . Other factors permanently determine the boy's relations to women: Horror of the mutilated creature or triumphant contempt for her . . . A little girl behaves differently. She makes her judgement and decision in a flash. She has seen it. She knows that she is without it, and wants to have it . . . She begins to share the contempt felt by men for a sex which is the lesser in so important a respect.[17]

Then, having had to publicly disparage her own and every other woman's anatomy, Anna Freud had to continue and do the same for their character. She had to read to her rapt audience, "I cannot evade the notion (though I hesitate to give it expression) that for women, the level of what is ethically normal is different from what it is for men.

Their superego is never . . . so independent of its emotional origins as we require it to be in men. Character-traits which critics of every epoch have brought up against women—that they show less sense of justice than men, that they are more often influenced in their judgements by feelings of affection or hostility . . . We must not allow ourselves to be deflected from such conclusions by the denials of the feminists."[18] George Bernard Shaw's great sexist Henry Higgins could not have written any more smugly.

At the time, Sigmund Freud's paper was received, according to the official congress report, "with cheerful gratitude." Ernest Jones wrote, "This mark of attention on his [Freud's] part, the content of the paper, and the way it was read all gave general pleasure."[19] Karl Abraham wrote to Freud, "But now I come to the best part of the whole Congress. The news that Miss Anna would read a paper of yours evoked spontaneous applause at the beginning of the Congress which I wish you could have heard for yourself. Her extremely clear way of speaking did full justice to the contents."[20]

At this time, when Anna Freud selflessly "did full justice" to her father's paper, one of her favorite poems was "Der Dichter" by Rainer Maria Rilke. One verse of the poem cries:

> I have no beloved or place for home,
>   no circle where I am at center.
> The things to which I give myself
>   grow rich—while I am impoverished.[21]

How, one may ask, did Anna Freud survive? How did she not only survive but do full justice to her own talents? I believe there were many sources for her resiliency.

If Anna's biological mother was distant from her all of her life, her nurse, Josephine, became, in Anna Freud's words, her "psychological mother." For the rest of her life, in women like Lou Andreas-Salomé, Princess Bonaparte, and Dorothy Burlingham, Anna Freud was to find a series of such sustaining psychological mothers. Surrogate loves often permit abused or neglected children to survive and flourish.

Help also came from another sector. If Anna's father exploited his daughter's capacity for self-sacrifice, he also gave permission for her aggression. Anger from his little Annerl was never for Freud a manifestation of the "death instinct," the aggressive anti-libido of Thanatos that Freud condemned in others. Rather, when Anna was angry and acting up, Freud wrote to his friend Wilhelm Fliess, "Annerl is becoming downright beautiful by way of naughtiness."[22] Her biographer Young-Bruehl, comments, "This naughty side of Anna Freud was later covered over with goodness, but it never disappeared—especially because her father loved it." Young-Bruehl quotes another passage from a letter to Fliess: "Recently Anna complained that Mathilda [her older sister] had eaten all the apples and demanded that [Mathilda's] belly be split open . . . she's turning into a charming child." If when she was 25 Anna's father gave her a ring which committed her to absolute loyalty to his psychoanalytic movement, when she was 29 he also gave her a black Alsatian puppy—a child of sorts. "She and her father treated the dog like a child," Young-Bruehl tells us, "enjoying the spoiling of him and making Martha Freud [Anna's meticulous mother] furious by feeding him scraps at her meticulous dinner table."[23]

Thus, if Anna Freud was outwardly modest, dutiful, and unassuming, there is no doubt that at another level she felt permission to be fiercely competitive. Her nephew Ernst Freud tells us, "When my mother died, Anna, who was the sibling next to her in age, assumed the role of foster mother, and not infrequently conveyed to me that a unique and superb aunt such as she was could fill it better than any mother. She was good with animals, and would usually win at games . . . and I think, enjoyed her sense of superiority though she may not often have shown it." After her forced emigration from Austria to London, Ernst tells us by way of example, Anna Freud heard that a golden eagle was roosting in Regent's Park. She expressed a wish to see the eagle, but after leaving the park commented smugly, "the Austrian eagle had *two* heads."[24] Anything London had, Vienna had—and better. More important, like the long-suffering, modest Cordelia, Anna became the dominant woman in her father's life until he died. Yet her ambition never jarred the observer; nor was the defense of splitting, invented by her arch-rival, Melanie Klein, ever in evidence. Unlike Sylvia Plath, Anna Freud showed none of the murderous rage or unbridled love of Electra or Oedipus. Her sublimation always made the perilous beautiful.

Throughout her life, Anna Freud's delicate balance between modesty and the quest for fame was an enduring theme. In 1929, when she was only 33, a Frankfurt newspaper described her as follows: "A slim young woman with dark hair crowning a serene and open face, stood yesterday on the platform of the little meeting house where every seat had been sold . . . Her presentation is so perfect in its smoothness and clarity, and, in its objectivity, so far from rhetorical pretension, that to listen to her becomes an aesthetic pleasure; intellectual grace which captivates without effort." [25] Although Anna Freud saw herself as the guardian of the heritage, the American psychoanalyst George Pollock wrote, "She was modest but assertive for the causes she felt were right . . . She led by example: hard work, high standards, generosity, love of truth, respect for the other and, overall, a sense of altruism." [26] Her altruism, Anna Freud had no doubt, came from the badness of her heart, from her intense wish to have something for herself.

The elegance of Anna Freud's altruism, of doing for others while serving her own instinctual needs, is dramatically illustrated by the following example. For a variety of reasons, she was deeply angry at Germany. Not only had the Nazis subjugated her country, forced her own emigration, and murdered her three aunts in concentration camps, but in 1938 she had been interrogated by the Gestapo under circumstances so perilous that she had carried means for suicide to the interview. She had spent the war years trying to meet the emotional needs of English children separated from their parents because of the German firebombing of London. After the war she had tended to the emotional rehabilitation of Jewish orphans rescued from the same death camps in which her aunts had been gassed. Then in 1964 the city of Munich offered her a cultural prize of 15,000 marks. Understandably, she wished to refuse, for she could not forgive Germany. But in order to avoid giving offense, her ego devised a benign—but thoroughly Machiavellian—solution. She accepted the prize on condition that the money would go "for help with the reconstruction of psychoanalysis in Germany." [27] As Anna's ego turned her anger into gold, Hitler must have writhed in his grave.

However constricted her childhood may have been, Anna Freud's solutions were highly creative. Beginning in 1934 she began making notes on a "kind of ego psychology." The notes became the monograph *The Ego and the Mechanisms of Defense,* which in 1936 she gave to her father as an eightieth-birthday present. If her father at one time or another had invented/discovered at least seventeen defenses, [28] Anna Freud for her father's birthday present invented/discovered two more: *identification with the aggressor* and *altruistic surrender.* Not surprisingly, these two defenses, which she described for the first time, were the same defenses that characterized her own adaptation to life.

With the first defense Anna Freud described, *identification with the aggressor,* the subject assimilates the qualities, behavior, thoughts, forms of aggression, or power symbols of a person seen as an oppressor. Thus, instead of scorning "Daddy" as did Sylvia Plath, Anna Freud identified with him. Her father's mission became her mission. Her father's sexism became her sexism. As part of her birthday gift to her father, she could write that a woman's "self love is mortified when she compares herself with boys, who are better equipped for masturbation, and she does not want to be constantly reminded of her disadvantage by indulging in the practise." "If the girl's attachment to her father comes to grief," she continued,

> it may give place to an identification with him . . . Her penis-wish, with its offshoots in the shape of ambitious masculine phantasies, was prohibited, so too her feminine wish for children and the desire to display herself, naked or in beautiful clothes, to her father, and to win his admiration. But these impulses were not repressed . . . She projected her prohibited instinctual impulses on to other people, just as the patients did whose cases I quoted in the last chapter. The only difference lay in the way these impulses were subsequently dealt with. The patient did not dissociate herself from her proxies, but identified herself with them.[29]

Just so did Anna Freud identify with her father. Throughout her professional life she saw herself, as her father had seen her, as the blind Oedipus's blindly loyal daughter, Antigone. Always she strove to be a daughter faithful to her father and *his* religion. From her lifelong efforts to give up her own self-interest and to obtain vicarious pleasure from the interest and pleasures of her father, she derived success and pleasure for herself.

When Sylvia Plath tried to identify with her father, an international expert on bees, and to maintain a small apiary, her identification turned her aggression inadvertently against herself. As she wrote, "Even my beloved bees set upon me today when I numbly knocked aside their sugar feeder, and I am all over stings."[30] But when Anna identified with the aggressor the result had to be classified as altruism, not masochism. Having taken Otto Rank's place as a member of Freud's secret inner circle, his "Old Guard," and having received a gold ring with intaglio from her father, Anna suffered no "stings." Rather, when in 1924 the Committee of Six announced that she would become the sixth member of the psychoanalytic inner circle in time for her twenty-ninth birthday, she wrote, "Sometimes the most beautiful thing is precisely the one that comes unexpectedly and unearned, hence something given truly as a present. Most beautiful, moreover, if it is for Papa's sake. The both of us were pleased together about it, he no less than I."[31]

By 1971 Anna Freud was in spirit the leading figure of the International Psychoanalytic Society. In that year I went to visit her and asked her to autograph my first edition of *The Ego and the Mechanisms of Defense*. I described the book, quite honestly, as the most important single book in my own psychoanalytic education. She modestly averted her gaze. She seemed not to hear what I had said; and then, abruptly, she waved her hand as if to draw my attention to the reception room— her father's former study, kept exactly as it was when he died. Her words followed almost as a reprimand: "Isn't this a lovely room?" I felt she meant, What right had I, in the presence of her father's ghost, to suggest that *her* work had been more important to me than *his*.

The purpose of *altruistic surrender*, the second defense that Anna Freud described, was the overcoming of "narcissistic mortification." In *The Ego and the Mechanisms of Defense*, Anna Freud editorialized:

> That the poet [Edmund Rostand] is depicting in Cyrano's "altruism" something more than a strange love-adventure is clear from the parallel which he draws between Cyrano's love-life and his fate as a poet. Just as Christian woos Roxane with the help of Cyrano's poems and letters, writers like Corneille, Molière, and Swift borrow whole scenes from his unknown works, thus enhancing their own fame . . . The personal defect [his oversized nose] which he thinks renders him contemptible makes him feel that the others who are preferred to himself are better qualified than he to realize his wish fantasies.[32]

Such is altruistic surrender. Decades later when Anna, the self-appointed guardian of her father's psychoanalytic legacy and the inventor of altruistic surrender, herself lay dying, her nephew Ernst was leaving for America on a lecture tour. In German she bade him, "If my friends in the States ask you how I am, tell them 'Go tell the Spartans, all ye who pass by, That here, obedient to their laws, we lie.'"[33] She was quoting Simonides' epitaph on the monument to the Spartans who fell at Thermopylae. She had sacrificed her life for her father, and yet to the end of her life she was proud to be such a Spartan, such a Cyrano de Bergerac.

But her own use of altruistic surrender did not force Anna Freud to deny her assertiveness, only to deal with it ingeniously. Her birthday gift to her father actually reflected a point of clear disagreement with him, a disagreement of a peculiarly ironic sort. Both in word and deed *The Ego and the Mechanisms of Defense* illustrated that aggression was not closely allied to Thanatos, Freud's "death instinct," but was the very fount of creativity. Anger was as much a part of life as the libido. In the gift she gave to her father, anger was transformed by her protagonists into play and healthy achievement. Properly harnessed, anger, the badness in our hearts, serves love. Over her father's lifetime, many people fell out of love with him, but in the biographical record of Anna Freud's long life there is no evidence that any of the many people who learned to admire her ever stopped. Such is the wisdom of the ego.

In the same birthday gift Anna Freud also illustrated the close parallel between personal conflict and scientific as well as artistic discovery. In an autobiographical illustration of altruistic surrender, she told the story of a young governess in analysis who "wanted to have beautiful clothes and a number of children . . . she wished to have and to do everything that her much older playmates had and did . . . better than they and to be admired for her cleverness. Her everlasting cry of 'me too!' was a nuisance to her elders." Recall that Anna Freud was the youngest, or as she put it "the littlest," of six children, and that she became, if not a governess, a teacher and an analyst of young children. As a child she, too, had shouted "Me too!" "What chiefly struck one about her [the governess] as an adult," she continued,

> was her unassuming character and the modesty of the demands she made upon life. When she came to be analyzed, she was unmarried and childless, and her dress was rather shabby and inconspicuous . . . Although she took no trouble about her own dress, she displayed a lively interest in her friends' clothes. Childless herself, she was devoted to other people's children, as was indicated by her choice of profession . . . Similarly, in spite of her own retiring behavior, she was anxious for the men whom she loved and followed their careers with the utmost interest.[34]

Anna Freud could have been writing her autobiography, not a case history.

Anna Freud never married, but she had been very fond of a man who was courting her older sister. She tells us that the "governess" at age 13 (the same age Anna had been as she watched her older sister be courted) "fell in love secretly with a friend of her elder sister who had formerly been the special object of her jealousy."[35] Like a female Cyrano, the governess

> remembered perfectly distinctly how, from having been at first paralyzed with disappointment, she suddenly began to bustle about, fetching things to make her sister "pretty" for her outing, and eagerly helping her to get ready. While doing this, the patient was blissfully happy and quite forgot that it was not she, but her sister, who was going out to enjoy herself. She had projected her own desire for love and her craving for admiration onto a rival and, having identified herself with the object of her envy, she enjoyed the fulfillment of her desire.[36]

> In her disappointment with herself she displaced her wishes onto objects whom she felt were better qualified to fulfill them. Her male friends were vicariously to achieve for her in professional life what she herself could never achieve, and the girls that were better-looking than herself were to do the same in the sphere of love.[37]

The thoughtful reader is entitled at this point to wonder if such altruism, such self-deception, such Pollyanna-like denial could really be adaptive. But for Anna Freud it was.

In real life, Erik Erikson was one of the men she helped and from whose success she drew vicarious satisfaction. When Erikson was in analysis with the childless Anna Freud, he recalled, "Anna Freud occasionally attended to her handiwork in my psychoanalytic sessions . . . I remember having referred to it once when I was speaking of Joan's and my newborn son [Kai]. A number of sessions later, Anna Freud, at the end of an hour, having said the usual goodbye with a firm handshake, smilingly handed me a small blue knitted sweater, saying, 'This is for Kai.'"[38] Admittedly, analysts are not supposed to give their analysands baby presents, but no one, I suspect, who ever knew her doubted the goodness in her heart *or* her professionalism. On another occasion in his analysis, Erikson talked of his fears that he would be unable to contribute to psychoanalysis. "I declared once more that I could not see a place for my artistic inclinations in such high intellectual endeavors. She said quietly: 'You might help to make them see.'"[39] Erikson never forgot. Sigmund Freud had given his analysand a ring to bind his daughter to *his* movement; Anna Freud had given her analysand gifts to help enhance Erikson's own creativity. As I suggested in Chapter 2, there are worse fates than becoming a nun.

In her compendium of defenses, Anna Freud wrote, "To these nine methods of defence . . . we must add a tenth, which pertains rather to the study of the normal than to that of neurosis: sublimation."[40] As she grew older her life was a model of sublimation as well as altruism.

In her twenties Anna Freud rejected all of her psychoanalyst suitors, for she believed they loved her only because she was her father's daughter. Until 1928, she said, she felt drained by the people around her: "because one is useful, one will be carried off piece by piece during the daytime; no one takes much interest in the unusable bit that is left by the evening—though strangely enough, that unusable portion is the real self."[41] Then, after she was 30, she found real joy and pleasure in her intimate friendship with Dorothy Burlingham. Estranged from a manic-depressive husband, Burlingham was an American woman who had come to Vienna with her young children. The women first met when the Burlingham children attended Anna Freud's play school and then later became her patients. Her unexploitable self—the self that did not desire to be exploited—flourished in Burlingham's company. Together they lovingly decorated an Austrian country cottage. Through this friendship, Anna Freud discovered a kind of retroactive, nonanalytic cure for her childhood unsociability. "It is funny," she wrote to Lou Andreas-Salomé in 1928, "but only last year and this did I really enjoy my birthday. Until then there were too many mixed feelings and now everything is much simpler: only more beautiful. I even had a big afternoon children's party."[42] A half-century later, on the occasion of his mother's death, one of Dorothy Burlingham's sons could say to Anna Freud, "You were everything to her and she had a most wonderful life with you . . . I keep thinking of all the happy times you had with each other, day after day after day."[43] Not a bad tribute to fifty years of friendship and unambivalent, if attenuated, commitment. Not a bad tribute to the goodness of Anna Freud's Spartan existence.

The Spartan life of Anna Freud also illustrated the defense of suppression. During 1938 as his family prepared their narrow escape from Hitler's Vienna to London, Sigmund Freud wrote, "Anna tries to make the present bearable by saying we now have a much needed rest between the exertions here and the tasks we have to face."[44] To Lou Andreas-Salomé, Anna Freud described her behavior during this stressful time a little differently: "I can't tell you how often I think of a sentence you spoke to me once. That it does not matter what fate one has if only one really lives it."[45]

After the death of her great companion and professional colleague, Anna took to wearing Dorothy Burlingham's sweaters and bought a chow, Jo-Fi, named after one of the chows that Dorothy had given to Anna's father in Vienna. In her funeral eulogy for her best friend of fifty years, Anna reminded her fellow mourners of her father's stoical wisdom: better to be grateful for a friendship than to lament its loss. The stoic knows that brave remembrance is the only honest antidote for grief. Perhaps the simplest example of her suppression was when Anna Freud wrote to a friend that each of her father's serial operations for cancer "takes a piece of me. But that is just the way it is. One cannot ask for the raisins without the surrounding bun. I understand that."[46]

Humor, like starlight, is much harder to capture; but it suffused Anna Freud's life. Those who knew her recognized her humor even if their anecdotes fail to capture it. She said of defenses, "One should not look at them microscopically, but macroscopically. You have to take *off* your glasses to look at them not put them *on*."[47] Thus, let me cite a macroscopic generalization to prove her use of humor even if I cannot cite specific examples. In a memorial volume for Anna Freud, Clifford Yorke wrote, "Her wit, of course, was boundless. If necessary, she had a joke for every occasion."[48]

Humor is also closely allied with play. Perhaps what transformed Anna Freud's reaction formation into altruism was that she never forgot how to play. "Even today," wrote her biographer Uwe Peters in 1985, "there are former students of Anna Freud's in Vienna who recall her unequaled talent for inspiring children with enthusiasm for the material."[49] When Anna Freud was well over 80 years old and just back from New York City where she had received an honorary degree from Columbia University, she asked her colleagues Clifford Yorke and Hansi Kennedy to wait in the hall. She rushed upstairs and then came down making a grand entrance resplendent in her newly acquired

Columbia academic robes. In her enjoyment of dressing up, she managed to retain the innocence of a child while simultaneously showing herself off as a distinguished woman. Indeed, Anna Freud is the only woman, and probably the only person without a college degree, to have received honorary degrees from the University of Chicago (1966) *and* Yale (1968) *and* Columbia (1978), *and* Harvard (1980) *and* even an honorary doctorate in medicine from the University of Vienna (1972).

Modesty, like altruism, provides its own rewards. As the years passed, Sigmund Freud became increasingly admiring of and modest toward his daughter Anna. In discussing the differential diagnosis of defense mechanisms, his own discovery, toward which he might have felt a proprietary interest, the usually competitive Freud advised the interested student, "There are an extraordinarily large number of methods (or mechanisms, as we say) used by our ego in the discharge of its defensive functions . . . my daughter, the child analyst, is writing a book upon them." [50] After *The Ego and the Mechanisms of Defense* was published, Freud wrote, "We call these procedures 'mechanisms of defense' . . . Anna Freud's book has given us a first insight into their multiplicity and many-sided significance." [51]

On another occasion he wrote, "I am glad that I am at least able to say that my daughter, Anna Freud, has made this study [the application of psychoanalysis to children] her life's work and has in that way compensated for my neglect." [52] Although Anna Freud complained that all of her patients—who shared a common waiting room with her father's patients—wanted to be in analysis with him, Freud's "rejoinder was short and to the point: all *his* patients would rather be treated by *her*." [53]

In 1935 Freud, in pain and dying of cancer, wrote to a friend, "Your description of the spring makes me sad and envious. I have still so much capacity for enjoyment that I am disappointed with the resignation forced on me. But one bright spot in my life is the success of Anna's work." [54] In the same year he wrote to Lou Andreas-Salomé, "My one source of satisfaction is Anna. It is remarkable how much influence and authority she has gained among the general run of analysts." [55] And four months later he wrote to her again: "In the end we all depend on creatures we ourselves have made . . . In any case it was very wise to have made her." [56]

To bring the curtain down on her book, of which her father thought so highly, Anna Freud had written, "The Ego is victorious when its defensive measures . . . enable it to restrict the development of anxiety and 'pain,' and so transform the instincts that, even in difficult circumstances, some measure of gratification is secured."[57] Like Beethoven, Anna Freud had emerged triumphant. She had elaborated a crucial link between her father's libido theory and the ego theories of her two young friends Erik Erikson and Heinz Hartmann. Thanks to her, defenses left the realm of metapsychology and became like the curvature of the earth, subtle phenomena but visible to everyone who really cared to look.

For her father, the alchemy of Anna Freud's ego had turned a leaden daughter into the purest gold. In contrast, Aurelia Plath wrote to a literary critic a decade after her daughter's death that Sylvia Plath "made use of everything and often transmuted gold into lead . . . the love remains—and the hurt. There is no escape for us."[58] Projection destroys; altruism mends. Both emanate from the pain within our hearts.

II

Eugene O'Neill: The Maturation of Defenses

Man is born broken. He lives by mending. The grace of
   God is glue!

Eugene O'Neill

Immature defenses are the building blocks of personality disorder. Immature defenses and personality disorder can create unbearable conflict, but they also help to relieve such conflict. Even as they distort and ultimately destroy relationships, immature defenses provide an illusion of intimacy. Since an unconscious purpose of immature defenses is to secure at least the illusion of stable love, it is not surprising that the immature defenses of others grip us, embrace us, and invade us even as they drive us to distraction. I believe that the explanation of this "contagion" lies in the capacity of immature defenses to penetrate, to bypass, and to ride roughshod over the barriers erected by sweet reason to protect the boundaries of our sense of self from intrusion by others.

What is so unforgivable—and so seductive—about people with personality disorders is that their longings and self-deceptions, unlike those of neurotics, do not just alter their own interior environment but also affect other people. But so do the longings and self-deceptions of the artist, the saint, and, as we have seen in the life of Florence Nightingale, the heroine. Vincent Van Gogh, Joan of Arc, and Florence Nightingale were all well qualified for inclusion in a casebook of personality disorders. Some contemporaries regarded each of them as a pariah and a misfit, and some considered each of them mad or bad. But each of the three was also extraordinarily creative, bringing into the world much that had not been there before, and today we regard them with admiration.

Just as creativity is different from psychosis, so the creative genius must deploy more mature defenses than those of personality disorder. In earlier chapters I have argued for an orderly developmental progression from psychotic to immature to neurotic to mature defenses. But I have also pointed out how Sylvia Plath's art and her psychosis incongruously merged. The irony-filled borderland between madness and great art is filled with such paradox. In order to understand this paradox we must understand the maturation of the ego and the evolutionary links between immature and mature defenses.

The life of Eugene O'Neill illustrates both the contagious nature of immature defenses—their transmission through close family interaction—and their evolution into mature defenses. The curse of immature defenses is that they make neglected children neglect *their* children. The blessing of immature defenses is that with a little love they can evolve into something beautiful. Thus, O'Neill's story begins as the case history of a neglected child turned alcoholic derelict and ends as the saga of an artist who was honored by a Nobel Prize and yet neglected all of his own children.

In 1885 a baby died in a hotel room of measles and neglect. His parents, James and Mary Ellen O'Neill, were not in town at the time but had left the baby and his older brother in the care of their grandmother, Bridget Quinlan. When Mary Ellen returned from traveling with her husband's itinerant theater company, she turned on the surviving child, Jamie, blaming him for killing his little brother. Then, although he was only 8 years old, she exiled him to a boarding school. He was not even allowed home at Christmas.

Two years later bereavement struck Mary Ellen again with the death of her mother, Bridget Quinlan, her only stable source of support. Then in 1888 another boy, Gene, was born in another hotel room. The parents had made no plans, the father was absent, and the birth was attended by a hotel doctor who entered the room smoking a black cigar and delivered the baby without washing his hands. Mary Ellen, still grieving for both her dead son and her dead mother, complained to the doctor of pain, not grief—and he prescribed for her pain, not her grief. Like many other bereaved persons before and since, Mary Ellen found that such "pain" was relieved by opiates. Gene, growing up neglected, dropped out of school and lived on the streets.

Gene grew up without friends, health, or family life. As a child in the care of a nurse, he moved from hotel to hotel. His brother was in boarding school and his addicted mother traveled nine months a year with her itinerant husband. As a child Gene nearly died of typhoid fever and also endured repeated respiratory infections and rickets. At 6 he was yanked away from his nurse and sent off to a Catholic boarding school, where he stayed until he was 12. True, he got to spend his summers with his mother. But his first boarding school Christmas was spent with just his nurse. Even the summers at home did not feel cozy, for his mother spent most of her days in a zombie-like state from morphine.

Just as his mother resorted to opiates to escape pain, Gene resorted to schizoid fantasy. Decades later he would be able to comfort himself by writing the truth: I will always be a stranger who never feels at home, who does not really want, who is not really wanted. But as a child he escaped into a world of dreams. Absorbing the nuns' teachings about the love and the peace of God, he tried to find comfort in religion. He began, in the loneliness of boarding school, to fantasize an ideal love that would enfold and protect him from the world. Years later he described this recurrent fantasy to his second wife: "It was a dream of my childhood—when I had to dream that I was not alone. There was me and one other in this dream. I dreamed it often—and during the day sometimes this other seemed to be with me; and, then, I was a happy little boy. But this *other* in my dream, this other I never quite saw. It was a presence felt that made me complete."[1] But, of course, his comfort was but a momentary illusion.

At age 14 Gene learned that his mother was a drug addict. Previously deeply religious, he now vowed, "To hell with church." And at 15, already a heavy smoker, he began to drink at the more colorful and notorious bars in town. In other words, abetted by the instability of puberty, the defense of acting out took the place of fantasy. In high school—the only formal education he ever got—he absorbed the works of literary outlaws: Nietzsche, Jack London, Dostoevsky, Oscar Wilde. His rebellious reading and petty delinquencies led his high school principal to predict that he would die in the electric chair.[2] But Gene learned another skill in high school. He was a hungry child who had learned to absorb what he saw, to write down what he saw. He began to keep extensive, systematic notebooks. These notebooks he was to keep all his life, for they were receptacles into which he could pour the raw truth of an everyday life too painful for him, or his family, to bear without elaborate self-deception.

After high school Gene entered Princeton University, where he continued his acting out. Whereas his other classmates drank beer and whiskey on campus or in straight bars in New York, Gene drank absinthe in gay bars in Trenton, New Jersey, and he was eager to try opium. He scorned school spirit, but since other students hated the college president, Woodrow Wilson, Gene rather liked him. Gene tried to shock his classmates by decorating his college room with a fishnet hung with bras and used condoms. He stole books from the college library. He hung out with anarchists. He failed three courses. He broke two college chairs and one washbasin. He threatened a classmate with a pistol, and his own drunkenness was so marked that he was blackballed by the hard-drinking college fraternities. He was suspended for throwing stones through windows, and shortly afterward he was expelled for his failing grades.

For the next two years Gene lived in New York, first at home while his mother toured with her husband, then with some impoverished bohemians. He consorted with prostitutes and was drunk much of the time. His only positive activity was to obtain, through his father's influence, complimentary tickets to the avant-garde theater. He saw *Hedda Gabler* ten times. Where does acting out end and an original mind begin?

In 1909 Gene impregnated his girlfriend, married her secretly, and immediately abandoned her to go goldmining in Central America. There, with a revolver on his hip, he lived in the jungle, fell in love with a married woman, and accomplished nothing except to continue to store up painful memories in his heart and in his journals. When he returned to New York his wife was about to give birth, but he did not contact her. Instead, he learned of his son's birth from a tabloid in a barroom. In a drunken tantrum, he entered his parents' empty apartment and tried to chop the legs off his mother's furniture with a machete.[3] Later he wrote of that period in his life in the words of a character, Jack Townsend: "At that time the whole thing seemed just a pleasant game we were playing; its serious aspects appeared remote, unreal. I never gave them a thought.[4] The defense of acting out abolishes the superego, soothes the self, and wounds others terribly.

A month later, on an impulse, Gene set off on what was to be a two-year drunken, homeless binge. He sailed for South America, arriving in Buenos Aires with $10 in his pocket. He soon became one with the urban homeless. Afternoons were spent begging for pesos or selling what he scavenged from trash; evenings were spent getting drunk on cheap Argentine rum; early mornings were spent sleeping on park benches or in a galvanized metal shack with a homeless adolescent waif for a mistress. In this first year on the road he also wrote one unpublished poem. Where does an original mind end and acting out begin?

In May 1911 Gene returned to New York on a tramp steamer. For a month he contacted no family member, not even speaking to his wife or seeing his son, now a year old, whom his wife had wistfully named after him. Instead, he lived in an unheated room in a vermin-infested flophouse called Jimmy-the-Priest's. A free lunch came with his room, and his cheap whiskey cost only 5¢ a shot. His only steady companion was a prostitute named Maude.

That July Gene impulsively sailed for London as an ablebodied seaman. This experience not only enriched him by $25 but allowed him to learn a useful trade called the soogie-moogie—scrubbing down ship bulkheads with caustic soda. Returning to New York, he resumed residence at Jimmy-the-Priest's for the rest of the year.

How are we to understand such a dissolute youth, a young man so selfish, so narcissistic, and so utterly incompetent? We could dismiss him as a pyschopath. But in Gene's case we have an alternative: he went on to write a brilliantly autobiographical play that can help us to understand why he believed he had to act out his feelings rather than share them.

Fortunately, immature defenses do not always last forever, and personality disorder, like adolescence, is often a self-limiting disease. Eventually Gene's capacity for fantasy allowed him salvation, if not solace, through remembering. In 1924 he wrote, "Writing is my vacation from living—so I don't need vacations."[5] But his writing was intensely autobiographical and anything but a vacation from the truth. The evolution of his dissociation allowed him to escape into real theater rather than into the dissociation of a Pollyanna. His fantasy and dissociation evolved into sublimation. For instead of being simple denial, his writing recreated every nuance of his recollected pain, pang by pang.

How the vagrant Gene's acting out of 1908–1912 became the Nobel laureate Eugene O'Neill's sublimated masterpiece *Long Day's Journey into Night* of 1940 is an odyssey of psychological recovery. O'Neill's biography helps to illustrate how maturation of the ego can cure character disorder and how real tragedy can evolve into cathartic art—how the hopelessness of twisted genes and twisted environment can also include triumph. As O'Neill himself wrote, "Human hope is the greatest power in life and the only thing that defeats death."[6] And yet the dark side of the story was that he also continued the family pattern by neglecting his own children.

A leading theater critic wrote of O'Neill's great autobiographical plays, "Today, *The Iceman* appears to be, along with *Long Day's Journey into Night*, the most substantial dramatic literature ever composed on this continent."[7] O'Neill himself said of *Long Day's Journey* and *The Iceman Cometh*, "These two plays give me greater satisfaction than any other two I have ever done."[8] In short, he was able to shape his memories of family agony during the crucial year of 1912 into a work that was a "faithful image of his fantasy" and yet could "link a large yield of pleasure" to a representation of his painful past and so produce a miracle of mental contagion. This is a process that no cognitive psychologist or computer simulation will ever fully explicate.

Long Day's Journey into Night is remarkably close to true autobiography. The family name is changed to Tyrone, but the first names of James, Jamie, and Mary Ellen O'Neill stay the same. Eugene O'Neill and his deceased brother, Edmund, simply have their names reversed. But the play is not only autobiography and great art; it is also a veritable textbook of immature defenses. It vividly illustrates the way immature defenses destroy souls even as at the same time it offers the theater audience catharsis and access to fresh truth.

It is no accident that the immature defenses are best illustrated in troubled but intimate settings, where the protagonists are too close for comfort. It is also no accident that the play's four principal characters are all alcohol or drug abusers, with pharmacologically regressed central nervous systems. Both social setting and biological impairment can facilitate the appearance of immature defenses. Nor was it any accident that when O'Neill wrote the play he was over 50, had been abstinent from alcohol for thirteen years, and was in a marriage where he was finally close enough for comfort. Social supports and a mature central nervous system both make it easier to deploy mature defenses.

Long Day's Journey illustrates a paradox. Although one of the major purposes of the immature defenses is to preserve the illusion of sustained relationships, another purpose is to hold the beloved at arm's length. Thus, after thirty-six years of marriage, the Tyrone parents remain faithful to and dependent on each other, yet when together, deploying the defenses of devaluation and projection, they berate each other:

> Tyrone: I understand that I've been a God-damned fool to
> believe in you!
> Mary: All I've felt was distrust and spying and suspicion.[9]

Nevertheless, when apart from her husband Mary can admit, "Oh, I don't mind. I've loved him dearly for thirty-six years. That proves I know he's lovable at heart and can't help being what he is, doesn't it?" And her maid, Cathleen, replies, "That's right, Ma'am. Love him dearly, for any fool can see he worships the ground you walk on."[10] Similarly, Mary is devoted to her sons, but in such a fashion that she leaves them feeling (in Edmund's words), "It's as if in spite of loving us, she hated us!"[11]

But *Long Day's Journey* does more than illustrate immature defenses; it illustrates their genesis. Unempathic failure to validate another person's pain is part of the key to the contagion of the immature defenses. In addition, the user of immature defenses not only fails to acknowledge the pain of others but also leaves his or her pain within other people to fester and to be regarded as their own. For example, Mary Tyrone's own morphine-catalyzed projection and dissociation catalyze in her son Edmund the somewhat different defenses of acting out and fantasy. The process of the transmission of defenses is sometimes referred to as projective identification.

Mary's projection encourages Edmund to lie, and more dangerous yet, to believe the lie—the process at the heart of dissociation.

Early in the play Mary makes Edmund the source of her own shame and denies him permission to acknowledge his own anxieties. Knowing that Edmund has recognized her relapse to drugs, she challenges him: "Tell me the truth. Why are you so suspicious all of a sudden?"

> Edmund: "I'm not!"
> Mary: "Oh yes you are . . ."
> Edmund: "Now don't start imagining things, Mama."[12]

Their through-the-looking-glass argument of Mary's accusations and Edmund's insistence of her innocence escalates until Mary exclaims, "Stop suspecting me! Please, dear! You hurt me! I couldn't sleep because I was thinking about you [that is, his tuberculosis]. That's the real reason!"[13]

"That's foolishness," her son lies. Driven to ignore his own concern over his tuberculosis, he tells his mother, "You know, it's only a bad cold."[14]

Insidiously, Mary transfers responsibility for her behavior to others while appearing to take it on herself. Edmund not only is permitted no problems, he is made the cause of his mother's problems from the time of his birth. Mary's projections become part of her son's identity. She tells her husband:

> I was so healthy before Edmund was born. You remember, James. There wasn't a nerve in my body . . . But bearing Edmund was the last straw. I was so sick afterwards, and that ignorant quack of a cheap hotel doctor—All he knew was I was in pain. It was easy for him to stop the pain . . . I blame only myself. I swore after Eugene died I would never have another baby. I was to blame for his death. If I hadn't left him with my mother to join you on the road, because you wrote telling me you missed me and were so lonely, Jamie would never have been allowed, when he still had measles, to go into the baby's room. I've always believed Jamie did it on purpose. He was jealous of the baby.[15]

Mary blames three people rather than take responsibility for her own grief or for her role in the death of her child.

Throughout the play, Mary both protects herself and binds her loved ones to her with projections, projections that threaten to destroy everyone in the family. For example, Edmund pleads with his mother to take responsibility for her addiction: "You're only just started. You can still stop. You've got the willpower! We'll all help you." His mother, yet again, makes Edmund the shameful one: "Anyway, I don't know what you're referring to. But I do know you should be the last one—right after I returned from the sanatorium, you began to be ill. The doctor there had warned me I must have peace at home with nothing to upset me, and all I've done is worry about you." Then, with the brilliant illogic of the demagogue, Mary takes from Edmund even the chance to accuse her of projection. She rhetorically forbids him to pass responsibility back to her. She hugs Edmund to her and exclaims, "But that's no excuse! I'm only trying to explain. It's not an excuse! Promise me, dear, you won't believe I made you an excuse."[16]

Mary denies everyone's anxiety but her own. Many of us might be occasionally tearful at being sent to boarding school at age 6 and having a drug addict for a mother, but Mary treats such behavior in Edmund as a weakness. So she teases him in public: "It was Edmund who was the crosspatch when he was little, always getting upset and frightened about nothing at all. Everyone used to say, dear, you'd cry at the drop of a hat."[17] In his mother's eyes, Edmund's pain is invalidated.

From his flophouse existence, Eugene O'Neill developed tuberculosis. In life and in the play he tried to draw this unhappy fact to his mother's attention. In the play his mother dismisses his anxiety: "A boy of your age with everything before him! It's just a pose you get out of books! You're not really sick at all!" She continues, "Don't say horrible things . . . You've got me so frightened . . . You look ever so much better than you did this morning." Edmund's own anxiety must fester without validation. Mary even denies his right to seek help from others: "It's such a tiring trip uptown in the dirty old trolley on a hot day like this. I'm sure you'd be much better off here with me." Edmund appeals to her, "You forget I have an appointment with Hardy." His mother responds quickly, "You can telephone and say you don't feel well enough."[18]

A little later in the day Edmund again tries to get his mother to attend to his own anxiety over his tuberculosis, an illness that was often fatal. "All this talk about loving me," he complains, "and you won't even listen when I try to tell you how sick—." His mother cuts him off: "Now, now. That's enough! I don't care to hear . . ." Edmund shrinks back into himself. His mother keeps on in a forced, teasing tone but with an increasing undercurrent of resentment: "You love to make a scene out of nothing, so you can be dramatic and tragic." With a belittling laugh she adds, "If I gave you the slightest encouragement, you'd tell me next you were going to die—."

Edmund breaks in, his own panic building, "People do die of it. Your own father—." His mother responds with outrage, "Why do you mention him? There's no comparison at all with you. He had consumption." She continues angrily, "I hate you when you become gloomy and morbid! I forbid you to remind me of my father's death, do you hear me?"

Edmund loses control: "Yes, I hear you, Mama. I wish to God I didn't! It's pretty hard to take at times, having a dope fiend for a mother!" She winces—all life seeming to drain from her face, leaving it with the appearance of a plaster cast. Her son notices and is conscience stricken: "Forgive me, Mama. I was angry. You hurt me." [19] It is too late, of course. Once you have called your mother a dope fiend, the tantrum cannot be taken back. But then the morphine-enhanced selfishness of Mrs. O'Neill must have been infuriating. So, what was there left for Gene to do but chop the legs off his mother's furniture with a machete?

The creative artist, too, like Mary Tyrone, penetrates others with the virus of her or his own pain, but the artist does it in such a way that the world is grateful. Catharsis is different from infection. Mary winced, the blood drained from her face, and she was diminished by her son's attack. As theatergoers we wince, too; the blood drains from our face; and we are entranced. Personality-disordered individuals mislead, infuriate, or even destroy those around them. Heroines, saints, and playwrights bring truth, inspiration, and even health to those about them. But they do not necessarily bestow these gifts upon their closest relatives. The family transmission of immature defenses may continue even as some family members master other facets of their lives. Eugene O'Neill's paternal grandfather abandoned his family when his son, James O'Neill, was 10 years old; he later died a suicide. James O'Neill neglected *his* sons, Jamie and Eugene. He taught them to comfort themselves with alcohol by the time they were 6 years old, and he condoned their being sent away to boarding school by age 8. As in Greek tragedy, Eugene O'Neill passed on this tradition of neglect. He abandoned both his sons, the first before birth and the second at about the same age at which he himself had been sent away to school. Both his sons became chronic substance abusers and died of suicide. He abandoned his daughter, too, when she was 4, and formally disinherited her when at 18 she married a man her father's age.

Recovery

I believe that Eugene O'Neill recovered through love as much as through maturation. But the love was not of the sort that we receive from friends and children. The love that he received was more akin to the love that patients receive from therapists. For O'Neill, the year that encompassed the action of *Long Day's Journey into Night* began a rebirth that was to progress from the spring of 1912 when he published his first poem, to the fall of 1912 when he fell in love, perhaps for the first time, to the spring of 1913 when he wrote his first play. This process was catalyzed by an institution, by a whole group of people who validated that Eugene O'Neill did indeed have tuberculosis and who at the same time held him and allowed him to feel cared for. Severely personality-disordered individuals often need to be *held* by whole institutions. A single person may not do. This loving acceptance of O'Neill's pain was in stark contrast to his mother's anxious fear and self-distancing response to his tuberculosis.

In 1912 O'Neill developed tuberculosis, and in 1913 he was sent to Gaylord Sanatorium. There he was cared for by nurses and doctors who themselves had recovered from tuberculosis. They ran the sanatorium almost as a self-help group—a Consumptives Anonymous, as it were. For the first time, O'Neill found himself in a setting that offered him the maternal care of which he had dreamed as a child.

Lacking antibiotics or even accurate X-ray diagnosis, the Gaylord staff put their emphasis on a homelike benevolent atmosphere. Dr. David was the empathic senior physician whose "gray eyes," O'Neill wrote, "saddened by the suffering they have witnessed, have the sympathetic quality of real understanding. The look they give is full of companionship, the courage-renewing, human companionship of a hope which is shared."[20] How different from the hopeless morphine-glazed eyes of his mother. How much warmer than his fantasy of suicide—to swim out to sea along the track of the rising moon until he was swallowed, forever, by the sea-moon's maternal bosom.

Dr. David started all his patients out on complete bed rest. This was followed by a step-by-step rebirth from their helplessness. Milk was a regular feature of the sanatorium diet. Dr. David gave scrupulous instruction in self-care. To Eugene, who when young had had no one to care for him and who since leaving Princeton had taken such poor care of himself, such a regimen of focused care must have seemed extraordinary.

Shortly after leaving Gaylord Sanatorium, O'Neill wrote to Dr. David, "If, as they say, it is sweet to visit the place one was born in, then it will be doubly sweet for me to visit the place I was reborn in—for my second birth was the only one that had my full approval."[21] And O'Neill never forgot the kindness he had received from the women at Gaylord. He continued to write to one of the nurses for most of his life. In 1918 he told an interviewer about his goal in recreating the atmosphere of Gaylord Sanatorium on the stage: "My whole idea is to show the power of spiritual help even when a case is hopeless . . . I saw it at close quarters for I was myself an inmate of a tuberculosis sanitarium and through hope and spiritual help beat it."[22] "At Gaylord I really *thought about* my life for the first time, about past and future."[23] The development of mature defenses may depend upon an individual's being granted the capacity to mentally grasp time—past and future.

For the seven years that took him from expulsion from Princeton to matriculation at Gaylord, O'Neill's life had been all action—doing rather than feeling; and all fantasy—dreaming rather than being. For the next seven years, he "turned his fury inward—and made the miraculous discovery that he could be a creator instead of a destroyer." Fantasy evolved into sublimation and O'Neill learned how to play instead of run. Or as he put it, "I got busy writing one-act plays."[24]

The link between O'Neill's use of fantasy and his use of sublimation is illustrated in his words to a friend, Bernard Simon: "I hardly ever go to the theatre, although I read all the plays I can get. I don't go to the theatre because I can always do a better production in my mind than the one on the stage. I have a better time, and I am not bothered by the audience. No one sneezes during the scenes that interest me."[25] What differentiated Eugene O'Neill from someone with a schizoid character disorder was that O'Neill made his dreams come true. He took the plays out of his mind and placed them in the real world.

The year 1926 witnessed the occurrence of two additional events that led to O'Neill's recovery from personality disorder. Alcohol left his life, and Carlotta Monterrey entered it. Both sobriety and love were critical to his ability to abandon his dissociation. The evolution of mature defenses depends upon both biology and the internalization of kind people. In 1925 O'Neill began clearly to realize that his abuse of alcohol was destroying his writing. "I will never," he proclaimed, "nor ever have written anything good when I am drinking or even when the miasma of drink is left."[26] Eugene O'Neill went on the wagon on December 31, 1925, and except for brief slips remained abstinent for the rest of his life.[27]

In the following months O'Neill became, without consciously realizing it, increasingly unhappy in his marriage to Agnes Boulton, his second wife, who had probably covertly supported his alcoholism. For about six weeks he saw a psychiatrist Gilbert Hamilton, who was doing research on marriage. During his brief time as a psychiatric patient, O'Neill learned how to talk about and remember the truth about himself. During these six weeks he made the autobiographical notes about himself that fifteen years later would provide the outline for *Long Day's Journey*. He also began to realize consciously how unhappy he was in his marriage. That summer he became friends with Carlotta Monterrey. She was an actress who had been christened Hazel Tharsing and who had become both rich and cultured through several short-lived marriages and affairs.

During the fall of 1926 O'Neill continued with Carlotta the work of self-discovery that he had begun with Dr. Hamilton. In the process he fell in love. As Carlotta later said of O'Neill's early conversations with her, "And he started talking, and began with his birth, almost, with his earliest memories of babyhood. And he talked and he talked and he talked, the whole time looking as if he were *tortured* . . . He looked so *unhappy*."[28] Her maternal instincts were aroused after one or two such meetings, and she found herself taking care of him as one would a neglected child. An actress who had known her for many years observed, "Carlotta was an extraordinary woman. She went beyond the wifely duties for O'Neill. She did everything for him, was even his typist. She did nothing by halves. She was the most generous human being I've ever known."[29]

As at Gaylord Sanatorium, O'Neill's ability to absorb love became a critical catalyst to his healing and to his creativity. In 1928 Eugene and Carlotta ran off to Europe together. For the next twenty years, until they both became crippled by the infirmities of old age, they were inseparable. The bad news was that Carlotta was terribly possessive. The good news was that O'Neill, who up to then had felt that he belonged to no one, felt deeply grateful to be, at last, possessed by somebody.

If dissociation (neurotic denial) is in part the interpersonal result of a parent's failure to validate a child's emotional pain, its evolution into sublimation or insight is in part derived from having that pain validated. In order to understand how validation by Carlotta Monterrey helped O'Neill relinquish dissociation, consider the following sequence from *Long Day's Journey*: Mary Tyrone is wandering about in a drugged haze. In response, her oldest son, Jamie, bitterly quotes Swinburne:

Let us go hence, my songs; she will not hear . . .
She loves not you nor me as all we love her.
Yea, though we sang as angels in her ear,
She would not hear.

Edmund turns impulsively and grabs Mary's arm. As he pleads, he has the quality of a bewildered, hurt little boy: "Mama! It isn't a summer cold! I've got consumption!"

For a second he seems to have broken through. Mary trembles and her expression becomes terrified. She calls distractedly, as if giving a command to herself. "No!" And instantly she is far away again. She murmurs gently but impersonally, "You must not try to touch me. You must not try to hold me. It isn't right."[30]

No wonder Eugene O'Neill learned to lose himself first in fantasy, then in dissociation, and finally in acting out by running off to sea. At sea, as both Edmund Tyrone and his creator recollect:

> I lay on the bowsprit, facing astern, with the water foaming into spume under me, the masts with every sail white in the moonlight, towering high above me. I became drunk with the beauty and singing rhythm of it, and for a moment I lost myself—actually lost my life. I was set free . . . And several other times in my life, when I was swimming far out, or lying alone on a beach, I have had the same experience. Became the sun, the hot sand, green seaweed anchored to a rock, swaying in the tide. Like a saint's vision of beatitude. Like the veil of things as they seem drawn back by an unseen hand. For a second you see—and seeing the secret, are the secret. For a second there is meaning! Then the hand lets the veil fall and you are alone, lost in the fog again . . .[31]

In contrast, immediately after his "psychotherapy" with Carlotta, O'Neill wrote to her that he felt his capacity for dissociation and fantasy slipping away under the power of her love and empathy—as if forever. He wrote to her of his own days at sea:

> Life then was simply a series of episodes flickering across my soul like the animated drawings one sees in the movies, and I could not then see how the continuity of my own seeking flight ran through them as a sustained pattern. Now that old thrill is gone . . . The self that it excited to dreams was long since buried at sea . . . [He then has an imaginary character from a previous play ask him] "What did they give yer, Gene the

Yank, in place of the sea?" "Oh," I answer with forced airiness, "There's a little fame, you know" . . . "It don't go down with me, that tale," he retorts . . . Today, I said to him: "There's Carlotta." And I heard him give what sounded like a grunt of approval."[32]

In 1931 O'Neill wrote of Carlotta's validating role in his creation of *Mourning Becomes Electra*, "In short . . . you collaborated, as only deep love can, in the writing of this trilogy of the damned! . . . I want these scripts to remind you that I have known your love with my love even when I have seemed not to know; that I have seen it even when I have appeared most blind; that I have felt it warmly around me always . . . sustaining and comforting, as warm, secure sanctuary for the man . . . a victory of love-in-life—mother and wife and mistress and friend! And collaborator!"[33] Thus is the debilitating defense of dissociation catalyzed to evolve into sublimation.

———————

Another of the enduring and miraculous tasks of the maturing ego is to transmute self-destructive envy and desire for revenge into gratitude. O'Neill grew up with the theme of revenge. Again and again his father reenacted the drama of the Count of Monte Cristo. James O'Neill played out the Count's vengeance as he slew his tormentors one-two-three. Just so, in many of O'Neill's earlier plays revenge was a dominant motif; just so, in his real life, O'Neill viciously retaliated against and disinherited his own children, Shane and Oona, for what he projected, with Lear-like unreason, to be their ingratitude and abuse of their father.

For years Eugene O'Neill punished himself for being born. In *Long Day's Journey* he drew a vivid picture of the soul-destroying quality of what Melanie Klein called *envy*, what Anna Freud called *turning against the self*, and what in this book I term *passive aggression*. The sadomasochistic relationships that result from such deployment of envy and passive aggression bind interpersonal conflict. Such defense merges self and other and violates the need for safe separateness that is so essential to real intimacy. Thus in *Long Day's Journey* Jamie, simultaneously the sadist and the masochist, turns on Edmund and gloats, "You reflect credit on me. I've had more to do with bringing you up than anyone. I wised you up about women . . . And who steered you on to reading poetry first? Swinburne, for example? I did!

And because I once wanted to write, I planted it in your mind that someday you'd write! Hell, you're more than my brother. I made you! You're my Frankenstein!"[34] He continues:

> Did it on purpose to make a bum of you. Made getting drunk romantic. Made whores fascinating vampires instead of poor, stupid, diseased slobs they really are. Made fun of work as a sucker's game. Never wanted that you succeed and make me look even worse by comparison. Wanted you to fail. Always jealous of you. Mama's baby, Papa's pet! . . . I love you more than I hate you . . . But you'd better be on your guard. Because I'll do my damnedest to make you fail. Can't help it. I hate myself. Got to take revenge. On everyone else. Especially you."[35]

A few years later, Jamie O'Neill died. His pain was unabated.

In *Mourning Becomes Electra*, O'Neill tells how revenge, instead of being acted out, is turned by the protagonist upon herself. Lavinia Mannon deals with her grief as follows: "I've got to punish myself! Living alone here with the dead is a worse act of justice than death or prison . . . I'll have the shutters nailed closed so no sunlight can ever get in. I'll live alone with the dead, and keep their secrets, and let them hound me, until the curse is paid out and the last Mannon is let die! (*With a strange cruel smile of gloating over the years of self-torture*) I know they will see to it I live for a long time! It takes the Mannons to punish themselves for being born!"[36] Her words reflected O'Neill's own lifelong curse upon himself until he wrote *Long Day's Journey into Night*.

In that play, O'Neill learned to deal with his own dead in a different way. In that play, his final exorcism of "old sorrow written in tears and blood," O'Neill experienced no less pain than when he had used to punish himself for being born, but now there was greater resolution and greater gratitude. As Carlotta O'Neill typed the drafts of *Long Day's Journey*, she recalled O'Neill's agony while writing: "At times I thought he'd go mad. It was terrifying to watch his suffering."[37] She told a reporter, "I typed this play twice, because he went over it a lot. I wept most of the time, it upset me so."[38] "It nearly killed him to write this play," she said on another occasion. "Night after night I held him tight in my arms so he could relax and sleep . . . Thus the play was written."[39] A little theatrical, perhaps; but that is why O'Neill, too, chose the theater—and why great experts on the human condition like Shakespeare and Freud have chosen poetry and metaphor—in order to link the cortex and the limbic system, in order to link the mind with the heart.

In response to her care, Eugene wrote to Carlotta:

> Dearest: I give you the original script of this play of old sorrow, written in tears and blood. A sadly inappropriate gift, it would seem, for a day celebrating happiness. But you will understand. I mean it as a tribute to your love and tenderness which gave me the faith in love that enabled me to face my dead at last and write this play—write it with deep pity and understanding and forgiveness for all the four haunted Tyrones.
>
> These twelve years, Beloved One, have been a Journey into Light—into love. You know my gratitude. And my love![40]

Twelve years earlier O'Neill had described the same process of being transmuted by love and gratitude with greater immediacy. In February 1928, just after he and Carlotta had begun living together, he had written to a friend:

> God, I wish I could tell you how happy I am! I'm simply transformed and transfigured inside! A dream I had given up even the hope of ever dreaming again has come true! I wander about foolish and goggle-eyed with joy in a honeymoon that is a thousand times more poignant and sweet and ecstatic because it comes at an age when one's past—particularly a past such as mine—gives one the power to appreciate what happiness means and how rare it is and how humbly grateful one should be for it . . . It really seems to my mystic side as if some compassionate God, looking back at Carlotta's unhappy life and mine, had said to himself, well . . . they deserve each other if they have the guts to take the gift. And we did have— and here we are! . . . To say that Carlotta and I are in love in the sense of any love I have ever experienced before is weak and inadequate. This is a brand new emotion . . . It is so damn right in every way! We "belong" to each other! We fulfill each other![41]

For O'Neill, merging with Carlotta led to gratitude, not envy; and as he grew older he entirely forgot his obsession with revenge. Late in life he observed, "In all my plays sin is punished and redemption takes place. Vice and virtue cannot live side by side. It's the humiliation of a loving kiss that destroys evil."[42] And in the great scheme of things, whether you attribute such mending to "glue," "love," "the grace of God," or "mature defenses" does not make much difference.

In any case, by 1940 O'Neill's adaptive style revealed greater use of mature defenses other than sublimation. During the dark year in which he wrote *Moon for the Misbegotten,* O'Neill labored under a rare neurological disorder that crippled him with a Parkinson's-like tremor. "I've always had [the tremor] more or less," he wrote with humor, "but it was not bad in the period in which the Princeton scripts were written. Now, Mrs. O'Neill, who has typed all my plays for years, has to operate with a magnifying glass and a book on Egyptology. These are the times when she wonders if, after all, our marriage was not a grave mistake."[43]

Toward the end of his life, the once impulsive and dissolute sailor also became a master of suppression. He became as good a stoic as in his youth he had been a dissociator who stayed drunk on Swinburne, rum, and the sea. In December of 1942, when he was crippled with neurological disease and too ill and tremulous to write more plays, O'Neill painfully scribbled to a friend, "We've succeeded in finding someone—the hardware man in Danville—to drive me to the doctor's in Oakland every two weeks for the imperative treatments. Now that gas rationing is with us, it will take tough figuring to do this on an 'A' Book, but what the hell! We do have good times and will continue to get by some way and remain reasonably cheery. Compared to the farmers around here, who face an impossible situation in so many respects, we are on velvet and suffer no hardships."[44]

Immature defenses achieve their effect by allowing one person to penetrate the marrow of others' bones. In contrast, mature defenses are essentially honest and moral and permit safe, less invasive intimacy. Only the artist manages to combine the honesty and morality of the user of mature defenses with the capacity of the confidence man and the sinner to penetrate our innards and awaken our oldest longings. To paraphrase O'Neill: The tragic alone has that significant beauty which is truth.

12

Disadvantage, Resilience, and Mature Defenses

> The notion that adverse experiences lead to lasting damage to personality "structure" has very little empirical support.
>
> Michael Rutter

Human lives do not always turn out as expected. Sometimes the unexpected outcome is tragic: the promising youth ends up in prison or broken by drugs; the loving and vulnerable mother loses her only child to leukemia. From this sort of situation we learn little that we did not already know. We all know that Humpty Dumpty can fall off a wall and be shattered beyond repair—forever. The second sort of unexpected outcome has more to teach us: the disadvantaged youth becomes a loving and creative success; the child who "did not have a chance" turns out to be a happy and healthy adult. We have much to learn from once-fragmented Humpty Dumpties who ten—or even forty—years later become whole.

At the heart of this recovery from disadvantage is *resilience*. The concept of resilience is far more accurate and useful than the more popular—but unempathic—concept of invulnerability. In no way does the eventual survival and recovery of resilient youth convey invulnerability. Indeed, Emmy Werner, the intellectual mother of one of the great longitudinal studies of child development, the Kauai Study,[1] has called such mended Humpty Dumpties "vulnerable but invincible."

The phenomenon of resilience is not easy to understand. As with many terms in the social sciences, we all know perfectly well what resilience means until we listen to someone else trying to define it. Resilience conveys both the capacity to be bent without breaking and the capacity, once bent, to spring back. Thus, I like the definition that Emmy Werner and Ruth Smith give for resilience: "The self-righting tendencies within the human organism."[2] But does this merely mean survival in the face of vulnerability and multiple risk factors, or should we think of resilience only when it also permits happiness? Is it enough that the vulnerable patient survives the operation and that the orphan survives the concentration camp, or, to be called resilient, must they be able to run and laugh and feel joy as well? The reader must choose. All the men I discuss in this chapter will be vulnerable; most will be resilient and ultimately invincible; a few will be happy.

In previous chapters, most of my illustrative examples of the wisdom of the ego have been of highly intelligent people from middle- or upper-class backgrounds who enjoyed good health, unusual energy, and parents who were successful in some field of endeavor. In this chapter, I shall focus only upon the most disadvantaged Core City men. (Because there were no women in the Core City sample, I remain as curious as the reader as to whether the findings described here apply to both sexes.) As a starting point, I asked a rater who had reviewed the childhoods of all 456 Core City men to give me a list of the worst childhood environments. This list provided me with a group of men who manifested multiple risk factors *and* who lacked most of the protective factors thought to promote resilience in childhood. The eleven examples I selected from this group are summarized in Table 16.

Each Core City subject was rated for the presence or absence in childhood of those factors thought by general consensus to put children at risk for poor psychosocial outcome. Most of the risk factors in Table 16 are self-explanatory. "Low socioeconomic status" meant living in tenement housing supported by welfare or by fathers who had not finished high school and who worked at unskilled jobs. "Low self-esteem" meant receiving a score of 7–9 on a 9-point scale of self-regard. "Multiproblem family" meant growing up with 9 or more of the 25 objective signs of dysfunctional family structure (for example, separated from both parents, mother mentally ill, father alcoholic or mentally retarded) that the Gluecks had originally used to predict serious delinquency.[3] Each of the risk factors in Table 16 is one pole of a continuum; the other pole is usually a commonly cited protective factor. In other words, high self-esteem or intelligence or social status tends to protect otherwise vulnerable children. For the men in Table 16 such protective factors were lacking. The only two protective factors these Core City subjects enjoyed were, first, that all but one had rela-

Table 16. Eleven vulnerable Core City men and their risk factors

Risk factors	Kinder	Hope	Kowalski	Thoreau	Bright	Patriarcha	Mulligan	Penn	Heep	Grimm	Loman
I.Q. < 85 (Werner)[a]	99	90	110	101	79	60	91	98	79	87	88
Low socioeconomic status (Rutter)[b]	2	4	3	4	4	4	5	5	4	5	5
Low self-esteem (Garmezy)[c]	2/9	9/9	9/9	7/9	1/9	6/9	7/9	2/9	4/9	2/9	9/9
Severe marital discord (Rutter)	x	x	x	x				x			
Foster care 6+ months (Rutter)	x		x								
Mentally ill mother (Rutter)	x	x									
Delinquent father (Rutter)		x	x	x		x	x	x			
Person/room ratio over 1 (Rutter)		x		x		x	x	x	x	x	
<2 years to next sibling (Werner)		x		x		x	x				
Five or more children born to mother (Rutter)				x		x	x				
Alcoholic parent (Vaillant)[d]		x		x		x		x	x	x	x
Multiproblem family (Vaillant)		x		x				x	x		x
Total number of risk factors	4	8	4	8	5	6	5	5	5	3	3
Outcome											
Health Sickness Rating Scale score (age 47)	88	73	88	90	92	84	91	93	48	68	?
Maturity of defenses score (age 47)	2	3	1	4	1	1	4	3	9	9	?

Note: I.Q., self-esteem, and SES scores are underlined if low enough to be classified as risk factors. For other variables, x indicates that risk factor is present.

a. *Werner:* E. E. Werner and R. S. Smith, *Vulnerable but Invincible* (New York: McGraw-Hill, 1982).

b. *Rutter:* M. Rutter, B. Yule, D. Quinton, O. Rowlands, W. Yule, and M. Berger, "Attainment and Adjustment in Two Geographical Areas, III: Some Factors Accounting for Area Differences," *British Journal of Psychiatry* 125 (1974): 520–533.

c. *Garmezy:* N. Garmezy, "Stressors of Childhood," in *Stress, Coping and Development in Children,* ed. N. Garmezy and M. Rutter (New York: McGraw-Hill, 1983), pp. 43–84.

d. *Vaillant:* G. E. Vaillant, *The Natural History of Alcoholism* (Cambridge, Mass.: Harvard University Press, 1983).

tively good physical health, and second, that all but two were at least two years older than their next sibling. But in general, the childhoods of all the men in Table 16 embodied the very factors that characterized the bottom 20 percent of Werner and Smith's disadvantaged cohort of Kauai children who "lived in persistently disordered family environments that provided little support . . . The overwhelming majority in this group tended to develop serious and persistent coping problems."[4] If at least four major risk factors are present, according to Werner and Smith, a child's chances for success in young adulthood are less than one in four.

At age 25, after ten years of prospective study, all of these Core City men still appeared to be broken beyond repair. Had I not been blessed with the telescope of the Study of Adult Development, had I not had access to a fifty-year follow-up, I should never have known how their lives really turned out. Man is born broken. He lives by mending. The wisdom of the ego provides a significant share of the glue.

After fifty years of follow-up, eight of the eleven men manifested that ineffable quality—resilience. By middle life they had self-righted themselves and were often blessed with a modicum of joy. By middle life the first eight men in the table had turned out very well, as indicated by their Health Sickness Rating Scale scores—a reliable means of quantifying mental health on a scale from 1 to 100. Although in adolescence all of these eight had had at least four risk factors present, all but Robert Hope later fell in the top quartile in mental health. All eight exhibited relatively mature defenses (1–4 on a 9-point scale).

By way of contrast, the last three men in the table, Yuri Heep, Sammy Grimm, and Will Loman, illustrated the unfortunate fate of men who, although initially at less risk, later used far less mature defenses.

Thus, in explaining the resilience of very unpromising lives, it becomes useful to invoke the concept of mature defenses. I have been repeatedly struck by the capacity of such invincible individuals to spin straw into gold, to laugh at themselves, and to display empathy, a stiff upper lip, and the capacity to worry and plan realistically. Of course, these popular phrases are just alternative ways of describing the mature defenses of sublimation, humor, altruism, suppression, and anticipation.

Three leading investigators of childhood resilience, Michael

Rutter, Norman Garmezy, and Emmy Werner, have hinted at the importance of such ego mechanisms of defense. But then each investigator either has dismissed the concept or has discussed such defenses in language very different from mine. For example, using the California Personality Inventory, Werner notes that the key adjectives that distinguish resilient youth from their less resilient peers include "humorous"; "emotionally responsive, nurturant, idealistic" (in other words, altruistic); "ability to focus attention and control impulses" (stoicism and suppression); "enterprising and resourceful" (creative); and "ability to plan" (anticipation).[5]

In summarizing the factors responsible for competence in black children from urban ghettos, Garmezy notes that such children do not turn against themselves (passive aggression) but that their "dominant cognitive style appear[s] to be one of reflectiveness and 'impulse' control" (suppression).[6] Garmezy also notes, as does Werner, the importance of internal locus of control—a concept consistent with use of intermediate and mature internalizing defenses rather than the immature externalizing defenses that are associated with an external locus of control.

Rutter has pessimistically suggested: "Coping mechanisms are likely to be important, too, in determining whether or not people develop psychological disturbance following stress or adversity. However, whether or not it is fruitful to seek to classify coping mechanisms according to their inherently adaptive or maladaptive qualities is much more dubious."[7] Elsewhere he has written: "Intuitively, it seems that the coping process ought to play a role in determining the outcome following stress events. But, up to the present, both the concepts and the measures have proved elusive and there is a lack of evidence that the particular coping mechanisms adopted in fact matter at all in terms of the risk for psychiatric disorder (in adults or in children). But it may matter and the possibility should be studied."[8] As the last twenty years of research from the Study of Adult Development have shown, Rutter is too pessimistic about the explanatory power of differentiated defenses.[9] Let me use illustrative life stories from the men in Table 16 to show why.

Among the Core City men listed in the table are Sammy Grimm and Ken Kinder. Sammy Grimm enjoyed none of Sylvia Plath's, Florence

Nightingale's, or Eugene O'Neill's economic and intellectual advantages. When the somewhat intolerant Study social worker first investigated Sammy Grimm's home, she described his family as "primitive" and his home as "like a den of vice . . . something better described by Dostoevsky." As she entered the front doorway:

> I found the broken-down front stoop crowded with children of all ages. All were talking and screaming . . . Entering the dark hallway were two boys in a clinch, one screaming pitifully. The other had his teeth in the screaming boy's neck. They did not stop when I spoke . . . The house was the most dilapidated and filthy of any I had yet visited. A barking dog and a crying baby added to the vile odors of the rooms . . . Sammy's parents and a neighbor were seated around a greasy table on top of which was a large jug of wine, five or six glasses, a dirty cloth and some pieces of bread.

The house was without hot water or central heating.

Sammy Grimm's father had been arrested for drunkenness; his mother had been convicted of assault and battery; all four of his grandparents were illiterate. The boy said he was strongly attached to both parents, but their preferred method of discipline was physical punishment—inconsistently applied. As the father put it, "When Mother says yes, I say no." Not surprisingly, Sammy Grimm's school performance was characterized by lack of interest, truancy, smoking, and inattention. He repeated two grades. His I.Q. was 87, but his verbal I.Q. was thirty points lower than his performance I.Q.

Thirty years later, at the time of his midlife interview, Sammy Grimm was still living in a rundown apartment. He was a short man, overweight, with a pronounced pot belly. He described his work in a state sinecure as "not the best job in the world but satisfying . . . Every two weeks, you get a check." Long ago he had tried marriage; it had lasted for about one year. He had been living with his current girlfriend for ten years. The interviewer wrote, "My impression of the subject's relationship with this woman is one of dependence on both sides. There was a real lack of enthusiasm on the part of the subject about anything that was going on in his life." For recreation, Grimm gambled and watched TV. Every now and then, he said, "I hit the number and blow all the money."

Sammy Grimm remained as much a stranger to intimacy, career consolidation, and generativity as Bill DiMaggio (see Chapter 7) had been an expert. Grimm's and DiMaggio's childhoods were not so very different, but their adaptive styles were markedly different. All his life, Grimm had used the immature defenses of passive aggression and dissociation to deal with difficulties. His defenses were as immature as those of any man in the Study. When Grimm was younger, he had told the interviewer that when he got angry, "I got kind of crazy." In midlife he said that when he got angry, "I guess I probably go out and get drunk." At the time of his midlife interview, he was troubled by hypertension and was taking five kinds of medication. His biggest difficulty with his medical regimen was one of compliance, for passive-aggressive Grimm had never liked to do what authority figures told him. Two years after the interviewer noted his poor compliance with self-care, Sammy Grimm's high blood pressure killed him. The story is sad but congruent. How could the ending have been any different? The life of Ken Kinder was very different.

Sammy Grimm had endured inconsistent but stable parents without serious alcoholism. In contrast, Ken Kinder had a childhood in which everything went wrong. His mother was taken from her own mother when she was only 4. After being cared for by her grandparents, she went to live with her father and stepmother. Her father beat her so severely that as an adolescent she had to go to an orphanage. From the orphanage she went on to marry, become alcoholic, and give birth to Ken Kinder. When she was drunk, she would abandon her son outside bars. The police would find him and bring him to the police station. When Kinder was 4 years old his mother died from her alcoholism. The next year he, too, was sent to an orphanage. That same year he was struck by a car and knocked unconscious. (Head injury was very common among the Core City youth and was another source of adventitious vulnerability.) From the orphanage Kinder went to live with his paternal grandfather, whose wife had been hospitalized for psychotic depression. His maternal grandmother could not take him, for she was afflicted with both schizophrenia and syphilis. Kinder also had a sister who was schizophrenic; she was later hospitalized for ten years.

Ken Kinder's life, however, was to be very different from that of his mother. At 13 he was taken back in by his father. Trained as an architect, his father could only find work during the Depression as a clerk and a draftsman, but at least he was regularly employed. In addition, he had chosen well in his second marriage. Under his new stepmother Ken Kinder's discipline was decisive and firm. Household routine was regular, and the house was clean. At 13 he described his childhood in very positive terms with a clear recognition of his strong attachment to both his father and his stepmother. Unlike Sammy Grimm, he described firm but kindly discipline from both of his parents.

Ken Kinder was also blessed with a fortunate temperament. The social worker noted that adjectives describing Ken Kinder's dominant personality traits were "conscientious, self-critical, aesthetic." In school, he got A's for effort. Although when in the orphanage he repeated the second grade, he eventually graduated successfully from high school. The psychiatrist noted, "from discussion of the problem [juvenile delinquency], it is very evident that Ken always sees both sides of the situation and is always inclined to weigh the consequences." Kinder's capacity for anticipation boded well for the future.

In spite of his own disrupted childhood, Ken Kinder married a woman who came from a large, very close family. Her father had been tolerant of and loving toward his children. When Kinder was 32 his home was described as "spotless." At the time he told his interviewer, "I bought a home for my wife and family as soon as I could." By age 47 Kinder was a tall, distinguished-looking man with a slightly receding hairline, a pleasant smile, and a charming manner. He owned an attractive apartment in a well-landscaped condominium building and a vacation home on Cape Cod. He had spent most of the previous fifteen years working as a salesman.

At this point in the interview his wife interrupted to say that he loved his job and everything about it. Kinder added that he got on well with both his employers and his customers, but he particularly liked his customers. "You have to get to know the person you're dealing with," he said. "You have to get the most out of them. If there is something that seems to be going wrong, you have to try to be understanding. You have to put yourself in their position." Blessed with altruism, Ken Kinder did seem to love being a salesman. He said he had built up a clientele of two hundred devoted customers, and he felt sure that if something happened to his job they would find work for him in one of their own companies.

Ken Kinder's way of handling anger was different from Sammy Grimm's. Kinder used intellectualization and displacement; Grimm used dissociation. As a teenager, Kinder said, he had had to fight in order to survive; but he had not been in a physical fight since his marriage. Asked what he did now when he got angry, he said he had a very short fuse: "I blow up quickly, but my anger is short lived." His wife added, "You can tell when he's doing a household job, how well it's going, by how many swear words you hear." Kinder described his own coping style in marital conflict as talking until he got to the root of the problem: "I go on talking until it's over."

Kinder's resilience may have been a product of his capacity for empathy and altruism. But where did his defenses come from? He had hardly learned empathy at his dead mother's or his psychotic grand-mothers' knee. In reviewing Kinder's record, I saw his invincibility as a function of his wife's devotion and care. Early in the marriage, he had converted from his Protestant sect to his wife's Catholicism before telling her, and in midlife they went to church together regularly. But perhaps his identification with her went deeper. Their marriage had been strained by the tragic fact their six children, because of Rh-factor incompatibility, had not survived infancy. Kinder said (was it denial or stoicism?) that the jointly experienced tragedies had actually strengthened their marriage rather than weakened it.

Kinder told the interviewer that he had no hobbies, but his wife said, "Oh, you haven't asked him about all the things he does for other people. Bill spends all his spare time helping my nieces and nephews. He's always helping them get on their feet." In describing his best friend, Kinder described a man very much like himself: "He calls a spade a spade—he has common sense—he thinks the way I do—he's strict, but he's kind, understanding, and fair."

The interviewer concluded her interview of the Kinders: "To listen to people who have worked through problems without bitterness and who maintain a warmth and generosity is always a moving experi-ence . . . To observe a man with many deprivations, almost from the cradle, who has emerged into such a picture of mental and physical health is miraculous." Perhaps a greater miracle was the Kinders' joint altruism. The interviewer was pregnant. As she left the six-times-bereaved couple's apartment, Mrs. Kinder pressed a little hand-knitted baby suit upon her. Having lost six of her own children, she could still be generous to a well-to-do pregnant stranger who had intruded into her life to interview her. Perhaps the Kinders' home could better be described by Tolstoy than by Dostoevsky. Certainly, altruism was a dominant adaptive style for both husband and wife.

———

But our faults lie not only in our stars but also in ourselves—in our nature as well as in our nurture. What about young men who not only were cursed with bad childhood environments but also seemed cursed with poor temperaments? What about men whose difficult personalities in adolescence made them seem particularly unlikely to succeed? Again, to choose such examples I drew from a list of the most disadvantaged youth given me by a rater who was blind to the future but who had reviewed all 456 childhoods. One such young man, Will Loman, had enjoyed a relatively benign family environment, but his personality was most unpromising. On the one hand, there was no delinquency, no alcoholism, no mental retardation, no mental disease in the Loman family. Their home was clean, neat, and newly painted and papered, "the furniture was quite adequate," and the neighborhood was good. Will Loman's father was in excellent health, never sick a day, and worked regularly as a foreman. The mother was chronically physically ill, but the father took over and seemed very fond of his son.

On the other hand, Will Loman seemed friendless. On rare occasions he would play with children, but only those much younger than himself. He was frightened of water; he said to himself that he was "too yellow" to sneak admission to movies; and his relatives said he "never tells the truth." His aunt uncharitably described him as a "jerk, a sneak, and a mean bastard." In school he failed history, math, science, and geography. His teacher saw him as "living in a world of his own, a dull, listless lad who appears to be disinterested in everything about him. His classmates pay no attention to him, or he to them." He was described as lazy, slovenly in appearance, unsocial, inattentive, with his only skill being "imaginative lying." Occasionally he truanted. The school also described him as "a disheveled and disorganized lad, whose chief problem appears to be living up to the standards set by even a mediocre class."

The psychiatrist described Loman as "quite dirty, rather untidy, very constrained in his posture. He seemed very immature socially and emotionally . . . He seemed unusually timid . . . His teeth are very much neglected. He needs glasses. He says his mother keeps him in a great deal to help her around the house . . . He plainly has no confidence in himself physically or socially." The blind rater gave him the lowest possible score on a nine-point scale of self-esteem.

Loman dropped out of school in tenth grade, did menial work, and enlisted in the army, where he worked in the shipping docks. He received an undesirable discharge and reenlisted under an alias. This time, he drove a truck. At age 21 he was home on leave visiting with a group of much younger friends. He tried to impress his teenage friends by playing Russian roulette. The first few times he spun the revolver's chamber he won; eventually he lost. Will Loman was the first Core City man to die. He was temperamentally vulnerable and all too vincible.

———————

The shortcomings in the temperament of Robert Hope were also enormous, and unlike Will Loman, he grew up in a most unpromising environment. He had several relatives in state mental hospitals. In addition, many relatives on his father's side, including his father and his own two sisters, were alcoholic. After deserting the family several times, his father finally died when Robert was 9. His mother was also alcoholic and of limited intelligence. As an adult Robert Hope described his mother as "mentally incompetent" and said that he had "hated" her.

Robert Hope lived in a tenement, and the Study social worker noted that his siblings were "dirty and ragged and had no shoes." The flat had no electricity, lacked bedding and blankets, and was "dirty and damp." In school Hope got D's and F's in all his courses. At age 15 he was still in only the seventh grade. His global I.Q. was 90, but his performance I.Q. was only 72. His teachers described him as "lazy, depressed, unsocial, and shy." He was afraid of competition, and was described by the psychiatrist as "unhappy, shy, and unsocial . . . Tense, ill at ease, stooped, and timid." His self-esteem was terrible. As he told the psychiatrist, "I can't think of a thing I am good at." By early adolescence Hope truanted, smoked, and, like his father, had begun to drink alcoholically. Indeed, after his first drink at 15, he was drunk every night for two weeks. Neither nature nor nurture appeared to be his ally.

Robert Hope, too, was dishonorably discharged from the military. He returned to live with his alcoholic mother. During his interview at age 25 the interviewer noted that the previous meal was uncleared from the table and that beer bottles were everywhere. Hope acknowledged that he had been unemployed for the past five months, abusing alcohol and too asocial to go out on dates. How was his life to be any different from Will Loman's?

One answer was that he, too, found a sympathetic spouse who diminished his insecurity. Another answer was that he stopped abusing alcohol. By the time he was interviewed at 32, he had married. His wife, ten years younger than he, kept a "spotless kitchen" but "had feelings of inferiority too." After his marriage, Hope had stopped drinking, stopped smoking, passed his high school equivalency test, and begun to read Jung, Freud, physics, and Kant. Whereas at age 25 he had been brusque, curt, and suspicious of the interviewer, at 32 he was "friendly and cordial." Nevertheless, he still projected his own problems onto people around him. Social supports supply only part of the answer of how defenses mature.

In his early forties, Hope divorced, sought counseling, and on psychological testing appeared to be vastly overcritical of himself and, in his grief over the divorce, to have very low self-esteem. His positive traits, however, were being "sentimental, fair-minded, sensitive, imaginative, individualistic, frank."

By two years later, when he was interviewed at age 47, Robert Hope's paranoid adaptive style had clearly changed from what it had been at age 32. Reaction formation and suppression had replaced projection, and he had become steadily more broad-minded. Hope was critical of the prejudices of his neighbors and was learning to fix the blame on himself when it was due: "I've never been able to accept things the way they are until recently." Further, he "was both honest and open in his responses and was particularly at ease and talented in expressing himself." He saw himself as shifting from having been "depressed" to being "sad." He also noticed that (as he gave up projection) he was learning to express anger: "I may tell people directly what I think." He contrasted this to his time in the Coast Guard in his early twenties, when he had dealt with anger by stealing a truck and getting into fistfights with his commanding officer. Tantrums (acting out) are different from bearing and focusing one's own anger. More recently, in keeping with his newly developed reaction formation, instead of fighting with his boss, he had felt guilty because his supervisor let him get away with things and was too kind to him. He added, "I love the people I worked for. They are wonderful people." Throughout his life, Hope was able to elicit social supports and to use them.

Again, social supports were not enough. Although the people at work had seemed to like him and to be loyal to him, he had not liked his work because he had had repeated failures. In despair, he had resigned from his job. In an electronics firm, a performance I.Q. of 72 is hard to overcome. Nevertheless, Hope was stoical and showed great patience with the job market. During this midlife interview, he described a shift in his attitude toward himself. He remembered his school days as an agonizing time of unhappiness and failure. In retrospect, he recalled that his mother was "probably schizophrenic . . . I look back on the way I was and hate me, but now I know I am good."

Hope said that his greatest ambition over the next decade was to do a lot more for his children, who "make me feel like somebody." He was very close to them and saw them at least once a week. He was proud that his children's lives were different from his own: "They are aware of love in this home." "My mother had a lot of feeling for me but I couldn't see it." As of 1990 his daughters were both high school graduates, stably married with children.

Because of his divorce, low self-esteem, and short-term unemployment at age 47, in Table 16 Robert Hope receives only an average score—73—in mental health. But he deserves a high score for honesty. After his interview, he wrote to the Study: "I don't personally object to my being chosen, but I do think officially it is an error in judgment. That is to say, that I don't think I am now or ever was a well-adjusted individual, at least not by any standards with which I am familiar . . . I'm intellectually aware of why this problem exists, but in a practical sense, I find myself incapable of doing anything about it . . . I don't want to give you the impression that I don't want to take part in this project. As a matter of fact, I do very much so. I'm only interested in insuring that you do not acquire any erroneous data."

The Study staff were glad that Robert Hope remained a loyal member. After age 47 his mental health and life adjustment continued to improve. At age 60 his job was the best he had ever had—as an electronics customer service technician. He had told the Study, "If I can't solve a problem, I've learned to put it aside. There is no use in trying to change things I cannot change . . . Turning to others for help is not my nature. When I've got troubles that are my fault, I don't want to burden someone else with them." But what he particularly liked about his new job was that it permitted him to help and teach other people. He also enjoyed creating and learning new things and took pride in getting his work done.

In his late adult life, then, Robert Hope's adaptive style of reaction formation had evolved more clearly into suppression and altruism. He was nothing if not stoical. He was a former two-pack-a-day smoker who had been able to quit completely at age 26. He was an alcoholic who, without AA, by age 60 had been abstinent from alcohol for twenty-five years. Having earlier mastered his alcoholism and heavy smoking, he had recently mastered obesity. His weight was 160–170 pounds, down from 212.

To feel better, Hope now exercised two hours every day. When he got a cold, he took no medications: "You should let the body take care of itself." He said that in the past "I had always hoped to be someone special," but that "now I'm happy with what I got." He said that his current health and his daily weightlifting were sources of great satisfaction. In his adolescence he had believed that "the god of the neighborhood was physical strength, which I did not have." Now he realized that courage was more important; courage was a quality he knew he did have—and in spades. But how does one learn that it is not the size of the dog in the fight, but the size of the fight in the dog? How does one learn to have compassion for oneself? And why did Robert Hope learn it and not Will Loman?

Resilience is certainly as multidimensional a concept as intelligence or athletic ability. There are as many ways of being resilient as there are ways of being intelligent or of being a star in sports. To help clarify the subsequent case examples, Table 17 lists twelve major sources of resilience. Although I shall sometimes underscore facets of resilience that have not been discussed in earlier chapters, I shall continue to point to maturity of defenses as the "god in the machine" that seems to account for otherwise inexplicable resilience. However, all of the twelve sources of resilience listed in Table 17 are interdependent. All my case examples, despite my simplistic section headings, will illustrate the multifactorial nature of resilience.

In Chapter 1, I identified three broad sources of psychic homeostasis—cognitive strategies, social supports, and ego mechanisms of defense. I shall focus on these three sources of resilience again, but first I wish to acknowledge some other sources.

Risk factors and protective factors. Some investigators see resilience as simply a balance sheet of the relative *absence of risk factors* and the

Table 17. Potential sources of resilience

Cognitive strategies
  Attributional style
  Temperament
Social supports
  Ability to internalize social supports
  Psychosocial maturity
  Hope and faith
  Social attractiveness
Ego mechanisms of defense
Absence of risk factors and presence of protective factors
Luck
Timing and/or context
Self-esteem and self-efficacy

relative *presence of protective factors*.[10] This is the model I presented in Table 16. Enough environmental insults (such as neonatal complications, an alcoholic mother, poor schools) and we all fail. Enough protective factors (such as loving parents, good health, a college education) and we are all invincible. But Michael Rutter warns us that although apparently "people knuckle under because of the sum of accumulated risk factors minus the sum of accumulated positive experiences . . . [and] there is doubtless something to this idea . . . it appears inadequate to account for the phenomena."[11]

Consider the College man who was blessed with intelligence, a warm family, a Harvard education, and superb health, and yet ended up living homeless in Key West. He was alienated from his wife and children and slept with his dog in the back of a station wagon. Why? All his life he had felt vulnerable, and certainly his gradual development of alcoholism had not helped. But his alcoholism was not more severe than that of many men who fared better. At no point in his life did he ever manifest mature defenses or even the effective use of intermediate defenses. He was always overwhelmed by life.

Consider the Core City men like Ken Kinder and Robert Hope who initially lacked Ann Masten and Norman Garmezy's three broad categories of protective factors for stress resistance: (1) self-esteem and a positive social orientation, (2) family cohesion, and (3) the availability of an external support system that encouraged and supported their social skills.[12] Yet Kinder and Hope became successful, loving, and generative. Why? As Rutter points out, resilience is more than just an algebraic sum of risk factors and protective factors. Resilience reflects that which characterizes a twig with a fresh, green, living core: when stepped on, such a twig bends and yet springs back.

Luck. There is also the whole question of luck. Some may see resilience as simply the lucky reverse of bad fortune. Sometimes resilience results from a system of fate designed by Rube Goldberg, Dr. Seuss, or Chaos Theory. Good deeds backfire; mistakes are rewarded. For want of a nail, the battle is lost; by missing a plane, one saves one's life. Clearly, luck does play a role, in spite of Einstein's idealistic belief that God does not play dice with the universe. Sometimes a chance experience can change our lives. But, to paraphrase Louis Pasteur, in producing resilience chance favors sunny temperaments and mature egos.

Timing and context. John Milton told us that the human mind can make a heaven of hell and a hell of heaven. In part how we view an event is a product of our ego's efforts at self-deception and our cognitive style of attribution. But in part the subjective significance of an event is a product of timing and context. Change the timing only slightly and a joke ceases to be funny or lifesaving and becomes a disaster. It is the same with resilience. The death of a spouse at 40 is devastating; at 80 it is the will of God. Menopause at 30 can be profoundly depressing; at 55 it can be a blessing. Being fired at 22 may be taken in stride; but being fired at 55 can be a crushing blow. So it is with many facets of resilience. A time out, a vacation taken at just the right time, the needed interval for one wound to heal before the next wound is inflicted can be critical to resilience.

Sometimes resilience is only an artifact of context: resilience in one arena can become brittleness in another. For example, effortless adaptation to marine boot camp can lead to death due to assignment to the first wave to land in an amphibious invasion. The six College men who died in combat in World War II were better loved as children than were their classmates; in college, they were braver and healthier; and they possessed better eyesight and displayed better leadership skills. Their less well adapted peers were denied combat leadership roles and survived the war. Again, wounds that in civilian conditions would have been debilitating and painful, on the Anzio beachhead during World War II were virtually painless because they signified evacuation to safety.

To illustrate the importance of context to resilience, let me offer the example Butch Patriarcha. Patriarcha grew up in one of the most dismal families in the Study, and his I.Q. was only 60. His temperament and his extraordinary ability to deploy suppression helped him overcome such handicaps. But the context in which he adapted was also critical.

All his life, Patriarcha's parents had been on welfare, and they had lived in a "blighted" three-story wooden tenement. The mother's father was illiterate and the neighbors saw the entire Patriarcha family as feebleminded. The mother had been charged with alcohol abuse and assault and battery. Her house was described in a police report as "dirty," with a "filthy floor." The father not only was an alcoholic but was also so badly crippled that he could hardly walk. He had attempted suicide at least once and had received several court summonses for child neglect and nonsupport. When he was at home, he shared a bed with his son.

Butch Patriarcha grew up with almost no assets. Between ages 6 and 10 he suffered three skull fractures. The psychiatrist described him as "untidy, filthy looking . . . with stooped shoulders . . . obviously very dull," and suffering from a speech impediment. At age 17 he was still in the seventh grade with the reading ability of an 8-year-old. As for his bodily health, he had a cleft palate, a wandering left eye, and rickets. By age 18 he had lost all his teeth. He had no demonstrated athletic skills. With difficulty he finally gained entrance into the army, only to spend a month in the brig. His army psychiatric classification was "feebleminded."

Somehow in this Pandora's chest of horrors, if Butch Patriarcha did not find hope, he found stoicism. When he was 14, the psychiatrist did not fully realize the value of the lifesaving fact that he was "a fairly placid fellow who is content to plod along." It was noteworthy that despite the negative reinforcement of repeated failures, he stuck with school until he was 18. Perhaps it was also noteworthy that during all the years in which he failed to read, fell four grades behind at school, and was relegated to special classes, he nevertheless would check elaborate jigsaw puzzles out of the library and painstakingly complete them.

Up to the point of his marriage at age 25, Butch Patriarcha's only real accomplishments had been, as a teenager, to attend church and the Boys' Club and, as an adult, to work regularly for a trucking company. For the next thirty-five years, he continued to work for the same Cleveland trucking firm. He took pride in and was grateful for being assigned to the higher-paying graveyard shift on the loading dock. He was proud that he gave a day's work for a day's pay. Having spent his entire childhood on welfare, by age 60 Patriarcha was proud to be making almost twenty dollars an hour. He could now take his family to Florida in the winter and to a Maine cottage in the summer. In contrast to the shabby house in which he had grown up, he had fixed up and painted the inside of his well-cared-for apartment, still ensconced within an externally shabby tenement.

By age 47 Patriarcha had not only worked for the same company for twenty-five years but had stuck to the same network of close friends. His oldest friend went back to boyhood, and he was godfather to that friend's child. He had been a loyal member of his union for twenty years. He had been a member of the Kiwanis for eleven years, and he worked hard volunteering for the Boy Scouts. One of his sons became an Eagle Scout, another source of pride. Since Patriarcha worked nights, he would nap while his sons were in school so that he could play with them when they came home. When interviewed at age 50 he still nagged his sons to make sure they did their homework. He had paid tuition to send his children to parochial school. Both his sons graduated from high school and entered skilled trades.

When Patriarcha was 50, the interviewer, blind to his childhood intelligence tests, summed him up as follows:

> Butch and his wife were quite honestly interested in the Study. Their questions seemed unusually sensitive to the subtleties and significance of studying adult development. In the same way, both of them seemed to be able to grasp the intent of the interview questions without much explanation and responded as openly as they could. The subject seems to have survived his childhood with considerable productive energy. With virtually no support from schools or from luck, he has sustained his curiosity and human responses to the world and to people. He presented himself with dignity. He doesn't apologize for his education or his speech, although he knows he has paid a high price for both . . . He and his wife have been able to give pretty freely to their family and to their community and seemed to have fun doing it.

Butch Patriarcha had not used the dissociater's rose-colored glasses and denial. Instead, as a stoic and a master of suppression, he simply never missed noting the silver linings in the clouds of life. His coping style included being able to remember the past as a little better than it was. He said that he sometimes wished he was back in his childhood, but he could also recall having had to go to work and bring all the money back to his mother. He remembered his schoolwork as very hard and recalled having to attend special speech classes; nevertheless he remembered liking school and working at it every day. He dealt with his bad moods by saying nothing to anyone. Then, as the day went by, "I work myself out of my cranky mood." He never seemed to quit anything he started. After age 30, he finally even became a jock and played football for his town team.

Butch Patriarcha's wife was clearly more intellectually gifted than her husband, and he was grateful, not resentful, that she looked after him. He said, "She's a wonderful woman. I couldn't have met anyone better," and added that she "takes care of me" and "would do anything that I asked her to do." He had also stayed close to his family of origin. After his parents died, he became the family patriarch. During the interview at age 50, his sister called long-distance to ask him for help. He might not have done as well as his classmates on intelligence tests, but within the relatively less intelligent Patriarcha family, he had always been a smart fellow who could solve puzzles. Like timing, context is everything.

Self-esteem. Resilience is also a product of self-esteem, self-efficacy, and a stable sense of self. This is an area of human personality where behaviorists like Albert Bandura and self-psychologists like Heinz Kohut appear to be in general agreement. We are all more resilient when surmounting obstacles that we have surmounted before. We are all more resilient when we have a firm sense of who we are and that we are lovable. Success breeds success, whereas the expectation of the repetition of past failures can make us depressed and "brittle." But where do self-esteem and self-efficacy come from? How do we learn to love ourselves when no one else has loved us? How do we learn to expect success when we have often encountered failure? Or, conversely, what ails the child who has always received A's, who comes from a cohesive home, and yet who cannot believe in himself? My best guess is that self-esteem is simply a product of the eleven other factors in Table 17, but I keep an open mind.

Like the life of Butch Patriarcha, the life of Bill Penn illustrates the importance of unquenchable self-esteem. But biologically, Penn's eventual resilience also owed much to his temperament and to sobriety. Environmentally, his resilience owed much to a loving mother. Finally, his self-esteem seemed linked to his ability to accept social supports, especially religion.

Bill Penn's father had been arrested for assault with a deadly weapon and had been through several detoxifications for alcoholism. He had abandoned his family when his son was 6. A few years later he and his wife got back together, only to separate permanently when Bill was 10. He then worked off and on as a janitor until he finally committed suicide at age 60. After his parents' divorce, Penn grew up in an old tenement house in a bad neighborhood, and his family lived on public welfare. He slept on a couch in the living room and dropped out of school in the middle of tenth grade. Eventually, both his sister and his mother became alcoholic.

On the positive side, until Bill Penn reached late adolescence his mother was a responsible, hardworking stenographer and a good housekeeper. He enjoyed unusually good physical health as a child and was described as responsible and "amenable to reason." "Just born that way," his mother explained. He received A's in conduct at school, loved reading, and "always has a book." (The role of wide and fluent reading in promoting resilience is uncharted ground, but books must provide growth and healing for many.) He identified with the inner-city Episcopal church and served as an altar boy. He also worked after school and was described in childhood as "conscientious, emotionally stable, with good manners, self-contained, discriminating and farsighted." The upshot was that both as an adolescent and as a young adult Penn manifested unusually high self-esteem (2 on the independent rater's 9-point scale).

By age 30 Bill Penn succumbed to the family curse of alcoholism. His life became a disaster. He drank a quart of Scotch whiskey a day and was sexually promiscuous, both homosexually and heterosexually. At age 36 he was briefly addicted to Demerol. He also abused Librium and phenobarbital. He spent three months in a state hospital for anxiety and depression. He spent ten days in jail. He got divorced, and as soon as his ex-wife remarried he gave up his two children to their new stepfather. He was also an occupational failure. In three years in the army he never progressed beyond the rank of private, and in his young adult life he never became more than a handyman at work.

As with many men in the Study, the death of a parent catalyzed Penn's psychosocial maturation and his return to seeking social supports through organized religion. It was significant that he took his last drink one week after his father's suicide and just hours after attending his father's funeral. Penn was 40. After becoming sober, he became intensely identified with both Alcoholics Anonymous and the Quakers. Through the Quakers he met a new girlfriend.

Among the Core City men, alcoholism was an important source of vulnerability, and stable abstinence was an important source of resilience. However, Bill Penn did not write off his years of alcoholism as lost years. His interviewer noted, "He realizes that he was sick, but he also spoke with a certain defensiveness of some of his activities during those drinking years. During the period that he worked for Waldorf's, he boasted of his reliability on the job. He said that some of his drinking buddies were really good friends, and he still keeps in touch with them." Between binges, he would go to the public library and write poetry. Despite years of active alcoholism, Penn still managed to maintain some of his self-esteem.

At age 47, Bill Penn appeared particularly mature and mentally healthy. "Bill had a good sense of humor," the interviewer noted, "and often would answer questions with a joke before responding seriously. He had a tremendous awareness of himself at this time in his life." What he liked most about his job was the people. Although he had continued to work as a handyman for the past fifteen years, he could quote Gandhi and said that he hoped to become a freelance writer. Asked what he did when he was angry, he first responded with a joke and then said, "I count to ten. I try to begin to gain a little serenity." Asked what he would do if he had his life to live over, he answered, "I don't dwell on the past. I'm here today and I know that life is not over." About his childhood, he said, "I didn't have a hell of a lot to eat, but what we ate was nourishing. We felt like we were together." He said that when he was younger he had used to get into fistfights, but "that's pretty stupid when you're only 5 foot 6."

Asked if he turned to others for help, he said that he served as a sponsor to newcomers in AA and that this work helped him. He also leaned heavily on the support system of AA. Of his relationship with both AA and the Quakers, he said, "It's incredible the number of people I can depend on." In AA he remained active in "step groups" and spoke at various meetings. He actively participated in the Quakers' work for peace and social justice. He was involved in the boycott of nonunion grapes and had actively protested the Vietnam war and picketed nuclear power plants. He was active in his community food co-op.

One week of his vacation Bill Penn spent hiking in the White Mountains with his woman friend; another week he spent at a Quaker college taking seminars. He played tennis regularly, and his hobbies were writing and photography. When asked what he might be doing in ten years, he joked, "I hope to be 57 years old then because the alternative might not appeal to me." More seriously, he added that his ambition was to be still "active, enjoying life, and caring for people." Bill Penn is offered as an example of self-esteem, but his life also illustrates the importance of social supports and of the ineffable gifts of faith and hope. For purposes of classification, I have put hope and faith under social supports because they often seem to be a product of having been, say, an altar boy, a Quaker, and an AA sponsor. However, the unanswerable question is: Does self-esteem come from a capacity for faith in a "power greater than ourselves," or does self-esteem catalyze faith and hope? The answer, I suppose, is "all of the above."

Attributional Style

Let me now return to the importance of cognitive strategies and social supports to resilience. Under these two headings in Table 17 I have placed six related sources of resilience: attributional style, temperament, internalization of social supports, psychosocial maturity, hope, and social attractiveness.

It is possible to conceive of resilience as the capacity to employ appropriate voluntary coping strategies. In this view, resilience is nothing more than the application of intelligence, street smarts, planfulness, and education. But some undereducated Core City men with low intelligence fared far better in life than some brilliant Terman women and well-educated College men. Whence did their resilience spring?

To account for such exceptions, cognitive psychologists have noted the importance to resilience of attributional style. Attributional style means how we regard our responsibility for the good and bad events that befall us. When we get an A on a math exam, do we feel that it was a mistake or a unique event that will never happen again? Or do we take credit for our A in math and believe that our success will generalize to spelling also and that we probably will continue to

do well in the future? When we get an F in math, do we assume that
it is entirely our fault and that F's will always be our lot—even in
spelling? Or do we attribute the low mark to the fact that the math
course was an unusually difficult and unimportant subject taught by a
teacher who could not speak English very well, and do we believe that
since we plan to major in foreign languages in college, the failing mark
is unlikely to affect our future lives?

A more concrete example of attributional style would be how a
person might conceptualize being afflicted with diabetes. A resilient
attributional style would be to think: I am a normal person with a
disease called diabetes (a limited, not a global problem), which I have
the power to treat (responsibility) with daily self-injections of insulin
(controllability). A vulnerable attributional style would be to think: I
am a hopeless diabetic (globally defective) with an incurable affliction
(helpless) that will lead to inevitable impotence and blindness (hopeless).

The story of Harry Thoreau illustrates the importance to resilience of clever cognitive strategies that reflect both an optimistic
attributional style and a sunny temperament. Thoreau grew up with
all of the environmental odds against him; yet he seemed blessed with
a wonderful temperament and the genetic blessings of a paternal grandfather who was an engineer and a maternal grandfather who was a
skilled ironworker.

On the negative side, the grandfathers were far better adjusted
and more successful economically than Thoreau's parents, who since
their marriage had been known to seventeen different social agencies.
Thoreau grew up in a crowded tenement apartment without a tub,
central heat, or hot water. He either slept on a couch in the living
room or shared a bed with his brother. As a child he had pneumonia
and coughed up blood, but his parents were too poor to take him to
a doctor. One of his brothers, often arrested for assault and battery
and for larceny, was in and out of reform school. Another delinquent
brother, in spite of a tested I.Q. of 96, was diagnosed as mentally
defective.

Thoreau's parents' marriage was unhappy from the beginning.
His maternal grandmother had been diagnosed manic-depressive, and
when he was 2 his mother was first hospitalized with manic-depressive
psychosis. During the times when his mother was psychiatrically well
enough to care for her apartment, it was described as "fairly neat."

On other occasions, during her psychotic lapses, the home was described as "filthy . . . Mother stays in bed until late and seems to have no conception of how to care for herself or her children." Because of alcoholism, Harry Thoreau's father was without steady employment. He was described as a brutal man, with an "uncontrollable temper," who beat his children until they bled. His I.Q. was 87, and he was hardly able to read. He was described as passive and inadequate. He left home when Harry was 6.

In terms of strengths, Harry Thoreau, unlike his delinquent brothers, was described as having no antisocial habits. Although he was seen by his teachers as somewhat dreamy, unreliable, lazy, and with limited interest in his work, his grades were B's and C's and he skipped a grade in school. He went to church regularly, and his few friends were not delinquent. He was described as "self-critical, conscientious, emotionally stable, and conventional." He was involved in the Boys' Club. When the father abandoned the family, Thoreau turned to his siblings. His oldest brother became a father figure and a role model for him, and he also was close to his sister. The psychiatrist noted his squint and poor posture but also observed that he was a neat boy who appeared rather conservative in his outlook. In short, his temperament was placid, and he remained open to each good thing that happened to him.

When he was 19 Thoreau joined the army, where he worked in intelligence and electronics. After leaving the army he continued to work as an undercover agent behind enemy lines and won a brown belt in karate. His mother described him at 25 as always well behaved, ambitious, and hard-working, and said he "sticks to a thing until he gets it." The interviewer described him as "adaptable, completely confident of his own abilities," and "cultured." He noted that Thoreau never drank or smoked and "seems more intelligent than his I.Q. [101] would indicate." At age 31 Thoreau left government service and began working as a longshoreman. He had saved virtually all the money he had earned in the military. He was able to spend much of his spare time and his savings improving his mother's home. Along the way, he had become a "skilled decorator, and an expert craftsman in wood."

At age 33 Harry Thoreau joined the Buffalo fire department. What he liked most in the department was the camaraderie of the firefighters. "At a fire house," he explained, "people get very close." He was proud that he had built his own home "alone with no help at all." At age 42, after nine years of courtship, he married. His wife was a college graduate and made more money than he did. He described her as a "gentle and compassionate person." At age 47 he saw his marriage as getting better all the time. At age 60, asked on a questionnaire to describe his marriage as excellent, good, fair, or poor, he made his answer clear: he put *four* checks after excellent.

At age 45 Thoreau was an "energetic and rewarding man to interview": "He is bright, a verbalist, good natured and engaging. He maintained steady eye contact." He was witty and "his cooperation, frankness, and warmth made this a very successful interview." He seemed to use humor in dealing with his difficulties, and his current health was very good. He found his chief enjoyment in reading and filled his house with nonfiction books. He also had a snowmobile, kept carrier pigeons, and to make extra money he fixed TVs. He never smoked and allowed himself but four alcoholic drinks a year. The interviewer noted, "There was a sense of excitement while listening to this man."

Having worked in jungles for the CIA, Harry Thoreau now enjoyed being a woodsman with his dog in Vermont. "From learning to survive in the jungle and to fight the Cold War," his interviewer wrote, "he now seems to have turned around 180 degrees and has taken those skills to enjoy the woods and nature, with map and compass and appreciation of beauty. All his life there was a sense of learning new skills for his present enjoyment and future use . . . Although trained as a guerrilla by the government, there was some quality in Harry Thoreau that transformed him into a warm, humane and very engaging man." He continued to acquire new skills, including parachuting, radio and plumbing repair, and being an emergency medical technician.

At 45 Thoreau told the interviewer he planned to take early retirement from the fire department at 56. He would move to the Northeast Kingdom of Vermont to pursue his interests in handicrafts, woodwork, and house renovation. Ten years later, that is exactly what he did. He again began going to church every week. He regarded his life, his job, his marriage, his children, and his friendships as highly satisfying. He continued to see his mood and health as excellent.

Harry took a great interest in the Study and was always faithful in returning his questionnaires. As one of his interviewers noted, he was blessed with "a persistent optimism that almost bordered on the naive." At age 55 this man who had been beaten by his alcoholic father and who had learned karate for his behind-the-lines work for the CIA illustrated his attributional style when he responded to Jane Loevinger's Washington University Sentence Completion Test with answers like these:

> I feel sorry: "for people who aren't animal lovers."
> A man should always: "try to be gentle."
> I just can't stand people who: "are mean and brutal."
> My conscience bothers me: "if I hurt someone's feelings during an argument."
> Rules are: "necessary if mankind is to survive."

What made Harry Thoreau most proud of his twenty-two-year-old son was that "he is decent and gentle." Temperament, ingenious cognitive strategies, and an optimistic attributional style count for a lot. But since both Thoreau's life and his sentence completion test revealed mature ego development, we also must wonder where ego development comes from—a question to be addressed in Chapter 13.

Temperament

Some men in the Study seemed born with good egos and temperaments that transcended their limited intelligence. One such man was Simon Bright. His mother's brother had spent two years in a penitentiary; his father had been arrested for both larceny and alcohol abuse when young. Simon Bright grew up in a tenement without central heating, and he repeated ninth grade. His I.Q. tested at 79 on the Wechsler Bellevue and at 78 on the Terman I.Q. test. At age 25 he read only tabloids and comics, and as far as the interviewer could tell he was unable to add or multiply. At age 31 he described himself as "not too bright" and "kind of dumb." He was working as a truck driver's helper at only slightly above the minimum wage.

On the positive side, Simon Bright belonged to a three-generational family in which everyone stayed close together. His mother was a very good housekeeper, and by middle life his father had become hardworking, sober, and strict. Of her seven children, Simon was his mother's favorite. When he was 14 she said, "He never plays. He goes to school, works after school; and, in the summertime, he works all day." A little Calvinistic perhaps, but with an I.Q. only half that of the Terman women, Simon Bright had to try harder.

Bright saw both his parents in a positive light and experienced their discipline as "firm but kindly." On Sunday they went to church.

The adjectives the interviewer used to describe Bright at 14 were "extroverted, adventurous, emotionally stable, conscientious, practical, aggressive." In addition, he was viewed as "thrifty," "particularly adequate," and "direct and humorous." He said he wanted to be a mechanic when he grew up for he knew that he would have to use his body, not his intellect. At age 25, in spite of working at an unskilled job, he was married, and his wife kept their apartment "immaculate," with "starched, crisp organdy curtains." He was already part owner of a boat and the full owner of water skis and a significant savings account. He might not have been good at book learning, but he had street smarts, common sense, and a wonderful temperament.

Bright began work for the San Jose department of recreation in the early 1970s. At first he received $2.30 an hour, but very quickly he was promoted to supervisor. By age 47 he was making $15,000 a year, but still having to work two jobs. At that time he appeared to the interviewer as a "very virile looking man, muscular, good physical shape, appeared quite young for his age, talked easily with much candor, good eye contact, high energy level, responded to questions easily with his feelings." Again, "everything was spotless and neat." "He conveyed a certain excitement about playing sports and working with kids. He had self-assurance, confidence and candor." Bright liked being around kids and helped to coach several teams. He not only worked in the recreation department but was active as a volunteer in one of the local drug treatment centers. He said he had become interested in fighting drug abuse when a young friend died of heroin addiction.

In his park job, Bright sometimes lost his temper, but he never got into physical fights. In his use of aggression he illustrated sublimation. He used his anger to solve problems rather than to cause difficulty. The interviewer noted that most of his fights "seem to come from his protectiveness of his facilities or his staff." The resistance of others had to be forcibly overcome, but for worthy ends. He had used his assertiveness both to ensure playing field etiquette against aggressive coaches and, at a time when he had no money, to get his son's cleft palate repaired by a sluggish urban welfare bureaucracy. Family problems were solved by the entire Bright family gathering like a team around the dining room table to "get it out of our system and not carry it around inside of us."

By age 60, Simon Bright had been repeatedly promoted and was making $52,000 a year. Because of his learning difficulties he still had to delegate his paperwork, but as he boasted to the interviewer, "They love me because I'm rough and honest." He supervised thirteen people: "I treat them all like my sons. I started at the bottom and worked my way up to be director of the department."

At 60 Simon Bright still worked an eighty-hour week, but he found time to play tennis regularly with his sons and racquetball three times a week with friends. He spent his vacations visiting friends and relatives, and he still enjoyed waterskiing. He took his wife out dining and dancing once a week. His children had all graduated from high school, and one had attended two years of college. Two children, like their father, were working as managers. His two other sons had become policemen. In young adulthood, to be a policeman had been Bright's dream, but he had been unable to pass the written exams.

Social Supports

Resilience can also be viewed as a function of social supports. Under social supports, I would include parental social class, a warm cohesive childhood family, a marriage to an understanding spouse, and what Rutter calls "stable affectional relationships."[13] But mature defenses and social supports are inextricably bound. On the one hand, we are more likely to feel safe enough to deploy mature defenses if we are among friends. On the other hand, our ability to attract others to become our friends is very much dependent on both the maturity of our defense mechanisms and our psychosocial maturity. Capacity for intimacy and generativity and for mature defenses elicits warm relationships and social supports. Conversely, bleak relationships and poor social supports elicit immature defenses. Once again, the factors promoting resilience listed in Table 17 are bound together in a chicken-egg-chicken causal sequence rather than in a simple cart-and-horse causal sequence.

In other words, if social supports are important to resilience, their effect is mediated in complex ways. Let me look at three subordinate facets of social supports that I have outlined in Table 17: the ability to internalize past social supports, psychosocial maturity, and hope. First, social supports must not only be present, they must be recognized and then internalized. Social experience is not what happens to you, it is what you do with what happens to you. Just as part of the

skill of a good football running back is his ability to find blockers, just
so part of resilience is the ability to identify the loving and health-giving
individuals within one's interpersonal matrix. In addition, resilience is
often not only the ability to identify but also to bond with the one
good family member, teacher, or neighbor discovered within a matrix
of disappointing ones. Such bonding involves reciprocity. In tracing
how vulnerable, poor children in Kauai became effective adults, Emmy
Werner has stressed the importance of being a "cuddly" child who
elicits predominantly positive responses from others and who manifests
skill at recruiting substitute parents. Such good fortune often depends
upon a temperamental match or what Alexander Thomas and Stella
Chess call "goodness of fit."[14] We have seen that such a fortunate
choice of mates was clearly important to the resilience of both Robert
Hope and Ken Kinder who, up to that point, had experienced poor
success in recruiting love. Thus, social supports are often a product
of temperament and luck.

But using social supports goes beyond choosing well and finding
goodness of fit. The capacity to use social supports involves the ability
to metabolize, as it were, other people once they are found. This
capacity is inextricably bound to potential for psychosocial maturation.
As Harry Harlow demonstrated through his follow-up of monkeys
raised with inanimate mothers made from wire and terrycloth, we
cannot mature without social supports.

In order to treat the experience of being loved as if it were a gift
and neither a danger nor a right, we need the ego capacity of being
able to absorb those who love us. If we marry someone much richer
than ourselves, shall we feel grateful or envious? If our tennis partner
always beats us, does our game improve or does our self-esteem plum-
met? If our father is in some ways a disaster, are we determined to
avenge ourselves by becoming really good fathers, or do we do unto
others as was done to us?

Consider people from happy families who can absorb nothing.
What of people who are offered love but cannot use it? For most of
their lives, characterologically unable to take people inside, Eliza and
Algeron Young (Chapter 7) remained more like grammar school children than adults. Just as some people may regard a Rockefeller or
Rothschild trust fund as a destabilizing burden, just so some people
are panicked by love. Individuals with schizophrenia provide the
clearest example. Thus, a major difference between Will Loman and

Robert Hope was their differing ability to use the social supports they encountered. Admittedly, Will Loman died before he developed schizophrenia, but he was one of the seventeen youths in the Study predicted by blind raters to develop the illness.[15] I remember a schizophrenic patient of mine who said that the people in her life whom she had hated the most and who had threatened her the most were nurses. She perceived nurses as dangerous. When asked why, she said because nurses "take care of you." She used the term exactly as one might refer to the way the Mafia takes care of its enemies.

I suspect that the capacity to appreciate what is good and nourishing in available social supports is the social counterpart of an optimistic style of cognitive attribution. But, of course, the process of metabolizing social supports is far more subtle. We can teach people ideas. We can teach someone to view a glass as half full rather than half empty; we can teach people to have positive attributions. But how to teach people to treat an onrush of love as a gift and not a threat is a more daunting task, one that requires grace or at least consummate skill.

Resilience is also closely linked to the second facet of social supports listed in Table 17—maturity. By maturity I mean the ego capacity to appreciate the relativity of situations, the ability to take a historical point of view and to tolerate paradox. But maturity is not an easy concept to grasp. In Adolf Meyer's words, "Of all the inevitably relative human considerations, maturity is one of the most elusive."[16] Essential to maturity is the capacity to understand that all things are relative and that others have suffered worse and survived. Essential to maturity are the knowledge that this too shall pass and the ability to postpone, yet not repress, gratification. Such a definition of maturity is very close to the ego defenses of suppression and anticipation. But it is also very close to Jane Loevinger's definition of mature ego development, to Jean Piaget's concept of formal operations, to Lawrence Kohlberg's highest stages of moral development, and to Erik Erikson's concept of generativity.

The third facet of social supports that is important to resilience is the capacity to reach back into the past for memory of special sources of strength and to keep in mind the hope of finding love in the future. Indeed, love, hope, and faith are inextricably entwined. Can a child caught in the middle of a divorce or an exam failure, or a child who is languishing in a Thai refugee camp, remember that things used to be better? Can he or she continue to have faith that "this too shall pass"? Hope and faith are very simple words, but they encompass an essential facet of resilience. It is no accident that hope has long been seen, as in the myth of Pandora, as the psychic balm on which resilience depends. And hope and faith are inextricably bound to social supports.

The fourth facet of social supports listed in Table 17 is social attractiveness. Our social supports depend upon how we affect those about us. Thus, one way of identifying an individual's capacity to elicit social supports is to record a trained interviewer's subjective impressions of the individual. Such impressions are often dismissed as subjective bias or countertransference. But to the extent that social attractiveness depends upon mature defenses, such attractiveness becomes an important clue to resilience. Mature defenses do for adults what being "cuddly" does for infants. They make them attractive to others. Consider the different responses of interviewers to Yuri Heep and Stan Kowalski. Both men were short, stout, and not physically beautiful; but they made dramatically different impressions on others, and not just because Heep's 220 pounds seemed all blubber and Kowalski's seemed all tattooed muscle. It was the men's different styles of defense that most profoundly affected the interviewers. At age 47 the two men got under the skin of their interviewers in very different ways.

Heep's interviewer wrote:

> Mr. Heep emerged, looking rumpled and sleepy, wearing only blue pajama bottoms over which hung a rather huge stomach . . . As I was writing up the interview, I experienced a growing sense of anger at and contempt for Heep. While we talked I imagined I was being charmed by something like blithe insouciance, but with a little distance between us I realized I had been talking with a man so immature that what I first took for an unusual candor had really been infantile exhibitionism, a totally unreserved, conscience-free willingness to share and bare all and anything without discrimination about or moral distinction among the various aspects of his life—and behavior—he discussed so openly. I thought of him as *toddling* out of the bedroom, fat and happy (like a baby) in his pajama bottoms, and later had a fantasy of him as a baby, sitting at the kitchen table, banging on the table with a spoon. I started thinking, too, of his wife's presence at the interview, how he himself insisted on it and showed patent anxiety on the occasion when the phone rang and she left the room for a few moments—

like a child whose sense of security of his mother vanishes as soon as she is out of sight. The contempt I felt came, I think, from a sense he ought to know better and can't he see what's really going on? But clearly he does not know better and cannot see.

I thought I could trace my anger to his hypomanic self-presentation. That anger abated considerably as I went through the interview and began to feel the wretchedness and deep depression that underlay Yuri Heep's overt affect, and which began to peep through toward the end of our talk. This man is a middle-aged baby, utterly dependent on his wife and his parents.

The binding force in his relationship with Mrs. Heep seems somehow involved in his devil-angel, good boy–bad boy alternation, or, as she put it, his "Jekyll-Hyde" proclivities. The "game" I suspect is one of brinksmanship, alternately seeing how much he can get away with, what the limits are to the outrages that she will endure, then periods of promises, pacification, penitent sweetness, etc. I guessed that she is a full partner in this unhappy business.

In my interview of Stan Kowalski I was as biased as Heep's interviewer but my notes expressed nothing but admiration:

Stan Kowalski himself was bald, squat, 5' 8", 220 lbs., heavily tattooed arms, working-class shirt, and the very model of the tough sergeant, the bartender, the body shop mechanic. Kowalski was bubbling over with animal health. His lunchbox had a place of honor on the counter. He smoked Camels and wore a wonderful smile. I had arrived at his house exhausted after having already put in a fourteen-hour day, and yet his eye contact, and his capacity to hold my interest, led to the instant restoration of my own energy.

Kowalski's manner with me was extremely easy, and yet touching. It was self-confident without cockiness. It was the serenity of AA at its best, and he teased me when he thought I made mistakes about the AA philosophy. The interview was difficult in the sense that he was a natural raconteur and preferred to tell me cheerful, amusing stories than the often painful details of his life. He often had trouble remembering things and had to free associate to recover them.

Stan Kowalski was gruff, macho; and he began our interview with "I had trouble adjusting when I came out of the joint

[Sing Sing]." However, it was also extraordinary how appreciative he was of the people who had touched him. As I left, he told me how devoted he had been to his foster mother. His capacity to identify—to take people inside—and to love without ambivalence, was extraordinary. The contrast was all the more dramatic because I had just finished interviewing a College physician with a world reputation who had been totally broken by his alcoholism. My interview with the College subject and his wife had been utterly depressing. The physician had known that his broken ankle and his occasional slips into alcoholism were not enough to crush him, and yet he was crushed. And here was Stan Kowalski, who knew that he had had enough pain in his life to break three men and yet was invincible. He told me of the loss of his adopted son—the child of his whom he most loved, and I suspect that he had loved all of them. He spoke of the loss without rancor and without acknowledged sadness. But, he had already told me that a man should never cry, and besides it was not hard for me to see the sadness just underneath the surface of his prizefighter's mask of a face with its flattened nose.

When I had come in the door, I had been met by his wife who looked right out of a cartoon by George Price, with her dirty-blonde hair and bad posture. She looked ten years older than her stated age. There was little effort at self-care, and I assumed that Kowalski had married a feebleminded heroin addict. Yet, as I sat with her at the table, she offered me a second cup of coffee, and I accepted. With a smile, Kowalski complained, "He turned it down when I offered it to him." With a smile, she tenderly replied, "You're not nice, that's why." My view of her was transformed. As she looked at her husband with an adoring smile, her whole face became beautiful with love.

It was a most exciting interview but there was no question that Kowalski's capacity to make painful issues exciting and entertaining was in the service of defense. Nevertheless, when I asked him his mood over the past six months, this man who had been doing nothing but laugh and entertain me said, "I can't think of what the problem was, but I know there was one," and then he slowly associated back to what the problem was. "I was pissed off for a month," he told me. "Moving was at a slump; we'd been in debt for the first time. I never can remember that April is a slump for the moving business—

I have to rediscover it every year." Stan told me that when he had such troubles what he did to make himself feel better was to "either play some music or tell my troubles to my wife or daughter—they help me."

In other words, at the time of the interview, Stan Kowalski continued to experience pain, but he had mastered it. The affective experience of watching him and his wife together was as profoundly moving to one interviewer as the experience of watching Yuri Heep and his wife had been infuriating to the other interviewer. We all are more resilient when we evoke admiration rather than contempt, when we are viewed as stoics and not as selfish infants.

But if the men were so different when grown up, could these outcomes have been predicted in their childhoods? The answer is no. Heep grew up in a stable household. His childhood apartment was noteworthy only because of an "excessive number of pictures." His father was regularly employed and wanted his son to go to college. Both parents were wrapped up in their son, who repeated no grades and whose schoolwork and behavior were adequate. Heep's teacher even claimed, "He is very intelligent, has good power of concentration, and is one of the best in the class." The psychiatrist found him a tense but "neat appearing boy." He went to church regularly, and, except for smoking, he was involved in no school misbehavior.

In contrast, for Stan Kowalski's first thirty years, his life was headed nowhere. He was abandoned by his father at birth. His mother had lost her own mother in childhood to suicide. She died of tuberculosis on Christmas day when her son Stan was only 3. He was taken in by elderly female relatives who lived in a tenement without central heat. Until he was an adolescent, his aunts raised him as a sissy with long curls. Then, he learned how to truant, steal rides, and cheat in school. Despite above-average intelligence, he dropped out of trade school at eighth grade. By age 17 he was in reform school for stealing cars.

Kowalski got married at age 20 to a woman later diagnosed as schizophrenic. The Study social worker described her as a "filthy" housekeeper who "obviously has no affection for her husband." When angry, the couple would attack each other with knives. By age 25, when his next interview was scheduled to take place, Kowalski had gotten divorced and was in Sing Sing for rape. At age 32, when finally the Study staff were able to interview him, he was in the county jail for vagrancy. He had already been alcoholic for fifteen years, and at times had supported himself by prostitution—sometimes with men, sometimes with women. There was no question that Yuri Heep's youth had been the more benign.

Yet Yuri Heep's childhood, of course, had not been all roses. He was an only child who had to share his bedroom with his mother. His father was charged with assault and battery against his wife. Heep showed the psychiatrist a bruise that he had received during a paternal beating, but he denied that his father was alcoholic. Despite his teacher's optimistic appraisal, Heep's tested I.Q. was 79, and he spent two years in special classes. His Stanford reading test I.Q. was only 70. All his life he read only tabloids and comic books. When he went to camp, Heep was deemed "quarrelsome, a troublemaker, and a poor camper." The psychiatrist noted that he "seems a pretty apprehensive sort of fellow." In short, Yuri Heep had what Emmy Werner has called a "non-rewarding difficult temperament." Most of his working life, he drove a cab and lived in houses or apartments owned by relatives. Most of his life, he depended on his father's financial help.

Nor had Stan Kowalski's childhood been all bad. His "refined" great aunt loved him; and even if she sissified him, she kept the house neat. At an early age, he was able to ask for help; he attended Sunday school every week until he was 14, and as a young man, even as he was drinking himself in and out of state prison, he attended Bible school in order to become a minister. His I.Q. was 110 and his reading I.Q. was 112. He was gifted with good physical health, and better yet he was a superb athlete. He made money as a professional boxer and excelled at football and hockey. Stan Kowalski's criminal record was very reactive. He always committed his serious crimes on Christmas eve or Christmas day, the anniversary of his mother's death.

At age 25 Yuri Heep said, "Eventually, I think my father will help me get someplace to live and set up a home of my own." At age 30 the interviewer wrote of him, "Content to eat and gamble and work only when forced to . . . rather immature and dependent." Heep later divorced his wife, ran off to Las Vegas, and then returned to live with her, so they could all live on Aid to Families with Dependent Children. From age 44 Heep was "disabled" with dizzy spells, "curvature of the spine," "a kind of arthritis," and "an enlarged heart." Fifteen years later, on an objective physical examination complete with an EKG, his heart appeared quite normal. Prior to age 44 he almost boasted, "I never worked a full week in my life." At age 47 Heep, his wife, and their children were being supported by his father. The interviewer wrote, "A part of his day is devoted to driving his mother around to do errands"; but Heep assured the interviewer, "I really don't do anything."

When Heep was 32, his wife complained that he was "no earthly good around the house." She would paint and paper the house, and he would "look on and wonder." "When I go out with him," she said, "he looks fat enough to be my father." Asked in her presence to describe his wife, Heep replied, "She's a son-of-a-bitch. When I got married, that's when my health started to deteriorate." What pleased him most about her was "when I'm mad, she knows enough to be quiet . . . She'll be nice, try to calm me and I can be cuckoo." Mrs. Heep replied, "Verbal abuse is worse than using your hands sometimes." "You'll never leave," he said. "Time will tell," she retorted.

In the past Heep had been unfaithful to his wife in a manner that insured discovery. The interviewer asked what the couple did when they went out, and their daughter replied, "They fight." When very angry, Heep said, "I'm liable to bust something." His wife added that he would punch people. He said he no longer threw punches at the family; but their daughter piped up, "Oh yeah, what about a week and a half ago?"

In the ensuing years, Heep's life did not improve. By age 58 he was retired. He still viewed himself as disabled with back trouble (no objective evidence), and remained, as he had been as a youth, "*very* worried." He was 5'6" and weighed 240 pounds. He continued to smoke three packs of cigarettes a day. He perceived his own health as "poor," and was in chronic pain.

When I met Stan Kowalski, he was 47 and had not been in jail since his last interview at age 32. He owned his home, where he had lived for two and a half years. When I arrived two minutes late to the appointment, he greeted me with a broad grin and exclaimed, "You're late!" He told me with pride that for years he had been qualified to drive the largest eighteen-wheel moving vans, and that he was known as a good worker. He boasted that three years earlier he had achieved the ambition of every mover, to carry a piano by himself. He said his dream was to buy his own truck. (He achieved this goal three years after our interview.)

Kowalski told me how he had achieved abstinence from alcohol a decade before. After getting out of the county jail in 1961, he had lived on the New Orleans streets. In winter he would sleep in gutters and cover himself with leaves to protect himself from rain. Then, waking up, still covered with dirt and looking like something out of a horror movie, he would ask terrified pedestrians for money so he could go on drinking. He had first gotten sober in 1964, through the intervention of a friend. He had taken his last drink in 1967.

Clearly, abstinence from alcohol is a powerful means of altering a downhill life trajectory. But equally important was Kowalski's capacity to allow himself to be cared for. That was his salvation. But the care that he received was very different from the care solicited by Heep. Kowalski had not taken a vacation in five years, and he was an ex-prizefighter who carried pianos on his back. Nevertheless, when he got sick, he did not try to care for himself. As he put it, "I just lay down and take medicine." And his wife added, "And he complains— he's worse than the kids." But unlike Heep's wife, she said it with love. And unlike Heep's, Kowalski's dependency gave him the strength of two men. When he wanted to drink, he would call his sponsor: "When you walk into the phone booth and get out a dime, you know you're not going to drink." The person who was the greatest help in getting him sober had been his adopted son: "He worshipped me. I used to walk off my drunks, and he'd say, 'Daddy, I wish you'd stop drinking.' He used to walk with me and he'd say, 'I get awfully tired walking.'" And so Stan Kowalski stopped drinking. Somehow, he had the gift of taking people inside.

Kowalski got on well with people at work; and this erstwhile felon, prizefighter, and prostitute positively radiated empathy. "I try to give the people whose furniture that I move their ease," he told me, "but I'm no psychiatrist. I try to realize that this is one of the most upsetting days of their life. I try to explain to them that I know they're upset, and I try to calm them down."

Stan Kowalski had been married for five years to his fourth wife. When I asked him to describe her, he replied, "She's the greatest thing since the wheel. I trust her . . . We both got tired of being abused and kicked around." He said they each tried to treat the other one as they themselves wanted to be treated. Later, when I asked him what his greatest satisfaction in life was, he jerked his thumb in his wife's direction and said, "Being married to her. We're pretty tight. I have to pinch myself every now and then to find out if it's really true." Their marriage remained stable until his death ten years later.

Kowalski and Heep employed very different defenses. Kowalski's altruism appeared to be as chronic as Heep's passive aggression. While I was interviewing Kowalski, he answered two telephone calls from friends asking for help. He said the social club in which he was most involved was Alcoholics Anonymous. But perhaps the most memorable aspect of our encounter was the way his use of suppression, altruism, and humor transformed his social field and evoked in me admiration and affection.

I asked Kowalski what he had learned in the last twenty years and he replied, "I wasn't a bad kid, but I was a stupid kid. I believe in God, and I've had God learn me some awful lessons." Asked if he ever went to church, he told me that AA was his church: "God has been close to me all of my life. I almost became a minister. Do you have that in your records?" We did, but at the time no one had believed it.

Observer Bias

Sometimes the researcher's judgment *is* just countertransference. Thus, the "vulnerability" of some Core City men lay more in the eyes of intolerant beholders than in the men's own biopsychosocial risk. Sometimes the observer's opinion does reflect bias and a lack of understanding. In such cases an individual's resilience is more apparent than real; for in fact the individual was initially at far less risk than observers believed. The life of Mike Mulligan provides an illustration of such a case.

The error in Mike Mulligan's evaluation came from the fact that observers misinterpreted his family's untidiness. Among the well-to-do, excessive neatness and cleanliness are often evidence of Calvinism, psychopathology, or too compulsive a personality. Among the beleaguered poor families of the inner city, however, cleanliness is often a correlate of resiliency, high morale, self-esteem, and mental health. Neatness often reflects a successful effort to master an otherwise chaotic environment. But sometimes, as with the Mulligans, apparent squalor is only skin deep.

Mike Mulligan grew up in a tenement with only the bare necessities. His apartment lacked central heat or "facilities for bathing." The Mulligan children were repeatedly excluded from school because of lice and impetigo or for just plain being unwashed. Several child and family welfare agencies had been involved with the family. One note read, "Reverend X. feels family is a hopeless case. Mother is a habitual beggar." His church tried to look after the family, "but clothing and furniture were never cared for." The school superintendent wrote of the Mulligan household, "this is one of the worst cases of utter filthiness seen." The household routine was described as "haphazard, the conditions wretched, beds filthy, children dirty and half-clothed." On his original home visit the social investigator described Mike Mulligan's mother as shabbily dressed in an old kimono with uncombed hair and dirty nails. He described Mulligan's sister as follows: "though only 22 years old, her front teeth were entirely missing and only a few decayed teeth on one side of her mouth were visible." In an effort to be reassuring, the Boston City Hospital medical record revealed its own prejudices about Mike Mulligan's parents by noting that they were "constitutionally inferior but not feebleminded." According to the notes of the Society for the Prevention of Cruelty to Children, "the police don't believe Mike's mother has much intelligence."

Yet somehow none of these alleged difficulties seemed to tarnish Mike Mulligan. The psychiatrist described him as "conventional and suggestible" and observed that although "definitely an untidy boy with a torn shirt, uncombed hair, and rather careless in his posture [he] has a simple, cheerful friendly manner."

The truth was that the Mulligan family was different, not dysfunctional. Admittedly, Mike Mulligan's mother had dropped out of school at age 14 in fifth grade and her husband, a carnival worker, had not gone beyond eighth grade. But the father was a hard worker who would take his son to baseball games and play games at home with him, and of family life, the mother reported, "we have lots of fun together." Admittedly, Mike Mulligan's own reading quotient was only 82, his arithmetic quotient was only 68, and he repeated two grades in school. Yet except that the school believed he "needs more brains," his school behavior report was quite good. The teachers described him as "well liked, with a happy smile and willing to do anything." His physical health was good, and he was without delinquent habits. He went regularly to Sunday school, sang in the choir, and played with nondelinquents. If the neighborhood was terrible and Reverend X. pessimistic about Mike Mulligan, the church influence was strong and Mulligan absorbed that strength.

Mike Mulligan quit school at 16, as his father had done before him, to work with traveling carnivals. He enlisted in the army in time for the Korean War, and following gruesome combat in Korea he suffered post-traumatic stress disorder. He was discharged and received a 50 percent disability on psychiatric grounds. His less than empathic medical report noted that he showed "immaturity, poor judgment and attempts to control the environment by means of a superficial suicide gesture." (Adequate understanding of post-traumatic stress disorder was still thirty years in the future.) Mulligan's difficulties were considered to have existed prior to the service, but of course the military psychiatrists did not have, as did the Study of Adult Development, a prospectively gathered record. At one point the doctors even diagnosed Mulligan's post-traumatic stress disorder as a "schizophrenic reaction," and they discharged him as "depressive reaction." In 1952 he received nine electroshock treatments at Pilgrim State Hospital and was discharged as a "schizoid personality." After leaving the army he drifted from job to job and rooming house to rooming house, and began drinking to excess. He read only tabloids and comic books. In 1956 his landlady still considered him "slightly touched."

In 1960 Mulligan married a primary school teacher. He had begun steady work in a tool and die plant at $70 per week and had accumulated a significant savings account. By age 47 the real Mike Mulligan could finally become visible to his myopic middle-class Study observers. Thanks to his wife, the inside of his house was now "neat and clean," and the interviewer could see Mulligan more clearly:

> His eye contact was good and his affect quite appropriate. He has an enormous amount of energy and he is a good conversationalist with the ability to listen and respond easily. He expressed a good deal of interest in the Study and shared his own opinions about delinquency. Often saying life has its ups and downs and accepting them easily, Mike's easygoing attitude was impressive and so was his ability to shake off problems, yet not ignore them. He was definitely an interesting and enthusiastic man to talk with.

In short, Mike Mulligan was not schizoid by the wildest stretch of the imagination.

"It did seem," wrote the interviewer, "that Mike had a certain admiration for his boss, and that he had learned a great deal from his boss." He boasted, "I'm the best machinist in the whole country. My boss says I can do the work of two men." At great financial sacrifice, he sent all of his children to parochial school, and they all went on to college. Like his own father, Mulligan spent a lot of time with his children and was involved in the same sports in which they won trophies. Beside his children's sports trophies was a plaque given to Mulligan for his community service as a leader in the Little League. He was proud of this award. He had enjoyed "keeping 250 kids off the corner." He was also a safety officer and a Little League umpire. Reverend X. might have been surprised to learn that childhood cleanliness was not necessarily next to godliness.

Mike Mulligan said that what pleased him most about his wife was "just her—her company." The Mulligans seemed to have a very easygoing relationship. His mood over the last six months had been "good-happy." He said he now walked away from fights. "I smartened up. I'm not a very big guy, and after I was 19 years old I learned I couldn't protect myself against big guys." In terms of his Korean War experience, he said, "I'm pretty well normal now." The interviewer, blind to Mulligan's past, wrote, "He is a fascinating study in the evolution and maturation of an adult who was probably rated pretty poorly for mental and emotional health twenty years ago."

Mike Mulligan did not deny his past; he only made it understandable and now created empathy in the Study observers who in the past had not been able to generate empathy for the Mulligan family by themselves. "I'm the type who always has to pay the bills," Mulligan had boasted to his interviewer. "I never get into debt." Yet he told, without shame, of stealing food as a child because his family had been so hungry and so poor.

By age 60 Mike Mulligan, who had once moved from rooming house to rooming house, had had a stable address for more than twenty-five years. At age 25 he had belonged to Disabled American Veterans "to protect my pension"; at 60 he belonged to the organization in order to take part in their community service activities. At 58 he was making $25,000 a year as a machinist, and was in good health. He had stopped smoking, and he used alcohol rarely. He was active in volunteer activities and enjoyed an active social life. He no longer went to church, but his mother, the street beggar, and his father, the carnival worker, were still inside him as sources of inspiration. His hobby was still traveling, and in spite of being a settled, married man he had not forgotten his old days with the carnival. Now, he marched in his clown outfit to raise money for the Staten Island Little League, of which he was on the board of directors. He said his ambition for when he retired was to peddle things from door to door from a fruit cart. The dirt of his childhood had stayed outside; inside, Mike Mulligan had re-created the best of both his parents, the street beggar and the carnival clown. The defenses assigned to Mike Mulligan by the Study raters included humor, altruism, sublimation, suppression, and anticipation—all five mature defenses.

13

How Does the Ego Mature?

The Brain – is wider than the Sky –
For – put them side by side –
The one the other will contain
With ease – and You – beside –
. . . . .
The Brain is just the weight of God –
For – Heft them – Pound for Pound –
And they will differ – if they do –
As Syllable from Sound –

Emily Dickinson

How does the ego learn to spin straw into gold? How can maturing ego function undo Joseph Conrad's bitter prophecy: "Woe to the man whose heart has not learned while young to hope, to love, to put its trust in life"? I believe that the ego accomplishes this in adult life, as in childhood, by taking people inside. In this chapter I shall systematically examine the process through which we internalize those whom we love and who have loved us.

The life stories presented in the last two chapters identified several potential sources—both biological and interpersonal—of ego maturity. First, biology: the increasing maturity of Eugene O'Neill, Stan Kowalski, and Bill Penn owed much to their sobriety; and over the course of years, nearly all of the 25-year-old "adolescents" in Chapters 11 and 12 matured as they reached midlife. Second, in order to mature each person needed a safe environment in adult life in which to find validation and unconditional positive regard: for Kowalski it was AA, for Penn the Quakers, and for O'Neill the Gaylord Sanatorium. We all can deploy more mature defenses if we feel that our dependency needs may be met. Third, the protagonists needed to internalize new loves: O'Neill found Carlotta; Kinder, Kowalski, Hope, Patriarcha, and Thoreau also found supportive wives. Similarly, other investigators have found supportive husbands to be critical to adult resilience in women raised in orphanages.[1] A final, more mysterious, source of maturity identified in these life stories was the return of hope, morale, and renewed faith. This renewed faith was often explicitly religious, but such maturation can be mediated by psychotherapy and by support groups as well.

Models of Ego Development

The first three sources of ego maturation listed above are associated with three rather distinct conceptual models of ego development: a neurobiologic model, an environmental model, and an assimilation or imprinting model. Although for a complete picture all three models must be simultaneously entertained, in this chapter I will focus principally on the third model of ego maturation: assimilation of other people. I will also briefly discuss the more speculative relation of hope and faith to mature defenses.

First, there is the *neurobiological model* of the ego. This is the explicit model of hereditarians, and to a much more limited degree, the implicit model of developmental psychologists like Lawrence Kohlberg and Jane Loevinger. In this model the ego is created by an inexorably maturing central nervous system and its development is not critically dependent upon the environment. In support of this model, there is good evidence that myelinization (insulation of nerve fibers) continues into the third decade of life.[2] In addition, the way that the human personality will respond to an identical neurologic insult varies over the adult life cycle.[3] Both these findings suggest that the neurobiological complexity of the brain continues to evolve into adulthood. Another strong argument for biological predisposition to certain defenses is that for the members of the Study of Adult Development ethnicity, culture, social class, and education—all potent environmental influences on many facets of human behavior—had little effect on maturity or choice of individual defenses.

There is also evidence that a predisposition to some defenses is inherited. A tendency to use dissociative defenses runs in the families of antisocial and very extraverted individuals. For example, a family history of alcoholism correlated significantly with the tendency of College and Core City men to use dissociation even when they were not themselves alcoholic. The defenses of isolation and displacement are common in the relatives of people with obsessive-compulsive disorder. Fantasy and projection are common in relatives of schizophrenics. Evidence supporting the genetic (neurobiological) transmission of defenses also includes the influence of heredity upon special talents. Beethoven's musical genius and Nightingale's facility with numerical data must have been in part genetic.

Perhaps the most compelling evidence for a neurobiological model of ego development comes from research on twins. The inherited "wiring" of the brain appears to override the effects of family nurture: identical twins raised apart have far more similar temperaments and personality traits than do nonidentical twins raised together.[4] And with the passage of time the similarity of separated identical twins increases, not decreases.

In a classic study of moral reasoning in children, Jean Piaget observed that children's morality evolved with maturity, and that such moral development occurred quite independently of whether the child received religious instruction or attended Sunday school.[5] Similarly, in order to deploy mature defenses, one must have matured cognitively to the point of achieving what Piaget calls formal operations, or what Loevinger calls autonomous ego functioning. That is, cognitively the user of mature defenses must be able to separate principle from context—to tolerate paradox, ambiguity, and historical relativity.

Within a cognitive developmental framework, the capacity to sustain paradox is a hallmark of ego maturation. Neo-Piagetians stress that to mature beyond formal operations we must be able to entertain two competing viewpoints at once. So do those who study moral development. For example, Loevinger defines the most mature, "integrated" stage of ego development as toleration for ambiguity, reconciliation of inner conflict, and the ability to cherish another's individuality while simultaneously respecting interdependence. Students of creativity like Albert Rothenberg and Arthur Koestler also stress that in order to achieve creativity our minds must be able to encompass conflicting images simultaneously.

In such a model, ego maturity (some call it wisdom) reflects the ego's increasing capacity to tolerate paradox. This same capacity characterizes the mature defenses, which can maintain a creative and flexible tension between irreconcilables and allow conscience, impulse, reality, and attachment all to have places at center stage. For example, a College man who was both a model for mature defenses and a distinguished career diplomat to the Arab world told me that he was on his way to address a B'nai B'rith group. I asked him what he planned to say about the dilemma of Palestine. He replied that he would quote the wise man who observed, "When in a conflict both parties have the moral right on their side, that is the meaning of tragedy." A paradox. Yet Eugene O'Neill suggested that the tragic alone has that significant beauty which is truth. A second paradox. But where does the capacity to tolerate such paradox come from?

Consider the paradox inherent in each of the mature defenses. The defense of anticipation reflects an ability to experience the affects associated with future pain in the relative safety of the present. Altruism reflects the empathy to understand how another person feels and yet simultaneously maintain such separation that we do not fall prey to sympathy and thus merge affective boundaries. Suppression gives us the courage to change the things we can change, the serenity to accept the things we cannot change, and the wisdom to know the difference.

Sublimation and humor, too, grow out of the intrapsychic reconciliation of paradox. Both art and humor reconcile love and hate. As Koestler points out, both humor and sublimation are subtypes of creativity; both the artist and the humorist possess the capacity to feel part of and yet separate from simultaneously.[6] As we saw in the life of Sylvia Plath, sublimation can evolve out of bringing together two conflicting mental representations of someone we hate and love at the same time. And as we know from contrasting the cruel humor of children with the gentle self-mocking clowning in a Charlie Chaplin or Woody Allen movie, humor evolves from the bipolar conflict of sadomasochism. For protagonist and observer alike, the result of humor and sublimation is not conflict but catharsis.

The psychologist Phoebe Cramer has reviewed the literature documenting the maturation of the ego's mechanisms of defense in children. Cramer reminds us that to some degree defense mechanisms may be considered ideational representations of infantile reflex behaviors. Just as infants differ in their ability to filter out upsetting sounds and sights, just so there may be biological differences in adults' use of defenses like denial. Cramer also points out that "experimental studies of figure-ground reversal, using ambiguous figures, have suggested that the capacity to make such a reversal increases with age." Such a process is basic to humor in which one pretends to do something that in the past has been associated with pain but now is associated with the release of laughter. For example, consider the audience's response when a gun is aimed at someone, the trigger is pulled, and out pops a flag from the gun's barrel. Figure and ground, as it were, are reversed. Finally, Cramer observes, "As children grow older, the locus of control for their behavior shifts from being predominantly external to being predominantly internal. Thus, the child moves from assuming that others are responsible for his feelings and behavior to internalizing the responsibility."[7] The immature defenses externalize responsibility; the intermediate and mature defenses internalize responsibility. In short, with the passage of time and with only limited dependence on external stimulation, a great deal of the "wiring" for the development of mature defenses seems to grow into place.

The second model of ego maturation focuses on the effects of nurture and environment. This is the learning theory or *environmental model* of ego development, the model of social learning theorists like Albert Bandura and Walter Mischel, of behaviorists like B. F. Skinner and John Watson, of anthropologists like Franz Boas, and of sociologists like Karl Marx and Erving Goffman. It is epitomized by the eighteenth-century philosopher John Locke, who conceived of the brain as a *tabula rasa* on which experience writes. It ignores biological predisposition and considers the brain to be analogous to a new computer waiting to be programmed by the individual's experience. The ego processes are simply the software through which society programs the individual's infinitely receptive mind. In this model, without experience there is no ego. According to this model the brains of psychopaths have simply been incorrectly programmed, whereas hereditarians believe that the defect lies in their genes.

The psychiatrist Stuart Hauser and his colleagues have pointed out the importance of family life in promoting ego development. In a study of the effect of family environment upon adolescent maturation, they noted that parents who listened and actively recognized and clarified their sons' and daughters' voices advanced the adolescents' ego development. In contrast, parents who demonstrated impatience by turning away from their teenagers' voices ("especially when they were expressing a new rhythm or melody") retarded development. "Yet another family characteristic enhancing change and growth,"

Hauser tells us, "was tolerance of the adolescent's feelings. Families have various ways of handling emotions, especially those that are potentially disruptive, such as anger, aggression and envy. Some families abhor the expression or even the experience of these feelings . . . In such a climate, it is hardly safe for the adolescent to challenge a parent angrily."[8] Hauser argues that there is a greater likelihood of arrested ego development for children raised in such a repressive atmosphere.

This second model of ego development is also supported by the life histories in Chapters 11 and 12. Although their appearance might come quite late in a Study member's life, the presence of loving people in the environment seemed critical to the emergence of mature defenses. As suggested by O'Neill's difficulty in facing his tuberculosis without his mother's support, we learn to anticipate future pain effectively only if someone first sits beside us while we learn to bear our current anxiety. Characteristically, children from severely disrupted homes are not adept at either anticipation or suppression. Follow-up studies of children suggest that early separation from both parents impairs a child's capacity to postpone gratification. Lacking stable early love relationships, such children may have little sense of time, poor ability to plan for the future, and low tolerance of frustration.

How do we learn to master powerful affects? How do we as adults learn to say and to appreciate not that we are "tired" or "bummed out" or "upset" but that we are angry or sad or embarrassed or humiliated? Often, we learn to do so only by having another person help us to bear and identify our pain. Thus, our ego's development and our ability to know how we feel owe much to those who have held us empathically.

Evidence for the importance of environment in shaping ego function also includes the relationship of social systems to human behavior. Social supports facilitate mature defenses; loneliness fosters immature defenses. In the presence of people whose personalities, values, and language match our own, and who enhance our sense of safety and our self-esteem, our capacity to interpret conflict, to respond maturely, and to deploy the less distorting (that is, more mature) defenses is enhanced. For example, the U.S. State Department exhibits altruism toward its well-known friends and projection toward its poorly understood enemies. Similarly, a given defense in a companion may elicit a complementary defense in us. This is especially true in the case of the contagious immature defenses. Finally, group permission powerfully affects defense choice. Projection in Nazi Germany, acting out during wartime, dissociation during Mardi Gras are all examples of social permission determining defensive style. But note that all these examples are short-lived. Remove the environmental influence, and the effect may disappear. The effects of heredity are less transient.

Of course, maturation always requires both nature and nurture, but sometimes only a modest environmental priming experience is needed to allow mature ego function to occur. For example, if a fledgling chaffinch hears a mature chaffinch's song over and over again when young, it still cannot emit the song until the next year when it is more fully mature. The bird's ability to sing depends on preprogrammed, embryological development. Nevertheless, in order to sing when adult, the young chaffinch must hear a mature chaffinch sing at least once. Similarly, in order to love, people need to feel loved by someone when young.

To conclude, learning as well as heredity plays a major role in our choice of defenses. Sublimation hurts less than masochism; altruism is better paid than reaction formation; humor wins us more friends, or at least fewer enemies, than wit. An environmental model of the development of sublimation requires not only that innate talent be present, but also that such talent be reinforced by the outside world. If O'Neill's plays had not been produced, would he have derived the same comfort from writing them? What if Beethoven had been born in Great Britain, where aristocratic patronage of gifted musicians was the exception rather than the rule? Might he not have carried out his intention to kill himself instead of composing the Ninth Symphony?

In Chapter 12, however, it seemed clear that what was most critical to resilience was not social supports but the ability to internalize those supports. An *assimilation or imprinting model* of ego development posits that the ego is formed as a precipitate of early relationships, in a process analogous to the ethological concept of imprinting. This is an interactional model halfway between nature and nurture. The cognitive psychologists conceptualize the task of assimilation as forming mental schemata of relationships or "role-relationship models."[9] An imprinting model posits that complex behaviors are a product of early identifications. Thus, the Freudian view that ego development is catalyzed by stable internalized representations of people is in many ways the view of an ethologist. To a significant degree Piaget, too, saw the mind as formed by its capacity to assimilate social experience. If the ego's defense mechanisms help us to *accommodate* to life, the ego's identification with and internalization of people is analogous to Piaget's concept of *assimilation*. It is my respect for this third model that has led me to part company with many writers on defense mechanisms; thus I have not classified the processes of internalization and identification (to be defined below) as primarily ego defenses. Internalization and identification are too important to the actual creation of the ego for us to regard them as just defenses.

In this third model, the ego is not programmed like a computer with multiplication tables and social taboos, nor does it evolve spontaneously as our genitals do at puberty. Rather, this model regards the ego as an "organ" that develops by internalization of beloved people and their virtues and their prohibitions. The ego's values, allegiances, and defenses are not learned as we learn table manners or even courting rituals. Rather, Erik Erikson has suggested, our ego identity develops out of a gradual integration of all prior identifications.[10] The psychoanalyst Hans Loewald has also extensively discussed the ways in which the internalization of others promotes the growth of ego capacities.[11] If the neurobiological model attributes the ego to our genes and the environmental model attributes the ego to our cerebral cortex, this third model puts the adaptive capacities of the ego in the temporal lobe where memory, sex, religiosity, and attachment all meet.

In part, the capacity of our ego to internalize comes from its ability to distinguish among our emotional states. Mature defenses, after all, involve not only accurate reality testing and a clear sense of self but also issues of distinguishing competing emotions and attachments and of distinguishing where *I* end and *you* begin. Confusion between self and other turns empathy into projection, and projection makes it impossible to grow through the presence of another person.

The difficulty with this third model is how to make it scientifically plausible. For example, in psychoanalytic writings there is an elaborate, but experimentally undocumented, literature about incorporation. Some texts speak of good breasts being incorporated and bad breasts being spit out. Psychoanalysts speak of the ego being formed by a "precipitate" of other people around which the ego "nuclei consolidate." The psychoanalyst Joseph Sandler writes that the world of internal objects gives rise "to a (largely unconscious) phantom world in which we live at the same time as the real world. This inner world is a world of unconscious ghost object images . . . whose presence is gratifying, wish-fulfilling and reassuring." [12] Sigmund Freud makes the same point with still more jargon: "The character of the ego is a precipitate of abandoned object-cathexes and . . . contains the history of these object-choices." [13]

Such terminology is useful only if we remember that it is metaphor and do not let it harden into myth. Metaphors are open-ended and playful; myths are rigid and serious. Metaphors mean "analogous to" and "as if"; myths convey "so I've been told" and "it's right there in the Bible (or the Standard Edition)." Metaphors allow the truth of our dreams to become clearer with every retelling. In contrast, myth merges into dogma and may insist that all dreams reflect wish-fulfillment. Metaphors add leaven to theory and to poetry, but myths add dead weight to Thomistic and Talmudic prose. Metaphors conceptualize and myths enshrine. Myths retard science; metaphors advance science.

Consider Antoine de Saint-Exupéry's fable about a little prince, a fox, and an aviator, *The Little Prince*. Toward the end of the book the following exchange takes place:

> So the little prince tamed the fox. And when the hour of his departure drew near—
>
> "Ah," said the fox, "I shall cry."
>
> "It's your own fault," said the little prince. "I never wished you any sort of harm; but you wanted me to tame you . . ."
>
> "Yes, that is so," said the fox.
>
> "But now you are going to cry!" said the little prince.
>
> "Yes, that is so," said the fox.
>
> "Then it has done you no good at all!"
>
> "It has done me good, " said the fox, "because of the color of the wheat fields." [14]

You see, a little while before, the fox had told the prince: "I do not eat bread. Wheat is of no use to me . . . And that is sad. But you have hair that is the color of gold . . . The grain, which is also golden, will bring back the thought of you. And I shall love to listen to the wind in the wheat." [15]

Later, although he loses the little prince, the aviator, too, becomes enriched forever. Wheat fields and the sight of stars will never be the same for him again. Always the wheat fields will glow with the gold of the little prince's hair. Always the stars will laugh with the prince's laughter. And always these memories will remind the aviator of his painful and paradoxical concern that perhaps the little prince's pet sheep has eaten the prince's beloved rose. Attachment does not come free of pain, but often such pain is the flame that marks the process of object assimilation, a process integral to human development. For the aviator, because of his experience of identification with the little prince, grief will never again be so conflicted, nor the comfort of weeping such an anathema. We, too, sometimes forget that, contrary to folklore and psychiatric myth, loss in itself does not cause psychopathology. We forget that healthy grief hurts but does not make us ill. Grief produces tears, not patienthood. It is never having anyone at all to love that cripples us. It is the inconstant people who stay in our lives who drive us mad, not the constant ones who die. It is failure to internalize those whom we have loved, not their loss, that impedes adult development. And Saint-Exupéry's metaphors make this clearer than Kantian logic ever could. For not only does metaphor arise from strong feelings, metaphor also generates strong feelings. This can be an advantage. "Only connect," E. M. Forster tells us in *Howards End*, "the prose and the passion, and both will be exalted."

What about the men and women in the Study of Adult Development who failed to internalize? They were not those who had suffered repeated losses. They were those who continued to live all their lives with present but emotionally inconsistent parents. We have already seen that the deployment of immature defenses (such as projection and fantasy) is a means of trying to stabilize internal relationships, but such deployment does not permit full assimilation of the loved person. Sylvia Plath, for example, never enjoyed a stable or very comforting internal memory of her mother. The development of mature defenses requires more complete metabolism.

Michael Rutter makes this same point when he distinguishes between *privation* and *deprivation*.[16] Privation means never having loved, and privation can lead to even psychotic disability. Deprivation means losing those whom we have loved, and deprivation usually leads to emotional distress, not illness. The difference between disability and distress is the difference between being crippled and being pained, between behavior and talk. To mourn thoroughly for someone we have loved and been loved by produces grief, not psychopathology. Indeed, as we have seen in the case histories of Algeron Young, Bill Penn, and

Eugene O'Neill, grief can catalyze internalization and identification. Privation does nothing of the kind.

Jay Shurley, a psychiatrist specializing in survivors of extreme isolation, tried to explain a child's acquisition of syntactical grammar to a science writer. The writer was trying to understand why such grammar had never been acquired by a woman who had been utterly socially isolated in an empty room until puberty. Rescued from isolation at age 13, the woman successfully acquired language over the next fifteen years, but never an internalized syntax with which to organize her speech. "Our advancements take place in a relationship." Shurley explained. "In order for an infant to learn anything—and this takes you back to Victor, the Wild Boy of Aveyron—there has to be a relationship in which the child gets enough nurturance to proceed. Affective attachment plays the primary role. It is not an intellectual process. Intellect rides on the back of affective bonding."[17] Learning the syntax of mature ego defenses is surely as complex as acquiring proper grammar.

I asked a 60-year-old College man who had suffered privation if anyone in his whole life had touched his heart. He replied, "I think no one. That is my character. It is a terrible thing." As a partial explanation, he suggested, "When young I learned to steel myself." He had learned to do this during his mother's bouts of manic-depression. For in his childhood there had been no one else in his family. His alcoholic father had left home early; and he had neither brothers nor sisters, neither uncles nor aunts. On the one hand, by age 60 this man had given up all hope: he loved nobody, and he brooded glumly over his osteoarthritis. He was alone in the world. Although he was an artist who had won the full respect of his nation, he saw himself as a failure, and it seemed he had no one except his manic-depressive mother inside. On the other hand, he was not schizoid or anhedonic, he did not feel sorry for himself, and he had never sought psychiatric care. He had escaped the genes that led to his mother's major depressive illness. He was able to ask me extremely wise and mature questions about my longitudinal study. His only failing was to be without attachment. He was unable to remember loving anybody. True, if we wished, we could label him a narcissistic character. But often narcissism is only a polysyllabic synonym for the more empathic term "in pain."

Clearly, nature, nurture, and assimilation of others are all involved in the creation of the ego. For while the model of an ego that develops through internalization of relationships is a compelling one, in some respects it begs the question: Where does the capacity to internalize others come from? One answer is from our environment and from our nature. Certainly, identification and internalization are promoted by meeting the right person at the right time[18] (environment), and by a good temperamental fit with that person[19] (nature).

Before elaborating on the third model of ego development I wish to examine a thread that ran through the lives of many of the men as they matured, a thread of spiritual growth or, for want of a better term, *religious wonder*. Others may prefer to call the process moral development. In some respects the cognitive ability to sustain paradox reflects the same higher order of psychic integration as do some facets of deep religious conviction. But moral and cognitive development are not enough. The 60-year-old College man had both, but he lacked faith and wonder. Other men in the study like O'Neill and Bill Penn who shared the hopeless College artist's privation still managed to discover faith.

Mature defenses grow out of our brain's evolving capacity to master, assimilate, and feel grateful for life, living, and experience. Such gratitude encompasses the capacity for wonder. To see and comprehend the joy of a sunset or a symphony or to sustain a mature religious conviction is evidence that one's mind has experienced a hallucination or an illusion of sorts. Such wonder is in itself a transformation and a self-deception of the most sublime nature. But how does such wonder develop? How shall we understand such a paradoxical hope—the health-promoting, morale-restoring self-deception that transforms the lonely atheist in a foxhole into a true believer?

In general, in this book I have tried to stay away from mysticism and to play the role of psychoanalytic agnostic, but in this chapter God—the God of the reader's understanding—will be allowed a wider role. For the ego is a fascinating "organ," a remarkable synthesizer, and sometimes its achievements are nothing short of miraculous. In 1845 Wilhelm Griesenger, one of the first great psychiatrists, helped to move German psychology away from romantic and theological explanations of the mind toward a strictly empirical brain psychology. But in trying to be rational, Griesenger did not abandon the phenomena of synthetic mental activity. Thus, he wrote, "How a material physical act in the nerve fibres or cells can be converted into an idea, an act of consciousness, is absolutely incomprehensible; indeed, we are utterly unable even to settle the question of the existence or nature of the media existing between them . . . it is scientifically admissible to connect the faculties of the soul with the body in the same intimate relation as exists between function and organ . . . to consider the soul primarily and preeminently as the sum of all cerebral states."[20]

Our capacities for creativity, for mature self-deception, and for religious wonder are all facilitated by situations that create a virtual reality, a way of supplementing and enhancing the love we have received. One such situation occurs in *dreaming*—both day and night dreaming—as we review the past and rehearse the future. We humans also seek out *sacred places* in which to find the holding environments we need. Our abilities to *play* and to *integrate idea and affect* also help to create the conditions that encourage creativity, maturity of defenses, and wonder. Not surprisingly, these four, dreaming, sacred places, play, and the linking of idea and affect, are all also essential components of most psychotherapies and self-help groups. And all of them help to foster the spiritual and psychological growth that sometimes allows us to develop hope, faith, and gratitude even late in life.

First, dreaming, by allowing us, in our minds, to manipulate past and future, gives us a way to master the passage of time. As egg-laying mammals like echidnas and platypuses evolved from their reptilian ancestors, they developed dramatically enlarged frontal lobes, but not the capacity to dream. Such expansion of the frontal lobes is thought to reflect an increased capacity to associate, to comprehend, and to reflect prior to action. As the non–egg-laying mammals evolved from their reptilian ancestors, they failed to develop similarly enlarged frontal lobes, but they developed a capacity for nocturnal dream states. While the purposes of nocturnal dreams are arguable, one purpose appears to be to allow the organism to reflect upon, associate to, and remember the past while, because of the cataplexy (relative paralysis) of the dreaming state, being unable to act.

Humans have evolved both the hypertrophied frontal lobes shared with more primitive mammals and the capacity to dream at night shared with dogs and cats. Humans also have the capacity to rehearse both past and future through daydreams while awake. Daydreaming and, by inference, night dreaming allow us to re-create the past and to rehearse the future. Thus, the evolution of both dreaming and the associational areas of the frontal lobes allows the organism to link past experience to future choice. Perhaps imagination and daydreaming are the same thing—but they are essential to the mastery of time, to the development of mature defenses, and to wondering whence we come and whither we are going. Dreaming and the frontal lobes permit us to *imagine,* and imagination is essential to religion, psychotherapy, and mature defenses. Without imagination and the capacity to transcend time present, mature defenses and faith would be impossible.

Sacred places, too, allow us to imagine, to sustain paradox, and to wonder. In the painted caves of Altamira and Lascaux, or upon the artifact-surrounded, Oriental rug–draped couch of Sigmund Freud, or in an Aboriginal dance at a sacred site in Australia's Northern Territories—in such sacred places art, religion, ego, metaphor, play, and dreams intersect. The caveman's shrine, the analyst's office, the child's playhouse are places separated from and yet bound to reality. The same can be said of Stonehenge, the nave at Chartres, the studio of Picasso, and the stage of Shakespeare's Globe Theatre. In sacred places, wonder reigns supreme. Transitional objects (symbols of early relationships) are everywhere. Sacraments and tragedy, rage and ecstasy can all be tolerated. Land can belong to two moral peoples at the same time; wine can become a savior's blood, and straw can be spun into gold. Perhaps a better term than sacred places would be playrooms or spiritual kindergartens for adults.

The third link between creativity, mature self-deception, and wonder is play. Play allows self-deception and religious wonder to create order out of chaos and to *seem* to be true. As the psychoanalyst Anna Maria Rizzuto has demonstrated, when adults are asked to "play" and to draw their childhood family of origin and their image of God, the image they draw of God can be discerned in the images they draw of their families.[21] In the presence of psychological conflict, play can put into the world what was not there before. Play allows us to repeat and re-create conflictual relationships so that we can develop increasingly stable internalizations of those we love. Playful repetition offers mastery over past experiences of helplessness. Play, like religion and defenses, creates order. Indeed, play is order and "brings to our lives a wonderful if limited perfection."[22] In both play and in the evolution of mature defenses, the strength of a higher power may become ours. Play produces the very opposite of what we usually think of as illusion, for play is essential to the Piagetian concept of assimilation. But play has a beginning and an end; it is circumscribed and not to be confused with reality. Play, like religion and defenses, creates its own reality. To interrupt play creates disarray and anger. So it is with interrupting defenses and religious observance—a comforting virtual reality is destroyed and the spoilsport is resented.

Sometimes, ritual allows the virtual reality of play to become reality. When, through ritual or sacrament, we accept a transformed identity, the relationship between our old self and our new self is not adequately expressed by calling such a transformation just symbolic or just superstitious. Sometimes our new identity and the essential oneness of the old and the new identities go far deeper than the mere correspondence between a person and a symbolic image. It is a mystic unity. The one has *become* the other. In his magic dance, the Aboriginal dancer *is* a kangaroo; in the magic ceremonies of marriage and graduation, the girl becomes a matron and passes from medical student to physician.

The fourth motif common to mature defenses and to many religious practices is the capacity to link the world of emotion and attachment with the world of reason and perception. Funerals, weddings, circumcisions, and christenings all bring passion and reason to mind simultaneously. An outspoken neuroscientist might venture that mature defenses, creativity, and religious wonder all come from the associational areas of the brain, especially from the frontal and temporal lobes. If the cerebral cortex allows us to make distinctions, to read, to count, and to discriminate, the "sticky" temporal lobes allow us to blend, to attach, to condense, and to remember people and feelings. It is not coincidental that smell, creativity, attachment, memory, and religious preoccupations all involve the temporal lobe. Both temporal lobe epilepsy and stimulation of the temporal lobes can produce hypergraphia, hypersexuality, hyperreligiosity—and sometimes the reexperience of smells and old songs. Damage the frontal lobe and we lose our judgment and our ability to distinguish "right" from "wrong." Damage the temporal lobes and our memory, and thus our ability to love, is destroyed. Remove the rest of the cortex and we cannot move, speak, or calculate, but we may retain our affective attachments and our morality. Nevertheless, the affect-ridden temporal lobes and the logical, lexical parietal cortex are all part of the same brain; and it is their *integration* that produces mature defenses. As Piaget reminds us,

"The two aspects, affective and cognitive, are at the same time inseparable and irreducible."[23]

To integrate spiritual development with the three models of ego development and to illustrate the seemingly spiritual path by which projection evolves into empathy, let me continue the story of Eugene O'Neill's mother, Mary Ellen O'Neill (called Ella), beyond the time portrayed in *Long Day's Journey into Night*, to the time she achieved abstinence from opiates. To some degree, the spiritual growth associated with ego maturation mirrors the psychological steps necessary to progress from drug dependence to stable abstinence. For spiritual growth, biology, nurture, and the internalization of new loves are all also critical to getting sober. In Alcoholics Anonymous there is a world of difference between being "dry" (being temporarily abstinent from alcohol) and being "sober" (attaining maturity and thereby achieving resistance to relapse to alcohol abuse).

Long Day's Journey into Night gives us some understanding of why Eugene O'Neill might have run away to Buenos Aires and why he might have preferred drunkenness to being exposed to his mother's paranoid accusations. In this understanding, we can forgive O'Neill his immature defenses. But if we forgive O'Neill, then his mother becomes the witch. How can we come to understand and forgive her projection as well?

In reality, Ella O'Neill changed from the paranoid zombie she was in 1912 to an empathic dowager who in 1919 could write to her son Eugene two days after the birth of *his* son, "I am one of the happiest old ladies in New York tonight to know I have such a wonderful grandson but no more wonderful than you were when you were born and weighed *eleven pounds* and had no *nerves* at that time. I am enclosing a picture of you taken at three months. Hope your *boy* will be as *good looking*." She ended the letter with love to O'Neill's wife, Agnes, to his new son, and to "the biggest baby of the three, *You*."[24] By 1919 Ella O'Neill had become an effective, self-reliant, drug-free grandmother. From being a young woman who seldom smiled, she became animated and was noted to laugh a great deal. She followed the budding career of her son the playwright with pride, intelligence, and empathy.[25] At last, more than thirty years after his birth, Ella O'Neill, safe in her own recovery, could admit feeling real gratitude that her son had been born. As her addicted and broken brain was allowed to mend, God, maturation, and gratitude were all allowed to enter.

But before we can understand Ella O'Neill's recovery we must first understand her conflict. All his life, O'Neill had wondered if he was to blame for his mother's problems. In *Long Day's Journey*, Mary Tyrone blamed Edmund and almost every other relative she had for her addiction. As he searched back for clues to his mother's addiction, O'Neill got only as far as his own birth and no further. But what had gone on *before* Eugene's birth? What was the real pain that Ella wished to anesthetize? What was the source of the desperate self-deceptions that underlay her behavior? Let us look for the one relative to whom neither the playwright nor his grieving character Mary Tyrone paid attention. This missing player in the family drama was Ella O'Neill's own mother. Bridget Quinlan had died while Ella and James O'Neill were vacationing in Europe four months before Eugene O'Neill's conception, and the hotel-room loneliness that Mary Tyrone offered as a cause for her reliance on morphine was probably a displacement for her unacknowledged grief over the death of her mother.

But even before her marriage to James O'Neill it was noted that Ella Quinlan seldom smiled. Later, having proved unable to care for her first two children, she became chronically depressed. She depended heavily on her mother to help care for her children. She was also profoundly ambivalent about having a third child, and had several induced abortions, but shortly after her mother's death she allowed herself to remain pregnant with Eugene. Mary Tyrone says in the play, "I was afraid all the time I carried Edmund. I knew something terrible would happen. I knew I'd proved by the way I'd left Eugene [Edmund O'Neill, Ella's middle child, who died at age one] that I wasn't worthy to have another baby, and that God would punish me if I did . . . And now, ever since he's been so sick I've kept remembering Eugene and my father and I've been so frightened and guilty." Later in the play she moves her grief forward in time and reminisces that *after* Edmund's birth, "All [the doctor] knew was I was in pain. It was easy for him to stop the pain." And later she describes her morphine as "A special kind of medicine. I have to take it because there is no other that can stop the pain—*all* the pain—I mean, in my hands."[26]

Mary Tyrone, instead of grieving for her mother, clings to her wedding dress, the way Linus in the comic strip *Peanuts* does to his blanket. "What is it that I am looking for?" she keens. "I know it is something I lost . . . Something I miss terribly. It can't be altogether lost." But her mother is identified only in disguise. For example, Mary says to herself, "It's so lonely here. You're lying to yourself again. You wanted to get rid of them. Their contempt and disgust aren't pleasant company. You're glad they're gone. Then Mother of God, why do I feel so lonely?" Later, in the wish-fulfilling distortion of her morphine-induced reverie, Mary finds what she is looking for, but thanks to her drug-induced defense of distortion, she improves upon her real mother. She ends the play with "I had a talk with Mother Elizabeth . . . It may be sinful of me but I love her better than my own mother. Because she always understands." [27]

However, love is not enough. Cure seems impossible without hope and faith. Early in *Long Day's Journey*, Mary Tyrone tells us she has lost her faith in a higher power and cries out, "If I could only find the faith I lost, so I could pray again! . . . You expect the Blessed Virgin to be fooled by a lying dope fiend reciting words! You can't hide from her!" As a good middle-class Irish Catholic girl Mary Tyrone knew that only whores took dope. Her husband, too, understood her shame. He says of his wife, "She hasn't denied her faith, but she's forgotten it. Until now there's no strength of the spirit left in her to fight against her curse." Later, Mary expresses the same point more hopefully: "Some day when the Blessed Virgin Mary forgives me and gives me back the faith in Her love and pity I used to have in my convent days, and I can pray to Her again—when She sees no one in the world can believe in me even for a moment any more, then She will believe in me, and with Her help it will be so easy." [28]

At the end of the play, in her psychotic distortion, Mary Tyrone accurately anticipates the future: "I went to the shrine and prayed to the Blessed Virgin and found peace again because I knew she heard my prayer and would always love me and see no harm ever came to me so long as I never lost my faith in her." [29]

Two years after the day her son would later describe in his play, Ella O'Neill went to live in a convent in order to become abstinent from morphine. In her successful quest for abstinence, she illustrated several of the models that I have suggested may explain the maturation of defenses. First, external environment helps to stabilize our inner lives. An external reminder that immature defenses are maladaptive can help us abandon them. When we try to change any bad habit, an external superego and external reinforcement are helpful. By external superego I mean a source of motivation and discipline other than one's own willpower. It was probably no accident that Ella O'Neill entered the convent the same year that the Harrison Narcotics Act—federal legislation that made indiscriminate prescription of opiates by physicians illegal—was passed. Her physicians could no longer legally prescribe narcotics for her.

Second, if Karl Marx dismissed religion as the opiate of the masses, Carl Jung turned Marx's maxim around and offered Dr. Bob, cofounder of Alcoholics Anonymous, the prescription "spiritus contra spiritu." Fresh hope, heightened morale, and identification with a benign authority figure can all catalyze recovery in drug dependence. For people short on helpful internalized figures, AA and the church can replace drugs with real people as well as with an alternative source of dependence. In the convent, Ella O'Neill found real nuns to love and to be held by. She found surrogate mothers who were superior to her wedding dress security blanket and her fantasized mother. Her dependence on the social supports of the convent lessened her dependence on her beleaguered ego. Thus, in the convent Ella O'Neill not only could be dependent on an institution and find a surrogate for the mother she had been seeking but could find fresh hope and morale. Religion, psychotherapy, and spiritual reawakening all facilitate the identifications and improved morale that permit the ego integration required for mature defenses. Our egos may function more maturely in the holding environment of a convent than on a battlefield. Similarly, in the stable and safe holding environments of psychotherapy, we are reminded that passive aggression, dissociation, and projection win us nothing, and so we may replace immature defenses with mature ones.

Assimilating Those We Love

Let us now return to the third model of ego maturation and how adults can internalize loved ones in order to achieve maturity and the safety to deploy mature defenses. Six words beginning with *i*—*incorporation, introjection, imitation, internalization, idealization,* and *identification*—describe the ways in which people assimilate other people. These processes have often been categorized as defense mechanisms. However, defense mechanisms help individuals *accommodate* to—and defend against—otherwise unmanageable internal and external environments.

In contrast, after the internalizing processes of *assimilation* have taken place, the individual, like the aviator in *The Little Prince*, may never be the same again.

Granted, such internalizing processes may be categorized as merely one facet of memory; but such assimilation involves a very special kind of memory. Let me distinguish this specialized memory from more mundane, more purely cognitive examples. We remember our telephone numbers and the multiplication tables by rote; the process is cognitive and without feeling. We can retrieve such memories abruptly and voluntarily. We can recite such memories word for word. In contrast, we remember people, smells, melodies, and moments of personal crisis in a manner analogous to the way dogs remember their masters by their smell. Our awareness of smells begins gradually and lingers even when we try to escape them. Memories of either supportive or destructive relationships can come to mind involuntarily and alter our mood. Such memories are evoked by odor, music, and symbol, not by command. If we are not poets, we often cannot give words to our memories of loved ones. But our memories of a lover's perfume are often more vivid than our memories of the more easily verbalized multiplication tables. Put in simple terms, we assimilate the people we love by suffusing them with emotion, and taking them inside changes us. In contrast, we can learn the multiplication tables without any emotion at all, and in doing so we do not change.

Grief and assimilation of people are intimately, if paradoxically, entwined. The aviator identifies with and internalizes the little prince by losing him. Ella O'Neill finds her lost mother by grieving for her. No one we have ever loved is totally lost. And we rarely grieve for someone we have never loved. Admittedly, it is often painful to the point of mental illness to lose a person we have loved a little and hated a lot. Thus, as we grow older, resilience and freedom from psychopathology involve a chicken-and-egg process. On the one hand, by taking people in and by grieving for those we have loved and lost, we are able to shift from immature to mature defenses. On the other hand, by deploying mature defenses we are able to remember lost loves with affection and gratitude rather than with bitterness, and to attract new people to our side. As we grow older, we assimilate new people, and we more fully assimilate imperfectly "digested" people from the past. Indeed, the data from the Study of Adult Development suggest that both an increasing commitment to human relationships and a lessening of social anxiety may continue throughout adulthood.

To discuss the six concepts—incorporation, introjection, imitation, internalization, idealization, and identification—that underlie the third model of ego development, I must resort to metaphor. I shall use *metabolism* as a metaphor for Piaget's more abstract concept of *assimilation*. In addition, since there is no consensus on the meanings of these six terms (for example, Cramer reminds us that there are at least eighteen different definitions for *identification*),[30] the definitions that I use will be my own. I shall discuss the six concepts in terms of their hypothetical maturity.

The term *incorporation* will connote the least complete "metabolism" of another person, and *identification* will connote the most complete metabolism. The book *The Little Prince* begins with a painting of a boa constrictor that has swallowed a totally unmetabolized elephant—a vivid image of what I mean by incorporation. At the end of the book the aviator has gracefully assimilated the little prince. The aviator will now always be reminded of his affection for the little prince when he sees wheat fields; this image illustrates what I mean by identification and complete metabolism of another person. Contrast the aviator's psychic enrichment with the state of mind of a person fretfully humming Cole Porter's "I've Got You under My Skin" or Rodgers and Hammerstein's "I'm Gonna Wash That Man Right out of My Hair." These songs come closer to evoking the indigestion that a boa constrictor might feel having swallowed a pachyderm. And it is not by chance that I must turn to songs, not rational argument, to illustrate our inner representations of people.

The incomplete metabolism of other people that I am calling incorporation is manifested by individuals afflicted with involutional melancholia, a mental disorder often associated with pathological mourning. Such depressed patients use the defenses of distortion and delusional projection to hallucinate that the loved ones they mourn are alive and well or actually inhabit parts of their own bodies.

The second process of assimilation is *introjection*. In contrast to incorporation, in which we absorb the whole person, with introjection we take in only one facet of the person. Nevertheless, introjection may make us feel as if we had ingested a foreign body.

Taking people in without metabolizing them properly may exaggerate our immature defenses. Introjection is common among preschoolers, adults with personality disorder, and patients with severe depression. Both the defenses of hypochondriasis and of turning against the self (passive aggression) reflect the use of introjection. It is easiest for us to introject people who are themselves paranoid, that is, who project their feelings toward us; the demagogue inserts himself under our skin, and so we share his delusions. We may speak of the ego-alien precepts of our conscience as "Jiminy Cricket sitting on my shoulder" or "I can hear my mother's voice saying" or "I feel in my bones that it is wicked." In some ways, introjection is the opposite of projection. With projection, our own feelings and traits are projected onto the other person; with introjection, we experience the feelings or traits of another person inside ourselves.

One of the College men had a father who died suddenly of a coronary thrombosis after experiencing angina for many years. Following his father's death, the College man experienced unexplained chest pain that lasted for eight years. Rather than consciously grieve for his father, he took on his father's heart pain as his own. Despite normal electrocardiograms and physical examinations, the pain became progressively more severe and more angina-like. Finally, after reading an article in the popular scientific press on "imaginary" heart disease, he wrote to the Study internist of his mysterious heart pain. In so doing, for the first time he consciously linked his heart pain to his father's death. He recalled that at his father's funeral "I'd wondered what was expected of me emotionally," and that he had felt "inclined not to show grief." The Study internist, unlike other physicians he had consulted, reassured him that his heartache was not imaginary. At last, consciously aware of his grief, he could let go of his painful introject of his father. He has now been followed for another forty years, and has never again been troubled by "imaginary" heart pain. His assimilation of his father has become more complete.

The process of introjection is also dramatically illustrated by the phenomenon that Anna Freud has labeled *identification with the aggressor*. Such identification reflects incomplete metabolism of another person, often a tormentor. For example, when the Nazi concentration camps were liberated, the Allied soldiers were astonished to find that some of the oldest prisoners, originally imprisoned for their deep-felt opposition to the Nazi regime, were now wearing their caps bent up like their Gestapo guards and enforcing the rules of the camp with unquestioning dedication. But of course in their hearts the prisoners

did not want to be Gestapo guards; they felt corrupted. I remember a
medical student who with complete disbelief initially dismissed the
concept of identification with the aggressor. Then suddenly he remembered a teacher of organic chemistry whom he had particularly disliked.
Toward the end of the chemistry course he had abruptly realized that
he had grown a mustache identical to that of the professor. Once his
introjection became conscious, he shaved off what he had unwittingly
taken in. The prisoners and the medical student had absorbed the traits
of a powerful other but without modification or a sense of personal
enrichment. Digestion had not occurred.

If introjection has much in common with turning against the self
and with hypochondriasis, the third process of assimilation, *imitation*,
has much in common with the defense mechanism of dissociation.
Imitation is common among 5-year-olds. Playing house under the card
table, children can for a time become Mommy and Daddy. In adulthood, imitation can occur as an unconscious defense mechanism during
grief. When a mourner, as a means of defensive accommodation,
involuntarily imitates the person who has died, the process is labeled
hysterical identification. For example, after John F. Kennedy's death,
a friend of mine noted that every time he sat in a rocking chair he
pretended he was Kennedy.

Imitation is essential to play and to psychodrama. In the Stanis-
lavsky acting method, actors are encouraged to give up their own
personalities for those of the characters whose personalities they are
trying to assimilate. But wash off the greasepaint and the actors return
to their old selves. Such a process is also described in Anna Freud's
description of the defense mechanism that she calls *reversal*. She illustrates reversal by the story of the child who overcomes his terror of
ghosts by "pretending to be the ghost he might meet."[31] In this kind
of imitation one does not fully master the role, but only for a brief
time imagines that one *is* another person. As with identification with
the aggressor, imitation does not produce a sense of enrichment.
Cramer distinguishes such immature processes of assimilation from
mature identification as follows: "Through imitation and learning, the
child becomes functionally more like the parent: this paves the way
for identification with the parent to occur. Once the child has the
behaviors and understandings in his repertoire that allow him to *act* a
little bit like the parent, he can, through identification, *become* like the
parent."[32]

The fourth process of assimilation, *internalization,* is closely linked with the defenses of reaction formation and undoing. We take the rules and roles of other people inside of us and accept these rules and roles as if they were ours, but the rules often still belong to our conscience and not to our souls. The 10-year-old boy says, "Boys don't cry." He no longer experiences the mandate as coming from someone else, as he might with introjection. His internalization is "ego-syntonic," but such a mandate not to cry may not be what he truly wants for himself.

In many ways internalization is different from incorporation, introjection, and imitation. Taking people in through the three less mature processes does not make us truly stronger. Imitation has no staying power, and incorporation and introjection do not make us feel more complete, only more burdened. In contrast, the process of internalization begins to become a stable support to self-esteem. With internalization, we not only can take people inside but can also sing, "You touch my hand and my arm grows strong." O'Neill took in Carlotta Monterrey in this way. The stoical 10-year-old boy who does not cry feels more complete than does someone who identifies with the aggressor.

A dramatic example of internalization occurs in the films from George Engels's famous longitudinal studies of Monica, a child who was born with a defective esophagus.[33] This congenital defect meant that as an infant Monica had to be fed through a tube that went directly into her stomach. Thus, to be fed, she had to lie on her mother's lap with her head on her mother's knees and her feet pressing against her mother's abdomen, in contrast to the conventional breast- or bottle-feeding posture in which the child is cuddled at or near the breast with her face close to her mother's. As Monica grew older, although she never saw another child fed as she had been fed, she always fed bottles to her dolls with their head on her knees and their feet pointing toward her abdomen. When she grew up she fed her own children their bottles in the same awkward way. It was as if she had been imprinted by her mother's behavior.

Although we become what we internalize, the process of metabolism is still incomplete. Anybody who has ever taught a child to ride a bicycle knows that there is a certain point when the child can maintain balance on the two-wheeler only so long as he believes the parent still has a hand underneath the bicycle seat. Although the parent no longer actually has to hold the bicycle, the skill is not yet the unquestioned property of the child. When my son was five years old, I needed to push him and his tricycle up a certain hill. When he was five and a half, he could pedal up the hill on his tricycle by himself, but he could do so only if I touched the small of his back with my finger—as if I were pushing him. I touched his back and his legs grew strong. Like riding a bicycle, the deployment of mature defenses is an integrated, involuntary balancing act. At first, to deploy such defenses we need to believe that people who have loved us are still close by.

As was made clear in Chapter 12, a capacity for ready internalization of others is essential for the effective utilization of social supports. In the Study of Adult Development there were two brothers, one of whom flourished and one of whom did not. Both brothers were in their "oedipal" years when they lost their father to divorce, to alcoholism, and to the opposite coast. A strong, overbearing mother remained behind. One son became a champion wrestler, openly fought with his mother, and found that by crossing both the country and the barriers of his father's alcoholism he was able to become close to his father. Indeed, for the rest of his life this brother continued to experience repeated object losses and to heal those losses with an extraordinary capacity for fresh, intimate friendship. Each new friendship left him with new skills, new capacities for sublimation that he had not had before. He became a brilliant professor of humanities. The other brother floundered. He was overwhelmed by his mother; he never reformed a relationship with his father; and later he sought geographic separation from his remaining family. He died young. The first brother internalized others easily; the second brother did not.

Idealization, the fifth process of assimilation, is first cousin to altruism and is associated with the capacity to manifest real empathy. Idealization is more mature than internalization and comes closer to achieving a complete synthesis of other people. Idealization involves duty less and gratitude more. In adolescence our personal identities develop through a process of idealization. Freud suggested that the ego ideal was "a precipitate in the ego consisting of the two identifications, with mother and father, fused together." "It is easy," he continued, "to show that the ego ideal answers to everything that is expected of the higher nature of man . . . It contains the germ from which all religions have evolved . . . Religion, morality and a social sense—the chief elements in the higher side of man—were originally one and the same thing."[34]

Idealization, like other processes of assimilation, is often facilitated by the death of the idealized person. I recall the funeral of a friend at which only one of the three eulogies really described my friend as he had been. The other two accorded him two very different idealized persona that corresponded more closely to the persons the two eulogists themselves hoped to become than to our dead friend.

A College man provides an example of a shift in idealization. When originally interviewed, he perceived his mother as a much admired force in his life. She had selected his high school friends and had chosen his college major. She had asthma and hay fever, and as a Harvard sophomore he too had asthma and hay fever. His parents were of different religions, and he had chosen his mother's church. He described his father as a distant, passive man who suffered from dyspepsia and had played an unimportant role in his life.

At age 47 he was asked again about his parents. His father had died a year before. He now described his mother as an ineffective, psychoneurotic woman who had played a minor role in his life. He now remembered his father as an idealized figure—a man with a wonderful sense of humor. As our idealizations change, so may our identities. Although in recent years he had been untroubled by his mother's asthma and hay fever, his father's religion was now his religion and his father's dyspepsia—alas—was now his dyspepsia. The bad is often taken in with the good.

The sixth process of assimilation, *identification,* is not to be confused with identification with the aggressor, which I have classified under internalization. Identification is closely associated with the defense of sublimation. If sublimation is the most graceful example of adaptive *accommodation to* the external world, just so identification is the most graceful example of *assimilation of* the external world.

In the words of the psychoanalyst Otto Fenichel, "The empirical fact that sublimations, especially those that arise in childhood, depend upon the presence of models, upon incentives directly or indirectly supplied by the environment corroborates Freud's assumption that sublimation may be intimately related to identification."[35] Compared to internalization, identification is a more flexible, reversible, neutralized, differentiated, choice-determined way of taking another person in. With identification the metabolism, as it were, of the other person is both selective and complete. With identification we can say to ourselves, "He did it and, if I choose, I can do it too." Yet with identification, as with the other five processes of assimilation, we respond to how we are treated, rather than to what we are told or what we observe. We can learn how to use a washing machine from a manual, but we must assimilate how to use a violin from a teacher. We identify only by being shown, not by being told.

In other words, the process of identification takes encounters with the outside world and places them inside in order to create new ego structures. In contrast, projection takes internal mental representations and places them outside, to rid the self of sources of conflict. The psychoanalyst Roy Schafer has pointed out that the process of identifying with another person "is unconscious, though it may also have prominent and significant preconscious and conscious components; in this process the subject modifies his motives and behavior patterns, and the self representations corresponding to them, in such a way as to experience being like, the same as, and merged with one or more representations of that object." [36]

Often incorporation, like plagiarism, reflects envy. In contrast, mentors and teachers with whom we identify elicit not our envy but our gratitude. With incorporation and with introjection, the other person is treated like a thing. Even with idealization we have unempathic expectations about the other person: our idols are not allowed to have feet of clay. With identification, we assimilate a person's real strengths and they become our strength. We can also acknowledge the person's faults and leave those faults behind. We *imitate* or *incorporate* a whole person. We *identify* only with a person's behavior.

Identification enhances our capacity to gain self-esteem. Always, the aim of identification is to continue a relationship with another person by transferring the relationship from the outer to the inner world. This transfer makes the world safer and permits the luxury of mature defenses. In the words of a wise psychobiologist, Myron Hofer:

> Human relationships are conducted at the mental or symbolic as well as at the sensorimotor levels. Our lives are lived as much within the internal world of mental representations as among the actual people themselves. This enables us to endure temporary separations without full-scale bereavement responses. Therefore, the inner experience of our relationship with another person . . . [is] at least as important to consider as the actual interpersonal interactions themselves. Could these elements of our inner life come to serve as biologic regulators,

much the way the actual sensorimotor interactions with the mother function for the infant animal in our experiments? And could this link internal object relations to biologic systems? I think this may be possible.[37]

It is easiest for us to identify with those people who are empathic toward us; and as we acquire mentors for identification, such identifications serve to counter our need for immature defenses. Put differently, we can only rid ourselves of our primitive consciences and obtain more merciful ones by identifying with new loves.

To sum up what I have been saying, incorporation and introjection are ways of believing that one *has* the other person. Idealization and identification are ways of *being* the other person and yet being oneself at the same time.

The story of Leo Tolstoy's long life braids together the three threads of this book: adaptive creativity, adult psychosocial development, and the evolution of defenses. The close association between Tolstoy's creativity and his well-being is well known, and in Chapter 6 I discussed his sequential passage through the stages of psychosocial development. In this concluding section I shall note the maturation of his defenses from acting out, projection, dissociation, and hypochondriasis to reaction formation, and then to altruism, sublimation, and suppression. (Admittedly, in the last year of his life, perhaps because of his failing body and brain, Tolstoy returned to immature defenses.) I shall also trace his progression through the processes of assimilation that I have just described. In his lifelong effort to assimilate his mother and to transmute his memories of her as an external threat into a source of internal strength, Tolstoy illustrated all six.

In his twenties Tolstoy was a rich high school dropout who was busy gambling, whoring, raping his servants, and running away from home. Reasons for his alienation are not hard to find. His mother died when he was 2. His father died when he was 9. His grandmother, who had served as a surrogate mother, died the following year. Then when he was 13 two aunts, who had stepped in to fill the breach, died.

Thus in some ways Tolstoy, like Eugene O'Neill, remained all his life as (in Carlotta O'Neill's words) an "infant who had never grown up." As a bearded septuagenarian, Tolstoy wrote in his diary, "I walk in the garden and I think of my mother, of Maman! I do not remember

her, but she has always been an *ideal* of saintliness for me."[38] Two
years earlier he had confided to a scrap of paper, "Felt dull and sad
all day . . . I wanted, as when I was a child, to nestle against some
tender and compassionate being and weep with love and be con-
soled . . . become a tiny boy, close to my mother, the way I imagine
her. Yes, yes, my Maman, whom I was never able to call that because
I did not know how to talk when she died. She is my highest image
of love—not cold, divine love, but warm, earthly love . . . Maman,
hold me, baby me!"[39] Tolstoy could have said, like Arthur Miller's
Willy Loman in *Death of a Salesman*, "I still feel kind of temporary
about myself." For after seventy-eight years of life Tolstoy was still
not sure that there was anyone home inside.

And yet in 1908, when he was 80, the American press called
Tolstoy "the best-known man in the world." Since his youth as a roué,
both Tolstoy and his defenses had matured. He had evolved into the
author of two of the most mature novels in world literature, into the
respectful portraitist of one of the most compelling women in world
fiction, and into a Russian sage who was to inspire two of the most
mature world leaders of the twentieth century: Mahatma Gandhi and
Martin Luther King, Jr. I believe that what made this development
possible was that Leo Tolstoy, a lifelong stranger to object constancy,
learned how to internalize many people throughout his adult life.

Tolstoy's biographer Henri Troyat tells us that when Tolstoy was
2 his mother was definitely *outside*. On August 3, 1830, after taking
communion, Tolstoy's mother asked to see her loved ones to bid them
farewell. "The family assembled around her bed. In his nurse's arms,
little Leo, twenty-three months old, screamed in terror at the sight of
the livid mask whose eyes, full of tears, were fixed on him with unbearable tenderness. He did not recognize his mother. He hated this strange
woman. The nurse took him back to his bedroom, where he grew calm
again amidst his toys."[40] At that time, Tolstoy had little language, but
he already possessed a stunning capacity for observation. Twenty-two
years later, he told of his only slightly fictional memory of staring into
his mother's coffin: "It was only at that moment that I understood
whence came that strong, heavy odor, which, mingling with the odor
of the incense, filled the room; and the thought that that face, which
a few days before had been more full of beauty and tenderness than
anything in the world, could excite terror, seemed for the first time to
reveal to me the bitter truth, and filled my soul with despair."[41] Until

he completed *Anna Karenina,* Tolstoy continued to see women as potential tormentors.

Over the subsequent decades, through a series of approximations, Tolstoy endeavored to bring his mother inside. In the process, his defenses evolved from projection and dissociation to reaction formation, and then into altruism and suppression.

At first his modes of assimilation were congruent with introjection and incorporation. These immature modes of self-repair, depending as they do upon the primitive defenses of distortion and even psychotic denial, permitted little real self-enhancement. At age 17, having dropped out of school, Tolstoy returned in failure to his familiar boyhood home, Yasnaya Polyana. With dissociation bordering on psychotic denial, he wrote that "the same force of life, fresh and young, that filled nature around me" now coursed through him. That same night he dreamed (hallucinated) of the ideal woman, who had one black braid and provocative breasts: "But something told me that SHE, with her bare arms and searing embrace, was by no means all the happiness in the world . . . The longer I stared up at the moon high in the sky, the more it seemed to me that true beauty and true happiness were still higher, more pure, closer to Him, the source of all that is good and beautiful, and tears of joy, an unfulfilled straining sort of joy, came to my eyes . . . It seemed to me then that Nature, the moon and I were one and the same."[42] In short, Tolstoy incorporated the maternal moon, but such fantasy has no sticking power. Tolstoy had provided himself with an autistic mirror; it was like trying to hug himself—a chilly experience.

How could he internalize profound compassion for himself? For however much Tolstoy yearned to be one with the women outside of him and inside of him, it often appeared to him that women existed solely in order to incite men to behave like animals and then to frustrate them. Having organized his inner world through the defenses of projection and splitting, he had precluded intimacy. By age 21 he had become a compulsive gambler and patron of whorehouses. Projection and reaction formation ruled his life. Trying to overcome his lust for both Gypsy women and Lady Luck, he wrote in his diary: "Now I shall set myself the following rule: regard the company of women as a necessary social evil and avoid them as much as possible. Who indeed is the cause of sensuality, indolence, frivolity and all sorts of other vices in us, if not women? What causes us to lose our natural qualities—

courage, resoluteness, reason and justice, etc., if not women?"[43] Women were still not to be allowed inside of himself in a nurturant fashion. They remained outside as receptacles for his own disavowed feelings.

But emotional growth necessitates taking people inside from without. The following year, not abandoning his quest, Tolstoy found an idealized surrogate mother. She was his Aunt Toinette, a woman who had loved Tolstoy's father before his marriage and to whom, after Tolstoy's mother had died, his father had proposed. Sometimes Aunt Toinette accidentally called Leo by his father's name: "She showed me that my father's image and my own had merged into one in her love for us." Of Aunt Toinette he also wrote: "Her chief influence upon me was, from childhood, to make me feel the spiritual joy of loving. I could see how happy she was to love."[44]

For a moment, Tolstoy gave up his gambling and began to play four-handed sonatas with his faithful 57-year-old aunt. Other terms for playing four-handed sonatas with one's idealized, virginal surrogate mother might be "finding a holding environment" or "parallel play" or "mirroring by an idealized mentor." Tolstoy spent time with his aunt almost every evening. "Every time I see Aunt Toinette I find more excellent qualities in her," he wrote. "The only fault one can find with her is that she is too romantic, but that is because she has such a good heart and such a good mind, that she had to occupy her mind with something, so for want of anything better, she chose to build the whole world into one great romance."[45] Tolstoy was projecting. He too was a great romanticizer.

Through idealization of Aunt Toinette, Tolstoy was able to maintain a sense of himself as one who was beloved, and so he became able to create. He began to feel impelled to write a book called "The Study of Yesterday"; this evolved into his great first novel, *Childhood*. Initially the book was to be about Aunt Toinette, but Tolstoy became able to abandon projection and realized that it was about himself. He began the novel by building the world of childhood into one great idealized romance. In so doing he provided a striking example of pure dissociation. "When I wrote *Childhood*," the four-times-orphaned Tolstoy told a friend, "I had the impression that nobody before me had ever felt or expressed the wonderful poetry of that age."[46] But his dissociation and intellectualization were more adaptive than his earlier projection.

In *Childhood*, Tolstoy also illustrated that if he had internalized and idealized Aunt Toinette, his mother still existed in his mind only as an introject. He was able to describe only fragments of his mother. He could describe her personality only by making a tour of her body: "When I try to recall my mother as she was at that time, nothing appears to me but her brown eyes, which always expressed love and goodness; the mole on her neck a little lower than the spot where the short hairs grow; her white embroidered collar; her cool, soft hand which petted me so often and which I so often kissed; but her image as a whole escapes me." He understood the value of a clearer memory when he wishfully wrote, "Beautiful as was Mamma's face, it became incomparably more lovely when she smiled . . . If in life's trying moments I could catch but a glimpse of that smile, I should not know what grief is."[47] But he was not to escape grief so easily.

In part we remember people by remembering the feelings they arouse in us. If Tolstoy's mother was remembered only in pieces, she was also a ghost that haunted him. In *Childhood* Tolstoy tells of listening to his mother playing a concerto: "I dreamed, and light, bright transparent recollections penetrated my imagination. She played Beethoven's Sonata Pathetique, and my memories became painful, dark, burdensome. Mamma often played those two pieces; therefore, I well remember the feeling which they aroused in me. It resembled memories, but memories of what? I seemed to remember something which had never happened." Having thus initially disavowed, through the defense of undoing, the relevance of *pathetique* music to his rose-colored childhood, Tolstoy kept on writing, and the reality testing of his memory improved. Recollection of his mother became more vivid. The last two chapters of his tale about the "wonderful poetry" of childhood are called "Sorrow" and "The Last Sad Memories": "Mamma's eyes were open, but she saw nothing. Oh, I shall never forget that dreadful look! It expressed so much suffering. They led us away . . . Mamma died in terrible agony." And the very last words of *Childhood* are: "Sometimes I pause silent, midway between the chapel and that black fence. Painful reminiscences suddenly penetrate my soul. The thought comes to me: Did Providence connect me with those two beings [his mother and his grandmother] merely in order that I might be made to mourn for them forever?"[48]

If much pathological mourning illustrates introjection, successful mourning often involves what I choose to term internalization. Toward the end of the novel, Tolstoy offers us a model of internalization: "Only people who are capable of loving strongly can also suffer great sorrow; but this same necessity of loving serves to counteract their grief and heals them . . . Grief never kills."[49]

But how was Tolstoy to give up splitting women into either lascivious Gypsies or virginal Aunt Toinettes? For although the young Tolstoy could write about grief, he could not yet bear it in his day-to-day life. Just as he spent his young adulthood running away from the psychosocial task of intimacy with women, he also fled the ego task of confronting death directly, except through the dissociation and intellectualization of being a war correspondent. How did he evolve from wastrel gambler to saint? One answer was that he was blessed with a devoted extended family. Small nuclear families, like the Plaths, the O'Neills, and the Nightingales, can be crippling; but Tolstoy had a seemingly inexhaustible supply of relatives—both for loving and for grieving. At age 30 he was finally able to face directly the death of a beloved brother. At last he was able to love and grieve for the same person at the same time. In similar fashion, he used his myriad of female relatives to overcome his ambivalence toward women. For fifteen years he lived for long periods with one female cousin or aunt after another. Then finally, at age 33, he began to notice the 18-year-old Sonya Behrs, and within a year he mastered the task of unambivalent attachment to another person.

With intimacy mastered, career consolidation allowed Tolstoy further rediscovery. Career consolidation was facilitated by neurobiological maturation, by "holding" by Sonya, and by a great talent derived from generous genes. At last, Tolstoy's ego was able to reconcile grief, sexuality, anger, dependency, trust, and love. He began to write *War and Peace*. In this novel the once romantic home of *Childhood* was rechristened Bleak Hills, and his mother was no longer idealized. Tolstoy's mother's maiden name had been Marya Volkonsky, and in the Bleak Hills of his imagination lives one Princess Marya Bolkonsky. She is described very differently from the 17-year-old Tolstoy's "high in the sky" moon and from "the expression of goodness and love" of the Mamma from *Childhood*:

> Princess Marya went back to her room with the sad, scared
> expression that rarely left her and which made her plain, sickly
> face yet plainer . . . Princess Marya sighed and glanced into

the mirror . . . It reflected a weak, ungraceful figure and thin face . . . [Julie] "flatters me," thought the princess . . . But Julie did not flatter her friend. The Princess's eyes—large, deep, and luminous (it seemed as if at times there radiated from them shafts of warm light), were so beautiful . . . But the princess never saw the beautiful expression of her own eyes . . . As with everyone, her face assumed a forced un-natural expression as soon as she looked in a glass.

In the novel, Marya's older brother is one Andrey Bolkonsky, who represents one facet of Tolstoy himself. It should not surprise us, then, that Tolstoy's description of the fictional interaction between younger sister and older brother sounds more like the encounter of a mother with her young child. Princess Marya turns toward her brother: "Through her tears, the loving warm gentle look of her large luminous eyes, very beautiful at that moment, rested on Prince Andrey's face."[50]

After completing *War and Peace*, Tolstoy was able to say, "I am a writer." But he also became preoccupied with death. Like Mary Tyrone, he asked himself, "What can I want? . . . I went through everything in my mind . . . Nothing could satisfy this desire in me. And the desire persisted . . . I desire what does not exist in this world. But it exists somewhere . . . Where?" After quoting these words, Troyat goes on to tell us, "For the rest of his life, he was to live like a man who had been hit by a bullet that cannot be extricated. It is always there, lodged in one's head. Impossible to forget it, although one hardly feels it at all."[51] The introjection of pathological mourning is so different from the pain of simple grief.

So, at age 43, Tolstoy became increasingly hypochondriacal, the defense mechanism most closely associated with introjection. It seemed to him that death was assuming all kinds of mysterious disguises and was trying to worm its way into his body. "I am ill," he wrote to a friend, "but I don't know what's the matter with me; at any rate, it looks bad or good, depending on one's attitude towards the end of it all . . . My health is poor. I have never been so depressed in all my life. I have lost all joy in living."[52] Sonya encouraged him to undergo kumys treatments. To receive kumys treatments, Tolstoy was seques-tered in a felt tent, and six times a day a peasant woman thrust leather jugs of fizzy, fermented milk through a slit in the tent for him to drink. With such literal nursing, Tolstoy, like O'Neill at Gaylord Sanatorium, slowly recovered. His response was to buy a 6,700-acre farm; and then, to boost his morale further still, he invited his most extravagant admirer to his estate. Under this shower of praise, under such metaphorical internalization, Tolstoy's depression lifted.

Immediately after this sequence of self-enrichment, Tolstoy, at a provincial railroad station, first viewed the broken body of the woman destined to be the source of inspiration for *Anna Karenina*. He had "gone to the station as a spectator, while the autopsy was being performed in the presence of a police inspector. Standing in a corner of the shed, he had observed every detail of the woman's body lying on the table, bloody and mutilated, with its skull crushed . . . He tried to imagine the existence of this poor woman who had given all for love only to meet such a trite, ugly death."[53] I believe that this brutal reminder of the loss of his mother became a pathway to Tolstoy's artistic recovery of his attachment to her. The woman's death had originally attracted his attention because according to the newspaper account she had written to her lover, "You are my murderer. Be happy if an assassin can be happy."[54] More than one child who has lost his mother when young has fancied himself an assassin. Tolstoy was now able to begin his next great novel, *Anna Karenina*. It was to be a masterpiece in which he managed to bring the split internalized images of his mother together. His once loving mother and her ghost who filled his "soul with despair" were to become one.

In the early drafts of *Anna Karenina*, according to Troyat, "Her personality is that of a man-killer. One whole chapter in one of the early drafts of the book, devoted to a description of Anna, is entitled 'The Devil.' She is the agent of evil in the world. Both husband and lover are her victims." As Tolstoy wrote, however, he could no longer deny that his mental image of Anna also evoked love. "Do you know," he told a friend, "I often sit down to write on some specific thing, and suddenly I find myself on a wider road . . . That's the way it was with *Anna Karenina*."[55]

Anna turned out to be no devil. Instead, Tolstoy tells us that her lover, Vronsky,

> was drawn, not by her beauty, although she was a very beautiful woman, nor by the unobtrusive elegance she radiated, but by the expression of utter sweetness [the Modern Library edition translates this phrase as "the peculiarly caressing and soft expression"] in her charming face . . . For an instant, her gray keen eyes, which seemed darker than they were because of her

thick eyelashes, paused to give him a friendly glance as though she recognized him. Then she began looking for someone in the crowd . . . Her eyes and her smile revealed vast stores of repressed vitality.[56]

Tolstoy's mother's outstanding feature was said to have been her eyes with their bushy eyebrows. Although Tolstoy was quick to maintain that he was glad no pictures of his mother survived, such pictures did survive within his memory—within a temporal lobe that could remember his mother's smell, touch, and music better than it could summon up a cognitive image of her whole face.

At the end of the novel, Tolstoy's early defensive splitting of women into angels and she-devils is finally replaced by Vronsky's loving, but agonized, fusion of his two images of Anna. Tolstoy, who at age 2 had witnessed his own mother dying in agony, describes the inner world of Vronsky at the railroad station after Anna's suicide: "And all at once a different pain, not an ache, but an inner trouble that set his whole being in anguish made him for an instant forget his toothache. As he glanced at the engine and the rails . . . he suddenly recalled *her* . . . the bloodstained body so lately full of life, the head unhurt dropping back with its weight of hair, and the curling tresses about the temple, and the exquisite face, with red, half-opened mouth, the strange, fixed expression, piteous on the lips and awful in the still open eyes."[57]

Tolstoy then describes two images, separate in the novel but obviously assimilated in his own mind: "And he tried to think of her as she was when he met her the first time, at a railway-station too, mysterious, exquisite, loving and seeking and giving happiness, and not cruelly revengeful as he remembered her on that last moment. He tried to recall his best moments with her, but those moments were poisoned forever. He could only think of her as triumphant, successful in her menace of a wholly useless remorse never to be effaced."[58] Vronsky forgets his toothache entirely and bursts into tears.

I believe that in writing *Anna Karenina* Tolstoy recovered what he had loved in his mother. While Vronsky's guilt and his reproach toward Anna had been with Tolstoy all his life, the integration of the loving Anna was new; and perhaps this rediscovery of old love saved Tolstoy from the suicidal thoughts that had plagued him during the period preceding the novel's creation. In *Anna Karenina* he tells us about his alter ego, Levin, a happy father and husband, in perfect health, but several times so unaccountably near to suicide that he hides a rope that he might not be tempted to hang himself. At one time Tolstoy, too, had been afraid to go out with his gun for fear of shooting himself. But Levin did not hang himself, and Tolstoy did not shoot himself. Instead, having finished *Anna Karenina*, Tolstoy could editorialize about his autobiographical Levin: "Without knowing it, he had been sustained by those spiritual verities which he had sucked in with his mother's milk." In the novel he has Levin say, "And this knowledge I did not acquire. It was given to me, like all the rest; *given*. I could not know where to get it . . . Did I get it from reason? But would reason ever have proved to me that I ought to love my neighbor, instead of choking him? I was taught it in my childhood, but I believed it gladly because it was already existent in my soul . . . Reason has nothing to do with loving one's neighbor."[59] Rather, as Emily Dickinson reminds us, "The brain is just the weight of God." And in his own effort to master life, Tolstoy became an inspiration to the world.

But at age 76 he could still walk alone in his garden keening, "She is my highest image of love—not cold, divine love but warm, earthly love. Maman, hold me, baby me!" For in Carl Jung's words, "Many—far too many—aspects of life which have also been experienced, lie in the lumber room among dusty memories; but sometimes, too, there are glowing coals under gray ashes."[60] The unconscious does not respect the passage of time. But if the mature ego cannot make the past better than it was, it can face past pain honestly, leave it behind, and thereby soften the future.

In the nineteenth century the great British surgeon John Hunter wrote: "Inflammation in itself is not to be considered as a disease. Inflammation is not only occasionally the cause of diseases, but it is often a mode of cure, since it frequently produces a resolution of indurated [inflamed] parts by changing the diseased action into a salutary one."[61] In this book I have repeatedly told stories of how in potentially disastrous situations creative self-deception and madness have been lifesaving. Plato tells us of a similar observation by Socrates: "there is also a madness which is a divine gift and the source of the chiefest blessings granted to men . . . madness superior to a sane mind, for one is only of human, but the other of divine origin . . . He having no touch of the Muses' madness in his soul . . . is nowhere when he enters into rivalry with the madman."[62] But there is an enormous difference between the madness of psychosis and the madness of sublimation. As Charles Lamb has pointed out, true poets dream while awake; they are not possessed by their subjects but have dominion over them. And therein lies all the difference.

Beethoven's biographer Maynard Solomon reminds us that "Masterpieces of art are instilled with a surplus of constantly renewable energy—an energy that provides a motive force for changes in the relations between human beings—because they contain projections of human desires and goals which have not yet been achieved."[63] In short, Socrates' madness of divine origin allowed Beethoven to transmute self-deception into his Ninth Symphony, Nightingale's neurotic obsessions to reduce a hospital death rate from forty to two percent, and Tolstoy's longing for compassion to offer inspiration to Gandhi and to Martin Luther King, Jr.

Only in the last half-century have the two disciplines of medicine and surgery learned to listen to John Hunter. Only in the last half-century have medicine and surgery learned to become allies to the curative potential of the human body instead of its adversaries. By finally understanding homeostasis, immunology, and natural wound healing processes, both internal medicine and surgery have taken giant steps forward. In the same manner, to contemplate the ingenious self-deceptions of the mature defenses is to teach ourselves humility and to appreciate that the ego is wiser than we are. To understand the homeostatic value of defense mechanisms is to appreciate that we are servants to, rather than masters of, psychological healing processes. The human ego, like the human immune system, continues to provide us with better therapy than the best-trained physician or the most up-to-date pharmacy. We all must learn to understand and to work with this powerful ally.

Notes

Introduction

1. W. B. Cannon, *The Wisdom of the Body* (New York: Norton, 1932).
2. S. Freud, *The Ego and the Id* (1923), in *Standard Edition of the Complete Psychological Works of Sigmund Freud* (hereinafter abbreviated *SE*), ed. and trans. James Strachey (London: Hogarth Press and Institute of Psychoanalysis, 1953–1964), 24 vols., 19:17.
3. R. Kegan, *The Evolving Self* (Cambridge, Mass.: Harvard University Press, 1982), pp. 16, 17.
4. Ibid., p. 17.
5. H. Gardner, *The Mind's New Science* (New York: Basic Books, 1985), p. 6.
6. J. Nemiah, "Reflections of an Aging Educator: A Tale of Two Residents" (Teacher of the Year Award Address presented to the Association of Academic Psychiatry, Seattle, 1990).

1. Why Praise the Human Ego?

1. M. S. Gazzaniga, "Organization of the Human Brain," *Science* 245 (1989):947–952, p. 947.
2. D. Shutcliffe, ed., *Untriangulated Stars: The Letters of Edwin Arlington Robinson to Harry DeForest Smith* (Cambridge, Mass.: Harvard University Press, 1947), p. 325.
3. M. Konner, *The Tangled Wing* (New York: Holt, Rinehart and Winston, 1982), p. 20.
4. C. S. Sherrington, *The Integrative Action of the Nervous System* (London: Oxford University Press, 1911).
5. Konner, *The Tangled Wing*, p. 180.
6. M. S. Gazzaniga, *Mind Matters* (Boston: Houghton Mifflin, 1988), pp. 13–14.
7. P. G. Bourne, R. M. Rose, and J. W. Mason, "Urinary 17-OHCS Levels in Combat," *Archives of General Psychiatry* 19 (1988):135–144.
8. M. Rutter, "Resilience in the Face of Adversities," *British Journal of Psychiatry* 147 (1985):598–611.

2. A Matter of Definition

1. R. S. Lazarus, J. R. Averill, and E. M. Opton, "The Psychology of Coping: Issues of Research and Assessment," in *Coping and Adaptation,* ed. G. Coehlo, D. Hamburg, and J. Adams (New York: Basic Books, 1974), pp. 249–315.
2. Plato, *Phaedrus,* ed. I. Edman (New York: Modern Library, 1928), pp. 295–296.
3. S. B. Friedman, P. Chodoff, J. W. Mason, and D. Hamburg, "Behavioral Observations on Parents Anticipating the Death of a Child," *Pediatrics* 32 (1963):610–625.
4. N. Haan, *Coping and Defending* (New York: Academic Press, 1977).
5. G. L. Bibring, T. F. Dwyer, D. S. Huntington, and A. Valenstein, "A Study of the Psychological Process in Pregnancy," *Psychoanalytic Study of the Child* 16 (1961):25–72.
6. G. E. Vaillant, *Ego Mechanisms of Defense* (Washington, D.C.: American Psychiatric Association Press, 1992); M. Beutel, *Bewältigungs-prozesse bei chronischen Erkrankungen* (Munich: VCH, 1988).
7. S. Freud, "Three Essays on the Theory of Sexuality" (1905), *SE* 7:238.
8. H. Hartmann, *Ego Psychology and the Problem of Adaptation* (New York: International Universities Press, 1958), p. 43.
9. S. Freud, *Jokes and Their Relation to the Unconscious* (1905), *SE* 8:233.
10. Ibid.

3. Self-Deceptions of Everyday Life

1. R. White, *Lives in Progress* (New York: Holt, Rinehart and Winston, 1952), p. 4.
2. E. Forbes, *Thayer's Life of Beethoven* (Princeton, N.J.: Princeton University Press, 1969), p. 282.
3. Ibid., p. 284.
4. Ibid., pp. 304–305.
5. Ibid., pp. 909–910.
6. Ibid., p. 896.
7. Ibid., p. 306.
8. Ibid., p. 286.
9. Ibid., p. 892.
10. Ibid., p. 1053.
11. A. Rich, *Diving into the Wreck* (New York: Norton, 1973), p. 43.
12. R. Coles, *Children of Crisis* (Boston: Little, Brown, 1967), p. 299.
13. Ibid., p. 304.
14. Ibid., p. 315.
15. Ibid., p. 302.

16. Ibid., p. 112.
17. Ibid., p. 117.
18. Ibid., p. 122.
19. W. Wundt, *Lectures on Human and Animal Psychology* (New York: Macmillan, 1896); W. James, *The Principles of Psychology* (New York: Henry Holt and Co., 1983).
20. S. Freud, "Neuropsychoses of Defence" (1894), *SE* 7:45–61.
21. *The Complete Letters of Sigmund Freud to Wilhelm Fliess*, trans. J. M. Masson (Cambridge, Mass.: Harvard University Press, 1985), p. 65.
22. Ibid., p. 65.
23. Ibid., p. 136.
24. Ibid., p. 73.
25. Ibid., p. 67.
26. M. Schur, *Freud, Living and Dying* (New York: International Universities Press, 1972).
27. J. Masson, *The Assault on Truth: Freud's Suppression of the Seduction Theory* (New York: Farrar, Straus and Giroux, 1984), p. 202.
28. M. Krull, *Freud and His Father* (New York: Norton, 1986), p. 43.
29. *Complete Letters to Fliess*, pp. 230–231.
30. Ibid., p. 250.
31. Ibid., p. 249.
32. Ibid., p. 253.
33. Ibid., p. 261.
34. Ibid., p. 264.
35. Ibid., p. 272.
36. Ibid., p. 298.
37. S. Freud, *The Interpretation of Dreams* (1900), preface to the 2nd ed., trans. J. Strachey (New York: Basic Books, 1956), p. xxvi.
38. S. Freud, "My Views on the Part Played by Sexuality in the Aetiology of the Neuroses" (1906), *SE* 7:276.
39. S. Freud, *Id, Inhibitions and Anxiety* (1926), *SE* 20:163.
40. Ibid., p. 120.
41. P. Gay, *Freud: A Life for Our Time* (New York: Norton, 1988).
42. A. Freud, *The Ego and the Mechanisms of Defense* (London: Hogarth Press, 1937), p. 9.
43. C. Bernard, *An Introduction to the Study of Experimental Medicine* (1865; New York: Macmillan, 1927), p. 188.

4. Necessary Questions

1. S. Freud, *New Introductory Lectures* (1932), *SE* 22.
2. A. Freud, *The Ego and the Mechanisms of Defense* (London: Hogarth Press, 1937).

3. G. L. Bibring, T. F. Dwyer, D. S. Huntington, and A. Valenstein, "A Study of the Psychological Process in Pregnancy and of the Earliest Mother-Child Relationship, II: Methodological Considerations," *Psychoanalytic Study of the Child* 16 (1961):25–72.

4. J. Sandler and A. Freud, *The Analysis of Defense: The Ego and the Mechanisms of Defense Revisited* (New York: International Universities Press, 1985), p. 176.

5. S. Freud, "Fragment of an Analysis of a Case of Hysteria" (1901; 1905) *SE* 7:50.

6. J. Piaget, *The Moral Judgement of the Child,* trans. M. Gabain (London: Kegan Paul, 1932).

7. H. Hartmann, *Ego Psychology and the Problem of Adaptation* (New York: International Universities Press, 1958), p. 30.

8. A. Colby, L. Kohlberg, J. Gibbs, and M. Lieberman, "A Longitudinal Study of Moral Judgement," *Monographs of the Society for Research in Child Development* 48 (1983):1–2, Serial 200; S. T. Hauser, "Loevinger's Model and Measure of Ego Development: A Critical Review," *Psychological Bulletin* 83 (1976):928–955.

9. S. T. Hauser, *Adolescents and Their Families* (New York: Free Press, 1991); R. Kegan, *The Evolving Self* (Cambridge, Mass.: Harvard University Press, 1982).

10. G. E. Vaillant and L. McCullough, "A Comparison of the Washington University Sentence Completion Test (SCT) with Other Measures of Adult Ego Development," *American Journal of Psychiatry* 144 (1987):1189–1194; A. M. Jacobson, W. Beardslee, E. Gelfand, S. T. Hauser, G. G. Noem, and S. I. Powers, "An Approach to Evaluating Adolescent Ego Defense Mechanisms Using Clinical Interviews," in *Ego Mechanisms of Defense: A Guide for Clinicians and Researchers,* ed. G. E. Vaillant (Washington, D.C.: American Psychiatric Press, 1992), pp. 181–194.

5. How Can We Prove That Defenses Exist?

1. G. E. Vaillant, *Adaptation to Life* (Boston: Little, Brown, 1977).

2. G. E. Vaillant and C. O. Vaillant, "Natural History of Male Psychological Health, X: Work as a Predictor of Positive Mental Health," *American Journal of Psychiatry* 138 (1981):1433–1440.

3. C. Heath, *What People Are* (Cambridge, Mass.: Harvard University Press, 1945), p. 4.

4. J. P. Monks, *College Men at War* (Boston: American Academy of Arts and Sciences, 1957).

5. S. Glueck and E. Glueck, *Unraveling Juvenile Delinquency* (New York: Commonwealth Foundation, 1950), and *Delinquents and Non-Delinquents in Perspective* (Cambridge, Mass.: Harvard University Press, 1968).

6. A. Hollingshead and F. C. Redlich, *Social Class and Mental Illness* (New York: Wiley, 1958).

7. L. M. Terman, "Mental and Physical Traits of a Thousand Gifted Children," in *Genetic Studies of Genius*, vol. 1 (Stanford: Stanford University Press, 1925).

8. M. D. Terman and M. H. Oden, "The Gifted Group at Midlife," in *Genetic Studies of Genius*, vol. 5 (Stanford: Stanford University Press, 1959); M. H. Oden, "The Fulfillment of Promise: 40-year Follow-up of the Terman Gifted Group," *Genetic Psychological Monographs* 77 (1968):3–93; R. R. Sears, "The Terman Gifted Children Study," in *Handbook of Longitudinal Research*, ed. S. A. Mednick, M. Harway, and K. M. Finello (New York: Praeger, 1984), pp. 398–414.

9. The fifteen individual defenses used frequently enough to count were clustered into three groups: mature (sublimation, suppression, anticipation, altruism, and humor), intermediate or neurotic (displacement, repression, isolation, and reaction formation), and immature (projection, schizoid fantasy, passive aggression, acting out, hypochondriasis, and dissociation). In order to control for marked variation across subjects in the frequency of identified defensive vignettes, ratios of defenses at different levels of maturity, rather than absolute numbers of defenses, were employed. For example, suppression as a style of defense received the same weight if it was noted three times in someone for whom ten vignettes were counted as if it was noted nine times in someone for whom thirty vignettes were counted.

The relative proportion of defense vignettes in each of the three general categories was determined as follows: In order to obtain a nine-point scale of defense maturity, the ratio between immature and mature defenses was used to distribute a total of eight points. Each of the three categories of maturity could be assigned one to five points, but the total had to be eight, and every category had to be assigned at least one point. For example, someone who manifested ten examples reflecting sublimation and suppression, four examples reflecting displacement and reaction formation, and *no* examples of immature defenses would be scored mature defenses 5, immature defenses 1, and intermediate defenses 2. Someone who exhibited six examples of mature defenses, eight examples of intermediate defenses, and nine examples of immature defenses would be scored mature 2, intermediate 3, and immature 3. Subtracting the rating (1–5) for mature defenses from the rating (1–5) for immature defenses provided a total score of +4 to −4. For purposes of computation, the score for overall maturity of defensive style for each subject was transformed into a one-to-nine scale by adding five points to the total. Thus, a score of 1 reflected the most mature and a score of 9 reflected the least mature adaptive style. This procedure produced a normal (bell curve) distribution of scores, and a rater reliability of .84 for the Core City men and .87 for the Terman women.

10. G. E. Vaillant, M. Bond, and C. O. Vaillant, "An Empirically Validated Hierarchy of Defense Mechanisms," *Archives of General Psychiatry* 43 (1986):786–794.

11. N. Haan, "Proposed Model of Ego Functioning: Coping and Defense Mechanisms in Relationship to IQ Change," *Psychological Monographs* 77 (1963):1–23.

12. G. E. Vaillant and C. O. Vaillant, "Natural History of Male Psychological Health, XII: A Forty-Five Year Study of Predictors of Successful Aging at Age 65," *American Journal of Psychiatry* 147 (1990):31–37.

13. G. E. Vaillant and L. McCullough, "A Comparison of the Washington University Sentence Completion Test (SCT) with Other Measures of Adult Ego Development," *American Journal of Psychiatry* 144 (1987): 1189–1194.

14. G. E. Vaillant, *The Natural History of Alcoholism* (Cambridge, Mass.: Harvard University Press, 1983).

15. R. A. Levine, *Culture, Behavior and Personality* (Chicago: Aldine, 1973); A. Kleinman, *Social Origins of Distress and Disease* (New Haven: Yale University Press, 1986).

6. The Ego and Adult Development

1. S. Lightfoot, *Swarthmore College Bulletin,* Aug. 1989, p. 24.

2. H. Troyat, *Tolstoy* (Garden City, N.Y.: Doubleday, 1967), p. 139.

3. Ibid., p. 290.

4. Ibid., p. 297.

5. G. E. Vaillant and S. H. Koury, "Late Midlife Development," in *The Course of Life,* vol. 6, ed. G. H. Pollock and S. I. Greenspan (New York: International Universities Press, 1993); G. E. Vaillant and E. Milofsky, "Natural History of Male Psychological Health: Empirical Evidence for Erikson's Model of the Lifecycle," *American Journal of Psychiatry* 137 (1980):1348–1359.

6. B. L. Neugarten, "Personality and Aging," in *Handbook of the Psychology of Aging,* ed. J. E. Birren and K. W. Schaie (New York: Van Nostrand, 1977), pp. 626–649; R. Kegan, *The Evolving Self* (Cambridge, Mass.: Harvard University Press, 1982); J. Stevens-Long, *Adult Life* (Palo Alto, Calif.: Mayfield, 1984).

7. R. Havinghurst, *Developmental Tasks and Education* (New York: David McKay, 1972).

8. E. Hancock, *The Girl Within* (New York: E. P. Dutton, 1989), p. 83.

9. A. H. Barr, Jr., *Picasso: Fifty Years of His Art* (New York: Museum of Modern Art, 1946), pp. 247, 264.

10. E. Erikson, *Childhood and Society*, 2nd ed., (New York: Norton, 1963).

11. J. Loevinger, *Ego Development* (San Francisco: Jossey-Bass, 1976); L. Kohlberg, "Continuities in Childhood and Adult Moral Development Revisited," in *Life-Span Developmental Psychology: Personality and Socialization*, ed. P. B. Baltes and K. W. Schaie (New York: Academic Press, 1973).

12. C. Gilligan, "In a Different Voice: Women's Conception of the Self and Morality," *Harvard Education Review* 47 (1977):481–517.

13. E. Erikson, "The Problem of Ego Identity," *Journal of the American Psychoanalytic Association* 4 (1956):56–121.

14. G. W. Goethals and D. S. Klos, *Experiencing Youth* (Boston: Little, Brown, 1976).

15. D. Levinson, *The Seasons of a Man's Life* (New York: Knopf, 1978).

16. J. Kotre, *Outliving the Self* (Baltimore: Johns Hopkins University Press, 1984).

17. V. P. Clayton and J. E. Birren, "The Development of Wisdom across the Life Span: A Re-Examination of an Ancient Topic," in *Life-Span Development and Behavior*, vol. 3, ed. P. B. Baltes and O. G. Brimm (New York: Academic Press, 1980); P. B. Baltes and J. Smith, "Toward a Psychology of Wisdom and its Ontogenesis," in *Wisdom: Its Nature, Origins and Development*, ed. R. J. Sternberg (Cambridge: Cambridge University Press, 1990), pp. 87–120.

18. Erikson, *Childhood and Society*, p. 231.

19. Erikson, "The Problem of Ego Identity"; E. Erikson, "Identity and the Life Cycle," *Psychological Issues* 1 (1959):1–171.

20. Hancock, *The Girl Within*, p. 66.

21. Ibid., p. 13.

22. Ibid., p. 6.

23. I. Broverman, S. Voger, D. Broverman, F. Clarkson, and P. Rosenkrantz, "Sex-role Stereotypes: A Current Appraisal," *Journal of Social Issues* 28 (1972):59–78.

24. R. Helson and G. Moane, "Personality Change in Women from College to Midlife," *Journal of Personality and Social Behavior* 53 (1987):176–186.

25. D. Guttman, "The Cross-Cultural Perspective: Notes toward a Comparative Psychology of Aging," in *Handbook of the Psychology of Aging*, ed. J. E. Birren and K. W. Schaie (New York: Van Nostrand, 1977), pp. 302–326; G. E. Vaillant, *Adaptation to Life* (Boston: Little, Brown, 1977).

26. Baltes and Smith, "Toward a Psychology of Wisdom," p. 102.

27. Kotre, *Outliving the Self*, p. 14.

28. S. K. Whitbourne, "Openness to Experience, Identity Flexibility, and

Life Change in Adults," *Journal of Personality and Social Psychology* 50 (1986):163–168.

29. A. H. Maslow, "Neurosis as a Failure of Personal Growth," *Humanities* 3 (1967):153–170; Kohlberg, "Continuities in Childhood"; Loevinger, *Ego Development*.

30. Gilligan, "In a Different Voice," p. 504.

31. G. L. Klerman and D. J. Levinson, "Becoming the Director: Promotion as a Phase in Personal-Professional Development," *Psychiatry* 32 (1969):411–427.

32. B. L. Neugarten, *Personality in Middle and Late Life* (New York: Atherton, 1964), p. 189.

33. T. S. Eliot, *The Confidential Clerk* (New York: Harcourt, Brace, 1954), p. 43.

34. D. Offer and J. Offer, *From Teenage to Young Manhood* (New York: Basic Books, 1975); M. P. Farrell and S. D. Rosenberg, *Men at Midlife* (Boston: Auburn House, 1981).

35. Erikson, *Childhood and Society*, p. 270.

36. K. W. Schaie, *Longitudinal Studies of Adult Psychological Development* (New York: Guilford Press, 1983).

37. R. R. McCrae and P. T. Costa, *Emerging Lives, Enduring Dispositions* (Boston: Little, Brown, 1984).

38. Erikson, *Childhood and Society*, p. 274.

7. Life Histories

1. G. Pollock, "The Morning Process and Creativity: Organizational Changes," *Journal of the American Psychoanalytic Association* 25 (1977):3–34.

2. G. E. Vaillant and E. Milofsky, "Natural History of Male Psychological Health: Empirical Evidence for Erikson's Model of the Lifecycle," *American Journal of Psychiatry* 137 (1980):1348–1359.

3. M. Horner, "Toward an Understanding of Achievement-Related Conflicts in Women," *Journal of Social Issues* 8 (1972):157–174.

4. E. Fibush and M. Morgan, *Forgive Me No Longer: The Liberation of Martha* (New York: Family Service Association of America, 1977).

5. Ibid., pp. 207–208.

6. Ibid., p. 207.

7. Ibid., p. 129.

8. Ibid.

9. Ibid., p. 131.

10. Ibid., p. 129.

11. Ibid., p. 285.

12. Ibid., pp. 222–223.
13. Ibid., pp. 223–224.
14. S. Plath, "Daddy" in *Collected Poems,* ed. T. Hughes (New York: Harper and Row, 1962), p. 203.
15. Fibush and Morgan, *Liberation of Martha,* p. 224.
16. Ibid., p. 293.
17. J. Kotre, *Outliving the Self* (Baltimore: Johns Hopkins University Press, 1984), p. 10.
18. These pages and their phrases owe much to Sara Koury, a valued collaborator.
19. D. Levinson, *The Seasons of a Man's Life* (New York: Knopf, 1978).
20. E. Erikson, *Childhood and Society,* 2nd ed. (New York: Norton, 1963), p. 266.
21. J. Loevinger, *Ego Development* (San Francisco: Jossey-Bass, 1976), p. 59.

8. The Ego and Creativity

1. C. Woodham-Smith, *Florence Nightingale* (London: Constable, 1950), p. 93.
2. Ibid., pp. 94–95.
3. Ibid., pp. 95–96.
4. Ibid., p. 46.
5. Ibid., p. 76.
6. M. Goldsmith, *Florence Nightingale* (London: Hodder and Stoughton, 1937), p. 72.
7. A. Koestler, "Three Domains of Creativity," in *Challenges of Humanistic Psychology,* ed. J. F. T. Bugental (New York: McGraw-Hill, 1967); quotation from p. 31.
8. H. Gardner, *The Mind's New Science* (New York: Basic Books, 1985), p. 6.
9. S. Freud, *Introductory Lectures on Psychoanalysis* (1916–17), *SE* 15:376.
10. Ibid.
11. Ibid.
12. Ibid.
13. Woodham-Smith, *Florence Nightingale,* p. 7.
14. Goldsmith, *Florence Nightingale,* pp. 23–24.
15. Woodham-Smith, *Florence Nightingale,* p. 17.
16. Ibid., p. 59.
17. G. Pickering, *Creative Malady* (New York: Oxford University Press, 1974), pp. 131–132.
18. Z. Cope, *Florence Nightingale and the Doctors* (London: Museum Press Ltd., 1958), p. 100.

19. Woodham-Smith, *Florence Nightingale*, p. 178.
20. Ibid., p. 207.
21. Ibid., p. 257.
22. Ibid., p. 232.
23. Ibid., p. 200.
24. Ibid., p. 397.
25. Ibid., p. 220.
26. Ibid., p. 222.
27. Ibid.
28. Freud, *Introductory Lectures*, p. 376.
29. Pickering, *Creative Malady*, p. 131.
30. Woodham-Smith, *Florence Nightingale*, p. 86.
31. Ibid., pp. 300–301.
32. A. Storr, *The Dynamics of Creation* (Harmondsworth, England: Penguin, 1976), p. 13.
33. H. C. Lehman, "The Age Decrement in Outstanding Scientific Creativity," *American Psychologist* 15 (1960):128–134.
34. C. Heath, *What People Are* (Cambridge, Mass.: Harvard University Press, 1945), p. 27.
35. Ibid.
36. N. C. Andreason, "Creativity and Mental Illness: Prevalence Rates in Writers and Their First-Degree Relatives," *American Journal of Psychiatry* 144 (1987):1288–1292.
37. S. Freud, "Creative Writing and Day-dreaming" (1908), *SE* 9:144.
38. A. Storr, *Dynamics of Creation*, p. 139.
39. J. Huizinga, *Homo Ludens* (London: Temple Smith, 1971), pp. 28–29.
40. A. Rothenberg, *The Emerging Goddess* (Chicago: University of Chicago Press, 1979).
41. Woodham-Smith, *Florence Nightingale*, p. 33.
42. Koestler, *Three Domains of Creativity*, p. 38.
43. Freud, "Creative Writing," p. 144.

9. *Sylvia Plath: Creativity and Psychotic Defenses*

1. N. H. Steiner, *A Closer Look at Ariel: A Memory of Sylvia Plath* (New York: Popular Library, 1973), p. 22.
2. S. Plath, "Daddy," in *Collected Poems*, ed. Ted Hughes (New York: Harper Row, 1981).
3. Steiner, *A Closer Look at Ariel*, p. 20.
4. S. Plath, *The Bell Jar* (1962; New York: Harper and Row, 1971), p. 47.
5. A. Stevenson, *Bitter Fame* (Boston: Houghton Mifflin, 1989).
6. J. L. Lowes, *The Road To Xanadu* (Boston: Houghton Mifflin, 1927).

7. Stevenson, *Bitter Fame*, p. 228.

8. L. Ames, "Sylvia Plath: A Biographical Note," in Plath, *The Bell Jar*, p. 213.

9. Plath, *The Bell Jar*, p. 62.

10. S. Plath, *The Journals of Sylvia Plath*, ed. T. Hughes and F. McCullough (New York: Random House, 1982), pp. 184–185.

11. Ibid., p. 209.

12. Stevenson, *Bitter Fame*, pp. 123–124.

13. Plath, *Journals*, p. 255.

14. Ibid., p. 272.

15. S. Plath, *Letters Home—Correspondence, 1950–1963*, ed. with commentary by A. S. Plath (New York: Harper and Row, 1975), p. 467.

16. Plath, *The Bell Jar*, p. 135.

17. Ibid., pp. 136–137.

18. S. Freud, "Letters to Arnold Zweig," in *Letters of Sigmund Freud*, trans. T. Stern and J. Stern (New York: Basic Books, 1960), p. 430.

19. Plath, *The Bell Jar*, pp. 2, 105, 106.

20. Ibid., p. 148.

21. Plath, *Collected Poems*, p. 203.

22. Plath, *The Bell Jar*, pp. 121, 116.

23. Ibid., p. 112.

24. Ibid., p. 132.

25. Ibid., p. 182.

26. S. Plath, "A Mad Girl's Love Song," in Ames, *Sylvia Plath*, p. 216.

27. Plath, *The Bell Jar*, pp. 46, 41.

28. M. Solomon, *Beethoven* (New York: Schirmer Books, 1977), p. 246.

29. Ibid., p. 241.

30. Ames, "Sylvia Plath," p. 214.

31. Plath, *The Bell Jar*, p. 98.

32. Ames, "Sylvia Plath," p. 215.

33. Plath, *Journals*, pp. 265, 281.

34. Ibid., p. 265.

35. Plath, *Letters Home*, pp. 131, 478, 481–482.

36. Plath, *The Bell Jar*, pp. 152, 165.

37. Plath, *Letters Home*, pp. 239–240.

38. Plath, *Collected Poems*, pp. 225–226.

39. Plath, *Letters Home*, p. 468.

40. Stevenson, *Bitter Fame*, p. 62.

41. Plath, *Collected Poems*, pp. 75–76.

42. Stevenson, *Bitter Fame*, p. 126.

43. Plath, *Letters Home*, p. 31.

44. Plath, *Collected Poems*, pp. 239–240.

45. Plath, *Letters Home,* p. 458.
46. G. Steiner, "Dying is an Art," in *The Reporter* (Oct. 7, 1965), p. 54.
47. S. Freud, "Three Essays on the Theory of Sexuality" (1905), *SE* 7:130–243, p. 238.
48. Ames, "Sylvia Plath," p. 209.

10. Anna Freud: Mature Defenses

1. E. Young-Bruehl, *Anna Freud* (New York: Summit Books, 1988), p. 459.
2. Ibid., p. 211.
3. S. Freud, *The Interpretation of Dreams* (New York: Basic Books, 1955), p. 257.
4. Young-Bruehl, *Anna Freud,* p. 90.
5. Ibid., p. 75.
6. S. Freud, "The Theme of the Three Caskets" (1913), *SE* 12:291–301, pp. 293–294.
7. S. Freud, *Letters of Sigmund Freud,* ed. E. L. Freud (New York: Basic Books, 1960), p. 301.
8. A. Freud, *The Ego and the Mechanisms of Defense,* trans. C. Baines (London: Hogarth Press and the Institute of Psychoanalysis, 1937), p. 163.
9. P. Roazen, *Freud and His Followers* (New York: Knopf, 1976), p. 440.
10. Young-Bruehl, *Anna Freud,* p. 62.
11. "Anna Freud Memorial Issue," *Bulletin of the Hampstead Clinic—Part I* 6 (1983):1–135, p. 31.
12. Young-Bruehl, *Anna Freud,* p. 52.
13. U. H. Peters, *Anna Freud* (New York: Schocken Books, 1985).
14. E. Jones, *The Life and Work of Sigmund Freud,* vol. 3 (New York: Basic Books, 1957), p. 96.
15. Young-Bruehl, *Anna Freud,* p. 130.
16. A. Freud, "Beating Fantasies and Daydreams," in *Complete Works,* vol. 1 (London: International Universities Press, 1966), pp. 146, 157, 153, 138.
17. S. Freud, "Some Psychical Consequences of the Anatomical Distinction between the Sexes" (1925), *SE* 19:248–258, pp. 251–253.
18. Ibid., pp. 257–258.
19. Jones, *Sigmund Freud,* p. 112.
20. Peters, *Anna Freud,* p. 69.
21. Rilke quoted in Young-Bruehl, *Anna Freud,* p. 128.
22. J. M. Masson, *The Complete Letters of Sigmund Freud to Wilhelm Fliess* (Cambridge, Mass.: Harvard University Press, 1985), p. 358.
23. Young-Bruehl, *Anna Freud,* pp. 43, 39, 99.

24. E. Freud in "Anna Freud Memorial Issue," pp. 5–6, 8.
25. Ibid., p. 22.
26. Ibid., p. 47.
27. Young-Bruehl, *Anna Freud*, p. 397.
28. G. E. Vaillant, "The Historical Origins and Future Potential of Sigmund Freud's Concept of the Mechanisms of Defense," *International Review of Psychoanalysis* 19 (1992):35–50.
29. A. Freud, *Ego and the Mechanisms of Defense*, pp. 105, 136.
30. S. Plath, *Letters Home* (New York: Harper and Row, 1975), p. 465.
31. Young-Bruehl, *Anna Freud*, p. 150.
32. A. Freud, *Ego and the Mechanisms of Defense*, p. 144.
33. "Anna Freud Memorial Issue," p. 8.
34. A. Freud, *Ego and the Mechanisms of Defense*, pp. 134–135.
35. Ibid., p. 137.
36. Ibid.
37. Ibid., p. 142.
38. "Anna Freud Memorial Issue," p. 52.
39. E. Erikson, *Life History and the Historical Moment* (New York: Norton, 1975), p. 30.
40. A. Freud, *Ego and the Mechanisms of Defense*, p. 47.
41. Young-Bruehl, *Anna Freud*, p. 191.
42. Ibid.
43. Ibid., p. 443.
44. Ibid., p. 229.
45. Ibid., p. 230.
46. Ibid., p. 197.
47. J. Sandler and A. Freud, *The Analysis of Defense: The Ego and the Mechanisms of Defense Revisited* (New York: International Universities Press, 1985), p. 176.
48. "Anna Freud Memorial Issue," pp. 13–14.
49. Peters, *Anna Freud*, p. 23.
50. S. Freud, "Disturbance of Memory on the Acropolis" (1936), *SE* 22:239–248, p. 245.
51. S. Freud, "Analysis Terminable and Interminable" (1936), *SE* 23:235–236.
52. S. Freud, *New Introductory Lectures on Psychoanalysis* (1932), *SE* 22:146.
53. "Anna Freud Memorial Issue," p. 15.
54. Jones, *Sigmund Freud*, p. 195.
55. Peters, *Anna Freud*, p. 131.
56. Young-Bruehl, *Anna Freud*, p. 234.
57. A. Freud, *Ego and the Mechanisms of Defense*, p. 193.
58. Stevenson, *Bitter Fame*, p. 302.

11. Eugene O'Neill: The Maturation of Defenses

1. L. Sheaffer, *O'Neill: Son and Playwright* (Boston: Little, Brown, 1968), p. 67.
2. A. Gelb and B. Gelb, *O'Neill* (New York: Harper and Row, 1962), p. 78.
3. Sheaffer, *O'Neill: Son and Playwright*, p. 156.
4. Gelb and Gelb, *O'Neill*, pp. 137–138.
5. Ibid., p. 235.
6. Ibid., p. 383.
7. J. H. Raleigh, "Introduction," in *Twentieth-Century Interpretations of The Iceman Cometh* (Englewood Cliffs, N.J.: Prentice Hall, 1968), p. 17.
8. Ibid., p. 20.
9. E. O'Neill, *Long Day's Journey into Night* (New Haven: Yale University Press, 1955), p. 69.
10. Ibid., p. 101.
11. Ibid.
12. Ibid., p. 45.
13. Ibid., p. 47.
14. Ibid., p. 48.
15. Ibid., p. 87.
16. Ibid., pp. 92, 93.
17. Ibid., p. 110.
18. Ibid., pp. 90, 91, 92.
19. Ibid., p. 120.
20. Gelb and Gelb, *O'Neill*, p. 227.
21. Ibid., p. 235.
22. Ibid., p. 383.
23. Sheaffer, *O'Neill: Son and Playwright*, p. 252.
24. Gelb and Gelb, *O'Neill*, pp. 233, 231.
25. Ibid., p. 559.
26. Sheaffer, *O'Neill: Son and Playwright*, p. 424.
27. L. Sheaffer, *O'Neill: Son and Artist* (Boston: Little, Brown, 1973), p. 187.
28. Gelb and Gelb, *O'Neill*, p. 962.
29. Ibid., p. 706.
30. O'Neill, *Long Day's Journey*, pp. 173–174.
31. Ibid., p. 153.
32. T. Bogard and J. R. Bryer, *Selected Letters of Eugene O'Neill* (New Haven: Yale University Press, 1988), pp. 220–221.
33. Gelb and Gelb, *O'Neill*, p. 735.
34. O'Neill, *Long Day's Journey*, p. 164.
35. Ibid., pp. 165–166.
36. E. O'Neill, *Nine Plays: Mourning Becomes Electra* (New York: Modern Library, 1941), pp. 866–867.

37. Gelb and Gelb, *O'Neill*, p. 836.
38. Ibid., p. 838.
39. Sheaffer, *O'Neill: Son and Artist*, p. 509.
40. O'Neill, *Long Day's Journey*, dedication page.
41. Bogard and Bryer, *Selected Letters of O'Neill*, pp. 277–278.
42. Raleigh, *The Iceman Cometh*, p. 22.
43. Gelb and Gelb, *O'Neill*, p. 848.
44. Ibid., p. 845.

12. Disadvantage, Resilience, and Mature Defenses

1. E. E. Werner and R. S. Smith, *Vulnerable but Invincible* (New York, McGraw-Hill, 1982).
2. Ibid., p. 152.
3. The 25-item Childhood Environmental Weakness Scale: (1) *Lack of cohesive home:* (a) 8 or more moves; (b) loss of parent before age 6; (c) 6 months or more apart from both parents; (d) parents divorced or chronically incompatible; (e) 9 or more social agencies involved. (2) *Lack of maternal supervision:* (a) boy says so; (b) mother alcoholic or delinquent; (c) mother severely disabled; (d) housekeeping substandard (2 observers); (e) no supervision when mother absent. (3) *Lack of maternal affection:* (a) multiple observers say so; (b) boy says so; (c) mother absent more than 2 years; (d) boy indifferent to or dislikes mother; (e) mother mentally ill. (4) *Lack of paternal supervision:* (a) father alcoholic or mentally retarded; (b) father delinquent; (c) father absent more than 6 years; (d) multiple observers say discipline is inadequate; (e) boy says discipline is inadequate. (5) *Lack of paternal affection:* (a) boy says so; (b) multiple observers say so; (c) voluntary desertion by father for more than 2 years; (d) father mentally ill; (e) boy indifferent to or dislikes father.
4. Werner and Smith, *Vulnerable but Invincible*, p. 133.
5. Ibid., p. 88.
6. N. Garmezy, "Stressors of Childhood," in *Stress, Coping and Development in Children*, ed. N. Garmezy and M. Rutter (New York: McGraw-Hill, 1983), p. 75.
7. M. Rutter, "Myerian Psychobiology, Personality Development and the Role of Life Experiences," *American Journal of Psychiatry* 143 (1986): 1077–1087, p. 1083.
8. M. Rutter, "Stress, Coping and Development: Some Issues and Some Questions," *Journal of Child Psychology and Psychiatry* 22 (1981):323–356, p. 346.
9. G. E. Vaillant, *Adaptation to Life* (Boston: Little, Brown, 1977); G. E. Vaillant and C. O. Vaillant, "Natural History of Male Psychological

Health, XII: A Forty-Five-Year Study of Successful Aging at Age 65," *American Journal of Psychiatry* 147 (1990):31–37. G. E. Vaillant, *Ego Mechanisms of Defense* (Washington, D.C.: American Psychiatric Press, 1992).

10. Garmezy, "Stressors of Childhood." Werner and Smith, *Vulnerable but Invincible.*

11. M. Rutter, "Resilience in the Face of Adversity: Protective Factors and Resistance to Psychiatric Disorder," *British Journal of Psychiatry* 147 (1985):598–611, p. 600.

12. A. S. Masten and N. Garmezy, "Risk, Vulnerability and Protective Factors in Developmental Psychopathology," in B. B. Lahey and A. E. Kasdin, eds., *Advances in Clinical Child Psychology*, vol. 8 (New York: Plenum, 1985), pp. 1–52.

13. Rutter, "Myerian Psychobiology."

14. A. Thomas and S. Chess, "Genesis and Evolution of Behavioral Disorders: From Infancy to Early Adult Life," *American Journal of Psychiatry* 141 (1984):1–9.

15. E. Hartmann, E. Milofsky, G. Vaillant, M. Oldfield, R. Falke, and C. Ducey, "Vulnerability to Schizophrenia: Prediction of Adult Schizophrenia Using Childhood Information," *Archives of General Psychiatry* 41 (1984):1050–1056.

16. A. Meyer, *The Collected Papers of Adolf Meyer*, vol. 4, *Mental Hygiene* (1908), ed. E. Q. Winters (Baltimore: Johns Hopkins University Press, 1950–1952).

13. How Does the Ego Mature?

1. D. Quinton, M. Rutter, and C. Liddle, "Institutional Rearing, Parenting Difficulties and Marital Support," *Psychological Medicine* 14 (1984):102–124.

2. P. I. Yakovlev and A. R. Lecours, "The Myeogenetic Cycles of Regional Maturation of the Brain," in *Regional Development of the Brain in Early Life*, ed. A. Minkowski (Oxford: Blackwell Scientific Publications, 1967).

3. D. R. Weinberger, "Implication of Normal Brain Development for the Pathogenesis of Schizophrenia," *Archives of General Psychiatry* 44 (1987):660–669.

4. T. J. Bouchard, D. T. Lykken, M. McGue, N. L. Segal, and A. Tellegen, "Sources of Human Psychological Differences: The Minnesota Study of Twins Reared Apart," *Science* 250 (1990):223–228.

5. J. Piaget, *The Moral Judgement of the Child* (London: Kegan Paul, 1932).

6. A. Koestler, *The Act of Creation* (New York: Dell, 1964).

7. P. Cramer, *The Development of Defense Mechanisms* (New York: Springer-Verlag, 1991), pp. 48, 74.

8. S. T. Hauser, *Adolescents and Their Families* (New York: Free Press, 1991), pp. 239–240.

9. M. J. Horowitz, *Introduction to Psychodynamics* (New York: Basic Books, 1991).

10. E. Erikson, "Identity and the Lifecycle," *Psychological Issues* 1 (1959):18–164.

11. H. W. Loewald, *Papers on Psychoanalysis* (New Haven: Yale University Press, 1980).

12. J. Sandler, "On Internal Object Relations," *Journal of the American Psychoanalytic Association* 38 (1990):859–880.

13. S. Freud, *The Ego and the Id* (1923), *SE* 19:29.

14. A. de Saint-Exupéry, *The Little Prince* (New York: Harcourt, Brace and World, 1943), p. 68.

15. Ibid., p. 67.

16. M. Rutter, *Maternal Deprivation Reassessed*, 2nd ed. (Harmondsworth: Penguin Books, 1981).

17. R. Rymer, "A Silent Childhood—II," *New Yorker*, April 20, 1992, p. 77.

18. Quinton, Rutter, and Liddle, "Institutional Rearing."

19. A. Thomas and S. Chess, *The Dynamics of Psychological Development* (New York: Brunner/Mazel, 1980).

20. W. Griesenger, *Mental Pathology and Therapeutics* (London: New Sydenham Society, 1867), pp. 5–6.

21. A. Rizzuto, *The Birth of the Living God* (Chicago: University of Chicago Press, 1979).

22. J. Huizinga, *Homo Ludens* (London: Temple Smith, 1971), p. 10.

23. J. Piaget and B. Inhelder, *The Psychology of the Child* (New York: Basic Books, 1969), p. 158.

24. L. Sheaffer, *O'Neill: Son and Playwright* (Boston: Little, Brown, 1968), p. 4.

25. A. Gelb and B. Gelb, *O'Neill* (New York: Harper and Row, 1962), p. 434.

26. E. O'Neill, *Long Day's Journey into Night* (New Haven: Yale University Press, 1955), pp. 88, 87, 103.

27. Ibid., pp. 172–173, 95, 175.

28. Ibid., pp. 107, 78, 95.

29. Ibid., p. 176.

30. Cramer, *Defense Mechanisms*, p. 40.

31. A. Freud, *The Ego and the Mechanisms of Defense* (London: Hogarth Press, 1937), p. 4.

32. Cramer, *Defense Mechanisms*, p. 88.

33. G. L. Engel, F. Richsman, A. S. Dowling, V. Harway, and D. W. Hess, "Monica: A 25-Year Longitudinal Study of the Consequences of Trauma in Infancy," *Journal of the American Psychoanalytic Association* 27 (1979):107–126.

34. S. Freud, *The Ego and the Id*, p. 37.
35. O. Fenichel, *The Psychoanalytic Theory of Neurosis* (New York: Norton, 1945), p. 195.
36. R. Schafer, *Aspects of Internalization* (New York, International Universities Press, 1968), p. 179.
37. M. Hofer, "Relationships as Regulators: A Psychobiologic Perspective on Bereavement," *Psychosomatic Medicine* 46 (1984):183–197, pp. 194–195.
38. H. Troyat, *Tolstoy* (Garden City, N.Y.: Doubleday, 1967), p. 14.
39. Ibid.
40. Ibid., p. 13.
41. L. Tolstoy, *Childhood, Boyhood, Youth* (1852; New York: Scribners, 1904), p. 103.
42. Troyat, *Tolstoy*, pp. 49, 50.
43. Ibid., p. 59.
44. Ibid., pp. 63, 17.
45. Ibid., p. 63.
46. Ibid., p. 98.
47. Tolstoy, *Childhood*, pp. 7, 8.
48. Ibid., pp. 35, 98, 113.
49. Ibid., p. 109.
50. L. Tolstoy, *War and Peace* (1868; London: Oxford University Press, 1930), vol. 1, pp. 114–115, 122.
51. Troyat, *Tolstoy*, pp. 336–337.
52. Ibid., p. 344.
53. Ibid., p. 361.
54. Ibid.
55. Ibid., pp. 377, 384.
56. L. Tolstoy, *Anna Karenina* (1877; New York: Modern Library, 1950), p. 908.
57. Ibid., p. 909.
58. Ibid.
59. L. Tolstoy, *Anna Karenina* (1877; New York: Scribners, 1904), vol. 3, pp. 371–372.
60. C. G. Jung, "The Stages of Life," in *The Portable Jung*, ed. J. Campbell (New York: Viking, 1971), p. 122.
61. H. E. Siegrist, *The Great Doctors* (New York: Doubleday, 1958), p. 209.
62. Plato, *Phaedrus*, ed. I. Edman (New York: Modern Library, 1928), pp. 284–285.
63. M. Solomon, *Beethoven* (New York: Schirmer Books, 1977), pp. 315–316.

Acknowledgments

This book represents the fruits of a vast collaborative effort that has continued for half a century. The effort began in the late 1930s as two separate studies: one of inner-city men at Harvard Law School, and one of college men at the Harvard University Health Services. Sheldon Glueck and Eleanor Glueck assembled the Core City sample as part of the research for their classic criminology text, *Unravelling Juvenile Delinquency*. In their work many helped them—especially Mildred Cunningham, Mary Moran, Ernest Schachtel, John Burke, Sheila Murphrey, and George McGrath. Arlie Bock and Clark Heath, with philanthropic help and imaginative interest from William T. Grant, created the College sample, often called the Grant Study of Adult Development. Among the many who helped them were Frederic Wells, Carl Selzer, and especially Lewise Gregory Davies. Charles McArthur was the director of the College sample from 1954 to 1972 and was responsible for its survival.

Since 1972, the College and the Core City samples have been consolidated into the Study of Adult Development, of which I have been fortunate to be director. Many people have played critical roles in keeping contact with the study members and assessing data: initially, Eva Milofsky, Robert Richards, Caroline Vaillant, and Phyllis Remolador; and, more recently, Sara Koury, Sally Allen, Kimberly Lee, Leigh McCullough, Tara Mitchell, and Darsie Riccio. In addition, the book includes data from the study of gifted women begun at Stanford University in 1920 by Lewis Terman. I am grateful to Robert Sears and Albert Hastorf for their generosity in allowing me and Caroline Vaillant to join their research team, and to Eleanor Walker for her unflagging help in facilitating our interviews with the women. The mere listing of names here can only hint at the enormous devotion and painstaking hard work required to follow more than one thousand individuals for fifty to seventy years.

Clearly, I am also indebted to the several hundred erstwhile

Boston schoolboys, California schoolgirls, and Harvard sophomores who are the book's chief protagonists and its most valuable collaborators.

Among the early financial benefactors who helped fund the Study of Adult Development were the William T. Grant, Nathan Hofheimer, Field, and Ford foundations. Generous help was also received from the Commonwealth Fund and the National Institute of Mental Health. Since 1967 I have received funding from the William T. Grant Foundation, the Spencer Foundation, the Milton Fund, Grant AA-01372 from the National Institute of Alcohol Abuse and Alcoholism, and Grants MH-38798, MH-32885, and KO5-MH0364 from the National Institute of Mental Health. I owe special thanks to the anonymous donor of the Raymond Sobel Professorship at Dartmouth Medical School, an endowment that for the last ten years has given me the freedom to study and to write. As directors of the Harvard University Health Services, first Warren Wacker and then David Rosenthal have provided a good home for the study.

For six years the several hundred Harvard College students who attended Social Sciences 169 listened to the ideas in this book as they were first formulated. Their sensitive and challenging questions gave me both inspiration and a crucible for my ideas.

Many people reviewed one or more chapters and made valuable suggestions. I am especially indebted to Nancy Andreasen, Anne Colby, Charlene Drake, Stuart Hauser, Kimberly Lee, Annmarie McDonagh-Coyle, Christopher Perry, William Phillips, Diane Roston, Caroline Vaillant, Emery Vaillant, Joanna Vaillant, John Vaillant, Nancy White, Anna Wolff, and Elisabeth Young-Bruehl. I am particularly grateful to Linda Miller and Joan Thomson for their dedicated help as typist and medical artist respectively. Camille Smith edited the book with a care that was above and beyond the call of duty and that greatly enhanced its clarity. Finally, Leigh McCullough spent many hours reading every chapter, generously sharing her ideas. She has made this a warmer and a wiser book.

Credits

Index

Note: Page numbers in italic indicate tables and figures; names in italic are pseudonymous case examples.